A Day in the Life of a CISO

Personal Mentorship from 24+ Battle-Tested CISOs —
Mentoring We Never Got

David J. Gee

A Day in the Life of a CISO

Portfolio Director: Vijin Boricha

Relationship Leads: Dhruv Jagdish Kataria and Rahul Nair

Program Manager: Ankita Thakur

Project Manager: Gandhali Raut

Content Engineer: Rebecca Youé

Technical Editor: Nithik Cheruvakodan

Copy Editor: Safis Editing

Indexer: Hemangini Bari

Proofreader: Rebecca Youé

Production Designer: Vijay Kamble

Growth Lead: Ankita Thakur

First published: September 2025

Production reference: 2061125

Published by Packt Publishing Ltd.
Grosvenor House
11 St Paul's Square
Birmingham
B3 1RB, UK.

ISBN 978-1-80611-069-8
www.packtpub.com

Chapter	Chapter Names	Author	LinkedIn	Autograph
1	*Sunrise on a New Day*	David J. Gee	https://www.linkedin.com/in/davidjordangee/	
2	*Hand-to-Hand Combat with Lazarus*	James McLeary	https://www.linkedin.com/in/jamesmcleary/	
3	*Priorities for the New CISO*	Keith Howard	https://www.linkedin.com/in/keithjhoward/	
4	*Cyber Threat Intelligence That Is Actionable*	Teresa Walsh	https://www.linkedin.com/in/teresa-w-9b068130/	
5	*How I Got to Be CISO*	Silvia Lam Ihensekhien	https://www.linkedin.com/in/silvia-lam-ihensekhien/	

Chapter	Chapter Names	Author	LinkedIn	Autograph
6	*The Journey to CISO: From Humble Beginnings to Leadership*	Krzysztof Kostienko	https://www.linkedin.com/in/kkostienko/	
7	*Stepping Up into a Global Role*	Sam Coco	https://www.linkedin.com/in/samcoco7/	
8	*Diverse Paths to Cybersecurity Leadership*	Catherine Rowe	https://www.linkedin.com/in/catherine-rowe-35648a14/	
9	*Overcoming Doubt*	Stéphane Nappo	https://www.linkedin.com/in/stephane-nappo/	
10	*How to Defend with Less*	Adam Cartwright	https://www.linkedin.com/in/adam-cartwright-5344966/	

Chapter	Chapter Names	Author	LinkedIn	Autograph
11	*Being Brilliant at the Basics*	Sandro Bucchianeri	https://www. linkedin.com/in/ sandrobucchianeri/	
12	*A CISO in Japan*	Osamu Terai	https://www.linkedin. com/in/osamu-terai/	
13	*Navigating the C-Suite, Boards, and DOPE Dynamics*	Shamane Tan	https://www.linkedin. com/in/shamane/	
14	*Systems Thinking CISOs*	Phoram Mehta	https://www.linkedin. com/in/phorammehta/	
15	*The CISO as a Change Agent*	Fal Ghancha	https://www.linkedin. com/in/falghancha/	

Chapter	Chapter Names	Author	LinkedIn	Autograph
16	*Alternative Career Paths to Consider*	Abbas Kudrati	https://www.linkedin.com/in/akudrati/?originalSubdomain=au	
17	*So, You Lost Your Job*	Dr Matthew Ryan	https://www.linkedin.com/in/dr-matt-r-70b96581/	
18	*Rebuilding after a Breach*	Daryl Pereira	https://www.linkedin.com/in/darylpereira1/	
19	*Cyber Strategy That Makes a Difference*	Jim Boehm	https://www.linkedin.com/in/jim-boehm/	
20	*Do's and Don'ts for CISOs*	Yabing Wang	https://www.linkedin.com/in/yabingwang/	

Chapter	Chapter Names	Author	LinkedIn	Autograph
21	*Developing Cyber Talent*	Maryam Betchel	`https://www.linkedin.com/in/maryambechtel/`	
22	*Managing Critical Vulnerabilities*	Steven Brown	`https://www.linkedin.com/in/steve100/`	
23	*AI: The Promise and Challenge*	Jacqui Kernot	`https://www.linkedin.com/in/jkernot/`	
24	*Protecting the USA*	Camilo Sandoval	`https://www.linkedin.com/in/camintel/`	
25	*Why Risk Management Matters*	Tim Callahan	`https://www.linkedin.com/in/tim-callahan-4b39241/`	

Chapter	Chapter Names	Author	LinkedIn	Autograph
26	*Driving Cyber Transformation*	Dr David Ng	`https://www.linkedin.com/in/david-ng-bb08a723/`	
27	*My Metrics Playbook*	Peter Troy	`https://www.linkedin.com/in/petetroy/`	
28	*Career Resilience*	Meg Anderson	`https://www.linkedin.com/in/andersonmeg/`	
29	*Lessons in Leading Yourself, Cyber Teams and Through Crisis*	Richard Johnson	`https://www.linkedin.com/in/richard-johnson-366b1490/`	
30	*Sunset*	David J. Gee	`https://www.linkedin.com/in/davidjordangee/`	

Among life's most common regrets is failing to express love to those who matter the most. Let me start by saying my deepest love goes to my wife Anna and our wonderful adult children – Nathan, Amber and Jeremy. All are now married to exceptional partners (Sabrina, Samson and Virginia), and together they've blessed us with two brilliant grandchildren, Azalea and Harrison. I am profoundly grateful for this family and love you all immeasurably.

As I expressed in my first book, I owe immense gratitude to my parents, David and Cindy Gee, for their selfless devotion. Few people know that I was adopted at a young age from Ernest and May by my dad Ernest's brother after his courageous battle with cancer.

In fact, I won the lottery in life with parents who not only cared deeply but consistently told me I could accomplish anything. Their unwavering encouragement undoubtedly inspired my career and this book.

My humble objective with this book is, with the assistance of these distinguished leaders, to help develop and nurture the next generation of cybersecurity leaders and professionals. Hence, my heartfelt thanks to everyone who contributed to making this book possible – the many CISOs and executives who generously took the time to share their career stories have made this book possible.

And finally, my thanks to the great team at Packt for their amazing support – Dhruv, Rebecca, Rahul, Ankita, and many others made a real difference in supporting this process.

David J. Gee

Foreword

Among the most valuable components in my career as a **Chief Information Security Officer (CISO)** is the interaction with other CISOs. The forum could be in-person meetings through private or public organisations, sharing articles or one-on-one conversations. One of the most distinctive occurrences in my career was when financial institutions were threatened by politically motivated cyber-attacks. The threat actors were publishing lists of who they would attack on a sketchy social media platform. My company was on the list. In the first round of attacks, there was a large financial institution that was attacked, and their website was shut down. They recovered, but the attack impacted customers. I had met the CISO of that institution through our joint association with the Financial Services Information Sharing and Analysis Center. I reached out to that CISO, who agreed to have a private conversation about how the attack occurred. The CISO was transparent with me because of our trusted relationship. The CISO gave me information that my team was able to use to harden our environment. The very next week, we were attacked. Because of the advice and transparency of that CISO, our financial institution was able to deflect and defend against the attack. At the time, it was the largest volume of malicious traffic ever pointed towards a company's network. The threat actor group was surprised and began to throw everything they had at us, but we never went down. I credit the CISO's transparency and partnership with that success. The very best advice one can receive is from others who have gone through similar experiences. There are countless stories of how organisations have participated with information sharing initiatives and through that have been able to build programs tailored to specific threats.

This book is at that level of sharing. These chapters contain the wisdom and experience of some of the world's leading security professionals. There is more than 700 years of experience across multiple industries, including banking, insurance, energy, postal services, technology, consumer products and consulting industries. These stories are learnings that can be tailored and applied to your organisation, whether you are an experienced security executive or just starting out. This book is a must-read for the next generation of CISOs and can be used as experienced CISOs mentor their up-and-coming champions. At a minimum, by reading through these accounts, one can identify with the challenges and successes of an operating and effective cybersecurity program.

Tim Callahan

Global CISO, Aflac Insurance

Contributors

About the author

David J. Gee is a globally recognised CIO, CISO, risk executive and thought leader with over 25 years of distinguished C-suite experience spanning some of the world's most prominent financial institutions and multinational corporations. Born in Darwin, Australia, David is a Buddhist whose core philosophy centres on helping others achieve their potential.

Prior to retiring, David was Global Head of Technology, Cyber & Data Risk at Macquarie Group. He has held senior cybersecurity leadership positions including **Chief Information Security Officer (CISO)** at HSBC Asia Pacific and Chief Information Officer roles at MetLife Japan, Eli Lilly USA and Credit Union Australia. His unique perspective combines hands-on operational experience with strategic governance expertise across diverse global markets.

David is a non-executive director and strategic technology advisor who acts as board advisor to multiple organisations. He is also a prolific author and speaker who previously wrote *The Aspiring CIO & CISO*, which was recognised among the "Top 10 Must Reads" for security leaders. David also writes for several magazines on technology and digital change, cybersecurity and data/AI.

With significant contributions from his global CISO network, David's new book, *A Day in the Life of a CISO,* provides an authentic, behind-the-scenes look at modern cybersecurity leadership. This collaborative work is a testament to David's core philosophy of empowering others and his dedication to cultivating the next generation of cyber leaders.

This book contains content from 28 additional cybersecurity leaders from around the world, who have each contributed a chapter. These leaders are listed on the previous pages and introduced formally at the beginning of their chapters.

You'll see that there's a space beside each contributor's name on the previous pages for their autograph, should you cross paths with them and wish them to sign your book.

About the reviewers

Simon Blanchet has 25 years of international experience across 3 continents, including 15 years in banking, 10 of which were with HSBC, where he was the Global Head of Security Testing, managing a global team of 70 strong security testers. Between HSBC and his current position at the Hong Kong Jockey Club, he was the **Chief Information Security Officer (CISO)** at Serai, a wholly owned fintech start-up by HSBC, after being the Director of Threat Vulnerability Surface of Attack at Bullish.com, a GFSC-regulated crypto exchange. Simon started his career as a software developer of cryptographic and security-related software and quickly became an expert in software security, application security and vulnerability management. He has also presented at major events, including BSIMM Europe, AppSec Forum Switzerland and DragonCon Hong Kong.

Matthew Ryan is a cybersecurity practitioner and researcher whose work focuses on the intersection of cybersecurity risks, economic valuations and strategic risk management. He currently serves as the Head of Cyber, Data, and AI Risk at the National Australia Bank, and has previously held senior roles with the Australian Prudential Regulation Authority, Macquarie Group, Commonwealth Bank, Deloitte and the Australian Defence Forces. Alongside his industry leadership, Dr Ryan serves as a cybersecurity researcher at the University of New South Wales Institute for Cyber. He is the author of *Ransomware Revolution: The Rise of a Prodigious Cyber Threat* and produced the world's first doctoral thesis on ransomware. He holds a doctorate in cybersecurity from UNSW, alongside four additional degrees spanning counterterrorism, strategy, security and diplomacy.

Debra Baker, with 30+ years of experience in information security, served as **Chief Information Security Officer (CISO)** at RedSeal. As CEO of TrustedCISO, she provides vCISO services and advises on cybersecurity strategy, risk management and compliance frameworks. A CISSP and CCSP holder, she's recognised among the Top 100 Females Fighting Cyber Crime and authored *A CISO Guide to Cyber Resilience* book.

Yoshimasa Kobayashi is a partner at a professional firm with a global network, where he leads advisory services in cybersecurity and IT risk management for the financial services sector. With over 20 years of experience in IT and security, his career is marked by significant roles in both the private and public sectors, including his tenure at the **Japanese Financial Services Agency (JFSA)**. At the JFSA, he served as a Deputy Director, overseeing and monitoring cybersecurity and IT risks for major financial institutions. He has experience in planning and conducting the JFSA-hosted cybersecurity exercise 'Delta Wall' and actively participated in initiatives aimed at strengthening cybersecurity in collaboration with international financial regulatory authorities, such as the G7 regulators. Kobayashi san provided specific support to review Chapter 12 in Japanese for Osamu Terai, and this content is available for download from `https://github.com/PacktPublishing/A-Day-in-the-Life-of-a-CISO`.

Table of Contents

Part 1: Advice to the New CISO 25

Chapter 2: Hand-to-Hand Combat with Lazarus 27

Chapter 3: Priorities for the New CISO 41

Chapter 4: Cyber Threat Intelligence That Is Actionable 59

Chapter 5: How I Got to Be CISO 71

Part 2: Building Your CISO Skills   143

Chapter 10: How to Defend with Less   145

Chapter 11: Being Brilliant at the Basics   159

Chapter 12: A CISO in Japan   173

Chapter 13: Navigating the C-Suite, Boards and DOPE Dynamics   189

Chapter 14: Systems Thinking for CISOs 207

Chapter 15: The CISO as a Change Agent 229

Chapter 16: Alternative Career Paths to Consider   243

Chapter 17: So, You Got Fired   257

Part 3: Advanced CISO Toolkit   269

Chapter 18: Rebuilding after a Breach   271

Chapter 19: Cyber Strategy That Makes a Difference   289

Chapter 20: Do's and Don'ts for CISOs 305

Chapter 21: Developing Cyber Talent 329

Chapter 23: AI: The Promise and Challenge 367

Part 4: Advice from CISO 'Yoda Masters' 381

Chapter 24: Protecting the USA 383

Preface

When I was in high school, I was appointed captain of the Newington College Basketball First Team. I felt elated; it was an ambition I had held for many years. Then, my coach, Mr. Herb Barker, who had played rugby for the Australian Wallabies and represented the country at the Commonwealth Games, asked me to 'pass' the ball rather than 'shoot'. Having always been the best shooter on the team, this was a mental challenge as I found myself conflicted. Herb wanted me to make the team better. This was my first lesson in leadership.

This same transition from individual contributor to team enabler defines the CISO journey. The (probably technical) expertise that got you noticed must evolve into something broader: the ability to guide, influence and elevate others while navigating complex organisational dynamics.

A Day in the Life of a CISO is a personal mentoring and coaching session with **24+ CISOs and other cybersecurity leaders**. This is not classic textbook material, but career lessons from each leader, told through real stories of crisis management, board presentations, team building, organisational change and the countless unexpected challenges that define our profession. Each story captures both the experience of what happened and the behaviour these leaders had to model in response.

My first book, *The Aspiring CIO and CISO*, was written to help you get the job. This book is intended to help you be successful as a CISO, once you are appointed to a CISO role. In many ways, that is when the real learning starts, as there will be many situations you will not have experienced before or had the opportunity to learn about firsthand.

To produce this book, I reached out to my network and the network of my contacts to invite CISOs and senior cybersecurity executives to join me in sharing their own scar tissue of learning. These battle-tested insights represent knowledge forged under real-world pressure, the kind that can only be gained through lived experience, not theoretical study. I wanted each leader to tell their own story and provide the advice they themselves wished someone had shared with them earlier in their career.

How to read this book

Each chapter in this book stands as an individual mentoring session, allowing you to learn from the experiences of the leaders who have contributed, whether you read the book sequentially or turn to specific chapters as situations arise in your own leadership journey.

Who this book is for

This book is intended to help aspiring, new and current **CISOs** and **cyber leaders** learn from others who have walked the same or similar paths, and stood in the same CISO shoes. It is for those wanting to learn their craft from experienced CISOs and avoid making their mistakes. The book is your **personal mentorship** guide to being a CISO.

The **CIO** can also use this book to learn more about cybersecurity and help them to coach their own CISO. Today's CISO position demands more than technical expertise; it requires strategic thinking skills, organisational influence and the ability to translate security concepts into business outcomes. Whether you're leading security initiatives or supporting those who do, the real-world insights in this book from successful practitioners will help you understand not just what effective CISOs do but why they do it.

There is also another audience: the **vendor ecosystem** that needs to understand how CISOs think, evaluate solutions and make decisions rather than operating on assumptions about their needs. By providing insight into the CISO's decision-making process, day-to-day work pressures and success metrics, this book will help vendors to build more meaningful relationships and deliver solutions that truly address CISO challenges.

What this book covers

Chapter 1, Sunrise on a New Day, by David J. Gee, marks the start of the CISO's day. There is a real sense of physical and mental rejuvenation from the night's rest and the stark realisation that significant challenges await before you can rest again. Just as your mind prepares for the myriad tasks and meetings that will fill the hours ahead, this chapter introduces the parts and chapters of this book, and the CISOs and other cybersecurity leaders who have contributed, providing a strategic overview of your day ahead.

Chapter 2, Hand-to-Hand Combat with Lazarus, by James McLeary, explains how he was confronted with a real nightmare scenario: brand new in the job, he found himself with a serious cyber incident to manage. This is a powerful chapter to start your day in the life of a CISO journey. As you read this, reflect on how you would handle this scenario yourself.

Chapter 3, Priorities for the New CISO, by Keith Howard, covers Keith's personal insights into his strategic priorities as a new CISO and guidance on what he'd recommend you focus on in your first six months. This chapter is a great reference point for you in starting your CISO career.

Chapter 4, Cyber Threat Intelligence That Is Actionable, by Teresa Walsh, introduces the strategic importance of cyber intelligence to the new CISO through the form of a letter. Her letter to the CISO puts forward a proactive approach to defining what good looks like for cyber intelligence. Without attempting to address everything, the letter introduces key questions to be addressed and provides a starting point for further industry collaboration.

Chapter 5, How I Got to Be CISO, by Silvia Lam Ihensekhien, covers Silvia's own journey into the CISO role and the lessons she learnt along the way. She also discusses the challenges of being a woman in a male-oriented industry and shares advice for the next generation of women in cybersecurity leadership.

Chapter 6, The Journey to CISO: From Humble Beginnings to Leadership, by Krzysztof Kostienko, contains Krzysztof's story of moving into a CISO role, from Poland to the UK and then Hong Kong. Lessons he shares include being adaptive, taking calculated risks, being a good manager, developing trust networks and the importance soft skills.

Chapter 7, Stepping Up into a Global Role, by Sam Coco, takes us through Sam's career journey from individual contributor to leader. This shift required a mindset change, which included learning how to build a new team, delegating and personal resilience.

Chapter 8, Diverse Paths to Cybersecurity Leadership, by Catherine Rowe, covers Catherine's atypical journey from law to being a CISO. Catherine explains how she applies the skills she gained in law to cybersecurity and advocates for broader cybersecurity leadership recruitment practices.

Chapter 9, Overcoming Doubt, by Stéphane Nappo, explains how to operate in a world where uncertainty is normal, by embracing doubt and using it to your own personal advantage. The absence of doubt can lead to false levels of confidence, so getting the balance right takes some calibration.

Chapter 10, How to Defend with Less, by Adam Cartwright, covers prioritising to protect your most critical assets when you must make trade-offs due to budget constraints. As a CISO, this is where you really earn your pay, and if you get it right, then you reduce the risk for your enterprise.

Chapter 11, Being Brilliant at the Basics, by Sandro Bucchianeri, shares a commonsense approach to cybersecurity: getting the basics right. To be 'brilliant at the basics', you and your teams must be disciplined and focused. When your role as CISO has the added dimensions of leading geographically diverse teams, this task can be more complex. Sandro also shares his approach to managing teams effectively across different countries in this chapter.

Chapter 12, A CISO in Japan, by Osamu Terai, contains an overview of the unique challenges that are faced by CISOs in Japan, arguably one of the toughest assignments for a cyber leader in the world. This is a fascinating insight into managing cybersecurity with the odds stacked against you, across a number of dimensions.

Chapter 13, Navigating the C-Suite, Boards, and DOPE Dynamics, by Shamane Tan, shares an innovative approach to effective stakeholder engagement, particularly with the C-suite and board. All CISOs must prioritise advanced stakeholder management to be able to be successful.

Chapter 14, Systems Thinking for CISOs, by Phoram Mehta, is a way to reframe how you tackle your role. There is a complexity and focus on details within cybersecurity, and it is very easy to be drawn into these and to not see the bigger picture. In this chapter, Phoram shares the approach of systems thinking – a holistic approach that can provide you with a larger, more joined-up perspective.

Chapter 15, The CISO as a Change Agent, by Fal Ghancha, covers Fal's approach to stretching into the role of driving change. This is not a natural role that the CISO has traditionally played but is becoming increasingly critical for enterprises. This is a mindset shift for the CISO and requires some new thinking to approach this responsibility.

Chapter 16, Alternate Career Paths to Consider, by Abbas Kudrati, explores some alternative career paths for CISOs, opportunities that are both complementary and supplemental to this position. As market demands continue to increase, these options can also provide a transitional path in between CISO assignments.

Chapter 17, So, You Got Fired, by Dr Matthew Ryan, explains how to reassess and bounce back should you find yourself in the position of losing your job. There are some days in the life of a CISO when you might indeed find yourself here. In this chapter, you'll discover how you learn from and reframe this experience.

Chapter 18, Rebuilding after a Breach, by Daryl Pereira, is the start of the Advanced CISO Toolkit part of the book. In this chapter, Daryl shares some engrossing and pragmatic lessons in how he tackled the significant task of rebuilding following a major breach. Re-building the long-term trust of your stakeholders and customers takes a combination of many factors across governance, technology improvements and executive engagement.

Chapter 19, Cyber Strategy That Makes A Difference, by Jim Boehm, covers the essential components of a good cyber strategy, from Jim's extensive experience helping many companies to develop their strategies. The approach that he outlines will help you to translate technical risks into business language for improved stakeholder management.

Chapter 20, Do's and Don'ts for CISOs, by Yabing Wang, shares her personal approach to the role of CISO, including how you must build and prioritize your cybersecurity uplift program. Her thoughtful approach starts with the first 90 days as a CISO in a new role and moves from there into guidance for the CISO as a business partner.

Chapter 21, Developing Cyber Talent, by Maryam Betchel, provides an approach to the complex issue of finding, recruiting and retaining cyber talent, with some supplemental thoughts from David Gee on the topic. How to find and onboard the right talent is an existential challenge for the CISO – if they cannot attract and retain this talent, then they simply will not be successful in their role.

Chapter 22, Managing Critical Vulnerabilities, by Steven Brown, contains a practical approach, based on industry best practice, to vulnerability management – a critical task for CISOs.

Chapter 23, AI: The Promise and Challenge, by Jacqui Kernot, explores the fast-moving hot topic of AI: a double-edged sword that can be used both to defend yourself and for others to attack you. This is not a domain that the CISO has traditionally had much, if any, focus on, but the CISO must now act on this as it will become essential for organisational resilience.

Chapter 24, Protecting the USA, by Camilo Sandoval, contains Camilo's career stories and advice from the unique and challenging positions he held in the White House, most notably as the third CISO for the USA. The stakes are off the charts in terms of complexity and impact. The principles and leadership lessons from this chapter offer profound lessons for CISOs across every industry and organisation size, however.

Chapter 25, Why Risk Management Matters, by Tim Callahan, covers a 'guru'-level CISO perspective on why risk management is so important. Tim has a considered and mature outlook on how risk management should operate and shares this with us here.

Chapter 26, Driving Cyber Transformation, by David Ng, shares the personal story of driving significant cyber uplift for his bank. This maturity uplift is not a short-term fix, but a consistent, planned series of improvements over a multi-year period. David provides a great 'guru'-level overview of the approach he's taking and how the bank's maturity was improved by this uplift.

Chapter 27, My Metrics Playbook, by Peter Troy, covers Peter's personal approach to measuring cybersecurity and selecting and presenting metrics to executives. The most effective CISOs always anchor their decisions in empirical evidence rather than intuition; as Peter says, "If you are not measuring it, you are not managing it!"

Chapter 28, Career Resilience, by Meg Anderson, contains Meg's story of being in a CISO role for over 17 years in the same company, and her advice on resilience being the secret ingredient of success. There are some great lessons for every CISO to learn from Meg's incredible career in this chapter.

Chapter 29, Lessons in Leading Yourself, Cyber Teams and Through Crisis, by Richard Johnson, shares Richard's story, learning and advice from his extraordinary 16-year tenure as CISO at a major bank (one of the longest continuous security leadership roles in the financial sector). Richard has seen everything in his tenure, and his career is an exemplary example of leadership. There is invaluable wisdom Richard has gained and shares with us in this chapter.

Chapter 30, Sunset, by David J. Gee, provides a synthesis of the key themes and learnings across each of the chapters, revealing some patterns and specific advice from the CISOs and other leaders. Like sunset itself, this chapter offers a moment to pause, reflect and consider what you will take away from this book. Passing these lessons on to you to help you develop as a leader is our very reason for writing this book.

To get the most out of this book

I'd suggest taking the traditional approach of starting at the beginning of this book; however, I'm aware that each reader will come with a different set of expectations and perhaps also a very specific learning objective. If that is the case, then you may want to turn to a specific chapter of interest and read that first, then the next that sparks your curiosity.

Some readers will perhaps personally know of one or two of the CISOs or other cybersecurity leaders who have contributed a chapter. In this case, their chapter may be the logical place to start.

Most of all, enjoy the read, however you read the book. Reflect on the relevance of the material to your own journey and consider the changes you might need to make to yourself and your team.

Finally, please do connect with me on LinkedIn (https://www.linkedin.com/in/davidjordangee/) and share your feedback and any questions on the book with me.

Best regards,

David J. Gee

Download the color images

We also provide a PDF file that has color images of the screenshots/diagrams used in this book. You can download it here: https://packt.link/gbp/9781806110698.

Conventions used

There are a number of text conventions used throughout this book.

Bold: Indicates a new term, an important word, or words that you see on the screen. For instance, words in menus or dialog boxes appear in the text like this. For example: "Lazarus is renowned as an **Advanced Persistent Threat (APT38)** actor that has a successful track record of attacking payment systems."

> Warnings or important notes appear like this.

> Tips and tricks appear like this.

Get in touch

Feedback from our readers is always welcome.

General feedback: If you have questions about any aspect of this book or have any general feedback, please email us at customercare@packt.com and mention the book's title in the subject of your message.

Errata: Although we have taken every care to ensure the accuracy of our content, mistakes do happen. If you have found a mistake in this book, we would be grateful if you reported this to us. Please visit http://www.packt.com/submit-errata, click **Submit Errata**, and fill in the form. We ensure that all valid errata are promptly updated in the GitHub repository at https://github.com/PacktPublishing/A-Day-in-the-Life-of-a-CISO.

Piracy: If you come across any illegal copies of our works in any form on the internet, we would be grateful if you would provide us with the location address or website name. Please contact us at copyright@packt.com with a link to the material.

If you are interested in becoming an author: If there is a topic that you have expertise in and you are interested in either writing or contributing to a book, please visit http://authors.packt.com/.

Share your thoughts

Once you've read *A Day in the Life of a CISO*, we'd love to hear your thoughts! Scan the QR code below to go straight to the Amazon review page for this book and share your feedback.

https://packt.link/r/1806110695

Your review is important to us and the tech community and will help us make sure we're delivering excellent quality content.

‹packt› _secpro

Stay Relevant in a Rapidly Changing Cybersecurity World — Join Thousands of SecPro Subscribers

_secpro is the trusted weekly newsletter for cybersecurity professionals who want to stay informed about real-world threats, cutting-edge research, and actionable defensive strategies.

Each issue delivers high-signal, expert insights on topics like:

- Threat intelligence and emerging attack vectors
- Red and blue team tactics
- Zero Trust, MITRE ATT&CK, and adversary simulations
- Security automation, incident response, and more!

Whether you're a penetration tester, SOC analyst, security engineer, or CISO, _secpro keeps you ahead of the latest developments — no fluff, just real answers that matter.

Scan the QR code to subscribe for free and get expert cybersecurity insights straight to your inbox:

https://secpro.substack.com

1

Sunrise on a New Day

The sun rises early in the day in the life of a CISO. There is a sense of anticipation as you consider yesterday and reflect on where you will focus your energies today.

There is a catalytic aspect to sunrise that is both refreshing and tiring. While you physically feel fresh from your sleep, there is also a reload of your short-term memory's to-do list. This shift kicks your brain into action.

Figure 1.1: Sunrise (photo credit – David Gee)

As your brain shifts into 'on' mode, in a microsecond all the relaxation of sleep and family life comes to a sudden end. As CISO, you are in a dream job that you have worked your entire career to attain, but with the pressure and stress of the role, you may not appreciate it. How, then, do you make this position fulfilling and enjoyable? The last thing you want is to dread your work as this is such a large part of your life and everyday activity.

This book was designed to provide glimpses into the days of CISOs from around the world. The CISOs and other cybersecurity leaders who have contributed to this book come from different industries, countries and backgrounds. Some have been born into cybersecurity as 'lifers' and others have reinvented themselves and moved into this domain.

Their stories and their life lessons are what I have aimed to capture in this book. This is not meant to be textbook cybersecurity, but how each of the leaders has learnt to succeed and overcome their own personal challenges. The insights that you will gain from this book will be a collection of 'aha' moments, probably with some 'I already knew that' moments too. Either way, you will learn from ~740 years of accumulated experience.

Getting the most out of this book — get to know your free benefits

Unlock exclusive **free** benefits that come with your purchase, thoughtfully crafted to supercharge your learning journey and help you learn without limits.

Here's a quick overview of what you get with this book:

Next-gen reader

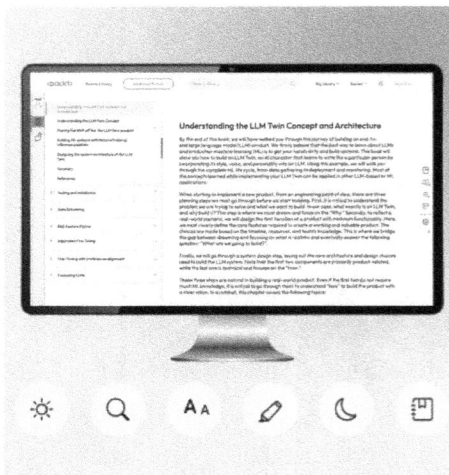

Figure 1.1: Illustration of the next-gen Packt Reader's features

Our web-based reader, designed to help you learn effectively, comes with the following features:

- Multi-device progress sync: Learn from any device with seamless progress sync.
- Highlighting and notetaking: Turn your reading into lasting knowledge.
- Bookmarking: Revisit your most important learnings anytime.
- Dark mode: Focus with minimal eye strain by switching to dark or sepia mode.

Interactive AI assistant (beta)

Figure 1.2: Illustration of Packt's
AI assistant

Our interactive AI assistant has been trained on the content of this book, to maximize your learning experience. It comes with the following features:

❖ Summarize it: Summarize key sections or an entire chapter.

❖ AI code explainers: In the next-gen Packt Reader, click the Explain button above each code block for AI-powered code explanations.

Note: The AI assistant is part of next-gen Packt Reader and is still in beta.

DRM-free PDF or ePub version

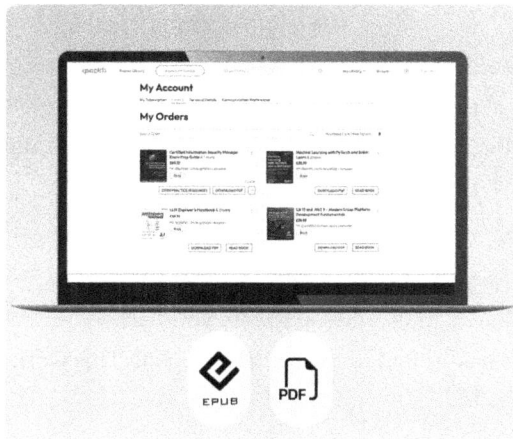

Figure 1.3: Free PDF and ePub

Learn without limits with the following perks included with your purchase:

🖺 Learn from anywhere with a DRM-free PDF copy of this book.

🖺 Use your favorite e-reader to learn using a DRM-free ePub version of this book.

Helping the next generation

I started writing this book at the same time as *The Aspiring CIO and CISO* – my first book. Then I realised that, as I had not retired, I had bitten off more than I could manage. *The Aspiring CIO and CISO* has been a great success commercially and has provided me with a platform for public speaking and coaching IT talent around the world.

Doing this first, and the experience I gained from it, has helped me to refine my own 'voice' and informed this second book. Sharing life lessons learned in an honest and humble manner is extremely powerful. My mission for this book, therefore, was to search the world to find CISOs and a few other senior leaders in this ecosystem to join me in sharing their own stories of how they learnt and flourished within their trade.

The essence of this book was to help the next generation of leaders, as well as those already in the CISO role, learn from the successes and mistakes of the current and previous generations of leaders. This mantra to 'help the next generation to learn by sharing our own mistakes and learnings' was shared by every CISO and contributor to this book.

This book has been designed to share career stories, mentorship and coaching from 24+ CISOs and other cybersecurity leaders that you otherwise would not be able to access. These are the stories and life lessons that we wished someone had told us when we were younger and full of ambition. Alas, we had to learn the hard way by the traditional route of trial and error. This works, but it is much slower and much more of a bumpy ride.

Allow me to use a story from the Holy Bible to illustrate my point (although I'll disclose that I'm personally a Buddhist). In a way, this book is a Noah's Ark moment. There is a perpetual flood of cyber-attacks that is impacting the world and creating crises globally. It is clear that we all need to learn from those who have been through their own trials and tribulations and have come out the other side. This is the foundation of this book, a Noah's Ark, a safe haven, for CISOs and cybersecurity leadership.

While my first book, *The Aspiring CIO and CISO*, was designed to help you develop yourself into the role of CISO or CIO, and provide some guidance for this accension, *A Day in the Life of a CISO* will help you to be successful and stay in this role.

We all want to leave a legacy, and in a small way, we can do this by sharing our personal stories with others, distilling our learnings so that they can themselves consider adopting them, or at least remembering them.

I want to express my personal gratitude to everyone who contributed to this book. The insights shared by this remarkable group of leaders are truly exceptional, and if we can each absorb even a handful of lessons from their experiences, our personal and professional growth will advance significantly.

How this book is structured

The book is divided into four logical parts. Allow me to introduce these and the CISOs and leaders who feature within each of them.

Part 1: Advice to the New CISO

We all must start somewhere as a CISO. This first part has specific stories that provide great advice to the newbie, but I'd add that the lessons learnt here actually have much wider appeal, and I would recommend that even an established CISO pay attention to the insights from these leaders.

The new CISO is on borrowed time; they are learning their trade, and attackers may be aware that they are still getting their grip on the new role and cyber controls that are in place. Where do you start, and what should you look out for in this challenging role? There are insights here that answer these questions and more.

Advice to the New CISO	
Author	**Chapter title**
James McLeary	2: Hand-to-Hand Combat with Lazarus
Keith Howard	3: Priorities for the New CISO
Teresa Walsh	4: Cyber Threat Intelligence That Is Actionable
Silvia Lam Ihensekhien	5: How I Got To Be CISO
Krzysztof Kostienko	6: The Journey to CISO: From Humble Beginnings to Leadership

Author	Chapter title
Sam Coco	7: Stepping Up into a Global Role
Catherine Rowe	8: Diverse Paths to Cybersecurity Leadership
Stéphane Nappo	9: Overcoming Doubt

Table 1.1: Part 1 chapters

Part 2: Building Your CISO Skills

At the CISO level, building skills means transitioning from technical security expertise to strategic business leadership. This means that you need to focus on translating security decisions into business outcomes and developing executive thinking and communication skills to influence across the C-suite.

The key is mastering business acumen, crisis leadership and strategic planning while positioning security as a business enabler rather than just a cost centre.

But sometimes, you won't succeed. In this case, how do you recover from career setbacks. Should you consider some alternative CISO paths?

You'll find all this and more in this part of the book.

Building Your CISO Skills	
Author	**Chapter title**
Adam Cartwright	10: How to Defend with Less
Sandro Bucchianeri	11: Being Brilliant at the Basics
Osamu Terai	12: A CISO in Japan
Shamane Tan	13: Navigating the C-Suite, Boards and DOPE Dynamics
Phoram Mehta	14: Systems Thinking for CISOs

Author	Chapter title
Fal Ghancha	15: The CISO as a Change Agent
Abbas Kudrati	16: Alternative Career Paths to Consider
Dr Matthew Ryan	17: So, You Got Fired

Table 1.2: Part 2 chapters

Part 3: Advanced CISO Toolkit

The most successful CISOs will be those who can balance deep technical knowledge with strong business acumen, excellent communication skills and the ability to think strategically about cybersecurity's role in enabling business success.

There are some specific experiences that the CISO will need to master. This includes driving a strategic roadmap, rebuilding after a breach, managing critical vulnerabilities and developing talent. Personal mastery takes time and practice with a continuous learning mindset. This part of the book will help you with this.

Advanced CISO Toolkit	
Author	**Chapter title**
Daryl Pereira	18: Rebuilding after a Breach
Jim Boehm	19: Cyber Strategy That Makes a Difference
Yabing Wang	20: Do's and Don'ts for CISOs
Maryam Betchel	21: Developing Cyber Talent

Author	Chapter title
Steven Brown	22: Managing Critical Vulnerabilities
Jacqui Kernot	23: AI: The Promise and the Challenge

Table 1.3: Part 3 chapters

Part 4: Advice from CISO 'Yoda Masters'

The CISO role is one that is typically 3–4 years in length; however, there are some CISOs with exceptional skills who have held the role of CISO for much longer.

I compare veteran CISOs to Yoda (the fictional character from the *Star Wars* series, a Jedi Master who trained Luke Skywalker and is known for his profound wisdom and ability to see the bigger picture beyond immediate circumstances) in this part of the book. This is apt because Yoda represents the archetype of a master who has transcended technical skill to achieve deep wisdom – someone who can guide others not just through specific techniques, but through the fundamental principles and mindset needed to succeed in a challenging, ever-changing environment. The wisdom of these 'Yoda Masters' means that they have mastered the art of strategic execution and business language fluency. They can distinguish between genuine threats and 'noise', while translating security needs into business outcomes rather than technical jargon.

Most importantly, they truly understand that cybersecurity is about building trust across all stakeholders, using simple and well-executed controls rather than complex systems and prioritising influence over authority.

These are all executive leaders who have ~20 years of experience at a senior leadership level, and their insights are gold. Thus, there are vital lessons from them around career resilience that even the most experienced CISOs can learn from. Allow me to introduce these Yoda Masters to you:

Advice from CISO 'Yoda Masters'	
Author	**Chapter title**
Camilo Sandoval	24: Protecting the USA
Tim Callahan	25: Why Risk Management Matters
Dr David Ng	26: Driving Cyber Transformation
Peter Troy	27: My Metrics Playbook

Author	Chapter title
Meg Anderson	28: Career Resilience
Richard Johnson	29: Lessons in Leading Yourself, Cyber Teams, and Through Crisis

Table 1.4: Part 4 chapters

Diverse voices

In reading this book, it's important to recognise that every CISO and cybersecurity leader is different, with diverse backgrounds and experiences. There are life lessons here that have never been shared before, including what has worked and not worked for each CISO/leader.

The geographical and sector diversity was deliberate. Hence, many of the chapters in this book have been written by new contacts and friends of friends. I did not want 'group think' and sought to find willing volunteers to work with me on telling their own personal stories. I also wanted to have CISOs from different-sized organisations to reflect the reality that we face.

There is incredible geographical diversity of voices represented in this book. The 29 CISOs and leaders who have contributed to this book originate from 13 different countries, although I admit somewhat of a bias towards my own country, Australia.

Having leaders from 13 different countries out of a cohort of 29 demonstrates significant international representation, showing how cybersecurity leadership is drawing talent from a truly global pool.

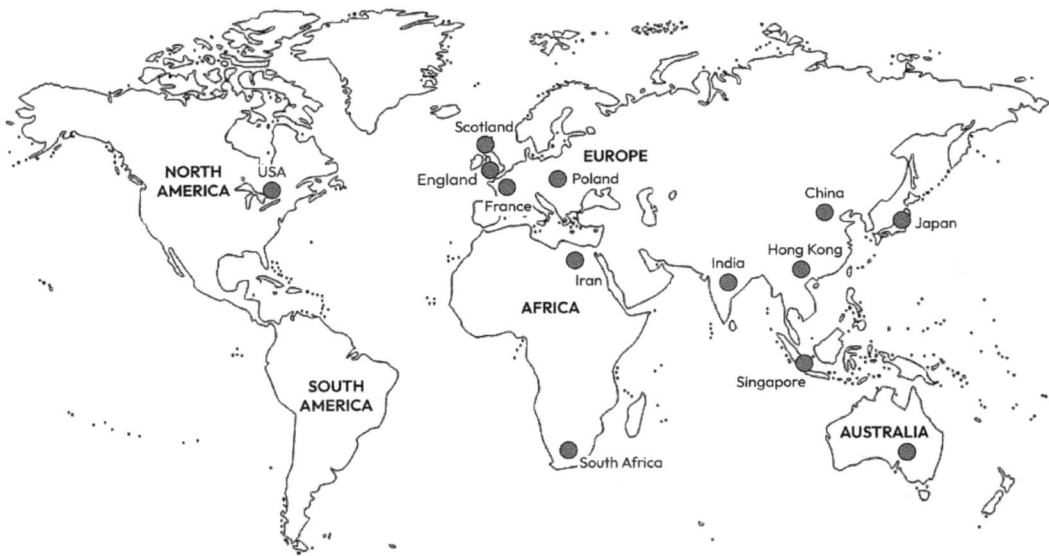

Figure 1.5: The countries of birth for the CISOs and leaders in this book

Diversity is also reflected in the gender and ethnic representation of the contributors to this book. There are 8 female leaders, roughly 28% of the book team, which is above the typical industry average for cybersecurity leadership roles. There are 12 leaders who identify as people of colour (about 41%), which indicates strong ethnic and racial diversity.

The other perspective to consider is which industry and sector these leaders operate in. I admit that there is a sight bias to financial services CISOs here. This sector has been historically better prepared and has invested more in cybersecurity. Otherwise, there is a good distribution across sectors:

	Industry	Number of CISOs/Leaders
$	Financial Services	15
[− +]	Energy	1
☁	Technology	4
🍾	Consumer, Services & Healthcare	4
👥	Government & Consulting	5

Table 1.5 – The working industry of each leader

A few of the contributors are retired, but most are still active in their careers.

This level of diversity in cybersecurity leadership can bring valuable benefits – different cultural perspectives on risk, varied approaches to problem-solving, diverse networks and relationships across global markets and, importantly, leadership teams that better reflect the global nature of cybersecurity threats and the organisations they're protecting.

Each to bring their own voice

The format for this book is that I have invited each of the CISOs and other cybersecurity leaders to talk about their area of personal passion. Rather than dictating the topic, I really wanted each leader to bring their own 'voice' and stories to life to illustrate their life learnings.

For each chapter, this started with each leader nominating their own area of passion: cyber strategy, vulnerability management, etc. The most important criterion was a real personal passion for the topic, and that this would come through in their chapter.

How to read this book

You will notice as you read this book that there is a consistent pattern in each chapter. I start each chapter with an introduction to the topic and to the guest author. I provide context as to why each chapter deals with a difficult subject for a CISO to address and how a CISO might find this challenging. This ensures that we start with a foundation of the problem that is to be addressed in each chapter.

The author of each chapter brings with them their own natural language and style. This will be evident as you read each chapter, and this is aligned with my earlier point that CISOs are all different. An example to highlight is that a CISO who writes in British English will write *centre* and a CISO from the US will write *center*. Note that most publishers and authors will make a conscious choice to write a book with one form of spelling, but given that I want this book to capture as close as possible each contributor's natural voice, we have chosen to adopt this approach.

At the end of each chapter, you will see that I provide a summary of the key points ('takeaways') and learnings from the chapter.

Allow me to expand on how each chapter is woven into the fabric of this book.

Part 1: Advice to the New CISO

Taking on the role of CISO is a major career step. While you feel elated with this accession, there is also a sense of 'oh my gosh – how will I manage this role and be successful?'

As mentioned earlier, the intention of this set of chapters is to provide guidance to the new CISO. It can be read in preparation for this promotion and, of course, in real time as you are undertaking your first days and months in the role. Indeed, the first year as a CISO will be a challenging one, and there will be learnings that you make every day of this journey.

When I was very young, I went to Judo class, and I was never very good at it. I did learn to 'fall', which is in many ways more important than to 'throw'. But there is a famous story about Jigoro Kano, the founder of Judo, who, as he neared death, asked his students to bury him in a white belt rather than his black belt. This symbolised his belief that death makes everyone a beginner again. In life, true mastery depends not on accumulated expertise, but on maintaining the open, curious mindset of a novice throughout one's journey. Hence, for those already in a CISO position, there are lessons in the pages of these chapters that are worthy of your attention.

We start with an incredible story of a new CISO in the first few days in his job having to deal with a major cybersecurity attack (Chapter 2, *Hand-to-Hand Combat with Lazarus*). Just imagine yourself in this position! While you couldn't be blamed for the current cyber defences, you would feel incredibly vulnerable. You wouldn't really have much understanding of the company or the team that you have inherited, or even how your management and board will react. CISO and CIO **James McLeary** explains, in a light-hearted fashion, how he managed to survive this nation-state cyber-attack.

Keith Howard, CISO for Suncorp, provides great insights into his first year as a CISO in the next chapter (Chapter 3, *Priorities for the New CISO*), including what he focused on and what he ignored – some great lessons based on his own successful career.

For most new CISOs, it is unlikely that they have come from a cyber intelligence background. They may not appreciate and value the strategic importance of this capability. Former FS-ISAC Chief Intelligence Officer **Teresa Walsh** writes a letter to the new CISO in Chapter 4 (*Cyber Threat Intelligence That Is Actionable*) – an interesting approach to explaining the importance of cyber intelligence.

Silvia Lam Ihensekhien, CISO at Swire Coca Cola, discusses in Chapter 5 (*How I Got to Be CISO*) how she got to be a CISO and the challenges of being a female CISO in a male-dominated profession, and offers advice to the next generation of female leaders.

> We know that our industry suffers from a lack of diverse talent, but not enough strides have been made to address this.
>
> In one CIO role that I held at Eli Lilly, I worked in Japan, where diversity has not traditionally been strong. Diversity of gender, race and thought are all important dimensions. My boss, Newt Crenshaw, president at Eli Lilly, used to say that he supports diversity as this gives us "a strategic advantage".

Krzysztof Kostienko, Asia Pacific Head of Security at Qube Research and Technologies, former CISO at Morgan Stanley, in Chapter 6 (*The Journey to CISO: From Humble Beginnings to Leadership*), shares the story of his own leadership journey, including studying and working in foreign countries. This is an incredibly grounded account of his personal struggles and challenges.

In Chapter 7 (*Stepping Up into a Global Role*), **Sam Coco,** Head of Global Information Security at Fidelity, shares his path into a global role. He explains what he did to 'step up' into the more complex and challenging assignments that this entailed.

We know that every CISO had a different career path and journey into the role, even if there does tend to be some common ground. **Catherine Rowe**, CISO at Teachers Mutual Bank Limited, in Chapter 8 (*Diverse Paths to Cybersecurity Leadership*), highlights her own, less common career path: how her strong legal background helped her move into the CISO role. She also advocates for broader cybersecurity leadership recruitment practices, expanding recruitment beyond more traditional routes.

Finally, **Stéphane Nappo,** Director of Cybersecurity and Head of Information Systems Security, in Chapter 9 (*Overcoming Doubt*), tackles what is a less obvious but still crucial topic for CISOs: doubt. As a new CISO, there will be those doubting your ability; then, of course, you yourself will have doubts. Indeed, the whole domain of cybersecurity is filled with doubt; we never have full information to make decisions. Stéphane's fascinating thinking provides a great foundation for addressing and reframing doubt and building your own career towards a successful outcome.

Part 2: Building Your CISO Skills

This part deals with navigating the challenges of uplifting cybersecurity maturity, while supporting business operations and innovation. At the same time, you will be developing your own CISO skills that are not fully shaped. While you no longer have '*L*' learner plates displayed, you are still learning the ropes, and mistakes will be made when there is extreme pressure.

This section begins with **Adam Cartwright,** now Group CISO at Australia Post, who wrote a chapter (when he was CISO at Asahi Brewery) about how to defend when you have a smaller budget (*How to Defend with Less*). Having previously worked in financial services, he had to really consider how to allocate dollars when he had less than he was used to investing in the past.

In Chapter 11, the National Australia Bank's Group Chief Security Officer **Sandro Bucchianeri** (*Being Brilliant at the Basics*), who has significant experience working globally and residing in different countries, shares his thoughts around how, as CISO, there is a need to focus on basics, more than anything else, and to do these brilliantly.

On the topic of working in different cultures, we next go to Japan and hear from **Osamu Terai,** Group CISO at Mizuho Financial Group (one of the largest financial services in Japan with $1.9 trillion of total assets), in Chapter 12 (*A CISO in Japan*). Every CISO will struggle to have the right resources, and there is always a shortage of suitable talent. Terai-san shares insights into how he operates in a country that is not blessed with exceptional cyber-trained staff.

The CISO, to be successful, must engage well with the board and management. **Shamane Tan,** Chief Growth Officer at Sekuro, provides a fascinating approach to cyber risk messaging with different stakeholders in Chapter 13 (*Navigating the C-Suite, Boards, and DOPE Dynamics*). She explains how you can tailor your individual approach for the CEO, CFO, CRO, CIO and other members of the C-suite. The CISO's own success is based on getting this done right.

Phoram Mehta, international CISO at PayPal, explores problem-solving, which is a critical competency for the CISO, in Chapter 14 (*Systems Thinking for CISOs*). Systems thinking for a CISO involves viewing cybersecurity as a complex, interconnected system rather than a collection of isolated issues. His approach provides a sense of the bigger picture when stuck in the weeds every day.

The modern CISO must drive change. **Fal Ghancha,** CISO at JIO Blackrock, tackles this topic in Chapter 15, on the CISO as a change agent (*The CISO as a Change Agent*). I'd say that this is not a 'natural' strength of most CISOs, but this can definitely be developed with focus and commitment. For the majority of CISOs, this is a strength that they will need to develop to grow their influence in the business.

For some CISOs, their role will not be enjoyable, and they will want to consider pivoting their career into some alternate paths. **Abbas Kudrati**, himself an accomplished author and Chief Identity Security Advisor at Silverfort, in Chapter 16 (*Alternative Career Paths to Consider*), shares some alternative career options that may not have been obvious to you. Knowing these alternatives will provide you with another 'string to your bow'.

Finally, the CISO will undoubtedly face a moment of truth where it doesn't matter how hard you try, your career comes to an end. It may feel like the end of the world, but it really isn't. Your own personal resilience to deal with these circumstances is very critical to your long-term success. My ex-colleague Dr **Matthew Ryan,** now Head of Cyber, Data and AI Risk at NAB, writes an insightful chapter (Chapter 17, *So, You Got Fired*) on how to bounce back when you do lose your job. This is a topic that many CISOs will encounter and may be unprepared to deal with.

Part 3: Advanced CISO Toolkit

This part I've labelled *Advanced CISO Toolkit*, which is itself a broad topic and will cover items that you perhaps do not need to perform regularly and hence have not mastered. The topics in this part address the most complex, strategic and high-impact challenges that senior cybersecurity leaders face.

Knowing how to rebuild after a breach is not a common attribute that you would see on an average CV. **Daryl Pereira,** Asia Pacific CISO at Google, explores a topic in Chapter 18 that most CISOs have not had to tackle themselves (*Rebuilding after a Breach*). This is an advanced lesson in crisis leadership, and the CISO must know how to orchestrate technical recovery, manage stakeholder communications, conduct forensics, implement lessons learned and rebuild organisational trust to allow the business to rebuild from the ashes and start again.

Jim Boehm is a Chief Digital Risk Officer at McKinsey & Company who specialises in assisting CISOs to develop their cybersecurity strategies. In his career, he has seen many enterprises make efforts to craft a strategy. He will share his approach in Chapter 19 (*Cyber Strategy That Makes a Difference*) to strategic thinking that separates senior CISOs from tactical security professionals. The cybersecurity roadmap must align cybersecurity with business objectives, building long-term roadmaps, securing executive buy-in and translating technical risks into business language that boards understand.

There are many do's and don'ts in your tenure as CISO. **Yabing Wang,** CISO at Justworks, details in her chapter (Chapter 20, *Do's and Don'ts for CISOs*) her own personal perspectives on these.

We all have heard about the global talent shortage. The advanced CISO must be an organisational leader who can build, retain and scale security teams. This includes succession planning, skills development, creating career pathways and addressing the cybersecurity talent shortage strategically. I'd note that this is not necessarily a traditional strength of many CISO peers. **Maryam Bechtel** is CISO at AGL Energy, and she shares her insights in Chapter 21 into what she does to accelerate this capability (*Developing Cyber Talent*).

Managing critical vulnerabilities is a thankless and endless task. If you do this well, then your enterprise will have a reduced risk position. **Steven Brown,** a former CISO at Macquarie Group, shares his thoughts in Chapter 22 (*Managing Critical Vulnerabilities*) on enterprise-wide vulnerability governance, risk prioritisation across complex environments and coordinating responses that balance security with business continuity.

Finally, AI provides a new double-edged sword of both promise and challenge. CISOs must navigate AI's dual nature as both a powerful security tool and a new attack vector, while addressing governance, ethics and the transformational impact on cybersecurity operations. **Jacqui Kernot,** VP at Thales Cyber Security Services and Managing Director at Tesserent, shares her own thoughts and insights on this emerging field in Chapter 23 (*AI: The Promise and Challenge*). Mastering AI will require the CISO to enhance their strategic thinking and organisational leadership.

Part 4: Advice from CISO 'Yoda Masters'

Many of you will have watched *Star Wars* and know the character 'Yoda'. He is a wise warrior who shares wisdom from his long and successful career.

This section includes cybersecurity CISO veterans who, like Yoda, are incredibly wise, with a wealth of CISO experience. I can guarantee you will learn lessons from every leader in this section. They have successfully managed strategic delivery and uplift with stakeholder engagement plus navigating regulators to help their businesses succeed.

Firstly, in this part, I'm personally thrilled to introduce **Camilo Sandoval** (Chapter 24, *Protecting the USA*), who served as **White House** Federal CISO during President Trump's first administration. Camilo held this critical role during an unprecedented time – navigating cybersecurity challenges throughout COVID-19. In his chapter, he provides a compelling behind-the-scenes account of his experiences in the White House and reveals the extraordinary complexity of coordinating cybersecurity across the 24 major federal agencies under his purview.

Tim Callahan, global CISO at Aflac Insurance, shares his thoughts in Chapter 25 (*Why Risk Management Matters*) on why risk management is so crucial to CISOs. The experienced CISO understands that this is the language and lens of the board.

David Ng, CISO at OCBC Bank, has also had a long and distinguished career as a regulator at **Monetary Authority of Singapore (MAS)**. David shares, in Chapter 26 (*Driving Cyber Transformation*), his thoughts around cybersecurity transformation and driving this maturity uplift over many years. His experiences are unique, and as a result, he has valuable learning perspectives to share in tackling a multi-year cyber uplift.

In Chapter 27, **Peter Troy,** former CISO at **Morgan Stanley,** shares practical tips on developing effective metrics (*My Metrics Playbook*). Peter understands that 'facts are friends', and his framework is simple but powerful.

Meg Anderson, formerly of **Principal Financial Group,** had a 17+ year tenure as CISO. In Chapter 28 (*Career Resilience*), she shares her learnings around career resilience and, indeed, how this is her secret ingredient for success.

Finally, I'm honoured to introduce **Richard Johnson,** Group CISO at **Westpac,** who has served 17 years in this capacity. In his chapter (*Chapter 29, Lessons in Leading Yourself, Cyber Teams, and Through Crisis*), he shares the key lessons he's learnt during his long tenure as a CISO with us.

Richard, Meg and David are indeed unicorns in this world, where the average CISO lasts 3–4 years. Their life lessons are worth reading this book for if nothing else. Their survival skills are indeed incredible, and it's important that these are shared with the next generation.

My approach to developing this book

There are 24+ different CISOs (current and former) featured in this book. (Actually, there are 25 CISOs, with me included.) There are also 4 others that work closely with the CISO across their ecosystems as cyber strategy consultants or vendors, or, like Dr Matthew Ryan, an aspiring CISO. A few of these contributors are already authors and have published one or more books themselves, but for the majority, this is their first published work. As such, the approach has been quite agile, with every engagement slightly different.

The process worked this way: following my initial Zoom call with each CISO, we agreed on the concept and topic for the chapter. I would then write an introductory page before sharing it with the author and providing some prompts and questions for the content.

Each contributor's approach to writing the content was also incredibly diverse – some chapters were completed after a series of interviews and using voice transcripts, into a draft that was manually edited into a document for review. Others were more traditional drafts, which were then reviewed.

Most chapters were developed in a very interactive manner, with editing and reviews from multiple parties, including corporate communications departments. There was also technical editing from two past colleagues of mine – **Simon Blanchet,** ex-HSBC executive, and **Dr Matthew Ryan,** ex-Macquarie Group executive (and one of the contributors to this book). I'm extremely grateful to both Simon and Matt for their assistance on this project and, moreover, their amazing work with me in my past career where they provided intelligent and challenging 'hard core' delivery of cybersecurity.

As I also wanted to include a chapter from **Osamu Terai** in Japanese, we enlisted the expertise of **Yoshimasa Kobayashi,** who generously provided support for this (you can download the Japanese version of this chapter from: https://github.com/PacktPublishing/A-Day-in-the-Life-of-a-CISO).

A sneak peek — some common themes

As I read the chapters, it became clear that there are some common themes that came through in the learnings of a few of the leaders. Noting that each leader did not have the opportunity to read each other's chapters during development, this is purely a coincidence. Allow me to highlight a couple of these here for you, as a sneak peek (I will reflect on and talk about key themes in more detail in *Chapter 30, Sunset*).

The first thing I should highlight is **imposter syndrome.** Several of the CISOs noted that they felt they were not ready to be a CISO and had the dreaded 'imposter syndrome' when they attained their new role.

Another key theme that I noticed was how the CISOs dealt with the stress of their roles and managed their own mindfulness to be able to effectively cope with the challenges they faced. In a typical CISO's day, there will always be conflicting requirements, meaning that you have to make quick decisions about where to and where not to focus. Some CISOs talked about exercise as an approach to clearing their mind and helping them to be prepared for the challenges that they faced each day.

No doubt, as you read these chapters, there will be some other key themes and patterns that you will start to recognise. As a leader who aspires to be a CISO, or someone who wants to be a better CISO, there are some great lessons that you can learn from your predecessors. Some of these you will want to adopt and try yourself and, in other cases, you may decide to take on part of these learnings only, or they may become part of a future-facing list of things that you desire and can use as clues to help you progress along your own path. In the era of AI, the CISO will have more to defend but also more new attack vectors to address. There is no better time than now to invest in your own development.

Enjoy your day with our CISOs and leaders!

Sunrise has always been a symbolic time that marks a new beginning with new opportunities and challenges. Our ancestors would feel safer in the daylight as the sun rose and the darkness faded, and one could better see the dangers lurking in the shadows.

For the CISO, cyber-attacks can occur at any time. What will we face in this new day? What will this day bring to the CISO, and what learnings can you gain today to prepare yourself, your team and your company to defend against the new threats you will face tomorrow?

As the day unfolds alongside fellow CISOs and leaders, remember that the progress we forge today lays the groundwork for a more secure tomorrow – for our organisations, our teams, ourselves and, indeed, the very leaders who guide us.

Today's mentoring engagements with these global CISOs and leaders offer invaluable opportunities to not only safeguard our present but also glean the insights and lessons that will shape the next generation of cybersecurity defence, benefiting us all.

See you at Happy Hour drinks at the end of the day!

Best regards,

David J. Gee

Part 1

Advice to the New CISO

Every leader must start somewhere. Like children playing hide-and-seek who call out "ready or not, here I come", new CISOs must step into their roles regardless of their own skill gaps, limited experience, or possible imposter syndrome. Unfortunately, you can't hide, and the challenges are not going to wait until you're perfectly prepared – it is all about learning to lead effectively while acknowledging what you don't yet know.

The stories and guidance in this part of the book will help the new CISO, and indeed some current leaders, with lessons to help them succeed as a CISO.

This part has the following chapters:

- *Chapter 2, Hand-to-Hand Combat with Lazarus*
- *Chapter 3, Priorities for the New CISO*
- *Chapter 4, Cyber Threat Intelligence That Is Actionable*
- *Chapter 5, How I Got to Be CISO*
- *Chapter 6, The Journey to CISO: From Humble Beginnings to Leadership*
- *Chapter 7, Stepping Up into a Global Role*
- *Chapter 8, Diverse Paths to Cybersecurity Leadership*
- *Chapter 9, Overcoming Doubt*

Unlock this book's exclusive benefits now

UNLOCK NOW

Scan this QR code or go to https://packtpub.com/unlock,
then search this book by name.

Note: Have your purchase invoice ready before you start.

2

Hand-to-Hand Combat
with Lazarus

Receiving a phone call on a Friday afternoon about a potentially serious cyber incident is something that every CISO dreads. Having your heart skip a beat in such a scenario is inescapable.

Whenever a CISO must manage a serious incident, this must take priority over anything else on their schedule.

Imagine if the Lazarus Group, the infamous hacker group from North Korea, which has strong suspected links to the national government, pays you a visit. Lazarus is renowned as an **Advanced Persistent Threat (APT38)** actor that has a successful track record of attacking payment systems.

Now pause and consider how you would feel as a new CISO, dealing with this in your very first few days on the job. This can, and does, happen, as you will learn in this chapter.

While it is true that there will always be gaps in your knowledge, when you are brand new in your CISO role, there are more unknowns than knowns.

The cyber hackers and researchers who work for Lazarus have been trained in China, and only the best students undertake this extensive training. How would you feel if you were face to face with such an adversary, especially as a new CISO? There would, of course, be some element of fear as you wonder how to get yourself out of the tough situation.

When such incidents occur, there is usually missing information, and the root cause is rarely understood in the early stages. Being calm and considered is the only way to manage incidents such as this. There will always be further investigations involved, often with third-party vendors and partners. However, the incident will need to remain confidential, with information being shared on a 'need-to-know' basis.

At this stage, some preliminary internal communication with the CIO, COO, CEO, and so on will be carried out. Where required, some external communications can also be prepared. The amount of internal 'noise' can be disproportionate to the cyber incident itself, as many stakeholders will want to know what's going on to protect themselves and their own interests.

As a CISO, your role is to defend the enterprise; it is when major incidents occur that you really earn your salary. There are endless crisis calls and briefings that are required, and the pressure on your own team is at extreme levels.

I'd like to introduce **James McLeary**, a CISO who earned his pay when he found himself in the very situation I have described – his enterprise was attacked by Lazarus, within his first few days as CISO. James is currently **CIO** and **CISO** of a hospital in Thailand. He has previously served as an MD in cyber consultancy and was CISO at various banks in Thailand and the wider region, including risk executive roles at HSBC and GE. It is fitting that James is also a Six Sigma Master Black Belt, and he applied all his problem-solving skills in a similar way in hand-to-hand combat with Lazarus.

Lazarus is well known for their sophisticated and adaptable tactics approach – their most famous attacks include the Sony Pictures (2014), WannaCry (2017), and Harmony Bridge (2022) attacks. James will share what happened and how he felt during this event with 'warts and all' details (where that is feasible).

What James has experienced is unique, and the fact that he has survived to tell this tale is a testament to his own cyber abilities, and perhaps a slice of luck!

This chapter reflects James' personal experience and interpretations. While based on real events, specific names and institutions have been omitted or generalised to maintain confidentiality.

The Incident

James McLeary

With the weekend approaching, I was making plans to go down to the relaxing beachside resort of Hua Hin and escape the hustle and bustle of Bangkok. Friday evening traffic when getting out of Bangkok is horrendous, though; I'd need to leave the office around 4 pm. to avoid at least some of it. However, this particular Friday had other things in store for me that did not involve relaxing, as I was about to find out.

Just before noon, my head of SOC came running over anxiously. He proceeded to explain that we had received an encrypted email from the **Computer Emergency Response Team (CERT)** with separate instructions on how to decode it. The email contained details from BAE Systems and law enforcement authorities explaining that they had been tracking known IP assets belonging to the notorious North Korean state-sponsored threat actor, Lazarus APT38, and that one of those assets had suddenly come online after some significant dormant period. The asset in question was directing traffic to and from IPs belonging to the bank I was working for. The email then went into details of traffic observed at different dates and times and ended with the recommendation to initiate investigations and incident response immediately.

My head immediately began spinning and I felt nauseous. Was this really happening? I mean, obviously, I'd heard of Lazarus from their Bank of Bangladesh heist, their attack on Sony, and other banking SWIFT and ATM attacks, but why Thailand, why this bank, why me?!

7th September is a day that I will remember for a long time. The events that proceeded to play out over a three-month period would in fact redefine my whole career.

Escalation

There was no time to feel overly sorry for myself. This was now a crisis that needed to be managed. I instructed my team to check the asset IP ranges identified in the email and to scan for any recent traffic to the provided malicious address. In the meantime, I needed to get this escalated to the executive level. My immediate boss, the COO, was overseas, so I requested urgent meetings with the CEO and CRO whilst setting up an afternoon meeting with the COO.

In the meantime, I gave a call to an **Incident Response (IR)** company that I had recently met with, and they offered to start gathering threat intel immediately and have boots on the ground from Israel by Monday. After explaining the gravitas of the situation to the executives, I was given the authority to engage the IR firm and to arrange crisis management meetings, but I was also left with the view that their sense of crisis was not anywhere close to the level of concern that I had.

The IR firm was a company from Israel and was made up largely of ex-military cyber red-teamers. They flew in over the weekend and set up in the **WAR (Work Area Recovery)** room on Monday morning. There was a definite air of no messing around with them, and they started to make their presence felt immediately.

Thai culture is very polite and respectful; 'losing face' is a real consideration in getting things done in the workplace. However, the IR team approached it as a mission and, quite quickly, the local IT team was caught in the headlights of the speed of response activities and the demands to improve defensive and responsive capabilities. This was no time for sensitivities, though; remediation must be done, reported back on when it is done, and it had better be done properly.

The infrastructure visibility gaps, the skillset maturity gaps with the current SOC provider, the cultural and language barriers, and, importantly, the general misunderstanding of how serious in nature this attack was all made for an incredibly challenging first few days in my new job.

The nightmare begins

On the following Monday, we received notice of unusual, attempted logins to the SWIFT operator PCs. There had been multiple unsuccessful login attempts – eight events within one minute at 17.09 UTC on 10th September. Destination account: `mstrswift`; Result: Unknown username or bad password.

This event really caught everyone's attention, including the **Crisis Management Team (CMT)**. Now they knew that we had a serious matter on our hands. I had already updated them on who exactly Lazarus are and what they are capable of. So now we initiated daily CMT meetings to review the situation and make decisions in response to the unfolding situation. I was tasked with daily briefings, which would include a status update, activities taken, planned actions, and, importantly, the allocation and tracking of emergency budget to aid the response. For most (actually, all) members of the CMT, this was the first major cyber event they had experienced.

We ordered a full reconciliation of all recent SWIFT transactions and manual checking on all payments. This put a lot of demand on the operations teams, who, of course, did not appreciate the additional workload, but it was a very necessary move. We needed to account for every transaction that had been sent out, because it seemed like just a matter of time before there would be rogue transactions, and then we had better be ready to pull out the plug.

The IR team was tasked with looking at the SWIFT operator's machines, and they reported back that they were not sufficiently secured. The machines were not built in a sufficiently hardened way that would protect and isolate them from a skillful attacker. A decision was made to create new secure images, restricting internet access and access from other network resources. This would take some time, though, to get in place, so in the meantime, careful manual oversight was needed.

By this stage, we had identified several staff workstations that had been compromised, from the contact centre, to operations, to **Information Technology** (**IT**), and even the cyber security team. We initiated the collection of some physical forensic images, including the SWIFT operator's PCs and some compromised laptops of high-privilege users, to submit through the MySWIFT customer portal, allowing SWIFT to conduct their own forensics investigation.

At the same time, our own investigation was underway using the **Endpoint Detection and Response** (**EDR**) available to determine how broad the compromise had gone. A key obstacle, though, was the current lack of visibility across all endpoints. The EDR solution was not sufficiently deployed across the organisation to get full coverage. So, we embarked on additional deployment with a goal of getting to around 90% coverage across client and server sides. This, amongst many other matters, started to raise real conflicts between the IT function and IT security! We were doubling, no, tripling, their workload, and for them it was a security issue – why were they having to work day and night and weekends now for these additional demands that would typically take months to implement?

Now, to make matters even more complex, we decided to bring in another IR firm, the Ghostbusters team from Microsoft. At the same time, we decided to appoint an IR retainer firm, Mandiant. So, there I am now, having to manage three separate IR companies, plus a whole host of additional vendors (EDR, network, desktop support, forensic imaging, local MSSP, and more!). The WAR room was starting to really fill up, and the entire office floor was just a hive of activity, with people running and shouting and marking up whiteboards of actions.

The overall response mission was given the code name 'Operation Sunset,' which was a fitting name for Thailand, I guess, but for sure it was going to be quite some time before I would get to see one of those famous sunsets – I had a crisis on my hands!

Managing external stakeholders

Managing internal stakeholders during a major crisis is difficult enough, but as the CISO, you typically must deal with a whole host of external stakeholders in addition – especially in an emerging economy and an institution that is going through its first major cyber-attack.

First up, the regulator.

The regulator

Upon notification of the situation, the regulator instigated daily updates and briefings. The words "zero-day" and "data exfiltration" raised concerns with them. We had to provide very detailed summaries each morning of the prior day's events and actions, but it was always received with the additional query of "what and how much data has been taken out by the attacker?" Our explanations became frustratingly repetitive. We had a rough idea of the size of the data but couldn't determine its content as it was encrypted data. Moreover, we explained that for this threat actor, Lazarus, data exfiltration was not normally the modus operandi.

Visa got wind of the situation through their own threat intel. They were concerned about ATM jackpotting (using malware to manipulate ATM software, causing it to dispense cash on demand). This opened a whole new front in my investigation of this incident: now, I was not only dealing with a SWIFT attack, but a possible ATM heist! Following that statement, Visa instructed us to appoint a PFI investigation firm of their selection, to which my reply is better not repeated here – I had no intention of going from three IR firms to four!

Counterparties and other banks

Counterparties and other banks were other external stakeholders. One of our key SWIFT counterparties connected through their own threat intel of the situation. Despite the initial reservations of being completely transparent, this proved to be one of the key successes of the entire situation. Our security teams worked collaboratively, and we were able to instigate a series of measures to help in the protection, monitoring, and response should the endgame be affected. Make no mistake, we were very clear that this would be on us if all hell broke loose, but I highly appreciate the assistance that was provided; you know who you are!

At the same time, some friendly CISOs of other banks were keen to reach out to me and advise that their threat intel had identified something. My response was prepackaged – thank you for the information, we are aware of the situation and are taking all necessary measures to resolve it.

The press

The press was not something I considered I'd personally have to be involved with, but remember, this was an emerging economy in the last decade. I was informed that if this situation went wrong and there was a successful SWIFT compromise, then I would need to be part of the press spokesperson team. Given that the local press was in a language that I still only had a basic grasp of, this was a huge concern and an additional source of stress – but an important point to consider in your incident communication plans.

Whilst I was busy managing stakeholders, the IR teams were busy determining the scope of the incident.

Malware and compromise detections

The IR teams were reporting back regularly on the malware that they had uncovered. Much of it was benign or not related, such as identifying crypto-mining malware that had been there for some time. However, the malware detected that was specific to the Lazarus attack was both frightening and recognisable as having the hallmarks of the threat actor.

A destructive malware was found that had the capability of wiping out the boot records of servers. This one truly had my stress levels through the roof. I was informed by the Microsoft team that a similar malware was used as a decoy tactic in a SWIFT attack on a Latin American bank. APT38 had launched the destructive malware, wiping a whole bunch of application servers that had the IT teams scrambling to put out the fire, then launched the SWIFT attack in parallel!

A whole series of custom-built malware, remote access trojans, backdoors, PowerShell in-memory execution commands, and deletion of activities was uncovered, including what was classified as a zero-day malware. This really concerned all stakeholders, and I had to give a series of briefings internally and externally on the meaning and significance of those simple words "zero-day."

The number of endpoints classed as compromised really started to rack up.

To my dismay, they included:

- IT infrastructure, where both keylogging and video recording evidence was found that had been extracted by the threat actor, as well as all the sensitive architecture documents
- SWIFT IT architectecture, where detailed SWIFT diagrams and other related artefacts had been obtained
- IT identity and access management, which allowed them to gain very high privileges to move within the network
- IT security team members, where one of the artefacts discovered was a stolen Notepad file that contained names, IP addresses, and logon credentials for much of our cyber solutions (SIEM, WAF, IPS, etc.)

Other significant findings included the modification of genuine Microsoft binary files that enabled the attackers to bypass some multi-factor authentication. It included a recording of an EDR scan on a compromised laptop with the message "no malicious activity found," despite there being malware on this device! It also included the early determination that the Active Directory had been compromised with a legacy domain admin account that was used for basic admin activities by IT across the network – later, we would find out that it took just five days to take over the domain controller.

As the investigation moved along, I shared some of the malware and imaging with the key authorities in accordance with their instructions. They, of course, came back and informed me that the evidence provided was consistent with prior attacks by Lazarus APT38 on SWIFT environments and ATMs in other banks.

Red herrings

I have to give mention to some of the red herrings that occur when in the middle of such a significant cyber crisis, because they do indeed take the CISO's stress levels to whole new levels, as well as wasting valuable response time and efforts.

Was I, as CISO, compromised? It was raised to me that this could be the case, and no doubt, as a high-profile position for a cyber attacker, the probability was high. However, what did not help with this suggestion was the possible scenario put forward that the SWIFT communications I had received were from the threat actor who was phishing me for information. Put that one on the first page of the pending newspaper article! Thankfully, I was able to put this scenario to rest after verification via the MySWIFT portal of the genuine nature of the communications that had been received up to that point.

During this period, I also had several messages in this vein: "The mobile banking application is having performance issues. Is it associated with the cyber-attack? Customers are complaining!" It didn't seem likely. I mean, we'd already pretty much established the threat actor and their motives, so causing performance issues didn't seem like something we needed to involve the IR teams in. However, I was quickly realising that all IT operational issues were being tagged with the "it's because of the cyber-attack" brush, and these just dragged us down a whole new series of rabbit holes.

A similar event occurred that was termed as an internal DDOS attack, which initially we thought was the attacker. This was actually more likely a result of the heavy workload of IT operational activities going on across the network for both the day-to-day IT operations, the cyber response operations, and the addition of new cyber solutions to protect, detect, and respond.

The biggest false flag, though, turned out to be the whole ATM jackpotting attack that Visa was convinced was at play. From early in the investigation, we had indicators of attempts to compromise SWIFT, but nothing around the ATM environment. Nonetheless, we put major response activities in play to try to determine whether there was any compromise of ATM-related assets, as well as preparing detailed plans of what would be done if such an event were successful. Although nothing was found across the ATM assets, the investigative response was warranted as such an attack would have been a significant loss financially and reputationally.

A lucky escape

After several weeks of gruelling IR activity, I was confronted with making a key decision that would indeed prove pivotal to the whole affair. I was informed that on the coming weekend, IT had a scheduled upgrade planned to the overall SWIFT environment, one that would result in significant changes to the architecture. The question posed to me was, should the upgrade go ahead as planned?

I consulted my team and the incident responders, and there were clearly mixed opinions. On the one hand, if we did the upgrade, the attackers would absolutely know that we are on to them: they would know that we knew they were there. That could result in drastic action, such as an immediate launch of the attacks on the SWIFT system or execution of the destroy malware that would wipe out who knows what. Perhaps we would be better off continuing to covertly investigate, build defences, and be ready for a future eviction of the threat actor from the environment.

On the other hand, this was a planned upgrade. We should, in theory, be continuing with our normal activity, including upgrades, maintenance, and other changes to infrastructure. Behaving differently could also trigger the threat actor into aggressive action because it was likely they had obtained details of our planned activities.

This decision was being placed squarely on me due to the gravity and nature of the overall situation, and after much discussion and deliberation, I decided that we would go ahead with the planned upgrade to the SWIFT environment, with around-the-clock monitoring of any adverse response.

The days that followed the upgrade were, you could say, tense, but although unnoticed at the time, we started to see a drop in the daily counts of compromised assets. We started to see a drop in the number of artefacts being retrieved by the IR teams. Until such time as we started seeing no more assets compromised and zero additional artefacts being recovered. Could it just be that the upgrade to the SWIFT environment and redesign of the architecture had the surprising effect of causing the attackers to leave our network? This really was not expected, nor intended, but just maybe the new complexities introduced by the upgrade had given us the lucky escape of the attackers deciding to move on elsewhere.

Around the same time, our 'patient zero' was confirmed. Patient zero being the point of entry of the attack, the day it all started, the first person compromised. It turned out to be a phishing attack, originating from Vietnam, which included some Microsoft objects that bypassed email protection. When our patient zero, a front-line staff member, clicked on the attachment, it opened a whole world of pain for the organisation. The attacker was able to quickly establish persistence, move laterally across the network, build up privilege access, and compromise the Active Directory.

Interestingly, though, we noted that the date of the patient zero compromise was just around three weeks before we received the threat intelligence notification of the attack. This would prove crucial and the second lucky break. Very often, the dwell time (that is, the time that the attacker is inside the network before being detected) is very long – months, even years. Certainly, with prior Lazarus SWIFT attacks, the dwell time has been shown to be quite significant, allowing a very comprehensive understanding of the organisation by the attacker and a very robust capability established that would allow them to complete their final mission.

By receiving that encrypted threat intelligence notification after just three weeks from the initial compromise, that fateful day was, in hindsight, my luckiest day! Who knows what the outcome would have been if it had been a month or several months later? That said, threat intelligence must be acted upon, and my immediate escalation and response to the information that was given to me was undoubtedly critical to coming out successful and avoiding a SWIFT attack – that part was not luck, that was skill.

The compromise recovery

So, it appeared we had successfully contained the incident, without any financial or reputational loss resulting from a completed cyber-attack. Time to pack our bags, go home, and enjoy the beach, right? Not quite. Now came the strenuous job of recovery.

We still could not guarantee that the attackers were simply dormant. For all we knew, they could come back at any time and pick up where they left off. We needed to perform an eviction! Over a weekend, a very long weekend, we planned to rebuild the domain controllers, reset the passwords and Kerberos KRBTGT (the default key distribution account in Active Directory), and bring it all back online clean and secure – only then could we have confidence that the threat actor had been evicted from our systems.

The preparation for this proved to be a six-week exercise and a lot of overnight shifts for everyone involved. The clean builds had to be meticulous to ensure that we were not simply rebuilding with already-compromised assets that would allow a backdoor to the attackers. We followed best-practice guidelines to the letter in getting the new domain controllers prepared to go live, where we would swap out the old and bring in the new.

We had to gather all the threat intelligence and artefacts that had been uncovered during the investigation and work with our key IT partners, such as network providers, EDR provider, and more, to get ready to receive this threat intelligence the evening before our eviction weekend so that they could ensure that their devices had these new signatures and could block against them accordingly. This had to be done in a time-sensitive fashion as it contained zero-day artefacts that, once known, would no longer be zero-day, and the threat actors would know that also.

All this preparation work for the eviction weekend included the very tough decision on whether the weekend would involve a complete shutdown of the internet, a partial shutdown, or no shutdown at all. The intention of the eviction was to minimise the risk of the attacker coming back into the network, so closing all internet access during that time when the Active Directory was being reset would minimise the risk. However, it came with key business operational issues for a bank that operates 24x7. An alternative approach was to do a partial shutdown by whitelisting certain services that needed to operate over that weekend. A partial shutdown, though, ran the risk that the attacker would come back in via the whitelisted channels. More importantly, though, a partial approach is extremely difficult in a complex banking environment because you need to be sure of all the different components of the infrastructure that make up the business service to whitelist them. The last approach, no shutdown of the internet, is, of course, the highest risk as the attacker could come into the network as the eviction is taking place, making the whole thing pointless.

We decided to go with a partial shutdown – there were too many 24x7 business operations on the weekend that could not accept a full closure. This resulted in digging out **Business Impact Analysis (BIA)** documents and realising that we did not have full coverage of all the IT dependencies.

Asking such questions as "If we whitelist the Fleet Card function, could they operate if the mobile banking was offline?" is not the sort of scenario you want to brainstorm during a crisis.

My final thoughts

The battle wounds you gain as a CISO from a major cyber-attack are what make you. Without them, it's like learning to read music but never playing an instrument. You truly learn so much, teachings that can only be learnt by practical experience. It is for sure one of the most terrifying and stressful experiences of your life – as I recall telling my wife, either this goes well and I am going on a speaking tour, or it doesn't and we are moving to New Zealand (it was as far away as I could manage!).

After the event, I decided that I wanted to go into consulting and take what I had learned to assist other companies, so the attack was pivotal in my career. In those years of consulting, I've been involved in many such major incidents globally, and I always look at the CISO. Often, it's their first incident, and I understand exactly what they are going through. I tell them that I am there for them, whatever they need, and I gently lay out how matters might progress and what steps should be considered. For that is exactly what one of the incident responders did for me, and it was exactly what I needed at exactly that moment in time.

Cyber-attacks will, of course, continue to occur day after day around the globe, and who knows, tomorrow it could be you who is dealing with one. If it is, then just know that with some quick reactions, help from trusted advisors, and a huge dash of good luck, it might just be all okay.

David's key takeaways — Hand-to-hand combat with Lazarus

James's real-world experience here demonstrates that surviving a sophisticated nation-state attack requires both technical preparedness and strong crisis management skills, with success often depending on how quickly you can mobilise resources and make critical decisions under extreme pressure. As a CISO, a major incident is always a test, but a nation-state attack when you are a few days into the role is an incredible personal challenge.

James' story is both exhilarating and exhausting. Remember his experience on the job as CISO was measured in days. I just love his insights and felt that I was there with him; just imagine and put yourself in his shoes. How would you cope? Indeed, many may not make it through and the day in the life of the CISO for James turned into night – I mean *nightmare*!

Here are the key learning points from James's cyber incident story, where he survived his battle with a nation state and lived to tell us his lessons learnt:

- *Immediate executive escalation is critical.* When receiving threat intelligence about sophisticated attackers such as the Lazarus Group, escalate immediately to the CEO/C-suite level regardless of initial executive concern levels. The gravity of state-sponsored attacks requires executive buy-in and emergency budget allocation from day one to mount an effective response.

- *Build comprehensive IR partnerships early.* Establish relationships with multiple specialised IR firms before you need them, as complex attacks require diverse expertise (forensics, threat intel, malware analysis).

- *Infrastructure visibility gaps amplify a crisis* – insufficient endpoint coverage and monitoring capabilities will severely hamper your response when under attack. Prioritise achieving 90%+ endpoint visibility across your environment before a crisis hits, as trying to deploy these capabilities during an active incident creates additional operational stress and delays critical investigation work.

- *Stakeholder management is half the battle* – managing internal teams, regulators, counterparties, and potentially also the media requires as much attention as the technical response itself. Prepare standardised communication templates and designate clear roles for stakeholder management, as you'll be fielding constant updates while trying to coordinate the technical response.

- *Distinguish real threats from 'noise.'* During a major incident, every IT issue will be attributed to the cyber-attack, creating false flags that waste precious response resources. Maintain focus on confirmed threat actor activities and don't let routine operational problems derail your IR teams from their primary mission.

- *Timing and luck matter, but preparation is key* – early threat intelligence notification helped prevent a successful SWIFT attack, but quick escalation and decisive action were equally crucial. While some elements are beyond your control, having robust response procedures and trusted advisor relationships positions you to capitalise on any lucky breaks that may come your way.

3

Priorities for the New CISO

Your very first day as a CISO is a momentous one. This is a role that you have likely aspired to and coveted for some time. You enter the office with a sense of self-doubt and a degree of imposter syndrome. At the same time, you feel a growing weight of responsibility that you carry with this strategically important position.

As you walk around the office on that first day, you are noticed, and staff take a second glance at you. Each step feels weighted – not just by your own physical presence, but by the somewhat invisible architecture of expectation and responsibility around you.

My own credentials were impeccable – years of cybersecurity experience, advanced certifications, and a track record of successful defence strategies. And yet, there I was, feeling like an apprentice on the first day of an impossible quest.

"This is the new boss," the other staff were perhaps thinking, or there may have been more complex thoughts swirling around but remaining unsaid. I was sure that I knew what they were thinking:

> *Another CISO executive. Another cyber strategy.*
>
> *Another temporary guardian.*

Moving that aside, what indeed should you try to tackle in your first six months, or year, in the role of a CISO? You understand and realise that the clock is ticking and the positive outcomes that you drive will either keep you in the role or could lead to your demise.

The first 90 days are critical, and I dedicated a chapter to this in my book, *The Aspiring CIO and CISO*. Taking this a step further, this chapter will explore what to do in the first six months as a CISO.

It is my pleasure to introduce **Keith Howard, CISO** at **Suncorp.** Keith has been group CISO at Commonwealth Bank of Australia (CBA) and served as a CIO in various customer-facing roles. Prior to CBA, he worked at BP and at SAP. Keith is one of the new-age CISOs with a strong CIO business change background.

I'm personally fascinated to read Keith's learnings and compare them to my own story of making the transition from CIO to CISO.

Priorities for new CISOs: the first six months

Keith Howard

"Well done, I didn't think you'd last more than six months!" Always straight to the point, my mentor had called me on my third anniversary as a CISO. As this was a new revelation, I asked why.

"Well, you were just a projects and tech transformation guy; I thought the stress would get to you!"

Defining your key priorities as a new CISO – together with their what, why, and when – is crucial. During the initial six month period, you'll establish your leadership presence; meet senior stakeholders eager to hear your plans; gain a deep understanding of the organisation's security posture; seek and receive multiple views of what is going well, and not so well; establish, maintain, or super-charge your security program's momentum; and begin implementing a strategic vision that aligns with business objectives and an effective operating model to deliver it.

In this chapter, I outline five key priorities I have found helpful during this period. My intention is to lighten the load that concerned my mentor and help you set the foundations for long-term success!

Priority 1: Before you accept the offer...

There are a few things to consider prior to accepting the role to ensure you get the best possible 'scaffolding' to support you:

- What are the expectations of your role in terms of visibility with key stakeholders and the ability to influence at the highest levels? Having regular time in front of the board, executive leadership team, regulators, and so on is an important aspect of driving the understanding of, and support for, the cyber agenda.

- Are you comfortable that who you are reporting to will also effectively represent and support the cyber agenda?

- Over time, I've become less concerned with the 'should the CISO report to the CIO/CRO/CEO and so on' debate (provided the position has a 'seat at the table' to influence the key decisions required). My perspective is that the attributes, efficacy, support, and understanding of the person you report to are more important than their title in enabling you to successfully advance your priorities.

- Have you had an opportunity to meet with the people in roles that you will be working heavily with, such as the head of infrastructure, the chief risk officer (CRO), and the head of audit? Establishing solid and productive working relationships with people in roles such as these from the outset will be essential to delivering your agenda and will also give you a flavour of what you are walking into!

- Ensure there is agreement in principle for building your personal support network, such as a retainer for a small (preferably global) group of external advisors; membership of a CISO peer group (e.g., FS-ISAC; CISO Lens [Australia & New Zealand], etc.). Such networks provide excellent support, insights, peer review, intel, and occasional gallows humour, which are essential in a crisis.

- Work on yourself. The role of CISO in an ambiguous and demanding world – within an evolving threat landscape where perfect security does not exist – can be all-consuming. It's never too early to consider how you will best manage yourself and your time, pressures, hobbies, health, work-life balance, and breaks to ensure you retain the energy to enjoy the ride, rather than be burnt out by it.

These points are not intended to be exhaustive. My main point is, take the time to step back and think about what would be helpful to set you up for day one and beyond.

Priority 2: What's your reference point?

At the end of the day, a CISO's *raison d'être* is to continuously identify, prioritise, and address the most significant cyber risks faced by your organisation based on the threat landscape, risk appetite, and business objectives.

To be effective in doing so, I've found there are six interlinked elements: the threat landscape; the cyber risks you face and measure; business and external expectations; your strategy; the capability you have built or have access to; and governance. To tease this out, some enquiries I found useful include the following:

- How well does the organisation understand the **threat landscape**?

  - What mechanisms and feeds are in place to understand and then counter, mitigate, or avoid a given threat?

  - How does that connect to your operating context and environment, so the true threat is understood?

- What are the key **cyber risks** the organisation faces?

  - Are they clearly articulated, known across the business, and appropriately rated?

  - Do they accurately represent the board and executive team's perspective?

  - How well connected are these to the threats, but also metrics that define our position against these risks, and can they support tracking of progress?

- What other **expectations** are there within the ecosystem? Regulators, other government departments, major customer obligations (e.g., significant contracts may require ISO compliance, etc.), and suppliers ('material' or otherwise).

  - Does the existing **cyber strategy** make sense?

  - Is it intuitive, relatable, and balanced (e.g., between technology and culture; enforcing and enabling; supportive of business goals...)?

  - Does it set the flag on the hill? If so, for what period, and is it achievable?

- Having reviewed the strategy, threats versus internal environment, key risks and measures, and additional 'expectations', we come to the crux of the matter: what **capability** do you have to manage all of this to the optimal outcomes?

  - In this, I take a broad view of capability: **people**, **technology**, **policies** (including standards and controls), and **processes**.

  - Where are the gaps? What/where needs strengthening, what needs rebalancing, and what's half-done but could be so much more efficacious? Are policies and processes encouraging subversion? What initiative didn't work out as expected and should be jettisoned?

  - What is the mechanism for delivering security improvements/maturity uplift? What is its current and future scope, and how well is it connected to the risks, strategy, and executive/board reporting?

- Finally, how is this all prioritised, reported, and **governed**?

  - What are the key annual, quarterly, and monthly rhythms, and where do you fit into them – board meetings, executive management meetings, risk committees, business reviews, investment cycles, regulator meetings, and so on?

  - How well established is your team in not only feeding this machine, but also influencing and utilising it?

- How about your team's governance structure, and how you provide assurance that security advice, rules, and policies are being appropriately followed?
- What independent reviews of your organisation exist, and what were the insights? An illuminating sub-question can be what happened to the recommendations and the formality with which they were tracked, rejected, closed out, and so on.

Having a risk-based framework and a reference point represented by these interconnected elements will support you in determining where your security posture is today, how well it is understood, and how it needs to mature over time. Crucially, it will also inform the capability needed to shift the dial, measures to validate progress and course correct as needed, and ensure your security investment continues to align with business priorities.

Priority 3: Building relationships, listening, and learning

Inevitably, the first weeks will focus on building relationships, understanding expectations, and setting the tone. During this period, prioritise listening over talking, ask open-ended questions, carefully extract the insights, and note the recurring themes.

Key areas to focus on are as follows:

- Your team (and slightly beyond):
    - Meet your direct reports. Honour the past; clearly outline that you are in learning mode with no intention to immediately enact significant change (unless warranted); actively listen to their ambitions, successes, and concerns; pay attention to their personal values, signals, and development opportunities.
    - Now extend this to the wider team – gold is sometimes found sitting on the surface, but usually, you need to work for it. Seek out the leaders within and closely aligned to your team, those that have an outsized influence on the rest of the team (irrespective of formal titles). What's their story, where are their pain points, and how willing are they to speak up? Be very clear that you value a constructive conversation on any subject, at any time.
    - Consider whether you have a healthy diversity of opinions and skills within the team. Diversity makes for rich debates and improved decisions. Cyber is also a broad church – from deep security practitioners, to communications specialists, to people that can run a business – and the team should reflect that.

- Analyse the comments from whatever system your company uses to define staff/team engagement. Comments can highlight what the scores hide.

- Assess the current construct: does it make sense? Are roles and responsibilities clear? Are the right people in the right roles? Would you be able to credibly present this as the optimal model to cyber insurers, your regulator(s), and so on?

- Work out the team rhythm. I've tried weekly all-team scrums to monthly all-hands meetings, and everything in between. My preference is the latter – make your debriefs detailed, ensure the team is the first to hear the important things from you, celebrate, and mix up the subject matter to keep it interesting. Honour the past, of which they have all been a part.

- Your internal partners:

  - By internal partners, I mean the key internal partners that support you in both running your business and important initiatives (e.g., culture change, retention, and retainers for key response partners): HR, finance, procurement, legal, etc.

  - Cyber must often move at an uncomfortably fast pace, and the best function partners are, of course, SMEs who are also part lawyer and police, meaning they advocate and support the cyber team in moving swiftly, but within appropriate guardrails.

  - Assess whether you have receptive professionals in the right roles. Support them in understanding the key imperatives, and ensure they are part of your extended leadership team, with a voice.

- Audit and line 2:

  - Be open and transparent with the audit function (and Line 2, if applicable to your organisation). I honestly believe that this is essential to the success and maturity growth of a cyber function.

  - It is also a great place to start in terms of understanding some history of the security function's development from an audit/Line 2 perspective (remember they are asked their opinions on such matters by regulators, boards, etc.): key considerations, recent findings, and probably most importantly, the common themes that persistently arise during reviews across the organisation.

- Executives, business leaders, and your peers:

    - Establish strong partnerships with C-suite, board members, and business unit leaders. You need to deeply understand what motivates them, understand their business, customers, and objectives, and define their awareness of – and attitude towards – security.

    - Repeat with your peers, but with an understanding that constructive relationships with clear expectations on both sides here will make your life – and crucially, the life of your team – much more productive.

- Who's who during an incident?

    - It's never too early to build the muscles in case of an incident: as a wise CEO once said to me, "During a crisis, you don't rise to the occasion, you fall to the level of your preparation".

    - Meet those who are involved in the wider incident and crisis management processes. This is not meant as an exhaustive list on how to build resilience, but, for example, are the roles, responsibilities, escalation paths, stakeholder management responsibilities, and corporate affairs approach clear, particularly if the incident has a cyber flavour? Take any opportunity that arises to observe the process in practice.

- Strategic partners/suppliers:

    - Who are your strategic cyber partners – intel partners, response partners, vendors of your critical tech, advisory, and reviews?

    - Begin to arrange time to connect with them at a senior level to ensure that they understand your key expectations; ensure they have an opportunity to provide open and constructive feedback on the working relationship to date, and define a plan to drive the maximum value from the relationships.

Finally, and having reflected on listening to CISOs joining organisations in periods of turmoil – if this happens to you, embrace it – I've found there is no quicker method than understanding the organisation, the key people within it, and its culture, for you to personally add value straight off the bat!

Priority 4: Where are we on the journey, and what's the next horizon?

Given that there is no such thing as perfect security, we must settle for some occasional leaps forward and, more often, incremental maturity improvements.

For example, getting to a strong maturity on vulnerability scanning and patching is not a 'once and done' step, but each step is incrementally better. Having periodic scanning for known vulnerabilities is better than not scanning; more regular scanning supplemented by always-on attack surface monitoring is even better. Let's add software composition analysis (be ready for the uptick in volumes to deal with...!) and prioritising vulnerabilities based on threat intel and true risk versus just common vulnerabilities and exposures (CVE) delivers a further improvement. What's next? Self-disclosure program? Bug bounty?

You will hear multiple opinions on where the organisation is in your first few weeks. There will be some consistency in the key themes, but equally, there may be conflicting views. Either way, it is wise and pragmatic to get an external independent view of where you are now, and what you may consider as priorities going forward.

Here are some thoughts on independent reviews (and views):

- In addition to considering views from internal sources, independent reviews are of equal value to give you a sense of where you truly are in the maturity journey, where you are strong (and perhaps can give back to the wider cyber community), and where you have gaps and can learn from others.

- Independent reviews provide a strong platform for prioritisation and management awareness (it is always better for management to disclose the gaps rather than the audit), and can super-charge you up the maturity curve. To an extent, regulators also expect them, and they are valuable in giving boards and executives a sense of progress whilst reinforcing that there is more to do.

- A review can be a goldmine or an expensive hole in the ground that takes a lot of effort to extract yourself from. The choice of partner and scope is essential in an effective, meaningful review, and neither is an item that you should delegate and remain remote from. Equally, having regular check-ins along the way to ensure that the review is achieving your objectives is important.

- In scoping, consider what you want to achieve as the outcome: is this a detailed security posture review mainly for the cyber/technology practitioners, a compliance and governance review, a review of strategy, or key program deliverables? Will they achieve the desired outcomes, a review primarily for the executives/board, opining on whether they are discharging their obligations, and so on?

- Remember in your scope contemplations that 'compliance' and 'security' are two different disciplines, and you can be 'compliant' without necessarily being 'secure', and vice versa. Historically, I have preferred to obtain two views: one that is security posture-focused (threat vectors, attack surface, efficacy of solutions deployed, capability review, etc.), and one that is compliance-focused to enable a reasonable benchmarking of where we are versus industry and so on (e.g., NIST Cybersecurity Framework (CSF), CIS Controls, etc.).

- Once you have the review complete, ensure that you and the team document a detailed management response that considers each recommendation, explains the actions that will be taken, and why any given recommendation is not being actioned (e.g., low priority, improvement potential not worth the cost given compensating controls, etc.).

- Finally, I mentioned earlier 'reviews (and views)'. The cyber community is always willing to share and learn together, so having a trusted network across the industry is always a great opportunity to learn what others are doing, what worked, and what did not – in real time. In many ways, this persistent sharing of experience and knowledge is the most powerful instrument of all, and certainly the one that has benefitted me most.

Having established the 'here and now', the next natural step to consider is how we are positioned for the future. A well-considered strategy is a powerful artefact to document your approach to security, plant that symbolic 'flag on the hill', as well as highlight the key messages you want resonating throughout the organisation.

Here are some of my thoughts on strategy:

- An effective cyber strategy is not just a collection of objectives concerning security practices; rather, it should tell a coherent and compelling story – relevant to your organisation's context – that connects multiple elements into a meaningful narrative. Naturally, it is also important that your strategy integrates seamlessly into your organisation's strategy.

- Following the narrative approach predefines some components to create a natural high-level flow (but not an exhaustive list). This could be, for example: threat landscape > your attack surface > data driven insights (statistics highlighting some of the threats your intel, detection and response teams see) > how this translates into cyber risk(s) and ratings > state of associated key controls (suggesting investment requirements) >

how cyber maturity versus risk is measured > resultant security objectives and capability development needs > overlay of priorities, risk, controls, and expected outcomes (e.g., improvement in maturity, completing independent review recommendations, closing audit issues etc.) > governance and measurement framework.

- Other components to consider include cyber team structure; reference to frameworks utilised; reference architecture; hierarchy of policies, standards, and guidelines; how external perspectives are utilised; emerging risks; and so on.

- Whilst the resultant document will be useful in multiple ways, the most effective way to communicate your strategy is with some graphically attractive flair that summarises the key aspects – a strategy on a page.

- On crafting my first version of this some time ago, my team gave me some wise advice and locked me in a room until I'd followed it: Ensure that the strategy reflects your own voice, as you will be speaking to it multiple times and need to believe in it.

- For the strategy on a page, my preference for structure is to set a purpose – the 'why' – underpinned by three strategic objectives. These three objectives should be focused on the 'what' – your key outcomes – crisply described and sending a clear message of intent to the entire organisation (e.g., cyber is everyone's business). Each objective should be supported by two imperatives that add a useful drill-down on achieving the 'what'. Finally, include the enablers that make the achievement of the strategy possible (e.g., people, culture, a key value, data, and disciplined delivery).

- Finally, a strategy is not useful if left on the shelf. It must be embedded in the work and rhythm of the team. A simple example is that the six imperatives in the strategy can form the workstreams of your security program.

Priority 5: Bringing it all together – operating model and building capability

So, you've done the footwork, listened and learned, built key relationships, captured common themes, and received an independent assessment. You understand stakeholder expectations, the key cyber risks, the organisation's security structure and posture, the capability built to date, and where you need to go next.

Now, it is time to bring this all together to define the capabilities you need to initiate, mature, strengthen, optimise, change, or retire.

> In explaining my use of the word 'capability', I lean towards the belief that an organisation's culture is formed of four main elements: people, technology, process, and policy. For example, if we have policies that no one understands, we drive a culture of confusion and best-guesses, not adherence and hygiene. Likewise, if we develop processes that are sub-optimal, we drive a culture of people ignoring or working around those processes. Therefore, in explaining capability, those four elements are my reference point.

What we are also achieving here is the finalisation of an **operating model** to enable us to deliver our desired strategy and outcomes. That operating model includes organisation structure, governance and policy, processes, technology and systems, people and culture, metrics, and measurement.

Points to consider when forming your operating model include the following:

- For the **organisation structure,** what is your scope and intent?

    - Perhaps you are utilising a structure 'in the spirit of' NIST to make it more intuitive; maybe you have multiple business units and/or geographies and consider business information security officers (BISOs) important. Has your organisation become fully 'enterprise agile', and you need to work out what is federated versus centralised?

    - How do you ensure that you haven't just established a set of silos and that there is a culture of shared accountability, collaboration, and learning? How does the rest of the organisation navigate through cyber efficiently? Equally, how does cyber ensure we have the appropriate integration into the rest of the organisation to enforce and enable?

- For governance and policy:

    - Recognise first that there are increasing expectations of cyber being able to ensure that policy and standard edicts are being followed through and governed appropriately. Consider a thorough review of your policies and standards to ensure they are clearly written, with the audience in mind, and focus on what is critical (and needs assurance) versus optional.

    - Other key aspects of governance are: ensure that roles and responsibilities are clear within, and outside, of the team (e.g., vulnerability scanning is cyber, patching is the asset owner; accountability for cataloguing assets and the recovery of applications is with the technology infrastructure team, etc.); consider setting up a central coordination body (e.g., governance, risk, and compliance (GRC) function,

CISO office) to manage the demands of enacting cyber governance requirements and others' governance requirements, such as reporting to the board, audit and review co-ordination, regulator requests and reporting, and external requests for security posture evidence.

- Finally, what are your decision rights in peace times and during more stressful times (e.g., during an active incident, switching off systems, cutting integration links)?

- Optimal **processes** are critical to running an efficient security function. Some examples are:

  - How do security incidents integrate into the organisation's incident and, where relevant, crisis management process? What nuances are considered when the security incident is very sensitive (e.g., insider threat)? Are the appropriate roles and responsibilities in place for key activities (such as executive communications) so the cyber team is insulated to respond and contain?

  - For regulator reporting, is the process effective and integrated across all necessary geographic locations? Are the triggers for reporting security-related events clearly defined and approval rights documented?

  - How is the cyber voice heard in the change management process? Are there red lines baked into go-live criteria (e.g., no critical or high outstanding penetration testing results); has the change management process got more friction involved where applications are not meeting control standards; is it lean and fast where approved patterns have been utilised?

- With regards to **technology and systems,** I'm referring to the security technology estate:

  - In terms of delivery, it is vital to ensure that we achieve the security outcomes desired and do not allow a 'tick the box' mentality. For every initiative, we should consider a well-defined 'definition of done', be clear on the operating model for 'Run', the integration story, and 'drink our own champagne' in terms of the security posture of the solution delivered.

  - Naturally, we also need to carefully consider the needs of our users so that we remove as much friction as possible for people doing the right thing. Delivering a secure coding or secrets management solution that doesn't seamlessly integrate into the development pipeline would lead to sub-optimal results and frustration for all concerned. Delivering an identity management platform can be less effort with up-front consideration of the user experience and reporting needs.

- Once delivered, a clear plan for how to maximise the investment should be enacted – there is little point in buying a sports car that we drive like a wooden cart.

- Finally, in the threat landscape arms race, it has been tempting to focus on build, build, build. This can lead to an overly complex and inefficient security stack over time. It's important to have a reference architecture in place that maximises our capability, its integration to support secure coding through to containment and recovery, but that also promotes efficient usage of the company's resources.

- **People and culture** are subjects to which I cannot do justice in a couple of paragraphs, given their centrality in keeping (or not) the organisation secure. In the final analysis, cyber is a team sport, played in opposition to the threat actors (and their bots), where technology is the field of play. A few key thoughts on the subject, focusing on the cyber team, are as follows:

  - In your first weeks, prioritise a talent review. This will provide you with valuable insights into your leadership and the wider team.

  - Start as you mean to go on: what are your non-negotiables on values (courage, respect, excellence, etc.)? What's the tone you wish to establish? Consider working on a social contract with your leadership team to agree on your foundational ways of working.

  - Are there any current tension points between teams (within cyber or between cyber and others)? This is not unusual, and you need to spend time understanding the drivers to solve these. Inevitably, there are two (sometimes more) sides to every story. Ensure that the value expectations are understood by all parties. Don't over-promise on resolution, particularly where you can only influence, rather than control, the outcome.

  - How is your team's engagement and retention? What needs to change here? Are key roles competitively remunerated versus the market? What non-financial benefits can you offer – e.g., sponsorships with universities to provide opportunities for your SMEs to contribute to the curriculum and lectures? How seriously have development plans been considered in the past? Take a personal interest in these. What's the best use of the education budget for maximum benefit? How healthy is your culture of rotation through roles? This is good for retention, flexibility, and capability building.

  - What capabilities don't currently exist in the team that you think are required? What's currently outsourced that you think needs insourcing and vice versa?

- Often, a lack of metrics is not the issue, but rather a lack of insightful metrics. On **metrics and measurement**, consider the following:

  - What are the operational metrics you will rely upon to run your business (risk, finance, HR, procurement, etc.)? When all is said and done, your license to operate demands you run an efficient and professional business, so ensure you interrogate the operational metrics at least once a month with your leadership team.

  - Which metrics determine your true security posture, and how do you hold people to account for performance against these metrics? For example, consider a monthly Security Council that you chair with business units to run through threat landscape insights, patching, penetration test results, summarised applications' controls, security exemptions, usage of admin accounts, completion of user access reviews, phishing results, and so on.

  - Which metrics should be reported to the executive team and board? There are as many opinions on this as there are metrics. I tend to start from the board risk appetite statement (RAS). Ideally, the metrics that compose the RAS need to provide insight into your defence in depth, for many controls need to fail for a significant breach. At least some of the metrics should be leading indicators and driving towards an outcome, and thresholds should be challenging but grounded in reality (they can be progressively tightened).

  - Depending on maturity, sometimes you have to start from the basics with such metrics. However, given the other capability you are building, what's your maturity roadmap for metrics? Perhaps you started metricating detection and response with a percentage coverage of the latest EDR roll-out, then matured to a percentage of security events that became incidents, and in the future, you plan to measure and report the mean time to contain.

  - Finally, are there any key performance indicators (KPIs) that you need in others' scorecards to drive security outcomes? This can be a tricky area: go too specific and you end up with people only managing the one KPI you have measured and not truly building the understanding of why cybersecurity should be a priority for them in all its varied aspects!

An effective operating model – with capability at its heart – is the 'how' to complement your strategy's 'why' and translate it into day-to-day operations. By providing clear alignment between your strategy and its execution, you also benefit from built-in adaptability as things evolve.

My conclusion

Whilst this chapter has outlined key priorities across several areas, perhaps the most crucial insight is that security leadership requires balance. Balance between compliance and business enablement, between urgent risks and long-term resilience, between strategic intent and operational imperatives, between technology and, most importantly, human beings.

In joining a new organisation, it can be tempting to rinse and repeat your dance moves from the previous organisation. Whilst you should never discount your prior learnings, it is equally important to balance these with an understanding of the unique culture, risk appetite, and business imperatives of your new environment.

By following the priorities outlined in this chapter, you will be well set up to apply your experience within a new context and build a business leadership function that not only seeks to safeguard the organisation but also transforms how security can create value in an increasingly digital world.

David's key takeaways: Priorities for the new CISO

In this chapter, Keith has carefully reflected on where he focused his time and effort when he was first taking on the challenge of being a CISO. There is great wisdom here for those in similar positions, and crucial priorities to consider.

When taking on a senior role like this, there is always going to be demand exceeding the supply of personal bandwidth. Therefore, making good choices is key to success.

Key learning points from Keith's chapter include the following:

- *Establish the right foundations before accepting the role.* Ensure you have some level of visibility into key stakeholders you will be working with, and establish an agreement in principle for building a personal support network. And, of course, plan for your own well-being and work-life balance from the start.

- *Develop a comprehensive understanding of your security posture through a risk-based framework.* Assess the current threat landscape understanding and cyber intelligence processes to review key cyber risks and their articulation across the business. Evaluate the existing cyber strategy for alignment with business goals, including current security capabilities (people, technology, policies, and processes), governance structures, and reporting mechanisms.

- *Build relationships through active listening and learning.* Connect with your direct reports and wider team to understand their perspectives. Also, make an effort to start to form partnerships with key internal functions such as HR, finance, legal, and procurement, and transparent relationships with audit and second-line functions. It's also valuable to identify crisis management stakeholders in advance and engage with strategic security vendors and partners.

- *Balance independent assessment with industry perspective.* Commission external security reviews with clear objectives and scope, ensuring the line is clear between security posture and compliance assessments. It's also beneficial to leverage peer networks for industry insights and benchmarking.

- *Design an effective operating model allowing you to deliver your desired strategy and outcomes.* This includes organisational structure, governance and policy, processes, technology and systems, and people and culture, along with meaningful metrics that provide operational insights and track outcomes.

- *Be sure to balance compliance requirements with business enablement.* This means you first address the most urgent risks while building long-term resilience. This is how you connect strategic vision with operational execution, and it enables you, as a leader, to make baby steps to transform security from a cost centre to a business value driver.

4

Cyber Threat Intelligence That Is Actionable

In the age of digital, and the velocity that this entails, the importance of cyber intelligence shouldn't be underestimated. It provides valuable early warnings and helps CISOs ascertain whether there are any specific risks that require action to be taken.

Many new CISOs may not have a background related to threat intelligence, and as such, they may only have a limited perception of the value of cyber intelligence based on their previous experience. But as a new CISO, being able to understand new threats and act appropriately in response is a critical success factor for your role.

The CISO relies on cyber intelligence to scan the horizon and provide advice on threat actors. For example, many enterprises and organisations may be specifically targeted, or, in some cases, inadvertently exposed due to their technology stack.

Cyber intelligence teams operate at different levels of scale across industries. There are different-sized teams, but usually in the largest organisations, this is a highly specialised squad. These cyber intelligence colleagues often have a defence intelligence background, and their network is usually a source of their strength. These networks operate both formally and informally to share information. (We would expect, however, that the confidence level for some of the information they receive through these networks is low, and more likely to be only contemplated as a data point.)

In financial services and other industries, I note that we also have information-sharing communities that can be a conduit to collect and share cyber intelligence between peer companies.

My best analogy to represent this intelligence sharing is in nature and how animals such as the giraffe and zebra operate on the African plains. The giraffe and zebra have a natural synergy, with the zebra having sharper hearing than the giraffe, but not having the height advantage of the giraffe to have the perspective of seeing threats from a distance. Together, they are safer from the lion, as they operate more effectively as a team than individually. For me, this is the essence of cyber intelligence and how this helps make us all more secure.

It is my pleasure to introduce **Teresa Walsh,** former **Chief Intelligence Officer** for **FS-ISAC**, with 25 years' experience in intelligence, who has a wealth of experience in this domain.

Through a letter to the new CISO, Teresa emphasises the importance of actionable cyber threat intelligence and provides practical advice and guidance on building and managing an integrated intelligence team within your organisation.

My letter to the CISO

Teresa Walsh

Dear CISO,

Congratulations on your new role! As a new CISO, you have likely heard about threat intelligence already and the fact that you should be using it. But chances are that no one has really articulated why intelligence is important and how to use it within your information security department.

Firstly, let me dispel a few assumptions for you. Threat intelligence is not just about indicators of compromise (i.e., IP addresses and hash values) that you can just automate and forget about on the side, letting machines handle the workload. There are multiple levels of intelligence analysis that can address technical needs to feed into your tools, all the way to strategic-level assessments that can personally assist in your decision-making concerning investments and directions to push your team. Intelligence-driven security can and should be integrated throughout your entire department and beyond, assisting the infosec team with interacting with economic crime, technology risk, and other departments.

The rise of generative artificial intelligence (genAI) tools has caused some to question the need for intelligence teams, without understanding how genAI models can produce anything close to what a trained intelligence analyst could deliver, to first get established and then to be maintained. If intelligence is only IP addresses to someone, then it might be easy to suggest that a human can be replaced with technology, but as I mentioned before, it goes far beyond the technical domain. GenAI tools – if the investment is made – can provide valuable research capabilities to an analyst or a collector, but the role of the human is not easily replaced.

Intelligence collection and analysis that supports the various functions in your team can help them prioritize, build more realistic attack scenarios, and test against real-world tools. Finished intelligence analysis provides a crucial factor in your risk calculations, enabling your defense and risk teams to prioritize their focus, their budgets, and their staffing. It enables you as a leader in the company to not just be a cost center in the eyes of your shareholders, but a vital component in the fabric of your business and its success. Taking the time to train, integrate, and nurture your intelligence team can be more effective for both your company and your budget.

Building an integrated intelligence team

As the CISO, you lead this integration from the top down. This does mean investing in that intelligence function, though, which is a step many miss, picking at random people to do the deed without preparing them for this function. You wouldn't ask your dental surgeon to perform open heart surgery on you just because they are intelligent and have a medical degree, so why would you expect someone with no training in the profession to succeed?

Whether you are starting your own team or inheriting one, you will need to consider the following:

- Technical and non-technical intelligence analysis training for the team
- Strategic intelligence analysis and analytical writing training
- Budget for subscriptions to threat intelligence feeds, vendors, or groups
- Budget for tools, enrichers, and intelligence repositories (whether in-house or off the shelf)

While there is no one-size-fits-all solution to forming an intelligence team, the first step is to understand the needs of your company, in which you have a unique insight, being part of the C-suite of executives.

The knee-jerk reaction will be to focus on hiring technical incident response or security analysts who will focus on gathering indicators of compromise for your security platforms to search against. While this is undoubtedly needed, it is not the sole purpose of an intelligence team (and is often the reason why some assume machines and tools can take the place of a human in this capacity). Build an intelligence team to address the holistic needs of your department and the company.

Start by asking yourself a few questions as an initial assessment of what your company needs:

- What troubles your company in terms of attacks, or crown jewels they are protecting?
- What do you need to be well-informed about to help with your cyber risk calculations and mitigation strategies?
- What are your budgetary constraints for purchasing technology, vendor feeds, or hiring trained staff?

An intelligence team of 1 with clear direction and understanding of what affects your company can be just as useful as a team of 50 working without relevant requirements. Prioritization of your requirements – from the technical to the strategic – brings focus on the objectives the team needs to action on. As the CISO, you have oversight on how those requirements are both being communicated to your intelligence team and how they are addressed going forward. This will help you work with your intelligence manager on the expertise and tools needed to build out the team.

To build an effective intelligence team, you will need to hire the following roles:

- Technical analysts, for their experience and capability with researching different tools and the ability to objectively analyze what an attacker is trying to accomplish through the malware, exploits, or techniques they employ

- Intelligence engineers to build out your collection and enrichment capabilities, looking at various open and closed sources to bring in more information for the analysts to process

- Trained strategic analysts who can interact, learn, and communicate with the other cyber defense and lines of business teams who plan to use their analysis

When you do implement threat intelligence within your company, ensure that your multiple cyber defense teams are gaining value from it.

Maximizing your operational efficiency

The point of intelligence reporting is not just to give pleasant reading but to inform decisions and activities. The intelligence provided should be directly beneficial to at least one of your other teams, as in these examples:

- Vulnerability managers reprioritize patching timelines based on whether relevant threat actors are exploiting known vulnerabilities. Intelligence on active exploitation, especially against peer companies, can push certain patching jobs to the top of the queue.

- Red teams employ current real-world scenarios to determine how well your company's controls and defenses can prevent and detect attack activity. Intelligence on the tools and techniques used by threat actors currently targeting your peers can assist in spotting holes in your defenses.

- Threat hunters take known or suspected techniques used by the attackers to identify potential intruders in the environment. Intelligence on attacker behavior and patterns can assist in identifying potential intrusions or attempts already present in your environment and in creating rules for identifying future activity.

By using relevant, informed intelligence analysis, you can ensure that your teams are coordinated to maximize your defenses.

Key considerations for assessing how well your threat intelligence team is integrated into your organization include the following:

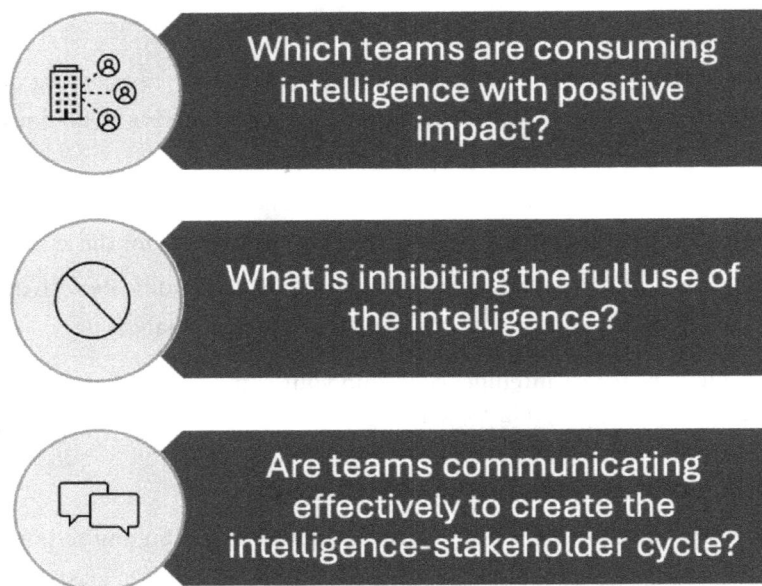

Figure 4.1: Key considerations for assessing integration

Communication between teams also needs to flow back to the intelligence analysts. Feedback is crucial for analysts to get it right, but unfortunately, communication between teams does not always happen effectively. This often gives rise to various teams deciding they need their own intelligence capability to address their own requirements, creating redundancies and inefficiencies.

When so many are complaining about the lack of talent in the industry, why duplicate effort needlessly? If the intelligence team is not performing to enable your cyber defense teams to succeed, then you, as the CISO, need to tell them and refine the inter-team dynamics. This is the nature of the intelligence-stakeholder communication cycle to ensure product delivery meets needs and expectations.

Troubleshooting breakdowns in effectiveness

The intelligence team provides a vital service to multiple stakeholders within and beyond your department, but those stakeholders need to feel the team is providing value to their functions, or else they will look elsewhere. If your other teams aren't using the intelligence, work with your intelligence manager to determine why. Here are some questions to ask:

- When doing their function, why do they need intelligence, and how do they use it?
- What do they need to help them succeed and work on priority risks for the company?

- Are the different functions using the curated intelligence or finished analysis coming out of the team?
- If the intelligence has not been usable by the function, what do they need in order to improve its value quotient?
- Is there a regular and honest feedback loop and requirements discussion occurring between the intelligence team and the function?

A valuable way for all teams to work together is to practice how they would use intelligence across teams and how the resulting actions affect one another (this may be conducted during strategy sessions you host with your department leads or even an off-site workshop), as in these examples:

- Finished intelligence analysis provides common techniques used across multiple threat actors that are prevalent against peers or critical third parties to your company.
- The SOC writes rules to alert on indicators related to the commonly observed infrastructure used by these attackers. Hits and resulting investigations can be shared back with the intelligence team to support their research and analytical findings.
- Threat hunters search for the described behaviors to determine whether the techniques are being used currently against the company. Indications of attackers inside the system should be escalated to the incident response process, which should include the SOC and intelligence teams to conduct further research into the observed activity.
- Red teams can employ their own attack scenarios to test external and internal defenses and detection tools. Gaps in the defenses can be fed back to the SOC for writing new rules and effective techniques provided to the threat hunters to search against. The red team can warn the vulnerability management team of exploits that were most successful during their tests as well.
- Vulnerability managers can adjust patching timelines according to the exploitation of known vulnerabilities and relevance to the criticality of internal systems. For Zero Days with no patches available, they can work with the intelligence and SOC teams to understand the methods employed by the attackers to exploit the Zero Day, to create controls or rules to prevent or detect the same attack pattern. These can be tested with the support of the red team.

The strategic use of finished intelligence analysis is often not understood by stakeholders as well, who often seek intelligence to drive daily operational activities instead. An off-site or strategy session would provide the opportunity for the team to take a step back from the day-to-day churn and understand the inter-team dynamics, such as the consumption of intelligence.

This is where you, as the CISO, can play a vital role for the organization as you are overseeing the security strategy for the company. By working with your cyber risk manager, you can drive investments, IT architectural changes, and other needs to enhance the external and internal security for the company.

Risk for the company is calculated by understanding the threat, knowing and testing the controls needed to counter that threat, and examining the residual risk that remains. You need good threat intelligence that is driving your teams forward for this.

> Threats are not the same as risks and are often confused with one another. For example, in a risk management sense, ransomware is not the risk; the inability to access critical and sensitive data is the risk. Ransomware is just the tool the attacker uses to realize that risk.

Using the finished analysis concerning tools and threat actor motivations and methods, you can reduce the risk your company faces from ransomware and other attacks that block access to corporate data.

This likely will require changes implemented in coordination with your IT teams, line of business teams, or others, as knowledge of how the relevant attackers plan and act will drive major decisions such as further segmenting your internal environment, implementing new controls for your employees, adding tools for authentication, or other modifications.

Working with an effective intelligence team that understands how to apply analytical findings to internal stakeholder needs can help your company connect the dots between what is needed and how to get there.

Investing in threat intelligence

As stated many times in this letter to you, relevant intelligence is the key for your teams to succeed. Many new teams will develop, thinking they need to duplicate what a government intelligence agency may do, looking at all threats and employing specialists. This is not only costly, but it's often not even useful.

Relevant intelligence analysis means that it is applicable to your company. If you are short on budget and trying to prove the value of an intelligence team, focus them on the actual threat against your company. For example, not everyone is likely to be a direct target for nation-state espionage activity, but financially motivated cybercriminals are much more prevalent.

If you have a limited resource, target the threat intelligence team on the most relevant and likely threats you can first. After these high-priority ones are addressed by the greater department (or beyond), you can start to branch out more into lesser (but still relevant) priorities. A clever way to ensure that this approach is being implemented is to formulate useful KPIs for the intelligence team to report.

If the only metric is how many indicators of compromise (IOCs) were pushed through the security information and event management (SIEM) system, it is likely that the team is not focused enough on strategic stakeholder needs. Metrics to demonstrate KPIs should be both quantitative and qualitative to state a clear value. This might be by demonstrating how the cyber defense teams and others used intelligence effectively, such as by asking the following:

- How many threat hunts were conducted based on intelligence production?
- How many scenarios did the red team test using their intelligence findings?
- What controls were adjusted by the SOC based on current threat actor activities?
- What type of malicious campaigns were stopped or prevented altogether by using the intelligence?

A note about working with your peers

One thing to keep in mind for even the smallest of intelligence teams is that they are not alone. In your industry, there are likely dozens to thousands of companies addressing the same threats, the same risks, and the same resource constraints. While you are looking internally at how to improve and integrate your intelligence, do not forget to look externally to crowdsource that intelligence.

Security should not be used for business competitive advantage, as threat actors are not particular about who they attack, usually. By working together and collaborating on these threats with others, you can multiply the resources and intelligence flowing into your company considerably.

Even if you only have one intelligence analyst working part-time, you can still crowdsource your priority requirements to feed into your cyber defense and cyber risk teams.

Some companies may have issues with this concept, but by showing how informed, relevant analysis can make your company more resistant against those attackers, you can hopefully win over the naysayers trying to prevent external collaboration.

Looking forward

As you embark on your CISO journey, look toward building a collaborative, integrated department where intelligence can be a key driver for communication and actionable improvements.

The attackers adapt as we work to defend our environments, which have now extended considerably via our third-party providers. Using not just technical intelligence collection but also strategic analysis can set the course for you to build a cost-effective and successful defense force.

Congratulations again on becoming the CISO. I look forward to seeing how the intelligence function flourishes under your leadership. If you have any questions or would like to discuss any of the points I've raised, let's meet for a strategy session.

Best regards,

Teresa

David's key takeaways — Cyber threat intelligence that is actionable

Sometimes it takes real strength to take an approach like this to threat intelligence to ensure that your key stakeholders have real context and information on how to act. This is very important because most CISOs don't come from a cyber intelligence background, and therefore, this is not always top of mind. Cyber intelligence is never an exact science, and the signals are often false positives, perhaps as high as 50% of them. This highlights the importance of establishing a position as a trusted advisor.

Teresa is not relying on a simple letter to set and clarify expectations on threat intelligence in this chapter; she is sharing a foundation for a great cross-team working relationship based on shared understanding.

I have never received such a letter when I commenced a CISO role. I wish I had! I had to learn about threat intelligence more organically and much more slowly.

The key points from Teresa's letter are as follows:

- *Cyber intelligence serves as an early warning system*, helping the organisation to identify and assess specific risks by scanning the horizon for threats. This intelligence is particularly crucial given the rapid pace of digital transformation.

- *Networks are everything.* The effectiveness of cyber intelligence teams often stems from their networks and relationships, both formal and informal. Many team members come from defence intelligence backgrounds, though team sizes vary across industries, with large organisations maintaining specialised squads.

- *Threat intelligence goes beyond indicators of compromise.* It requires trained analysts who can provide strategic insights that inform risk calculations, defence priorities, and business decisions. Even AI tools cannot fully replace human intelligence analysts.

- *Investment is required.* An effective intelligence function requires proper investment in both people and tools, including technical and non-technical training, strategic analysis capabilities, intelligence feeds, and appropriate tools for analysis.

- *Success depends on ensuring intelligence outputs are relevant and actionable for different stakeholders* (SOC, red teams, vulnerability managers, etc.) with regular feedback loops between teams. The focus should be on threats and risks specifically relevant to your organisation.

- *We are stronger when we work together.* Collaboration across industry peers is essential since security shouldn't be a competitive advantage. Organisations face common threats and can multiply their intelligence capabilities by working together.

5

How I Got to Be CISO

Every year, there are reports published that highlight the cyber talent shortage, and to no one's surprise, these numbers get worse, and the gap widens. There are literally millions of vacant roles that go unfilled every year, and these are not superfluous positions. This means that we are all less protected than we should be.

The answer is obvious, and in fact, I think that the way forward is right in front of you. Women are the secret weapon in addressing this gap.

Earlier in my career in Japan, as a CIO, I saw that all the candidates I received in my inbox were Japanese males who had the same work experience and were about the same age. In talking to my manager, Newt Crenshaw, we agreed that diversity is a competitive advantage when no one else is doing this. This is not about numbers or quotas, but strengthening the bench with diversity of sex, age, ethnic background, and thinking!

Following his lead, I embarked on doing just that and broke the mould on what was expected. It led to what was a renaissance of diverse new talent coming into Eli Lilly Japan, and many great executive careers.

At the time of writing this book, a reported 22% of the global cyber workforce is female (ISC2, 2025: `https://www.isc2.org/Insights/2025/03/Women-Comprise-22-percent-of-the-Cybersecurity-Workforce`). Now, these numbers come as no surprise; in fact 22% sounds much higher than I expected.

Who are the winners in the global market? Perhaps surprisingly, that is Mexico and Nigeria with 34% of the cyber workforce as women (The World Bank, 2023: `https://documents1.worldbank.org/curated/en/099111023150023703/pdf/P17785208994aa06d08eca094513904323a.pdf`). While there's still a way to go for gender equality in the cyber workforce, it's worth asking what the factors are that have assisted these frontrunners.

Industry studies indicate that this is due to a combination of more inclusive educational systems, supportive cultural attitudes towards women in technology, and emerging cybersecurity markets that developed with fewer historical barriers to female participation. These are points that we can learn from.

It is my pleasure to introduce **Silvia Lam Ihensekhien**, who is the **Group CISO** at **Swire Cola-Cola**, which covers China, Hong Kong, Taiwan, Southeast Asia, and Western USA. Indeed, Swire Cola-Cola is the fifth largest bottling partner for the Coca-Cola Company and one of the most iconic companies in the world. Silvia also served for 15 years as CISO and GM HK for ShipServ, a privately owned global online marine trading marketplace and platform.

Silvia's journey to cybersecurity leadership developed from a more generalist IT path. She is now a female role model for the cyber industry.

In her career journey, I'm fairly certain that there have been few, if any, female CISO role models that Silvia has been able to look up to learn or get some form of coaching from. She has succeeded in what is a male-dominated industry and is now very active herself in helping the next generation of women.

I'd love to hear from Silvia about her own career development and how she overcame obstacles and challenges along this journey, including the barriers she faced and who she spoke to when she was stumped. It would also be insightful to hear about Silvia's key strengths as a CISO.

There are some valuable lessons that can be gained from leaders who want to follow in Silvia's footsteps, and for CIOs and CISOs who understand that encouraging women in security can build a competitive advantage.

I invite Silvia to also cover aspects of her day and how she copes with the normal challenges and stresses. We all know that women are generally better at multitasking than men are, and it would be insightful to hear how she manages the velocity of her cyber workload.

Thanks, Silvia, over to you!

How I got to be CISO

Silvia Lam Ihensekhien

Thanks, David, for the introduction. I'm excited to share my journey and insights with you all. My path to becoming a CISO has been one that has evolved with me, shaped by diverse experiences, challenges, and continuous learning. In this chapter, I hope to provide an honest look at what it takes to thrive in cybersecurity leadership, especially as a woman in a predominantly male industry.

From the early days of discovering my passion for technology to leading cybersecurity in a global organization, I will share practical advice, lessons learned, and the importance of resilience, mentorship, and diversity. I'll also focus on empowering more women in security and building a stronger, more inclusive cyber community. Let's begin this conversation.

Where I started

I often get asked the question, "How did you start your career in cybersecurity?". I did not have the intention to choose cybersecurity as my career. In fact, when I was studying at the university, I had no idea what to do or what cybersecurity was.

I was born and raised in Hong Kong. After completing my secondary school education, I had to choose a major for university. Among the available courses, I found that computer science was the least boring and best suited to my personality, so I chose it without a second thought. Back then, I didn't consider my career path when selecting my major; I simply followed my interests.

I learned a lot during my four years of study at **Hong Kong Polytechnic University (HK PolyU)**. The best part of this time was the one-year job placement program, which was designed to provide us with some working experience. I was placed at a bank and learned the 4GL language, NATURAL.

Although the workload as a placement student was not very high, I gained a significant amount of knowledge during that period. I still remember making various mistakes, but those experiences were invaluable. Working in the placement program opened my eyes to the business world and showed me how teams collaborate to complete work.

Besides the technical knowledge that you need to pursue, I began to realize that people are a crucial element in getting the job done. I enjoyed my time there and learned a lot.

After graduating from university, I found a job as a teacher of computers and mathematics. Being a teacher also sharpened my presentation and teaching skills. I spent a lot of quality time with my students, and to this day, I keep in touch with a few, and I am very proud of their achievements.

After a few years of teaching, I decided to try working in the commercial field. Before reentering the business world, I obtained my MSCE qualification and secured a job as a systems administration team lead. Working in the commercial sector was very different from working at a school; it required meeting tight deadlines and handling ad hoc assignments.

Like many other IT teams, I had to schedule maintenance windows during off-peak hours, which often meant working late at night or at weekends to minimize the impact on operations. It was during this time that I realized I am a people person and wanted to help bridge the gap between technology and people to solve their problems.

As a result, I decided to join several start-ups where I could learn more due to the diverse opportunities each role offered. Among them, one provided me with the most memorable experience. This start-up was an e-commerce supermarket offering a variety of household products. I joined as a technical trainer before they launched the business. It was my first time working in such a large company, which had thousands of employees and included departments such as warehousing, delivery, product management, marketing, IT, and operations.

We worked long hours to prepare for the business launch, and I participated in various roles, including recruitment and training. I also supported store operations when they opened their doors. It was an exciting journey, being part of the team that made the business launch successful. I became more and more interested in handling operations.

Eventually, I landed a job at a company running a maritime **multinational corporation (MNC)** e-commerce platform, where I spent a significant amount of time. Working in an MNC allowed me to travel around the world, collaborate with different teams, and understand various cultures. I am truly grateful for the numerous career opportunities they provided, allowing me to develop and prove myself in areas such as project management, customer service, IT operations, and cybersecurity.

In the early days, cybersecurity was part of IT's responsibilities, involving the deployment of firewalls and network enhancements to protect the company. However, with the rise of the internet and the company's business nature, it was later decided that a separate cybersecurity function was needed to protect customer data in this digital world. I was honored to be assigned the role of head of cybersecurity, marking the beginning of my CISO journey.

Becoming a CISO

Studying in Hong Kong didn't encourage or provide me with the advantage of speaking up. I was shy and didn't ask questions during my school days. I rarely participated in discussions or joined any extracurricular activities or groups. It wasn't until I worked as a teacher that I began to come out of my shell. It required me to step out of my comfort zone and deliver lectures, which laid the foundation for my presentation and communication skills, which I needed to be a CISO.

Being a CISO is a demanding job. You must be constantly monitoring for new threats and vulnerabilities that could impact your organization and be prepared to act swiftly if necessary. Increased adoption of emerging technologies adds to the complexity of the role. However, understand that cybersecurity should be viewed as a facilitator for the business, rather than a blocker.

Our mission is to protect the organization's critical assets, recognizing that each organization has different priorities, business strategies, and risk appetites.

Another question I often get asked is, "Is the CISO role technical or managerial?". In my opinion, a CISO must possess technical knowledge, but more importantly, should have strong soft skills. These include the communication and presentation skills I have mentioned, as well as others such as negotiation and stakeholder management.

As a CISO, sometimes you need to make unpopular decisions, especially when you foresee challenges ahead. In such cases, you must use your listening and negotiation skills, working like a lobbyist to gain stakeholder buy-in. Storytelling and presenting facts clearly will also help you get this job done. Sometimes, you need to find a middle ground to progress.

> It's important to stay open-minded and avoid tunnel vision. Evaluate all comments and inputs you receive and use them to adjust your strategy and planning.
>
> Understanding that cybersecurity needs to align with business objectives is crucial for any CISO.

Logical and critical thinking are also essential CISO skills for prioritizing urgent and important tasks in this ever-changing field.

As a woman leader in a male-dominated industry, I have often been mistaken for a subordinate rather than a leader. At first, I felt a deep sense of disappointment each time this happened – it was frustrating to have my authority and role overlooked. However, as these incidents continued to occur repeatedly, I gradually became numb to them, almost expecting such misunderstandings as a part of the environment. In these situations, I found that the best approach was to remain calm, smile, be polite, and allow my teammates to correct the misunderstanding. Over time, my team became aware of this issue and began proactively introducing me, which helped reduce any awkwardness.

For others facing similar challenges, I would suggest a few additional strategies: clearly establishing your role early in meetings or conversations, using confident body language and tone, and, when appropriate, directly addressing any misconceptions in a professional manner. Building strong relationships and allies within your team can also create a supportive environment where your leadership is recognized and respected. These steps can help minimize misunderstandings such as those I faced and reinforce your position as a leader.

As a CISO, I work at a fast pace, which is essential in the field of cybersecurity, given that threats are always shifting and developing. Quick and effective responses are essential. However, I have learned that pacing differs among individual teammates when working to complete their tasks on time. Each of us has unique skills and strengths, and it's important that we complement each other rather than expecting everyone to move at the same speed. By letting your teams know that you recognize and value these differences (and encouraging them to do the same), you foster effective collaboration and help ensure that teams stay agile and resilient in the face of emerging challenges.

Thriving as a CISO

Being a CISO is a demanding job that requires maintaining both mental and physical fitness. In this section, I share my tactics for this with you.

Managing stress

Consistency and resilience are essential qualities for a CISO. To help me in this regard, I maintain a set of routines, starting with my morning workout before heading to the office.

I enjoy going to the gym because it helps relieve stress and allows me to take my mind off work. During gym classes, I need to focus on the tasks at hand, leaving no time to think about anything else, which helps clear my mind. Through years of consistent fitness workouts, I have pushed myself out of my comfort zone and achieved things I never thought possible, such as doing a full split or a headstand.

Much like in work, achieving these fitness goals requires constant practice, training, and overcoming failures. The motto 'no pain, no gain' rings true – you can't reach your targets and goals unless you take the first step. Through working out, I've learned to increase my endurance, resilience, and consistency, all of which I apply to my professional life as well.

Seeking out mentors

I was fortunate to find some mentors throughout my career. Although they were all male and not in the field of cybersecurity, this did not matter to me. They inspired and coached me on strategic thinking, **emotional intelligence (EQ)**, and developing in-depth skills in presenting and analyzing facts.

Personally, I believe mentors play a crucial role in everyone's journey. They are individuals you can look up to and learn from. By sharing their experiences, mentors can help you avoid making the same mistakes they did and guide you on the path to success. They can be your go-to person when you are facing challenges or celebrating achievements, which your friends and family might not always understand.

Continuous learning

Continuing to learn and improve yourself is something that cannot be underestimated. With attackers developing their methods constantly, you also need to keep up to date with what is happening and what the new threats and vulnerabilities are.

Throughout my career, one way I have kept updating myself has been by obtaining different qualifications, such as PMP, CISSP, CGEIT, and CCISO. Combined with my experiences, these qualifications further strengthen my profile and validate my expertise.

In addition to formal qualifications, I continuously stay informed about the latest cybersecurity threats and trends by regularly consulting threat intelligence sources. These include reputable news outlets, specialized cybersecurity blogs, and reports provided by leading vendors. Leveraging these resources helps me maintain a current understanding of threat developments and enhances my ability to anticipate and respond to emerging risks.

Stepping out of my comfort zone

I never thought of myself as a speaker before. My speaking journey started years back when I came across an opportunity to speak at a QA conference. My experience as a teacher in my first job made it easier for me to deliver the speech; however, no matter how many presentations I have delivered, I always feel nervous before my session starts. I believe this has taught me to 'be comfortable being uncomfortable.'

From then on, I committed to promoting cybersecurity and diversity on as many occasions as I can. I have also learned a lot from other speakers about the techniques for delivering a successful presentation, and I try to learn as much as I can from others.

Growing my brand and network

Besides local conferences, I have been invited to international conferences and speaking opportunities in Asia and the US. This really broadened my skills and experiences.

You might be curious about how I received all these new opportunities. Most of them came through brand building and networking. Building your brand on social media is a great way to help your peers understand more about you.

> I consistently post on social media twice a week. At first, it was difficult because I didn't know what to write. My tip for writing posts is to share articles and news along with your thoughts on these. Starting with short posts can help you get comfortable with writing, and from there, you can gradually expand your content.

Starting with social media posts, I have now progressed to writing articles and even contributing to sections of a book.

Through various conferences, luncheons, and other networking events, I was able to connect with various professionals, with whom I share knowledge from time to time. One of the good things about being in the cybersecurity community is that it is a small circle, and we are all willing to help each other. It is like a second home. When you attend conferences and events, it is exciting to see familiar faces. This is also a good chance to catch up with each other. It has also been especially rewarding to meet some other female CISOs. Engaging with them provides me with valuable perspectives and insights, enriching my understanding of leadership challenges and opportunities within the field. These connections foster a more inclusive network and inspire continued growth and collaboration. Fighting cybercrime is a team effort that requires 'all hands on deck.'

When I was attending my first speaking session, I met one of the alumni from HK PolyU, who nominated me as an outstanding alumnus. Through this nomination, I reconnected with PolyU and later became one of the **Computing (COMP)** alumni executive committee members. Reconnecting with PolyU also started my journey to becoming a mentor for the COMP department, which later extended to the whole PolyU.

As a mentor, I was amazed by how hard my mentees studied and how well they understood the challenges they faced. Reconnecting with PolyU also reminded me of my memorable university days. When I returned to PolyU, all the memories came flooding back – the lecture halls, the canteen, the library, and the podium all looked so familiar. It was also nice to see some of the professors still teaching there.

Later, I was introduced to the ISACA SheLeadsTech stream and became one of the committee members.

She leads tech

The ISACA SheLeadsTech program aims to "advance gender diversity and women in leadership roles within IS/IT professions." Through various SheLeadsTech events, I connected with like-minded women leaders, and we are committed to promoting gender diversity and empowering the younger female generation to enter the IT or cybersecurity domains.

I started my volunteer work when COVID hit, which halted all business travel and provided me the opportunity to give back to Hong Kong. As part of this work, I helped distribute free lunches to the elderly in need at a social enterprise restaurant that has operated for more than 20 years to support the elderly in finding work. During that time, I got close to these elderly individuals and felt their struggles. I learned that you shouldn't take things for granted and should always appreciate what you have.

I have been lucky to have my achievements recognized by various awards. It is not an easy task to be a female leader in a male-dominated field. I didn't expect to be nominated or to become an awardee in these events. I was impressed by the other awardees, how successful they are, and how they are making an impact. This inspired me a lot. You can always take the chance to learn from others.

The other question I always get is, "How do we breach the gender gap in cybersecurity roles?". I believe diversity is important in every industry, not only in cybersecurity, as it brings different perspectives that can be valuable. To address this challenge, we should start with the education phase, where we encourage girls to be interested in male-dominated industries. A mentorship program is a good way to go, as mentees can learn from their mentors how to tackle these challenges.

Companies can also help by offering internship programs to college students, allowing them to obtain real-world work experience and apply the skills they have learned. Finding a male ally to support you in the company is another way to help address this challenge.

My tips for success

Throughout my career journey, I have consistently faced challenging tasks and ambitious targets, which have strengthened my ability to deliver impactful results under tight timelines. For example, I was involved in operations support during the launch of an online supermarket, where I contributed to coordinating cross-functional teams and supporting their ERP systems. As another example, I successfully led a cloud migration project for an e-commerce platform, completing the transition within six weeks. This involved extensive planning, risk assessment, and collaboration with vendors to ensure minimal disruption to business operations while enhancing scalability and security. Furthermore, I doubled the cybersecurity maturity score within a year at a multinational corporation with 40,000 users by implementing comprehensive security frameworks, policies, guidelines, and procedures, conducting regular assessments, and fostering a culture of continuous improvement across teams. These are just a few examples of my experiences driving growth and resilience in dynamic environments.

I have always managed to overcome the challenges I have faced and achieve or even exceed the required targets. My tips for success are the following:

- Secure executive management support and sponsorship.
- Understand your stakeholders and identify the key influencers. Work closely with them to gain their alignment and buy-in.
- Ensure that the relevant teams fully understand their tasks and responsibilities.
- Identify important milestones to keep the projects on track.
- Stay focused and avoid getting distracted by other ad hoc tasks.
- Keep stakeholders constantly updated on progress to avoid last-minute surprises.
- Appreciate what your teammates have accomplished and celebrate both small and big wins along the way.
- Don't be afraid to escalate issues if your project is stuck and you can't find a way to push through.
- Remember, it's all about teamwork; no single individual can achieve success alone. Together, we can, and we will.

A day in my life

I usually start my day with a workout, followed by reading emails and cybersecurity news to see whether there is anything I need to address. I then follow up on the progress of various projects to determine whether any require my attention.

On a typical day, I spend more than half of my time communicating. I cannot stress enough how important this aspect is for success in the role.

Many teammates think cybersecurity is mysterious and prefer to work in the dark. However, I am the complete opposite; I value transparency and strive to ensure that my teammates understand our plans and priorities. We regularly share progress updates.

Another crucial aspect of cybersecurity is awareness training, which is essential to inform your teams about the latest threats and attacks so they remain vigilant. We conduct awareness training twice a year to ensure that everyone stays informed and prepared. When conducting awareness training, audits, or meetings, I take the opportunity to meet the heads of business units in different markets in person.

Sometimes, I meet with vendors and attend conferences to stay updated on the latest developments in the market.

At the end of the day, I review the tasks I plan to tackle in the coming days or weeks to see whether they need to be adjusted. I also take the opportunity to ensure that the planned tasks are aligned with our targets and roadmap.

How to be a great CISO

The final question I often receive is, "What makes a great CISO?". This is a million-dollar question. In my opinion, a great CISO should possess the following qualities:

- **Effective team management**: A CISO must be adept at motivating and inspiring their team. Understanding the strengths and weaknesses of team members as a CISO is crucial so that you can help them work together harmoniously and complement each other's skills.

- **Strategic and tactical vision**: A CISO should have both a long-term vision and the ability to translate that vision into achievable targets and goals for the team. These goals should align with business objectives and be clearly communicated to executive management and stakeholders.

- **High resilience**: A CISO must be capable of responding effectively to unexpected or ad hoc events. In incidents related to cybersecurity, the CISO should act as the commander-in-chief, remaining calm and using a logical mindset to handle the situation.

- **Project management skills**: Good project management skills are essential to ensure that projects stay on track and any exceptions are identified early.

- **Business acumen:** Understanding the business is crucial, as different businesses have different priorities. Cybersecurity should be integrated and aligned with business operations.

- **Listening and open-mindedness:** A good CISO should be an excellent listener, able to understand various perspectives, and remain open-minded to consider all feedback for continuous improvement.

- **Continuous learning:** With the constant emergence of new threats and vulnerabilities, a CISO must continuously update themselves with new technologies, attack strategies, and methods.

- **Analytical and communication skills:** Strong analytical skills are necessary for a CISO so that they can summarize and present findings to stakeholders and executive management. Coupled with good presentation and communication skills, this enables the CISO to effectively communicate across all levels.

These qualities collectively contribute to what makes a CISO truly great.

My final comments

My journey to becoming a successful CISO has been shaped by resilience, continuous learning, and the development of strong leadership skills in cybersecurity. Starting from a general IT background and progressing through diverse roles in teaching, IT operations, and project management, I have learned that there is no single path to cybersecurity leadership. Balancing technical expertise with essential soft skills – such as communication, stakeholder management, and strategic thinking – has been key to my success as a CISO.

As a woman leading in a traditionally male-dominated industry, I have faced challenges, including being underestimated and having my authority questioned. Over time, I developed strategies to assert my leadership with confidence and professionalism, turning obstacles into opportunities for growth. My experience has shown me the importance of mentorship, networking, and stepping outside of my comfort zone to embrace new challenges.

I am committed to promoting diversity and inclusion through initiatives such as ISACA's SheLeadsTech program, empowering the next generation of female leaders in cybersecurity. I believe in encouraging girls early on to pursue STEM fields, the value of mentorship, and creating supportive environments within companies through internships and male allyship.

To the next generation of female security leaders, my advice is to continuously build your skills, seek out mentors, cultivate strong communication abilities, and maintain resilience in the face of adversity. It's also important for you to view cybersecurity not just as a technical field but as a strategic enabler for business success.

By embracing diversity and fostering inclusive leadership, organizations can tap into a broader talent pool and gain a competitive advantage in addressing the global cybersecurity talent gap.

My journey is proof that with determination, support, and a growth mindset, women can thrive and lead effectively in cybersecurity. I hope more women will step forward, break barriers, and help shape the future of this critical industry.

David's key takeaways — How I got to be CISO

I never met Silvia on her journey to becoming a CISO. Instead, I only had the privilege of meeting her once she had. We actually connected on Zoom the first time, and when I asked her about writing about her passion, I recall she said that there were a few topics, but women in security was one that was high on her list.

This chapter is about Silvia's journey to becoming a CISO, and it's clear that she is role modelling the principles that guided her first and foremost, but the underlying message I get from her chapter is about diversity.

Being born in Darwin, I was always highly conscious of the teachings of the famous Sir Charles Darwin. He hypothesised that natural selection occurs in the world, and this too can be applied in the workplace. His core idea is that a diverse group is more likely to thrive in a constantly changing environment than a homogenous one.

Personally, I learnt in my CIO career from my Eli Lilly boss (President & CEO) that if we as a company embrace diversity, then we gain a competitive advantage, particularly if others are not doing this. This is not about quotas or just hiring female candidates (or those from other groups) for the sake of it; there are real advantages to a more diverse workforce, and you should be sharing this message with your own team and peers.

Here are the key learnings from Silvia's CISO journey and career insights:

- *Career paths to CISO roles aren't always linear* – Silvia started in computer science, taught school, worked in IT operations, and gradually transitioned into cybersecurity. Her diverse experience in different roles and industries helped her build a well-rounded skill set.

- *Technical knowledge is important, but soft skills are crucial* – a successful CISO needs strong communication, stakeholder management, and storytelling abilities, among others, to translate technical concepts into business language and gain buy-in for security initiatives.

- *Stepping out of your comfort zone is essential for growth.* From overcoming shyness to public speaking, taking on challenging assignments, and making unpopular but necessary decisions, professional growth requires embracing discomfort.

- *Building a strong professional network and personal brand is valuable.* Speaking at conferences, maintaining social media presence, and active participation in professional communities such as ISACA's SheLeadsTech create opportunities and support career advancement.

- *Work-life balance and stress management are critical* – maintaining consistent routines (such as morning workouts), pursuing continuous learning, and finding ways to clear your mind are essential for sustaining performance in the demanding CISO role.

- *Embrace diversity in the broad sense.* Every CISO has talent gaps, and making an investment in diverse talent will help you with these. It may also give your organisation a competitive advantage.

6

The Journey to CISO: From Humble Beginnings to Leadership

The CISO must ascend to their role, and often, there is a moment in their careers when they decide to really aspire for the CISO position. This then begins a journey from their current position and skill set, where they retool themselves to progress up the ranks.

Every CISO takes a different path to their peak, but what is similar is that they must all learn how to progress upwards while gaining the support of their supervisors and peers.

In simple terms, this is about working towards a vision and building trusting relationships that support your career ambitions. To become a CISO, there is a key lesson to be learnt around developing your communication skills (soft skills), but your technical skills still matter and should not be neglected.

To be a good leader, you must also learn to be a good manager – and that is not the same thing. The *leader's* role is to inspire and motivate people towards a shared vision, focusing on long-term goals and building relationships, while *managers* exist to plan, organise, and control resources to achieve specific objectives, prioritising efficiency and short-term tasks. The best leaders are those who can balance both leadership and management skills, adapting their approach to the specific situation and needs of their team.

When you are the CISO, there is also often the extra burden of extreme pressure and stress that comes with the role. A CISO does not automatically have superpowers to avoid stress and must manage it like any other leader. This requires that the CISO keep a clear perspective of what is important. The day in the life of the CISO is filled with different challenges.

The CISO must manage their own stress management and that of the cyber team in order to get the best performance from their team without breaking them and causing some longer-term problems. There are war stories of cyber team members who can't handle their work pressures and end up on medical leave or worse.

Perhaps the CISO is a super-person to have to deal with this? I'd like to introduce one such person – **Krzysztof Kostienko,** who is a former Asia Pacific CISO for Morgan Stanley and now **Asia Pacific Head of Security** at **Qube Research and Technologies (QRT).** Krzysztof is known as KK to his friends, so I will use this abbreviation. He has an extensive background as a security architect for more than 15 years. This is an extraordinary level of experience in such an emerging field.

I'd like to invite KK to share how he got to be a CISO and provide some insights into his journey and how he manages his life to avoid his own burnout and that of his team, while still finding enjoyment in his role and building a meaningful, long-term career.

My journey

Krzysztof Kostienko

There's no definitive runbook for building a meaningful and successful career in cybersecurity. The path is as unique as the individual walking it, shaped by personal experiences, challenges, and decisions made along the way. In this chapter, I want to share my journey from a humble upbringing in a small town in Poland to a senior role in a global bank. This is a story of resilience, leadership, and the lessons I learnt as I transitioned through different roles in cybersecurity. Writing this chapter hasn't been easy; it's deeply personal. But if sharing my story inspires even one aspiring CISO or helps someone navigate their own career, then every word is worth it.

The cybersecurity profession is saturated with technical guides and books covering cyber response, regulatory compliance, and domain-specific knowledge. These are essential resources, but in my experience, technical expertise is just the foundation. To truly thrive in leadership roles, you need a different set of skills. Integrity, discipline, selflessness, trustworthiness, resilience, and the ability to plan and execute with focus are the qualities that distinguish the great from the good. In this chapter, I'll share with you the key skills that made a significant difference in my journey, supported by real-life examples of how I applied them.

Humble beginnings

My story begins in a small town in post-communist Poland. I come from humble beginnings in a tight-knit family; my mother was a primary school teacher, and my father was a mechanic. Growing up in a lower-class but deeply caring family with two older brothers shaped my outlook on life. Many of my childhood friends faced tragic outcomes, succumbing to addiction or becoming trapped in a cycle of poverty with no way out. I was fortunate to have the support and opportunities to pursue a different path.

That path required resilience and hard work, starting with 5 summers of 12-hour shifts in German factories while studying at university. Those gruelling jobs, making sausages, car headrests, and chocolate powder, taught me humility, grit, and the value of perseverance. These experiences instilled a deep appreciation for hard work and reinforced a mindset that nothing should be taken for granted.

A passion for technology

My first exposure to IT came at the age of eight when I received a Commodore 64 as a gift for my Holy Communion. I quickly became fascinated by programming languages such as BASIC 2.0, Assembly, and C. My natural affinity for science subjects led me to pursue a career in computer science. It was during my BSc at Coventry University and, later, my MSc at Birmingham University that I discovered cybersecurity.

A pivotal moment came during my MSc thesis project at Hewlett-Packard Labs in Bristol, a global hub for cybersecurity research. Immersing myself in cutting-edge research solidified my decision to dedicate my life to this field. Early on, I knew I wanted to progress from being a hands-on security software developer to becoming a CISO.

I was fortunate to have exceptional mentors and managers, whom I am very grateful to: Brian MacDougal, Kevin Patel, Stuart Levison, Pete Troy, Patrick Lee, Darren Argyle, Gerard Bready, Richard Chum, Nick Harris, Krzysztof Wegrzynek, Omar Haq, and more. They entrusted me with increasingly challenging roles, shaping my career trajectory.

Clear vision

Having a clear vision for your career and executing on that vision is crucial. When I moved to the UK, I could hardly speak any English – I even needed a friend's help to translate during my registration at Coventry University. Despite this, due to my technical abilities, I excelled academically, earning high grades, scholarships, and even offers to continue my education with a PhD. However, I recognized that my communication skills, especially in English, were a major weakness.

My dream job after graduation was to join IBM's Management Trainee program. IBM had a legacy of groundbreaking innovation, from Deep Blue defeating Kasparov to the creation of the IBM personal computer and the first hard disk drive. I meticulously planned my job applications, scheduling 20 interviews in a particular order so that IBM was the last company I applied to. I failed with 19 companies and succeeded with the last one, IBM. Instead of viewing the failed interviews as setbacks, I saw them as opportunities to learn and prepare for my dream role. When IBM offered me a position at their South Bank office in London, it reinforced a crucial lesson for me: failure only exists if we fail to learn from it.

Shortly after joining IBM, I set a long-term vision for my career: to become a CISO within 10–15 years. At the time, I had no clear roadmap for achieving this, but I understood that continuous growth, both professionally and personally, was essential. As they say, if we don't grow, we die. While this may sound dramatic, it holds true for every living being, from humans to plants.

Periodically reassessing my path ensured that I remained aligned with my long-term objectives. Here is a simple graphic I would use to visualise my progress and ensure I was still moving towards my goal:

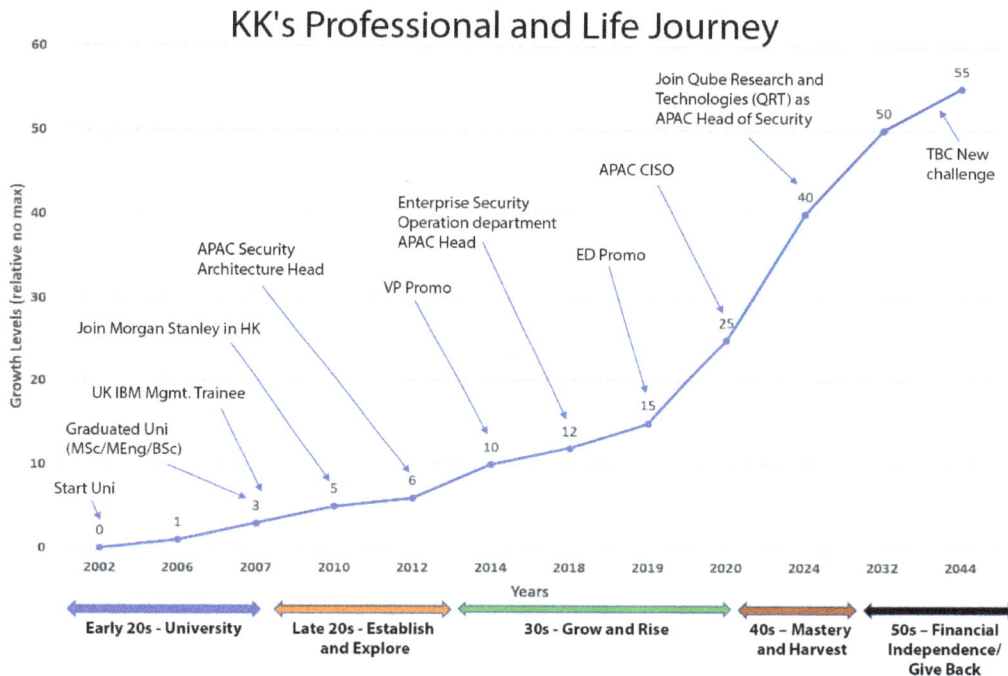

KK's Professional and Life Journey

Figure 6.1: KK's professional and life journey

🔍 **Quick tip:** Need to see a high-resolution version of this image? Open this book in the next-gen Packt Reader or view it in the PDF/ePub copy.

🔒 **The next-gen Packt Reader** and a **free PDF/ePub copy** of this book are included with your purchase. Scan the QR code OR visit https://packtpub.com/unlock, then use the search bar to find this book by name. Double-check the edition shown to make sure you get the right one.

Being adaptive and taking a calculated risk

Life, much like sailing, requires constant navigation. You must always know where you came from, where you are, and where you want to go. Whether adjusting your sail to stay on course or recalibrating your strategy after a setback, resilience and adaptability are vital. One of my defining decisions during university exemplifies this.

Initially, I planned to study in Germany and spent years intensively learning the language. However, just days before the application deadline, I realised that studying in an English-speaking country would be more beneficial for my career.

After a quick analysis, I pivoted to apply for a scholarship to Coventry University instead. I passed the English language exam with the lowest possible score, and even my teacher expressed doubt about my readiness. That decision, though difficult, became a turning point and one of the best choices I made during my academic journey.

This adaptability became even more critical as I transitioned into leadership. In cybersecurity, change is the only constant, whether it's shifting regulations, evolving threats, or organisational restructuring. The ability to assess a situation quickly, adjust course, and move forward with confidence is a skill every aspiring CISO must cultivate.

Building trust

Throughout my career, I've come to value trust as the foundation of effective leadership. I was struck by the simplicity and accuracy of the 'Trust Equation' when I first came across it (`https://trustedadvisor.com/why-trust-matters/understanding-trust/understanding-the-trust-equation`):

$$Trust = \frac{Credibility \times Reliability \times Intimacy}{Self - Orientation}$$

This equation highlights the importance of demonstrating expertise (credibility), dependability (reliability), and genuine care (intimacy) while keeping the focus on others rather than oneself.

One principle that has guided me is always asking how I can add value to others and help others rather than focusing on what's in it for me. As my dear friend Kevin often says, "What goes around comes around." A key example of this was my approach to team promotions. I have always considered the annual promotion case meeting for my team as the most important meeting in my annual calendar. Advocating for my team's growth and success is not only fulfilling but also reinforces the trust and respect that formed the foundation of our collaboration.

The power of soft skills

Cybersecurity is often viewed through the lens of technical expertise, and while technical capabilities are the foundation for this, they are only the beginning. What truly differentiates individuals in cybersecurity, and in any high-stakes profession, are soft skills: leadership, trustworthiness, resilience, and the ability to navigate uncertainty with discipline and focus. These attributes transform technical knowledge into real-world impact.

During my two years in IBM's Management Trainee program, I underwent rigorous leadership and soft skills training that was based on IBM Global Sales School. This highly regarded program covered essential skills such as relationship-building, consultative selling, negotiation, role-playing, and realistic simulations designed to prepare participants for handling complex business scenarios.

Graduating from this program had a profound and lasting impact on both my professional career and personal life, as many of these principles extend beyond the workplace.

Earlier in my career, I believed that technical skills were the most important asset; after all, they are tangible, measurable, and form the foundation of problem-solving. However, I soon realised that technical excellence alone is not enough to drive innovation or ensure the successful adoption of security initiatives. Soft skills are the true differentiator as they empower leaders to communicate effectively, influence others, build trust, and drive meaningful change. My time at IBM reshaped my perspective, demonstrating that technical mastery must be complemented by strong interpersonal and leadership abilities.

Never stopping being technical

For those early in their cybersecurity career, I strongly encourage gaining hands-on experience across multiple domains, including incident response, secure software development, penetration testing, red teaming, vulnerability management, security architecture, and governance. Ideally, spending two to three years in each function provides a well-rounded foundation that will set the stage for a successful and respected CISO career.

Avoid the temptation to rush into senior roles too quickly; while it may seem like the right move, taking the time to develop deep technical expertise will pay dividends in the long run.

If you are already a CISO, don't focus solely on strategy and high-level oversight. Roll up your sleeves and engage in the technical aspects of your cybersecurity program. Doing so ensures that cyber controls are effective, keeps your technical knowledge up to date, and earns the respect of your highly skilled team members. Leading by example is one of the most effective leadership styles I have adopted.

The CISO role requires balancing strategic oversight with technical depth. Each week, I set a goal to immerse myself in a specific technical area and schedule time in my calendar to ensure I follow through. This practice has allowed me to stay connected to the evolving field of cybersecurity while maintaining strong relationships with my technical teams.

Being a good manager

At a recent team-building event, I was reminded of what TEAM stands for: Together, Everyone Achieves More. This principle could not be more accurate. As Barack Obama highlighted in his Masterclass (`https://www.masterclass.com/`) on leadership, teamwork and collaboration consistently outperform individual brilliance when it comes to achieving long-term success. A single talented individual cannot accomplish nearly as much as a group of motivated, aligned people working towards a common objective.

One of the most important decisions you will make as a CISO is hiring the right people and then ensuring that you support and develop them. While there are many guidebooks on hiring and team management, my personal approach has resulted in a nearly zero attrition rate. Here are a few key lessons I have learnt:

- Have a clear hiring strategy. Prepare structured interview questions and focus areas, but allow room for flexibility. Taking time to discuss non-work topics helps you understand candidates beyond their resumes.
- Listen to your team's feedback. Even the most junior team member's concerns about a candidate should be taken seriously. Ignoring red flags during the hiring process can lead to long-term issues.
- Surround yourself with people you trust. Trust is built on credibility, reliability, and genuine care. However, do not mistake loyalty for trust. Prioritising loyalty over capability can lead to a toxic work environment where talented individuals become demotivated or leave.
- Treat everyone fairly. Regular one-on-one meetings are essential. Show respect, protect your team, and empower them, but always maintain fairness. Favouritism, even unintentional, can erode morale and cohesion.
- Support career growth, even if it means losing talent. If someone in your team finds an opportunity that better aligns with their goals, support them, even if it does not directly benefit you. Great leaders build careers, not just teams.

Managing people effectively is about more than leadership; it's about creating an environment where everyone can thrive. A strong, well-supported team will always outperform individual brilliance over the long run.

Keeping communication simple

Where I come from in Poland, and in many other Eastern European countries, there is a tendency to overcomplicate communication, whether through elaborate vocabulary, technical jargon, or overly formal phrasing. This communication style has historical roots, shaped by bureaucratic traditions during the communist era (1945-1989), where complexity is often equated to perceived credibility.

For much of my career, I also struggled with overly complex communication. However, in recent years, I have worked hard to adopt a simpler, clearer style in written and verbal communication. The impact has been significant; messages are more effective, and interactions are more productive. As a CISO, communication is one of the most critical skills, as it involves engaging with executives, technical teams, and employees at all levels. Clear communication enhances cybersecurity initiatives in multiple ways:

- Ensures understanding across all audiences
- Reduces misinterpretation and mistakes
- Builds trust and influence with executives
- Makes security awareness programs more effective
- Saves time and increases efficiency
- Improves incident response and crisis management
- Enhances the clarity of security reports and policies

Clarity is a superpower for a CISO. Success in this role is not just about technical expertise; it's about influencing others to take security seriously. Keeping communication simple ensures that security is accessible, actionable, and effective across an organisation.

The power of asking for help

Throughout my career, I have been fortunate to have great mentors who have guided me through challenges and shaped my leadership and cybersecurity perspectives. One of the most important lessons I have learnt is never to hesitate to ask for help.

Many people are willing to share their knowledge, experiences, and advice, but you have to be willing to reach out. Early in my career, I found that professionals genuinely want to help, whether they were colleagues, industry peers, or senior leaders. Asking for guidance not only helped me grow professionally but also strengthened relationships. As the saying goes, if you don't ask, you don't get.

Equally important is paying it forward. When someone seeks my advice, I make it a priority to find time for them, regardless of whether they are part of my team or my organisation. Mentorship is a two-way street; just as I have benefited from the generosity of others, I strive to provide the same support to those navigating their own career journeys.

CISO insights — the challenge and reward of leadership

Being a CISO has reinforced my belief that it is one of the most challenging roles in the C-suite. The role constantly demands a delicate balance between conflicting priorities, time to market, cost efficiency, risk reduction, and usability. Unlike the insurance industry, where risk quantification directly influences premium pricing, cybersecurity remains far from achieving the same level of precision. This makes it difficult to definitively measure how much risk reduction a specific investment will achieve.

In many ways, the role of a CISO mirrors the Greek myth of Sisyphus, who was condemned to roll a massive boulder up a hill, only for it to roll back down each time he neared the top. How many times have we worked tirelessly to patch all systems, only to be met with new critical vulnerabilities the following week? How often have we decommissioned end-of-life, outdated software, only to find that another critical platform is now obsolete?

For aspiring and current CISOs, it is essential to have a passion for the profession and a clear understanding of why you are willing to take on this Sisyphean task. Many people pursue the CISO role for the challenge, personal achievement, to feed their ego, or financial rewards. While none of these motivations are inherently wrong, they are often insufficient for long-term fulfilment. To truly thrive as a CISO, one must find deeper meaning in the work.

For me, being a CISO is about making a tangible impact – not just for the company, but for the industry and, most importantly, for individuals. When I graduated with my MSc, I had multiple invitations to pursue a PhD with scholarships included. However, I felt I could make a more significant difference in the industry than in academia. Instead, I accepted an offer from IBM's Management Trainee program and set a long-term goal to become a CISO within 10–15 years.

This journey proved to be the right choice for me. It allowed me to grow both professionally and personally, work in global institutions across EMEA and APAC, and mentor numerous professionals who have since achieved their own career aspirations. Knowing that my efforts have helped improve the lives of those around me, many of whom have become lifelong friends, is what keeps me motivated to return to work every day.

For me, being a CISO is synonymous with Sisyphus, not as a curse, but as a calling.

Personal resiliency and wellbeing

Being a CISO is a constant grind. The mix of long hours, endless firefighting, and the weight of knowing that the organisation relies on you to keep it safe takes a real toll. Stress from the role can bleed into every corner of your life. Vacations get cancelled, evenings disappear into incident calls, and even relationships with family and friends can feel the strain. Some people try to push through, but over time, it chips away at both mental and physical health.

When I talk to peers, the story is the same everywhere. Most are working far beyond a normal week, many admit they've lost the balance between work and home, and almost all agree that the role feels more stressful than other executive positions. The job doesn't really stop, and that makes it hard to switch off. There's a sense that if things could be simplified – fewer tools to manage, less duplicated effort – it would make a difference. But at the end of the day, much of the pressure comes from the culture and expectations that surround the role.

For me, sports became the antidote. After moving to Hong Kong, I took up squash and joined a squash section at a local private club. Playing squash two to three times a week, combined with gym workouts, interval runs, and hiking, allowed me to completely disconnect from work stress, maintain a healthy weight, and improve my sleep quality. There were times – especially in my first CISO role, during the COVID-19 crisis, and major regional transformation due to geopolitical challenges – when I neglected exercise, thinking extra hours in the office would make me more effective. I couldn't have been more wrong. Exercise isn't just a distraction from work; it's a foundation for sustainable high performance. It sharpens decision-making, reduces stress, and improves resilience. I learnt the hard way that prioritising wellbeing isn't a luxury; it's a necessity for long-term success in such an intense role.

Finding purpose as a CISO

As I mentioned earlier, the role of a CISO can sometimes feel like the myth of Sisyphus, endlessly pushing a boulder uphill, only for it to roll back down. You patch systems, only for new vulnerabilities to emerge. You train employees, only for someone to click on a phishing email the next day. It's easy to become disillusioned.

That's why knowing your life purpose and ensuring that it aligns with your company's values is crucial, especially during challenging and uncertain times. Decisions in cybersecurity and in life are rarely black and white; they often involve shades of grey and unpredictable consequences. In these moments, my 'Guiding Light,' as my dear friend Brian calls it, has been instrumental in my decision-making process:

- Live a fulfilling life with integrity
- Be better tomorrow than I am today
- Make a difference

These principles helped me navigate through difficult situations, including working under toxic corporate politics. Standing by my values sometimes felt like it might jeopardize my career; in hindsight, it allowed me to grow, overcome challenges, and land more senior roles.

Ultimately, I believe that being a CISO isn't just about managing risk; it's about having a platform to make a real impact. A CISO can influence a company, an industry, and, most importantly, the people they work with.

My final thoughts

If I could leave you with just a few thoughts from this chapter, they would be the following:

- The life of a CISO is not a smooth ride. You will be tested. You will get beaten up, face challenges that make you question your life choices. In those difficult moments, stay true to your integrity and focus on what's most important to the company you protect.
- Put the firm first, but within ethical boundaries. Neither your personal interest nor those of your team should come before what is right for the organisation – so long as it is legal and ethical.
- Find joy in what you do. If, over time, you struggle to enjoy your role, there is no shame in reconsidering your path. A career is a journey, not a prison sentence. If the CISO life no longer aligns with your values and aspirations, pivoting is a sign of strength, not failure.

I, too, have questioned my decision to pursue this career. And yet, looking back, I wouldn't change a thing. Despite the challenges, the stress, and the never-ending nature of the job, the impact, relationships, and sense of purpose make it all worthwhile.

My dear friend Brian summarizes it well: Life's struggles are what make it meaningful, just like the hero's journey in storytelling (as described by Joseph Campbell). If everything were easy, there'd be no growth, no triumph, and no real sense of accomplishment.

So, here's my advice to anyone considering or already walking the path of a CISO:

- Embrace the challenges
- Find your purpose
- And most importantly – enjoy the journey!

David's key takeaways — The journey to CISO

Krzysztof Kostienko (KK) has a wonderful story in this chapter, charting a path from his humble background, from Poland to London, and then to his role in Hong Kong, a major global hub for financial services.

KK's insights are very personal and relatable. The word 'humble' is a very adept description of KK, but this is not giving him full credit as a leader – I'd also add curious, intelligent, and collaborative.

True personal integrity means maintaining our authentic identity and perspective even as we advance professionally, never letting career success redefine who we fundamentally are. From my observation, KK role-models this in how he operates.

Here are some key points from his chapter:

- *There is no wrong path to take to the CISO role.* What is most important is that you are challenging yourself to grow and be 'uncomfortable'. Not taking opportunities to stretch yourself will only hamper your progress.

- *Building trust is key.* This has been foundational to KK's success. Trust involves developing credibility, reliability, and intimacy. It is earned, and trying to build this over time is worth it.

- *Don't underestimate the power of soft skills.* Being a CISO requires skills such as leadership, resilience, and the ability to communicate clearly and simply as much, or even more so, than it requires technical skills.

- *Ask for help if you need it.* Mentors are highly valuable, but you have to be willing to reach out to them. If you don't ask, you don't get. If you get approached with similar requests, pay it forward; mentorship is a two-way street.

- *Find your purpose as a CISO.* Finding your purpose is incredibly grounding and has helped KK define his own *raison d'être* – why he exists! Having this clarity will help you maintain your career rhythm. When motivation is unclear, performance can be inconsistent, and this can inadvertently become part of your brand.

7

Stepping Up into a Global Role

As your career progresses, there may be moments when you are promoted and fear that this will be both a personal and professional stretch. This is not due to a lack of confidence or competence; I'd argue that this is a natural reaction that everyone feels at some point.

For some senior executive roles, the position comes with the added knowledge that you will face some personal liability. Hence, this becomes deeply personal as it can impact your own back pocket, as well as your well-being.

A new promotion in this field brings increased scope of work, and most likely a broader scope with expanded geographic responsibility. This can be new territory for the average CISO, and how you embrace this change will play a huge part in your success.

In the first 90 days, there will be new challenges to tackle around building your new team, understanding the cybersecurity strategy, managing stakeholders and setting the tone for the organisation. Your own presence can create new stress for the existing team, as your questions will often be very different from those of your predecessor.

The new incumbent has to strike a balance between taking charge of their new accountability while also taking time to listen and learn from the existing team. Your new boss is expecting you to step up and lead, so there is no time to be sheepish and undecided.

There will no doubt be some changes that you will need to make; that is expected of any new leader. But also there may be some missing components in the cyber strategy, including technology, people and processes. Some of these may be significant shifts that will require you to engage broadly with executive stakeholders and may not all be seen as positive. That is why this chapter is all about stepping up into a global role.

It is my pleasure to introduce **Sam Coco, Head of Global Information Security** at **Fidelity**. Sam has had an extensive and long career at Fidelity, with more than 14 years in the information security field. As he started his career in technical and desktop support, he has a lot of 'hands-on' experience.

In this chapter, Sam will describe and explore his journey of stepping up into his current role and his learnings from it.

Setting myself up for success

Sam Coco

In this chapter, I want to share my experience of shifting career and the great learnings that I took from it that have helped shape my leadership.

Let me start by providing some background to this significant shift.

Early career transition to Hong Kong

In the initial stages of my information security career, I made a significant move to Hong Kong. This relocation wasn't just a personal shift; it also had profound professional implications. Hong Kong served as a bustling Asia Pacific hub, where I found myself surrounded by organisational leaders from various functions.

The learning curve was steep, but I embraced it eagerly. As the months passed, my responsibilities expanded, and I adapted swiftly to the dynamic environment.

From individual contributor to cybersecurity leadership

Over the course of six years, my role evolved dramatically. I transitioned from being a single contributor to leading the cybersecurity team in the region. By 2019, I had become the go-to person for security matters in the Asia Pacific region. My profile grew, and I relished the challenges that came my way.

While I wasn't a technical specialist, I excelled at building new functions within my remit and making positive change. During this period, I played a pivotal role in establishing a security operations centre and managing technology risk across the region. The teams I led expanded rapidly, and I found fulfilment in making a tangible difference.

Trust, impact and personal satisfaction

To me, success wasn't just about ticking boxes; it was about earning the trust of my management. I delved into the details, ensuring things got done efficiently. Most importantly, I loved what I did because I knew I was contributing significantly to the organisation's security posture. As the point person for security in Asia, I felt a sense of purpose and accomplishment.

I firmly believe that every step of your own journey is a testament to your adaptability, leadership and commitment to making a positive impact. Hence, my mantra is:

'Be ready for opportunity when it arrives.'

As the organisation underwent changes, so did the security team. This is a natural part of any successful organisation, and we should embrace such shifts. During one pivotal period of change, the global information security team faced a unique challenge: it lacked a leader, unlike other cybersecurity functions. Recognising this gap, my manager introduced a new role – the global head of information security. He encouraged me to consider applying for it, emphasising the opportunity more than once.

Suddenly, self-doubt crept in. Could I effectively lead a global team? Were there better-suited candidates out there? What impact would this have on my current work? Was I ready to leave my current position, which I loved? And could I manage this successfully while based in Hong Kong?

As a tough self-critic, I grappled with these questions. Ultimately, three key factors influenced my decision:

- **The rare opportunity:** When would an opportunity like this present itself again? I recognised its uniqueness.

- **Past encouragement:** This wasn't the first time someone had suggested a broader role for me. It echoed a recurring theme.

- **My personal mantra:** The saying, 'Be ready for opportunity when it arrives,' had guided me throughout my career at Fidelity, leading me to where I am today.

Without much hesitation, I decided to move forward. The journey involved a thorough three-stage interview process, complete with panels and presentations. It was an in-depth exploration of my capabilities and fit for the role.

After the interviews, there was a period of quiet anticipation. Then, one night, I dreamt that I was offered the role. I woke up feeling happy and excited. As fate would have it, on that very day, reality mirrored my dream – I received the official offer, and I gladly accepted!

There were some key learnings that I want to highlight from this period:

- Leadership isn't always about easy choices; it's about doing what's right for the team and the organisation
- Hiring, the tough decisions around this, and their impact
- Tackling stress to ensure career longevity

Let me go on to explain how these transpired.

Building the information security team

As the first piece of the new information security team puzzle, the responsibility fell squarely on my shoulders. Fortunately, the business was thriving, and I had three additional headcounts to fill, ready for me to begin hiring. These roles were specifically for new **Business Information Security Officers (BISOs)**, a capability we were introducing to the team. These BISOs would complement the existing information security team I was inheriting. The outlook was positive.

However, reality soon presented a challenge. One of the senior positions attracted particular interest – from within the information security team itself. I found myself torn between candidates.

On paper, the choice seemed straightforward, but the emotional impact surprised me. I opted for the candidate who had the experience to deliver on the functional goals and ultimately support the business requirements. However, managing disappointment and tension afterwards taught me valuable leadership lessons:

- **Evaluate beyond experience:** Experience matters, but it's essential to consider diverse perspectives. Fresh insights can drive innovation and growth.
- **Transparent communication**: Explaining decisions openly fosters understanding. Even when disappointment arises, clarity is crucial.
- **Resilience and self-reflection**: Leadership involves tough calls. When faced with challenges, resilience and self-reflection help us learn and improve.
- **People-centric leadership**: Balancing competence with compassion is key. People drive success, and tough decisions can impact relationships.

Despite the rocky start, one thing remained clear: I was comfortable with my decision. I resolved to continue making tough calls when necessary. As a technologist, I recognised that people are at the core of our success. Leading them brings both joy and personal growth. Yet, there are tough days delivering messages, not because we want to, but because we must, to propel forward. Cultivating **emotional intelligence (EQ)** and compassion is essential.

Hitting reboot

With a new senior team member on board, our focus shifted to the hiring process for new recruits. Meanwhile, the global information security team spanned across the UK, EU, India and China. However, it had lost its sense of purpose and direction over the past couple of years. Silos, inconsistency and a lack of spirit were evident.

My mission was clear: establish authority, build trust and foster harmony while redefining the meaning of information security. All of this had to happen virtually via Zoom due to the COVID lockdowns. I reminded myself that Rome wasn't built in a day; patience would be crucial. As a proponent of the Kaizen method, I aimed for incremental daily improvements that would accumulate into meaningful change.

The team comprised diverse personalities, each with their own motivations. Balancing my voice without stifling others became essential.

We lacked a shared purpose. To address this, I conducted workshops, listening to what people were doing and gathering views on how we could improve the value we provide to the organisation. We also defined a vision and core principles to provide everyone with clarity.

Progress was gradual, some team members embraced the changes sooner than others. What mattered was that they realised I (and all leadership) cared, remained engaged and held them responsible for achieving their objectives. Yet, challenges persisted. Hiring during the pandemic posed difficulties, and a few team members resigned as they grappled with new expectations and reality.

Over time, the team's energy surged. I emphasised our global unity – learning from one another, supporting each other and achieving success together. As a result, we witnessed unprecedented levels of engagement, consistency and delivery – the legacy of a team that had transformed and thrived.

Importantly, information security continued to improve visibility and engagement from the business. There was a growing list of ways to get involved, ways for us to educate and fundamentally improve our security culture.

The floodgates were beginning to open, and I had this realisation:

'Leadership is about adapting, inspiring and fostering a shared purpose.'

What about longevity?

Every information security professional knows the inherent stress of our field – the risks, incidents, vulnerabilities, stakeholder management and the constant need to stay ahead. Daily, we juggle multiple challenges simultaneously. Unfortunately, the average CISO career tends to be short due to stress and burnout.

As someone who tends to be anxious, I recognised that this level of stress wasn't sustainable. I wanted longevity, and I refused to become a statistic – another burnt-out security leader. Reflecting on my journey, I've identified three key strategies.

Being fit

When I moved to Hong Kong and immersed myself in my security career, I also embraced fitness. The more responsibilities I shouldered, the more I prioritised physical activity. Fitness became my foundation, not an add-on. It wasn't about squeezing it into my schedule; my fitness was integral to my well-being.

A healthy body supports a healthy mind and, ultimately, a healthy career. Many successful leaders I know carve out time for their own fitness routines.

Delegating

Transitioning from a hands-on role to a global leadership position posed challenges. Initially, I was entrenched in day-to-day details within the Asia Pacific region. Recognising this proximity bias, I hired a replacement for the local management. This shift allowed me to focus on broader goals, strategic roadmaps, resource management and delegation. As a director, I moved from doing to directing – an essential evolution.

Being resilient

And now, the most challenging part – the mental and emotional resilience required. Leading a team involves tough decisions, accountability and navigating interpersonal dynamics. It's about fostering trust, empowering others and ensuring execution. This balance, along with also seeking diverse perspectives, can be powerful, particularly as organisations and landscapes shift. Balancing empathy with results remains an ongoing journey.

Resilience didn't come to me overnight; it was earned through long hours, hard lessons and moments that tested both my technical judgement and emotional endurance. I learned to anchor myself in purpose, as well as process.

When the pressure mounted, I leaned into clarity, asking not just what the threat was but what the team needed from me. In information security the stakes are high and the unknowns constant. Over time, I found that resilience isn't a destination, it's a discipline.

> Leadership isn't just about technical expertise; it's about holistic well-being and effective management.

Trust and responsibility

As an information security professional, I'm continually amazed by the opportunities that lie just beyond the next corner – the unexpected email, the timely media post. Over time, I've gained exposure to various management roles. Recently, I've taken on regulated positions and even secured a seat on a non-regulated board.

While these achievements might look impressive on a LinkedIn profile (not that I ever updated mine), they come with significant responsibilities. They represent the trust my company places in me. I take this trust seriously, ensuring I operate at a high level and explore ways to fulfil my duties effectively. These roles are a culmination of the trust I've earned during my tenure across diverse senior management positions. What's more, it's a chance to change the executive narrative. We want security to be an enabler for the business that helps win clients and give the leadership group meaningful discussions to help them make decisions when it matters most.

Each new responsibility is an opportunity for growth. As a representative, I constantly evaluate how I can enhance the value I bring. What can I learn to improve my performance? But it doesn't end there. I also consider how I can pave the way for others who step into similar roles. Sharing knowledge and mentoring future leaders is part of my commitment.

Speaking at conferences remains a personal challenge. Panel discussions, in particular, excite me. When industry experts engage in healthy discussions on stage, it's invigorating. Over the years, my senior experience has led to invitations to some of Hong Kong's best events. It's all upside! These gatherings allow me to meet peers, discuss hot topics and learn from others.

But it's not just about taking, I also give back to the local industry. The rewards are immense: building my presence, boosting my confidence on stage and even identifying new talent for my team. People crave insights from CISOs, so if you haven't spoken at a conference, I encourage you to raise your hand. You'll likely find a flood of panel invites coming your way!

Leadership isn't just about titles; it's about seizing opportunities, learning and sharing knowledge.

You don't know what you don't know

In some past roles, I encountered managers who needed to be the smartest person in the room. They hesitated to hire people who might outshine them. As leaders, we must transcend this mindset. Self-awareness is crucial. Recognise your own strengths and acknowledge your limitations. Rather than seeing these limits as roadblocks, view them as opportunities.

Surround yourself with individuals who complement your skills and fill the gaps. Seek out strong, capable team members who exude potential for growth. Success, after all, isn't a solo journey – it is a team effort. Hiring individuals who excel in their areas doesn't diminish our own capabilities; it amplifies the team's collective strength. Be secure enough in your leadership to welcome brilliance around you.

Highly capable, trusted staff bring immense value. Their varied experiences, skills and thinking enrich the team. Diversity isn't just about demographics; it's about cognitive diversity – the different ways people approach problems. When you assemble a team with diverse backgrounds, you tap into a wellspring of creativity and innovation. Remember, it's not about finding clones; it's about finding complementary puzzle pieces.

Leadership demands humility. Acknowledge that you don't have all the answers or skills and leave your ego at the door. When you hire exceptional team members, you're not threatened, you're empowered. They become extensions of your capabilities. Trust them, empower them and let them shine. Your role shifts from doing everything to directing and orchestrating the team's symphony.

In the triad of 'people, process and technology,' people are the beating heart, and your team defines your success. In hiring strong, capable individuals who align with your mission, they'll look up to you, learn from you and contribute to the organisation's security posture. As you nurture their growth, you're shaping the next generation of leaders. It's a legacy worth building.

Leadership isn't about being the smartest; it's about enabling brilliance in others. As you lead, prioritise people – they'll be your compass on your security journey.

Pushing boundaries and making a difference

Finally, as I reflect on my career journey, a smile creeps across my face – not because it was revolutionary or because I was the best, but because I pushed myself beyond perceived limits. I raised my hand, said "yes", and supported those I managed with confidence. Sure, there were nerves, self-doubt and a few missteps along the way, but the end goal always drove me: making things happen and improving upon them each time.

Allow me to highlight a few key points in closing.

Protecting our business future

Like many organisations, the role of a CISO centres on safeguarding our business future. Our security posture shields us from the risks and threats we encounter daily.

While the challenges we face aren't unique, each day presents its own twists and turns. As security professionals navigating the ever-changing cyber landscape, we need to adapt to emerging issues and stay ahead of the curve.

Nurturing individual growth

Beyond organisational security, be passionate about individual growth. How can you empower team members to thrive in their careers?

This is about more than technical skills; it's about *leadership*. Whether encouraging team members to lead initiatives, learn from and gain visibility at senior forums, master people management, earn new certifications or mitigate security risks, each step contributes to personal and collective success.

Visibility and exciting projects

Visibility matters. As your function gains prominence, so do the opportunities for your team; engaging in exciting business projects becomes a reality. We're not just defenders, we're enablers. So, continue pushing boundaries, learning and making a difference – one secure step at a time.

Remember, leadership isn't about perfection; it's about progress and impact.

David's key takeaways — Stepping up into a global role

For the new CISO, there is good advice to glean from the experiences Sam recounts in this chapter. This includes the importance of being ready for opportunities, overcoming self-doubt and making tough decisions – particularly in hiring and team building.

These are not easy obstacles to overcome when you are yourself learning a new role.

Allow me to highlight other key learnings from this chapter:

- *Leadership involves being ready to adapt, and also being able to inspire unity*, as Sam learnt particularly while building a global information security team during COVID. It requires establishing authority virtually, breaking down silos and creating a shared purpose through workshops and clear vision-setting.

- *Making difficult personnel decisions is often necessary.* It's important to balance competence with compassion and maintain transparent communication about tough choices.

- *Stress is to be expected.* To help with your own leadership longevity in cyber, consider ways to tackle this, for example, by maintaining your physical fitness and developing mental resilience.

- *Build a strong team.* To be a successful security leader, admit what you don't know and hire team members who complement your skills. Seeking cognitive diversity and being secure enough to welcome those who might be smarter than you in certain areas is valuable.

- *The role of a modern CISO goes beyond organisational security* – it also includes nurturing individual growth, increasing visibility of the security function and enabling exciting business projects, making security an integral part of business success rather than just a defensive measure.

8

Diverse Paths to Cybersecurity Leadership

CISOs come from all walks of life, but mostly from a traditional IT path and a technical role. As the requirement for cybersecurity has intensified, there have been new entrants into this domain from outside the direct industry, however. This is likely due to the increasing strategic importance of cybersecurity, with expanding regulations.

There are requirements for the CISO to have strong credibility with the board and management. What attributes are particularly valuable in your career that could be of value in your future CISO role? This, of course, will depend upon your own starting position and learning agility.

We will see this trend of having more talent imported into cybersecurity continue. In fact, I myself moved from a CIO role into a CISO role by design. There are great advantages that you gain from taking talent with broader perspectives into a new domain, as they will be naturally curious and want to understand why things work the way they do, rather than just accepting anything at face value.

Take the example of a lawyer who moves into this area. What new challenges would they face? How would they make such a transition? Let me start by noting that any lawyer transitioning into a CISO role brings valuable skills in regulatory compliance, contract management, and incident response from their legal background.

To succeed, they should focus on developing technical knowledge and building an understanding of IT infrastructure and security operations. They can maximize their effectiveness by building a strong technical team, leveraging their legal expertise for governance and risk management, and actively pursuing professional development through security organisations and conferences.

I would argue that a legal background is particularly valuable as cybersecurity becomes increasingly tied to regulatory compliance and risk management. Lawyers bring both domain-relevant expertise and a naturally questioning mindset that demands logical, evidence-based arguments, thus making them well-positioned to handle the strategic aspects of the role while developing technical competencies – they make great CISOs for this reason.

It is my pleasure to introduce you to **Catherine Rowe**, who has a distinguished career, both in Australia and globally, including as **Global CISO** at **QBE Insurance** and **CISO** at **Teachers Mutual Bank Limited**. She has also served in executive roles at Commonwealth Bank of Australia and practiced as a lawyer in both private practice and in-house roles, advising on technology, cyber security, privacy, outsourcing and compliance.

Catherine has some excellent learnings to share that you can apply to your own career planning, particularly in how to make transitions into adjacent and new domains, giving you more scope and opportunity.

Diverse paths to cybersecurity leadership

Catherine Rowe

The role of a CISO demands a combination of leadership and influencing skills, strategic insight, risk management, and technical expertise. As cybersecurity has evolved from a purely technical issue to a fundamental business priority, people from diverse backgrounds such as law, finance, risk management, strategy and communications are joining the cyber profession.

CISOs commonly oversee a broad range of expert teams specialising in areas such as cyber education, awareness, governance, strategy, risk management and compliance, as well as highly technical functions. However, businesses still generally look to developing technical talent to grow the leadership and strategic capabilities required of a modern CISO, with only 24% of organisations actively looking to recruit talent into cyber from non-traditional backgrounds (World Economic Forum (WEF) Global Cybersecurity Outlook 2025: https://www.weforum.org/publications/global-cybersecurity-outlook-2025/).

Cybersecurity is a field that thrives on problem-solving, adaptability, collaboration and diverse thinking, as well as the skills to translate cyber risks into business impacts. I advocate for developing a broader CISO pipeline of talent by expanding recruitment strategies to encompass leaders from alternative career paths and investing in those professionals to grow the technical expertise required.

Such lateral hiring practices are essential in combatting both the current cyber skills shortage (according to the WEF report, the shortfall in cyber security professionals is estimated between 2.8 million and 4.8 million globally) and poor gender diversity in the profession.

Despite comprising 36% of broader tech roles, women represent only 24% of the cybersecurity workforce globally (Global Cybersecurity Forum, 2024 'Cyber Security Workforce Report': `https://gcforum.org/en/research-publications/cybersecurity-workforce-report-bridging-the-workforce-shortage-and-skills-gap/`) and 25% in Australia (Australia Cyber Network (ACN), 'State of the Industry 2024': `https://stateoftheindustry.auscybernetwork.au/`). Significantly, according to a report by Forrester, only 16% of CISOs are women (Forrester, 2023 'CISO Career Paths 3.0' report: `https://www.forrester.com/report/ciso-career-paths-3-0/RES178976`).

By sharing my personal story of moving from lawyer to CISO, and the lessons I learnt from it, I hope to inspire others to make the leap to a fulfilling and dynamic profession. Furthermore, I hope to inspire current cyber, technology and business leaders to also adopt broader recruitment and development strategies as we grow the next generation of cyber leaders. After all, cyber resilience is about people, not just technology.

My journey – from law to cybersecurity

My own transition into cybersecurity was a leap of faith fuelled by passion, purpose and a drive to take on new challenges.

I wanted to do more than advise on risks and compliance; I wanted to be accountable for delivering solutions that made a difference. Cybersecurity felt dynamic and tangible, a field where I could combine my passion for technology, risk management and data privacy with my drive to lead transformational change. At its heart, cybersecurity is about protecting people – our customers, employees and the broader community. That mission resonated deeply with me, and I was ready to step out of my comfort zone to be part of it.

This wasn't an easy decision. Like many women entering technical fields, I faced questions about whether I was 'technical enough' or 'qualified enough', but I saw those doubts as an opportunity to challenge outdated assumptions. Cybersecurity, after all, is not just about firewalls and encryption; it's about understanding threats, managing risks, and building resilience in the face of uncertainty.

Most importantly, I also had the support of a visionary CISO, who understood the need for a diverse and multi-faceted leadership team to lead the charge in facing the ever-evolving threat landscape and was prepared to take a bet on me.

Making the leap

While many lawyers make a transition into cybersecurity via risk and compliance roles, my first role in cybersecurity was purely operational – accountable for running and transforming key preventative cybersecurity controls across Australia's largest domestic bank. This meant leading a large and highly technical team including developers, engineers, architects, systems integrators, analysts and service owners.

I learnt quickly that successful leadership isn't about having all the answers; it's about creating the conditions for your team to thrive. I built trust by being honest about what I didn't know and showing a determined willingness to learn.

I also asked a lot of questions, even the so-called 'dumb' ones (and I still do). This not only helped me understand complex technical issues but also, refreshingly, often aided technical team members in challenging their own assumptions and rationales in the process of educating me. Interestingly, I encountered very little resistance from my team members and colleagues in having to spend the extra time they needed to dedicate to teaching and explaining. It provided an opportunity to demonstrate the significance of their work and the challenges they faced, and for me to understand not only the diverse technical aspects of cybersecurity but also the nuances and complexities faced by cyber experts in their day-to-day roles.

These were some of the most rewarding moments of my career – spending hours in a room with passionate cyber experts equipped with a whiteboard and post-it notes, sharing knowledge and designing innovative solutions to complex problems.

More challenging was building the confidence to represent cybersecurity and my team with other technology stakeholders, many of whom were far more technically proficient than me. The key for me was preparation, preparation, preparation. I spent many hours before stakeholder meetings ensuring I was comfortable with the subject matter, digging deep into any data or position being put forward, and seeking to understand the audience and where their interest or concerns may lie. Pre-socialising and getting feedback from significant stakeholders are vital in higher-stakes meetings with executives and boards. Of course, there were times (and still are) when questions arose that I could not answer on the spot, but dealing with this transparently and committing to revert with a considered response is imperative. Handling those tricky questions from executives and boards well is a skill that mostly only comes from experience.

When you first make the transition to a role outside your core area of competency, it's not a secret that you are learning a new area. Remember, you have not been engaged for your technical expertise; you have been hired for your judgement and leadership. It's important to recognise your role as a leader whose job it is to bring together technical expertise and resources to solve complex problems and achieve sound outcomes.

A key advantage of not being the most technical person in the room is being able to give your team the opportunity to shine. Empowering technical team members by involving them in high-stakes meetings and deferring to their expertise is crucial for fostering talent and building high-performing teams. For example, presenting to senior stakeholders can be an intimidating task for many technical experts. By leveraging my skills as an executive advisor, familiar with the executive suite and the boardroom, adept at translating complex technical issues into language that is meaningful for executives and boards, I could help bridge the gap. This approach not only enhances the visibility of technical experts but also provides valuable learning opportunities to understand how cybersecurity fits in the overall narrative of the organisation. It is a vital part of developing careers and ensuring effective communication across all levels of the organisation.

Don't underestimate the skills that you bring to a technical team. Having diverse experience in broader contexts and the skills to advocate and communicate at all levels of an organisation is critical in helping to develop the leadership skills of your technical teams, as well as securing the executive support and resources to succeed.

Making allies and securing buy-in

Inevitably, in corporate life, you encounter internal challenges to the outcomes you are seeking to achieve. This is particularly so in cybersecurity, which requires extensive interactions across technology and business, often in ways that others might not agree with, desire or even understand. Cyber professionals are, unfortunately, still frequently perceived as the people 'who say no,' or 'who negatively impact the customer experience', which can lead to friction and resistance.

To shift those perceptions, I learnt early on the importance of developing strong relationships with the broader business and executive teams. The more I was able to develop my understanding of the priorities and challenges they faced, including where our desired outcomes either met or diverged, the better and more transparent the conversation and the better the outcomes for the team and the organisation.

A CISO needs to cultivate a culture where cybersecurity is understood and valued as an integral component of an organisation's strategic objectives, rather than as an impediment or an afterthought. This requires actively seeking out opportunities and relationships that help you to understand the myriad dynamics and drivers of your organisation and, in turn, assist in promoting a broader understanding of the role of cybersecurity as a trusted partner. Don't focus only on developing relationships within the technology team; you will need to form good relationships across the executive team.

A key piece of advice is not to be shy about scheduling quarterly one-on-ones with executive stakeholders. Not only does this facilitate a shared understanding and improved risk culture, but it also helps to secure the executive sponsorship required to help you manage roadblocks and provide essential guidance in navigating organisational complexities and politics.

Network, network, network

Being well-networked in the cyber community is essential for cyber professionals to stay ahead of evolving threats and, importantly, to maintain personal resilience in a highly demanding and challenging role.

Australia is unique for its small(ish) and closely knit cyber community. This is a generous profession, and I was welcomed into this community and am grateful for the guidance and support offered, particularly as I was learning the technicalities of my profession. Crucially, cybersecurity is not regarded by cyber professionals as a competitive advantage; in fact, we are all too aware of the interconnectedness of the digital ecosystem and the imperative for collaboration across industry, government and the community to help keep that ecosystem secure. I strongly recommend seeking out and joining relevant networks early in your cyber career transition.

Meeting the challenges of being a woman in a male-dominated field

It is no secret that cybersecurity remains a male-dominated field, and was even more so over ten years ago when I made the transition. Seeking out and becoming part of women-led communities in cybersecurity and technology leadership has been an essential lifeline for me. These groups provide invaluable support, mentorship, and a sense of belonging, which is crucial for women navigating the challenges of this and other such professions.

There are several organisations that are dedicated to supporting and empowering women in cyber, such as Australian Women in Security Network (AWSN: `www.awsn.org.au`) and Women in Cyber Security (`www.wicys.org`). In addition to organisations like these, I encourage you to join and create informal support networks with other women throughout your cyber career.

Being part of such groups has provided me with guidance and solidarity, helping me manage the dynamics of all too often being the only woman in the room. They have helped me to maintain my voice, manage technical egos, and understand the unique value I bring to the table. The strength and support of such organisations and networks are critical as the gender imbalance remains prominent in cybersecurity.

Training and continuous professional development

Whilst I am a strong advocate for learning on the job and the direct hands-on experience it provides, gaining a certification in cybersecurity and ensuring your skills are continuously developed play an important role in the cyber profession.

As the diverse cyber industry continues to grapple with its professionalisation, certifications play a crucial role as benchmarks of technical proficiency and expertise in cyber risk management. I would encourage those taking the leap into cyber to pursue certifications or training programs that align with their specific needs (for certifications, see, for example, ISACA, ISC2 and SANS, as well as a range of organisations renowned for offering high-quality and diverse speciality training programs).

Numerous dedicated cybersecurity conferences held both in Australia and globally provide opportunities for professionals to remain engaged and informed about the latest trends and solutions in cybersecurity.

Shifting the hiring mindset

The traditional dynamic in hiring or creating cybersecurity leaders is to look predominantly to promoting technical experts to fill CISO roles. To shift this to one that encourages a more diverse talent pipeline, it's important to understand the role of the modern CISO and the skills that are required.

Whilst growing technical talent into multi-faceted leaders remains important, as the management of cyber risk becomes increasingly integrated into all facets of our lives and organisations, we should also recognise the importance of growing the technical skills of leaders from areas outside cyber.

The most important skill for a CISO is to be an adaptive leader, able to work across silos and multiple stakeholders, adapting to new and challenging environments in combination with understanding the strategic aims of the organisation. A great CISO strives always to understand the motivations and concerns of the board, business leaders, technology leaders, employees, customers and, of course, cybercriminals and threat actors.

Through my career journey, I have developed a keen understanding of the skills and value that non-technical leaders bring to cyber leadership. Here, I set out some of the key skills required of a CISO and explain how broader experience contributed to my role as a cybersecurity leader. Hopefully, this will provide guidance both to those considering moving laterally into cybersecurity and to those CISOs and leaders seeking to broaden their hiring approaches beyond the purely technical.

Risk and governance

The role of a CISO is one of risk management rather than risk elimination, requiring the management of cyber risks in accordance with organisational risk appetite. CISOs must be able to assess risks from multiple perspectives and help the organisation to balance competing priorities.

The ability to fluently articulate and demonstrate cyber risk posture is vital for effectively engaging with boards, risk committees, and other senior stakeholders. CISOs also need to engage in comprehensive and informed conversations with senior stakeholders and regulators regarding cyber governance, reporting, and accountability across the organisation.

My background in implementing governance and risk management frameworks for cybersecurity and other non-financial risks provided me with a strategic advantage, allowing me to effectively contribute to the critical balance between risk management and digital and technological innovation.

Strategic communication

Being able to develop effective communication strategies explaining cybersecurity risks to non-technical stakeholders, from board members to frontline staff, is critical to the CISO role. Working hard to translate technical jargon into clear, relatable narratives is key to fostering understanding and securing buy-in.

Broader cross-business experience is invaluable for crafting communication strategies that resonate with the intended audience. My experience as a legal advisor also helped me to break down complex technical issues into meaningful and actionable insights for boards and other senior stakeholders.

Ultimately, gaining the unwavering support of senior stakeholders is the key that unlocks the necessary funding and sponsorship to transform your cyber strategy from concept to reality.

Regulatory expertise and compliance

As a lawyer, navigating legal and regulatory frameworks was second nature to me, as it is to other compliance and regulatory professionals. This expertise was invaluable in ensuring our cybersecurity strategy and operational effectiveness adhered to the evolving and increasingly complex cybersecurity and broader technology regulations and standards.

A background in compliance and regulatory requirements equips a CISO with the confidence and capability to manage regulatory engagements and foster trust with both internal and external stakeholders.

Conflict resolution and collaboration

Cybersecurity necessitates cross-functional collaboration, requiring sound solutions spanning various departments with differing priorities. Experience in negotiation and mediation helped me to manage these demands by bridging gaps, resolving conflicts, and recognising valuable compromise.

Like the best contracts, effective achievement of the desired outcomes is best when it's a win-win – with all parties entering a workable and aligned solution.

Adaptive leadership

With adversaries constantly evolving their tactics, and organisations rapidly adopting new technologies, CISOs must possess the agility to adapt their approaches. They need to embrace change as a fundamental aspect of their role and be able to rally the team and the organisation to similarly adapt.

This requires not only a curious and adaptive mindset but also the agility to alter leadership styles. For example, empathetic leadership is essential to support and develop teams and foster innovation; influencing leadership is required to get peers and senior stakeholders on board and, in times of crisis, more directional leadership may be necessary to lead through significant high-stakes challenges.

I found my diverse leadership experience (not only as a leader of teams but as an individual contributor reliant only on my influence) helped me to adapt quickly and enhanced my ability to respond effectively to varying circumstances and constant change.

Critical thinking and decision-making

Critical thinking and decision-making are essential components of the CISO role. CISOs must identify, analyse, prioritise and resolve complex cybersecurity issues every day. The capacity to critically assess situations and make informed decisions, sometimes rapidly, with limited information and under significant pressure, is intrinsic to CISO responsibilities.

A background in analysing and resolving complex legal issues, evaluating various perspectives and desired outcomes and making strategic decisions based on facts provided me with a solid foundation for handling these challenges as a CISO. The adversarial stance often required by lawyers when advocating for their client's interests, and the need to think on your feet, also proved an advantage in dealing with the motivations of threat actors.

Project delivery, transformation and execution

All CISOs, whether they are building foundational cyber capabilities or continuing to mature those foundations, are required to drive technology and cultural change across their organisation. Program delivery experience and execution discipline are much-needed leadership capabilities for CISOs. The statistics for poor outcomes in technology and digital transformations remain high; however, the potential impact of failed cyber programs poses an even greater concern.

Having experience in delivering enterprise-wide risk remediation and transformation programs enabled me to ensure the required program disciplines and rigour were applied to drive the successful delivery of cyber change programs as a CISO.

Ethical leadership and integrity

As professionals responsible for protecting customers' data and ensuring operational security, CISOs must lead with integrity, trust and transparency. Ethical leadership and integrity foster trust within your team and among stakeholders, thereby strengthening the collective effort to maintain robust cybersecurity practices.

A comprehensive and ethical grasp of the role of cybersecurity in safeguarding data and communities is essential. Cybersecurity extends beyond warfare and adversarial tactics, and it is not limited to the stereotype of teenagers hacking in basements. It is imperative to have professionals who recognise cybersecurity as a social issue within our modern global digital and geopolitical landscape. Bringing in diverse leadership from professions focused on ethical and social outcomes brings nuanced understanding and dedication to the field.

Final reflections

As the fields of technology and business continue to evolve at pace, with organisations becoming increasingly digitised, borderless and customer-centric, the CISO can no longer be regarded simply as a technical expert with all the answers. They must be capable of establishing a shared vision across the organisation and remain adaptive to evolving business strategies and technological innovation, as well as developing threats. This necessitates leaders who are proficient influencers, able to lead upwards, sideways and downwards. They must be able to persuade CEOs and CFOs to invest, boards to set the tone from the top, technology teams to integrate secure-by-design practices and end users to adopt cyber-safe behaviours.

Over time, I found that not being the most technical person in the room was actually a huge benefit. It allowed me to bring an outside-in perspective, challenge assumptions, and foster innovation. By focusing on the big picture, rather than in-depth technical detail, I have been able to align individual strengths toward a shared vision and unlock the full potential of my teams.

For anyone considering the leap into cybersecurity, I encourage you to embrace the challenge. Bring your unique skills and perspectives to the table, lean on your team and your networks, and never stop asking questions. With the right mindset, it's an incredible opportunity to make a meaningful impact in a field that truly matters.

For businesses and leaders who wish to best secure their organisation, customer and stakeholder outcomes, hopefully by sharing my experience, you will gain an insight into the benefits of investing in building the technical skills of great and diverse leaders and challenge your assumptions in seeking only to develop great leaders from technical talent.

David's key takeaways — Diverse paths to cybersecurity leadership

Catherine has some compelling lessons that she has shared here in making career transitions from non-technical beginnings to taking on a complex and challenging career as a CISO.

It's clear that an adaptive mindset enables a leader to be successful in making these career shifts, and that using your strengths to build new muscle that can be applied helps you to lead successfully. With the shortage of global talent, it is inevitable that the role of the CISO will continue to attract diverse talents to take on the challenging opportunity it presents.

In particular, non-technical professionals can bring valuable capabilities to the field, such as risk governance, strategic communication, regulatory expertise, conflict resolution and project delivery experience. These complementary skills are essential for managing the complex, cross-functional nature of cybersecurity leadership.

Here are some of Catherine's key points:

- *Diverse backgrounds strengthen cybersecurity.* The modern CISO role requires more than technical expertise; it demands leadership skills, strategic insight and communication abilities, among others. Organisations should consider expanding recruitment to include leaders from non-traditional backgrounds (such as law, finance and risk management) to combat the skills shortage and also address the poor gender diversity in cybersecurity.

- *Leadership trumps technical expertise.* Successful CISOs are adaptive leaders who can work across organizational silos, understand business strategy and balance risk management with commercial growth. The role requires translating technical issues into business impacts, securing executive support and navigating organizational politics – skills often developed in non-technical roles.

- *Transitioning into cybersecurity from non-technical backgrounds requires honesty about knowledge gaps, asking questions, thorough preparation, and leveraging team expertise.* Remember that you're hired for judgment and leadership, not technical expertise; your role is to bring together resources to solve complex problems.

- *Give credit to others.* Not being the most technical person can be an advantage, allowing leaders to give their technical team members opportunities to shine. By involving technical experts in high-stakes meetings and translating their knowledge for executives, non-technical leaders can bridge critical gaps between technical teams and senior stakeholders.

- *Cybersecurity is about people protection* - this means protecting customers, employees, and communities, rather than merely securing systems, with privacy serving as an integral component rather than a separate discipline. Effective CISOs must view their role holistically, integrating privacy considerations into their security strategy to create comprehensive protection that addresses both technical threats nd the safeguarding of personal data.

9

Overcoming Doubt

The CISO operates in a world that is uncertain. Their key stakeholders on the board and management often have a limited understanding of cybersecurity. It is therefore not surprising that they have many doubts about it. This doubt can be transferred into doubting the 'messenger', in this case, the CISO. If the CISO loses the confidence of this audience, their role becomes increasingly difficult, making it nearly impossible to drive the cyber transformation required.

That is just one type of doubt that can affect CISOs. CISOs face several types of doubt that can undermine their effectiveness, including technical doubt and organisational doubt, as well as personal doubt.

Many CISOs have a deep technical background, where analysis competency has been a key strength. But the reality is that cybersecurity is a complex domain with many fine details. Even the most tech-savvy CISO does not have all the answers.

Technical doubt about emerging threats and security solutions can lead to analysis paralysis when quick decisions are needed. It is important, therefore, to know the right questions to ask and have a team around you that is willing to 'lean in' and support your own gaps.

The impact of cybersecurity on business resilience has made it the highest on the risk register. In this scenario, there can be **organisational doubt** about budget requests, policy changes, or **incident response (IR)** plans. This can result in insufficient security investments or delayed decisions on vital actions.

Then there are incidents, near misses and false positive issues. As the CISO, you are the messenger of these, bringing bad news and then sometimes even having to walk back and clarify that it was a false alarm. This can create **personal doubt** about your leadership capabilities, which becomes particularly damaging when communicating with executive teams in crisis situations, when confidence is essential for organisational trust.

Overcoming fear of doubt is critically important for CISO success, as the role inherently involves making high-stakes decisions with incomplete information amidst developing threats. The CISO must be able to adapt to the scenario and doubt that they are facing – this is the ultimate strategic tool to getting to a decision.

The consequences of not overcoming fear of doubt are significant. At worst, this could mean you lose your job as a CISO. But it is more likely that your day-to-day activities may be under extreme pressure of extra oversight. Your cyber strategic planning also suffers when doubt prevents bold but necessary security initiatives. Making the wrong decision can be costly, but indecision can stall all progress. Such indecision is a killer for your team and can completely demoralise a motivated group.

When doubt controls the CISO (rather than the CISO controlling doubt), some simple everyday tasks, such as risk assessments, become less about facts and more about opinion. *Too much* doubt can lead to over-cautious approaches that could stifle the business, while *too little* doubt can leave the enterprise open to security breaches by accepting this risk. The CISO has to have the ability to discern what the facts are and what is conjecture or human interpretation.

Highly effective CISOs cultivate the ability to differentiate between constructive scepticism, which sharpens analysis, and debilitating doubt, which impedes timely action. They embrace calculated risk-taking, recognising that decisions are often made under conditions of incomplete information.

Rather than seeking to eradicate uncertainty, they channel it into disciplined preparation, scenario-based planning and sustained learning. This approach can transform doubt into an asset that they can use to enhance both their planning and decision-making acumen and therefore also improve their organisation's overall resilience and impact.

It is my absolute pleasure to introduce **Stéphane Nappo**, who is a globally recognised leader in cybersecurity and a senior executive with over 25 years of experience in supporting the cybersecurity of major international financial, digital services and industrial groups.

As **Director of Cybersecurity and Global Chief Information Security Officer**, Stéphane Nappo has extensive experience at the Vinci Group, Société Générale International Banking, OVHCloud and Groupe SEB, the global leader in the small household appliances market, whose prestigious brands are present in 150 countries. Through his work, Stéphane remains at the forefront of the evolution and transformation of cybersecurity.

His diverse experience across financial, digital and manufacturing industries has allowed him to understand the challenges facing local and international organisations today. His experience in IT, **operational technology (OT)**, **Internet of Things (IoT)**, the cloud and AI provides a different, pragmatic perspective on the challenges our industries face in managing their growth in today's world, while ensuring their cyber resilience in the face of ever-changing technologies and threats.

As a recognised cyber leader, Mr. Nappo is a dynamic CISO who loves to share his knowledge. In this chapter, he shares his own experience in overcoming and reframing doubt, and discusses how he values this notion in the CISO role.

Overcoming doubt

Stéphane Nappo

Doubt has long been an intrinsic element of cybersecurity and risk management. Far from constituting a weakness, it complements established tools and methodologies, serving as a hallmark of seasoned CISOs. I have observed that when **applied with reason**, doubt becomes both a personal trait for navigating uncertainty and a strategic mindset that cultivates vigilance, strengthens resilience and drives proactive defence.

René Descartes, mathematician and philosopher, said:

> *'To determine whether there is anything we can know with certainty, we first have to doubt everything we know.'*

Marie Curie, scientist and Nobel Prize laureate, said:

> *'Nothing in life is to be feared, it is only to be understood.'*

These are just two quotes that reflect the actionable value of reasonable doubt and its importance in tackling uncertainty, reducing unnecessary fears and strengthening proactivity.

How should we view doubt?

In my experience, the first step in doubt management is to embrace its real nature and its impact on trust. Doubt is often perceived as a state of uncertainty or lack of conviction about the truth, reality or reliability of something. However, to dive deeper into the notion of doubt, it is important to look at its potential effects on us and our biases regarding doubt. This notably encompasses:

- The suspension of belief in the absence of sufficient evidence
- An emotional state marked by hesitation, between belief and disbelief
- A risky approach to the unknown, taking chances that have often not been thought out

In the context of cybersecurity, I have learnt that doubt handling requires one to **reframe doubt as a tool**, one that prompts questioning, validation and deeper investigation.

Once we conceive that doubt is not a Gordian knot (a complex, challenging problem) but a tool to enlighten shadowy areas, a question of rationality and equilibrium arises in risk treatment. In this respect, the boundary is thin between cyber proactivity and risky paranoia.

I wrote a statement years ago to materialise this challenging paradigm:

> *'One of the main cyber risks is to think they don't exist; the other is to try to treat all potential risks.'*

In my experience as a CISO, this demanding paradigm can at times place cyber decision-makers in a dilemma, adopting a *'glass half full'* perspective that emphasises technical accomplishments and progress against action plans. While remediation efforts are undeniably vital, the alternative, *'glass half empty'* view, acknowledging unknown risks and embracing doubt, remains an important standpoint and should not be neglected. Indeed, it is essential for safeguarding the organisation and addressing the threats that truly matter.

As a matter of fact, cyber blind spots and indecision often result from a lack of doubt valuation. At the same time, cybersecurity leaders' shoulders carry the weight of managerial expectation that strongly lies in the ability *to know what to do* regarding a predefined scenario, instead of **being prepared for what we don't know**. According to a persistent, outdated perception of cyber skills, taking doubt into account can still be frowned upon and considered a lack of leadership in decision-making.

One of my key cybersecurity mantras is to *'expect the unexpected'*.

Rationality drives us to define too deterministic plans to handle a non-deterministic and constantly shape-shifting threat. This posture leads to our increasing exposure to unexpected cyber issues, fueled by the ability of cyber predators to constantly surprise their victims.

As doubt lies in the shadowy areas researched, targeted and often destroyed by cyber offences, every new CISO (and cyber veterans as well) should consider doubt as a factor of success in risk reduction, and handle it with reasoned methods.

Although the notion of *shadow IT* is identified today as a concrete source of risk for organisations, for which there are prescribed actions to reduce, shadow cyber exposure is too often not taken into consideration, although it is often recognised.

How do we switch our perception of doubt from doubt as a challenging knot to *doubt as a tool?* As the human factor remains predominant in cybersecurity management, cyber philosophy plays an important role in interacting with all stakeholders (executive board members, employees, third parties etc.). In this respect, the parallel of cyber doubt with Karl Jung's shadow provides interesting insights.

In Jungian psychology, the 'shadow' represents the unconscious – often repressed aspects of ourselves, such as fears, instincts and weaknesses. This is akin to cyber weaknesses in an organisation, often known about but unconsciously repressed due to organisational and technological complexity.

When ignored, this *shadow* grows in power and can erupt destructively. In our cybersecurity context, this could mean that an organisation becomes a victim of their forgotten, unfixed or neglected cyber weaknesses. This teaches us that what is ignored can sometimes become very dangerous.

Jung advocates for conscious integration of the shadow to achieve a psychological balance and prevent an 'unconscious sabotage'. When it comes to cybersecurity, I have learnt that 'know thyself' and 'know your own shadow' are key notions to apply as a CISO. The famous 'know your enemy' notion remains important too, but dependent on your shadow exposures. This approach plays a pivotal role in illuminating doubt, exposing the shadowed areas where vulnerabilities lie and how they might harm the organisation. It enables targeted insight through methods such as opportunistic testing and detection/response, ensuring that weaknesses are revealed and addressed before they can be exploited.

Doubt in cybersecurity, like the shadow in Jung's theory, is essential. Just as Jung urges us to face our darkness to become whole, cybersecurity leaders must embrace doubt to build resilient systems.

Embracing doubt in cybersecurity

In the current digital world, cybersecurity has become a domain where the threats are invisible, ever-changing and often unknowable. Unlike traditional security challenges, where risks can be measured and addressed with clear strategies, CISOs operate in a realm of ambiguity and volatility where attackers can strike from anywhere, employing unpredictable methods designed to exploit both our risk management uncertainties and vulnerabilities that may not yet be identified. In such an environment of persistent uncertainty, the pressing question for CISOs is how organisations can mount an effective and adaptive defence.

There are three core factors to consider for cybersecurity, in the following priority order:

- **Evolving threats**: Attackers continually innovate, using methods such as AI, zero-day vulnerabilities and social engineering. Defenders are often one step behind, reacting rather than anticipating.

- **Information asymmetry**: Organisations rarely know the full extent of their own vulnerabilities, let alone the capabilities of their adversaries. The unknown is always greater than the known.

- **Complexity and interconnectedness**: Digital ecosystems are increasingly interconnected and interdependent, so a single vulnerability in a third-party vendor can trigger a chain reaction across multiple organisations, even over several continents.

This combination of factors makes cybersecurity a domain where absolute certainty really is a myth. Traditional risk management models, which rely on probabilities and big data *from the past*, often fall short in such an environment. This is why dealing with doubt is no longer optional in cybersecurity; it is, rather, **a strategic necessity**.

A team that acknowledges what it does not know is far more agile and resilient than one blinded by perceived control.

This is a mindset shift that transforms doubt from a threat into a tool that positively enlightens curiosity, vigilance and continuous learning.

As such, instead of trying to eliminate this uncertainty, the most forward-thinking cybersecurity leaders learn to adapt within it. Notably, this means:

- **Continuous monitoring**: Real-time threat intelligence and anomaly detection must replace periodic security assessments.

- **Assumption-based planning**: Assuming breaches will occur, and designing architectures that limit the impact of an attack, as well as putting measures in place to ensure speedy recovery, rather than relying solely on prevention.

- **Red team exercises**: Simulating attacks that exploit not just technical gaps but also organisational blind spots and human error.

- **Zero Trust architecture**: Replacing outdated perimeter-based models with a mindset that no user, device or system is inherently trusted. We'll look at Zero Trust in more detail next.

These practices acknowledge that uncertainty is not a temporary glitch, something to gloss over, but rather a permanent and fundamental condition of the cyber realm.

Doubt as a foundation of the Zero Trust approach

In this era of hyperconnectivity, hybrid working, and sophisticated threats, traditional security models (built on the assumption of clear perimeters and trusted internal actors) are no longer sufficient. The Zero Trust approach emerged in direct response to cope with this reality, and at the very core of its DNA lies doubt.

Far from being a sign of defect or a weakness, doubt is the strategic and operational cornerstone of the Zero Trust approach. It challenges dangerous implicit trust, demands continuous verification and assumes that any user, device or internal or external system may be compromised. It relies on doubt as a tool for clarity, control and strategic foresight.

Zero Trust has gained popularity as modern cyberattacks have shown that **threats often come from within,** or from external actors who gain internal access quickly after breaching a single vulnerability.

Zero Trust starts from a position of doubt, and asks, in priority order:

- Are these users who they claim to be?
- Is this device healthy and authorised?
- Should this action be allowed for this user, here and now?

Access is granted based on identity, context and verification, not from location or assumption. In essence, Zero Trust says: '*I don't trust you by default. Prove yourself every time*'.

Operationalising doubt

Doubt becomes operational through several key Zero Trust principles:

- **Least privilege access**: No one is granted more access than they need, limiting the potential damage of a breach
- **Continuous authentication and authorisation**: Identity and trust are never permanent; they are re-evaluated dynamically
- **Micro segmentation**: Network components are isolated so that compromise in one area does not automatically jeopardise the entire system

- **Real-time monitoring**: Behaviour is constantly analysed to detect anomalies, analyse them and respond in real time

These mechanisms all stem from an intentional distrust, not of people but of unchecked access. Doubt here is embedded in the architecture itself. It is transformed into a disciplined practice of legitimate scepticism and is what keeps security professionals from falling into complacency, with continuous questioning, testing and validation, not just of technologies but of assumptions.

Doubt, when institutionalised in harmony with business and user convenience, becomes resilience.

Building a culture of resilience

In the current climate, technical solutions such as Zero Trust are necessary, but are not sufficient on their own. Organisations must also build a culture that is comfortable with uncertainty. Zero Trust can serve as the foundation for this, with its shift in how organisations address trust, risk and security. Other means to establish a resilient culture include:

- Training employees to recognise and respond to developing threats
- Encouraging transparency so that when incidents occur, your staff understand that communication and signalling are key
- Fostering cybersecurity at the human level, where security-conscious behaviours are vital in maintaining cybersecurity and are embedded into the organisation at an individual level

Cybersecurity is not a domain of total control. It is a living system developing with dynamic threats, uncertain terrain and imperfect information. In this kingdom of uncertainty, success belongs to those organisations comfortable with doubt, who have embedded resilience into their culture.

Doubt as a counter to overconfidence

In cybersecurity, overconfidence can be a silent and severe threat. This is another reason why doubt is not something to fear or overlook, but something to embrace. The internal mindset of invulnerability can be just as dangerous as external threats to an organisation. Overconfidence is of great help to attackers.

Too many cybersecurity professionals fall into the trap of assuming that existing defences are sufficient: firewalls are deployed, antivirus tools are updated and running and compliance checklists are completed... So, the organisation must be safe, right?

Wrong. This illusion of control is comforting, but dangerously false. Threat actors evolve faster than security protocols, and no environment is ever fully immune to cyberattacks. The very moment a team believes it has everything under control is often when it is most vulnerable.

Overconfidence in cybersecurity can manifest in several ways:

- Neglecting threat modelling or risk reassessment
- Dismissing user-reported anomalies as false positives or one-off events
- Assuming compliance equals security
- Underestimating insider threats or social engineering risks

Attitudes such as these weaken an organisation's ability to detect and respond effectively to real threats, and they also hinder a culture of continuous learning, which is vital in such a dynamic domain (more on this later).

To counter overconfidence, organisations must institutionalise doubt, not as fear but as disciplined scepticism. This means continuously questioning assumptions and adopting a *'what if'* approach. For example:

- What if our perimeter has already been silently breached?
- What if our most trusted employees are compromised?
- Are we prepared for the unexpected? What if ... were to happen?

Routine red teaming, penetration testing and adversarial simulations can help with this, exposing gaps in defences and challenging the status quo. Regular audits and post-incident reviews can also foster cyber humility and drive security improvements.

Building a humble cyber culture

The best defence against overconfidence is a culture of humility and vigilance (and resilience, but I have covered that already), encouraging people to share mistakes, question decisions and remain curious. Cybersecurity decision-makers and leaders must model this by emphasising that security is not a destination but an ongoing process, and that overconfidence breeds complacency.

As discussed earlier, embracing doubt and questioning assumptions is important for CISOs. Because in this domain, **the greatest risk is believing you have none.**

Fostering a culture of continuous learning

In cybersecurity, new vulnerabilities, such as zero-day exploits, may appear overnight; tools and frameworks become silently obsolete and/or slip into a shadow IT blindspots, while regulatory requirements strengthen. In these conditions, relying on past knowledge or strategy alone creates an attractive technical or organisational surface of attack. As such, the cybersecurity response cannot be treated as a *one-time investment* or a fixed set of procedures; it must be viewed as a dynamic, learning-driven discipline. This means that fostering a culture of continuous learning is not just beneficial, it is essential!

> Note that a culture embedding continuous learning is not a different type of culture to those I have already discussed; it is instead another layer to the culture a CISO should seek to build – one that is resilient, vigilant and humble too.

Doubt in this case is the driver of continuous learning, which ensures that security teams remain resilient, adaptable and informed, empowering them to anticipate threats, recognise new attack patterns and improve their response strategies. Moreover, continuous learning fosters a mindset of curiosity, a valuable trait in cybersecurity, particularly in regard to identifying subtle anomalies and challenging assumptions.

To build continuous learning into your organisation's culture, I'd recommend focusing on:

- **Training and certifications**: Encourage staff to pursue up-to-date certifications (e.g., CISSP, CISM or CEH) and attend relevant workshops or conferences
- **Threat intelligence sharing**: Promote internal briefings and cross-functional discussions based on recent incidents and threat intelligence you have received
- **Red team/blue team exercises**: Use real-world simulations to test your defences, stimulate learning under pressure and expose gaps in your incident preparation
- **Post-incident reviews**: After every incident, conduct thorough reviews, not to assign blame but to extract lessons and improve
- **Mentorship and collaboration**: Facilitate and encourage peer-to-peer learning, where senior analysts mentor junior staff and insights are shared openly

Cyber and business leaders must set the tone for this by prioritising learning over optimal accuracy, celebrating lessons learned from failure and rewarding curiosity and initiative they see around them. When employees feel psychologically safe to ask questions, declare mistakes or anomalies, explore new ideas or admit knowledge gaps, security follows, with prompt, adapted and effective response to tricky situations.

> Note that it's important for cybersecurity leaders to allocate time for their own professional development as well.

In cybersecurity, yesterday's expertise can quickly become tomorrow's severe vulnerability. The organisations that thrive are not the ones with the most tools, but those with the most agile minds.

The role of doubt in driving threat detection and incident response

Doubt management plays a key role in threat detection and IR. This can be a critical pivot point for the career of the CISO – when they are able to manage incidents well then they are seen as a strong leader that is vital to the enterprise. From the early detection of anomalies to confirming a cyberattack, addressing doubt in this way allows us to provide an appropriate and timely response. In this context, it's important that CISOs identify and treat areas of doubt, such as blindspots and unexplained alerts received from tools, with discernment, the same way they would more tangible elements such as **indicators of compromise (IOCs)**.

Shifting from passive defence to proactive detection and rapid response is essential. The protean cyber threats organisations are facing are not just developing in sophistication and the level of impact they can have, but also increasing in volume. As such, driving effective threat detection and IR is a strategic imperative for any organisation and doubt management is a key component to treating cyber events and gaining relevance for enhanced response.

Threat detection is the process of identifying malicious activities or anomalies within an IT environment. To be effective, it requires a layered approach:

- **Security information and event management (SIEM)** systems to aggregate and correlate logs
- **Endpoint detection and response (EDR)** tools for real-time visibility on endpoints
- **User and entity behaviour analytics (UEBA)** and **identity threat detection response (ITDR)** to spot unusual activity patterns
- **Threat intelligence** feeds to provide context on known attack vectors

Together, these technologies empower teams to spot threats early, at a low signal level, before real damage is done.

Threat detection is only half the equation. Once a risk of impact is proactively identified, IR takes over with a set of processes, protocols and planned actions to contain, mitigate and recover from any attack resulting from the threat. It is at this stage that doubt management provides the most value, to reduce process wanderings and face rapid changes.

An effective IR is driven by these key elements:

- **Preparation**: Defining roles, responsibilities and playbooks in advance
- **Speed**: Responding quickly to incidents, to limit dwell time and impact
- **Coordination**: Ensuring effective cross-functional communication (such as to and between top management, IT, legal and PR teams) following an incident
- **Post-incident analysis**: Learning from attacks to prevent recurrence

As a cyberattack is a situation in motion, IR must also be flexible and versatile. In this respect, preparing alternative plans to face doubt is a key factor of success.

A mature IR program transforms cyber incidents from organisational crises into manageable disruptions.

The role of automation and AI in threat detection and incident response for CISOs

With the sheer scale of cybersecurity threats we are exposed to, human teams alone cannot keep up. That's where automation and AI can help. Automated tools can handle repetitive tasks such as massive log analysis, initial triage and even containment actions (such as isolating a suspicious or corrupted device), whereas AI can, amongst other tasks, enhance threat detection by identifying subtle patterns that might escape human analysts.

The insight I have gained is that these technologies do not replace humans; they augment them, allowing human security experts to focus on high-level investigation, decision-making and strategic defence.

Organisations that invest in systems combining technology, processes and human expertise will not only survive attacks but will grow stronger from each challenge, because cybersecurity is not just about stopping threats; it's also about **learning, evolving** and **staying ahead**.

My summary

In cybersecurity, **doubt is not a weakness; it is a necessity** to keep pace with continuously developing threats, technologies and regulations. Cybersecurity is defined by uncertainty, complexity and risks, so the ability to question assumptions, challenge complacency and probe for unseen vulnerabilities is what separates resilient organisations from vulnerable ones.

Overcoming doubt doesn't mean eliminating uncertainty or becoming paranoid; rather, it means **transforming doubt into a disciplined mindset** in order to fuel vigilance, innovation and strategic foresight. By embracing this mindset, CISOs can become more alert, adaptive and better prepared, to sharpen their detection skills and strengthen response strategies.

> Do remember – overconfidence and static knowledge lead to blind spots and even severe risks, while doubt, when harnessed correctly, leads to clarity, control and stronger cyber resilience.

A sound cybersecurity posture cannot rest on the illusion of invincibility; it must be humble and pragmatic, grounded in knowledge, and be refined through critical thinking and the disciplined examination of doubt. CISOs who cultivate cultures that respect uncertainty, encourage inquiry and reward continuous learning create systems (and teams) capable of navigating the unknown with resilience and adaptability.

In the end, overcoming doubt doesn't mean silencing it; it means **listening to it, learning from it and letting it drive smarter and stronger cyber defences.**

David's key takeaways — Overcoming doubt

The CISO must accept that they are always going to face some degree of ambiguity and uncertainty. This can be a good and bad thing for the CISO. Doubt can lead to fear and paranoia; however, as Stéphane has explained in this chapter, you can use doubt to your own, and your organisation's, advantage. Indeed, the complete absence of doubt could lead to your career downfall.

Overall, Stéphane's approach and thinking on reframing doubt can encourage a learning mindset, helping to avoid the temptation to be complacent by never allowing oneself to be comfortable. This is a powerful way to help the CISO stay relevant and drive the change required, despite the long-term fatigue that may come with the role. By working with and adapting to doubt, this becomes the frame of reference – a strategic tool that helps you to operate effectively.

Making sound decisions is a key part of the CISO role, and as such, indecision can mark the demise of the CISO. Getting yourself into the right mindset is vital for your success.

Some of the key learnings from this chapter are:

- *Doubt should not be viewed as weakness or indecision.* Instead, you should embrace it as a tool to drive continuous questioning of assumptions and investigate potential blind spots. This mindset shift transforms doubt into an advantage.

- *Expect the unexpected.* Be sure to take the time and effort to know your 'shadow' (your cybersecurity weaknesses and vulnerabilities). Embracing doubt in this way helps you strengthen your cybersecurity posture.

- *Zero Trust architecture is built upon doubt.* The approach succeeds because it operationalises doubt. This is one example demonstrating how doubt can enable resilience.

- *Make doubt your starting assumption.* Cybersecurity is a domain where absolute certainty is almost never the case – despite what the board may want. As a CISO, try to adapt to doubt, rather than fear or overlook it, for example, by adopting an 'assumed breach' mentality, which assumes breaches will occur and hence focuses on limiting the impact of these and ensuring rapid recovery from them.

- *Overconfidence is a killer.* Try to guard yourself against false assumptions that existing defences are sufficient. Regularly challenge the status quo through methods such as red teaming, penetration testing and scenario planning to expose gaps before attackers do it to you!

- *Foster a culture of resilience, humility and continuous learning.* In an environment where threats evolve daily, static knowledge can become a vulnerability. Create the psychological safety for teams to admit their knowledge gaps, share mistakes and explore new ideas, and reward the curiosity of your team. Make sure you also prioritise your own personal learning.

Part 2

Building Your CISO Skills

This part of the book will help you develop your cybersecurity leadership skills with proven strategies that successful CISOs use to protect their organisations and influence stakeholders. From learning how to defend on tight budgets to driving cultural transformation, these chapters reveal how to navigate complex challenges, communicate effectively with executives, and build resilient security programs that deliver real business value.

This part has the following chapters:

- *Chapter 10, How to Defend with Less*
- *Chapter 11, Being Brilliant at the Basics*
- *Chapter 12, A CISO in Japan*
- *Chapter 13, Navigating the C-Suite, Boards, and DOPE Dynamics*
- *Chapter 14, Systems Thinking for CISOs*
- *Chapter 15, The CISO as a Change Agent*
- *Chapter 16, Alternative Career Paths to Consider*
- *Chapter 17, So, You Got Fired*

Unlock this book's exclusive benefits now

10

How to Defend with Less

Every CISO must drive cyber transformation. However, not every business has the same deep pockets that some financial institutions, for example, may have to spend on cybersecurity. While this makes the role of the CISO more difficult, it is also fair to say that such organisations may be less attractive to attack than, for instance, a bank, but that does not mean that they should wait to be breached.

Being able to understand your own defence strategy and what you must respond to with regard to threat actors is the foundation of cyber transformation. Being a successful CISO is not about budget, although that can help. There is always an element of 'luck' involved, but better CISOs are able to focus on what is more important from a risk standpoint.

But, that being said, what do you do as a CISO with a small budget? There are clear lessons to be learnt in considering that 'less is more'. So many times I have seen large financial institutions buying multiple cyber solutions that are not fully implemented and embedded, meaning that only some of the actual risk reduction is achieved. Then, before this control is fully in place, there is a new project for implementing another tool.

Instead, I would argue that these industries have to be brilliant at the basics. This will provide the requisite detective and preventative controls to keep the business secure, and by being secure, the business can keep trading, hence the critical importance of being resilient.

Introducing **Adam Cartwright, Group CISO** at **Australia Post**, former CISO at Asahi Breweries. Adam has a strong background in incident response and has previously worked at ANZ Bank and Commonwealth Bank of Australia.

Coming into a new CISO role in the **Fast-Moving Consumer Goods** (**FMCG**) industry is very unlike banking, where cybersecurity is better understood as a threat and also significantly better funded. Adam has had to adapt from his experience to develop a defence strategy that would work within his new organisation and industry. This is where we can learn from his insights on how he approached this situation.

How to defend with less $$$

Adam Cartwright

The bulk of my IT and cybersecurity experience has been gained within large multinational corporations such as IBM, American Express, ANZ Bank, and Commonwealth Bank. However, this hasn't deterred me from diversifying my expertise by establishing security protocols in various sectors, including manufacturing.

Sectors such as manufacturing tend to have less regulatory oversight and often lag behind the financial sector in terms of cybersecurity maturity. Nevertheless, they operate critical processes that demand uninterrupted availability, offering a gratifying opportunity to formulate end-to-end cybersecurity strategies and assume full responsibility for their implementation.

For me, establishing teams, fostering a cybersecurity culture, implementing technology, and streamlining operations from scratch in a greenfield environment can be immensely rewarding.

But where does a CISO start?

Should you turn to NIST, ISO 27001, or (in Australia) the Essential Eight framework as your go-to approach? And how do you ensure that a cybersecurity capability is not gold-plated, that it exists to successfully counter the cyber threat and no more?

In manufacturing, especially within the FMCG sector, it is a fiercely competitive environment where every dollar is crucial, and profit margins are razor-thin. A cybersecurity strategy must respect these financial constraints while accomplishing the mission successfully.

Throughout my extensive involvement in cybersecurity over the years, one fundamental principle has consistently emerged as the cornerstone of strategy and defence: **the cybersecurity capability must be designed to address the specific threats unique to the organisation**. While this might seem like common sense, it's surprising to discover that many cybersecurity functions possess only a surface-level understanding of threats, often prioritising compliance and adherence to frameworks over tailored protection, and relying too heavily on technology.

A strategy is not about a product. CISOs should be very, very sceptical of vendor promises.

Every year, around 40,000 cybersecurity people and around 1,000 security vendors attend RSA (Rivest–Shamir–Adleman) in the US from around the globe. Each year, new cybersecurity acronyms are marketed, such as SOAR, XDR, AI, or HEAT, and vendors will warn you that extortion threat actors are becoming more sophisticated, and that you need their new tool to stay safe.

The reality is, sadly, somewhat different. Despite the growth in technology, the volume of successful extortion attacks continues to rise every year. There never has been, and probably never will be, a 'silver bullet'. That is not to say, however, that current tools aren't a vast improvement and allow better visibility, faster deployment, and easier integrations.

An overreliance on technology is perhaps the leading factor contributing to failures to prevent extortion intrusions. Technology will not prevent an intrusion without a robust threat-to-countermeasure operational cycle to identify and detect malicious actions.

I'd like to take a moment here to talk about threats at a high level and then discuss how an appreciation of threats links to strategic initiatives.

The following table is how I look at the various threat actors, and how they should be understood:

Actor	Goal	Motivation	Resources	Comments
Nation state	Espionage, theft, sabotage, or any other activity that furthers their national agenda	Political, economic, technical, and military agendas: strategic targeting. Focused on a set objective/target when they start planning an attack. Undetected persistence often a feature. Stealthy. Bespoke.	Highest skill. Nation states have significant skilled resources. They can spend large amounts of time planning and executing attacks against targets of strategic value.	Defending against nation-state attacks requires significant investment and process changes beyond the will of most commercial businesses.

Actor	Goal	Motivation	Resources	Comments
eCrime (extortion)	Financial benefit	Profit-motivated. Will use media to add pressure during a ransom negotiation. Usually crypto locking of assets (ransomware) is accompanied by theft of sensitive data with extortion based on denial of service and publicly sharing sensitive data.	eCrime is often perpetrated by a conglomerate of collaborating crime elements. One element will gain access and sell on access to another element or affiliate to execute the attack and monetise the ransom.	eCrime is a business. eCrime actors invest time in a breach and want a quick return. The business is based on volume. To meet these requirements, standard playbooks and associated malware are developed and provided as a service. These are reused against multiple targets with subtle variation.
eCrime (Business Email Compromise (BEC))	Financial benefit	Profit-motivated. Will exploit poor business processes and create a sense of urgency to induce a payment.	*As above.*	Actors who manipulate a victim into wiring funds to bank accounts under their control.

Actor	Goal	Motivation	Resources	Comments
eCrime (fraud)	Financial benefit	Profit-motivated.	High skill and knowledge of payment systems.	Payment card skimming, asset theft, or crypto mining. Skills vary but can involve nation state-level (particularly North Korea), where large USD amounts are targeted (e.g., banking SWIFT hacks, crypto exploits).
Hacktivist	Heightened awareness and media attention	Ideology-motivated. Media exposure.	Skill levels vary but can be high. Ideologically aligned staff may be exploited as insider threat vectors.	Attacks range from denial-of-service attacks on internet-facing web servers to sabotage and data theft.

Table 10.1: Threat actors

Why would I even mention threat actor categories?

A sound strategy should be underpinned by an understanding of the organisation you are protecting to determine the cyber threats it faces.

Factors such as the organisation's industry sector, any political or ideological influences, data of interest to a strategic adversary, and internet attack surface should all be evaluated. This is because each threat actor category requires distinct responses, in both an operational and technology sense, and therefore will alter the investment profile.

Within each category, there are significant nuances. Many eCrime groups confine their operations to specific geographical regions, presumably driven by linguistic or monetisation considerations. Some restrict their targeting based on ethical principles (a somewhat ironic twist), while others focus on sectors that they specifically possess technical expertise in.

This principle extends to nation-state actors as well. Even nation states have finite resources and face constraints related to subject matter expertise within specific industries, much like any other sector. Consequently, the most significant efforts and skills are typically directed towards compromises that promise the highest strategic gains.

Specialised teams will target different industries and cultivate the requisite knowledge to maximise their effectiveness. If your organisation lacks national strategic significance, for example, the likelihood of being a target for a nation state diminishes.

The adversary-victim relationship is depicted in the diamond model of intrusion analysis (Sergio Caltagirone, Andrew Pendergast, and Christopher Betz, 2013: `https://www.threatintel.academy/wp-content/uploads/2020/07/diamond-model.pdf`), which the following diagram is based on:

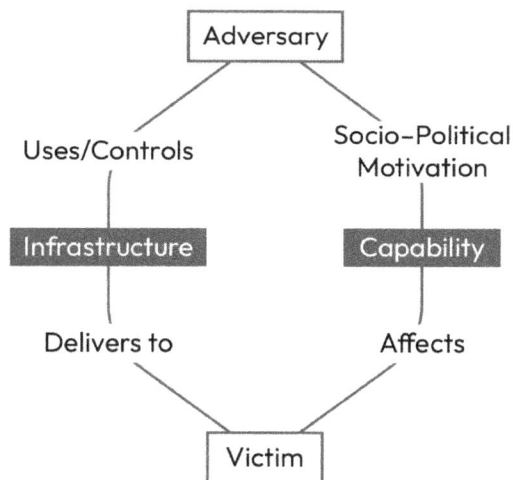

Figure 10.1: Intrusion analysis diamond, based on The Diamond Model of Intrusion Analysis

According to Caltagirone, Pendergast, and Betz, the degree to which a cyber adversary will target a victim and persist with an intrusion is determined by several factors, which include the following:

- The uniqueness of a victim to satisfy a particular need (such as strategic information)
- The relative strength of the adversary's needs, which the victim fulfils, compared to other needs
- The level of effort and resources a defender expends to resist persistence

An organisation can be either a **victim of opportunity** or a **victim of interest**.

If an organisation has been a victim of opportunity, it means that they were likely targeted (at least to begin with) as they were perceived as being vulnerable and/or available at the right time. In this case, they may be seen as expendable to the adversary. Losing access to the organisation (if they even notice) would therefore probably not drive the adversary to invest resources in regaining access (eCrime).

On the other hand, organisations that are victims of interest are likely seen by the adversary as highly valuable and non-expendable. They would no doubt notice if they lost access to them, and would intentionally invest in regaining access (for example, nation state).

To formulate a strategic intent, a CISO must first determine the relevant threat actor categories for their organisation and the reasons behind their relevance. These categories will serve as a foundation for cyber defence efforts, enabling the identification of possible specific adversaries, tracking their tactics, and facilitating a targeted response. This is the very essence of a cyber defence capability and the most important cybersecurity process.

To do this, start with a broad **threat actor category**. This, through intelligence, then leads to the identification of specific **threat actors** relevant to your company. In turn, looking into these then leads to hundreds of very specific **'atomic' tools, techniques and procedures (TTPs)**, which your cyber defence team can then construct **countermeasures** for, to prevent or detect each TTP. This is a continuous process and does not require a huge investment to establish.

I have worked at both ends of the spectrum, from well-funded, sophisticated intelligence feeds with dedicated threat intelligence teams to individuals using OSINT and Excel spreadsheets.

The extent to which CISOs may find themselves needing to address security concerns related to nation-state actors is heavily influenced by the strategic interests at stake and the level of uniqueness involved. At the highest level of strategic planning, comprehensive strategies encompassing areas such as human espionage, isolated enclaves, and deception will be essential. Organisations operating within a high-threat environment will need to implement effective behavioural controls and monitoring measures for both their staff and third-party entities.

A key concern when it comes to nation-state actors is safeguarding against disruptions to critical infrastructure, which is integral to complying with regulations such as Australia's **Security of Critical Infrastructure Act (SOCI)**. It is the responsibility of the CISO to develop strategies to defend against such potential acts of sabotage carried out by nation states.

One effective approach to mitigating sabotage within critical infrastructure is the concept of 'cyber-informed engineering'. This methodology draws inspiration from the framework developed by the US **Idaho National Laboratory** (INL) to protect nuclear installations.

For CISOs responsible for safeguarding critical infrastructure, such as electricity, water, or mining, I highly recommend reading *Countering Cyber Sabotage – Consequence-Driven Cyber-Informed Engineering (CCE)*, authored by Andrew Bochman and Sarah Freeman (2021, CRC Press). This resource provides valuable insights and guidance for enhancing cybersecurity within the context of critical infrastructure protection.

While some CISOs will need to consider nation states as a threat, the majority will not. However, all CISOs need to consider defending against eCrime actors who, given the opportunity, will compromise anything.

To deal with this ubiquitous threat, the CISO will need to consider how to prevent an intrusion. The good news is that, unlike their nation-state counterparts, eCrime extortion actors have very defendable characteristics:

- Initial access is divided between using stolen credentials, phishing, social engineering, and exploiting vulnerabilities. (The exploited vulnerabilities are most often aged.) To address this, focus on hygiene strategies to avoid becoming the latest victim of opportunity.

• Actors observed at the time of writing used many of the same techniques used by attackers observed in the previous four years, undermining the 'sophistication' rhetoric. Breaches demonstrated repeated use of techniques against multiple victims with limited deviations. Cybersecurity operations teams can turn this weakness into a critical advantage by implementing a targeted threat-to-countermeasure process.

Most public breaches that expose personal or sensitive data can be attributed to either eCrime extortion intrusions or employee errors. Consequently, when the threat from nation states is not a primary concern, the strategic focus should prioritise addressing eCrime intrusions to ensure robust privacy protection. Aligning strategic investments *with* the threat context serves multiple purposes, including facilitating discussions with the board and supporting discussions on setting target maturity scores when referencing frameworks such as NIST.

For instance, a CISO might explain that they are striving for a level 4 maturity in NIST dimensions related to logging, threat analysis, detection, and incident response. This alignment corresponds with the investment strategy aimed at preventing intrusions from eCrime actors. Such a conversation could then naturally lead to considerations of allocating lower investments towards achieving a lower maturity level in areas such as third-party risk management or awareness.

> NIST is not a strategy. It is a useful tool to highlight the troughs and peaks of your cyber maturity and promote discussion on elements that are missing or low scoring.

In my experience, board members are inundated with risk decisions across all aspects of the business, with cybersecurity playing a small, but important, part. A well-thought-out, logical pitch for cyber investment is likely to be well received if linked to a detailed threat discussion, and it avoids any rhetoric around 'gold plating'.

My views on cyber defence

Cyber defence is the operational aspect that, when executed effectively, prevents an intrusion. There is little value in excelling in areas such as awareness, supply risk management, and compliance if the organisation succumbs to a breach due to operational teams failing to detect and prevent the intrusion.

Too often, the operational function is outsourced. Be wary of doing this: you may outsource the function, but you cannot outsource the accountability...stakeholders will ultimately hold you responsible. I'm not advocating against outsourcing this specialised area; rather, I suggest doing so diligently while maintaining oversight and managerial control over the function.

A breach requires the execution of a significant number of individual actions within the victim's environment over an extended period. A detection of any one of the actions may have defeated the breach, so the manner in which cyber defence is performed is very significant. There are numerous breaches where an operational capability existed but failed to detect and respond effectively.

A robust cyber defence function should meticulously track individual attacker techniques, ensuring the organisation can both identify and contain them. This necessitates thorough testing of each technique within the environment, and there are available libraries and tests, such as atomic tests by Red Canary, designed to facilitate this process.

Strategic considerations

The level of cybersecurity maturity within an organisation, as of the time this strategy is being formulated, will dictate the roadmap for future actions.

For organisations with limited or no cybersecurity maturity, the initial objective should prioritise establishing fundamental capabilities to swiftly defend against intrusions. This can be achieved through the following steps:

- **Establish a basic technology stack**: Implement foundational security technologies such as **Endpoint Detection and Response (EDR)**, **Security Information and Event Management (SIEM)**, email filtering, and **Domain-based Message Authentication, Reporting, and Conformance (DMARC)**. These represent essential baseline controls that should be prioritised by all organisations, regardless of cybersecurity budget, to establish a minimum viable defence.

- **Instrument the IT environment**: Ensure you have visibility into the organisation's IT systems. Without comprehensive insight into ongoing activities, detecting potential intrusions becomes challenging.

- **Deploy a vulnerability service**: Set up a service that conducts regular scans of both internal and external assets while tracking the status of patching. Ideally, include real-time monitoring for internet-facing assets.

- **Enforce Multi-Factor Authentication (MFA) and privileged account protection**: Make MFA mandatory for all users without exception. Replace passwords with passkeys and consider implementing verification mechanisms such as Microsoft Verified ID to ensure employees can be positively identified when working remotely. Also safeguard privileged accounts, using tools such as CyberArk, and limit local access on devices.

- **Leverage the tools you have**: Incorporate Microsoft Defender **Attack Surface Reduction (ASR)** rules, or the equivalent controls available in, for example, Google Workspace, such as context-aware access and endpoint management policies, to strengthen protection against common attack vectors.

- **Monitor cloud assets**: Continuously monitor cloud-based assets for compliance and potential vulnerabilities, including misconfigured storage, overly permissive access controls, unpatched software, inactive or orphaned accounts, and deviations from established security baselines. Ensure regular scanning for exposed services, anomalous user behaviour, and alignment with regulatory or policy requirements.

- **Modernise standards and policies**: Update and modernise cybersecurity standards and policies to align with changing threats and best practices.

- **Enhance cyber incident response**: Review and update the **Cyber Incident Response Plan (CIRP)** and conduct drills to ensure preparedness for potential incidents.

Many of these points are included in the Essential Eight advice from the **Australian Cybersecurity Centre (ACSC)** (`https://www.cyber.gov.au/resources-business-and-government/essential-cybersecurity/essential-eight`). Essential Eight compliance serves as an invaluable guidance framework on the fundamental actions required to fortify an organisation's security posture.

Once your security basics are in place (ideally including Essential Eight recommendations – take a look at these), consider strategies to address the following:

- **The threat landscape**: Defences against actors (eCrime actors in particular, as discussed earlier, but others too) exploiting system vulnerabilities and conducting email-based attacks and social engineering, among other attack methods. Take the strength of your identity controls into consideration to counter credential theft and take **Operational Technology (OT)** security into account.

- **Regulatory compliance**: Regulator privacy mandates have expanded to cover staff and impose higher fines, with potential for even stricter obligations in the future. (Consider privacy responses such as data minimisation and tokenisation (de-identification) to help address this.) If relevant, also take critical infrastructure legislation into account, such as SOCI.

- **Security challenges with cloud:** The shift to cloud vendors has introduced new security vulnerabilities, including data exposure due to misconfigurations, complex network structures, and incorrect account associations.

- **Legacy infrastructure:** The persistence of legacy infrastructure and systems increases the risk of compromise, as many of these systems cannot be effectively patched.

My summary

In summary, in this chapter I have emphasised the importance of tailoring cybersecurity strategies to an organisation's specific threat landscape. This means understanding the unique threats the organisation faces, allocating investments effectively, and aligning strategies with the threat context.

I have also highlighted the importance of operational defence processes and noted that you will maintain accountability even if outsourcing this function. The goal is to achieve a balance between cybersecurity compliance and targeted defence measures while considering the organisation's specific needs and potential adversaries.

CISOs have choices when spending their investment dollars, and not everything in the frameworks should be weighted equally.

David's key takeaways — How to defend with less

Adam has a unique perspective, having had experience as a CISO across different industries. This experience has focused his lens on having to address risks with a limited budget, which he has shared with us in this chapter.

Every CISO needs to drive cyber transformation, but not all organisations have the same resources as financial institutions. CISOs should focus on being 'brilliant at the basics', regardless of budget.

Remember that technology alone won't prevent intrusions. Organisations need an effective threat-to-countermeasure operational cycle to identify and detect malicious actions. An over-reliance on technology is a leading factor in failing to prevent extortion intrusions.

Here are the key points from Adam's chapter:

- *A cybersecurity strategy must be designed to address specific threats that are unique to the organisation*, rather than just focusing on technology, compliance and frameworks. Understanding your organisation's defence strategy and threat actors is fundamental.
- *Threat actors can be categorised into different groups*, each requiring distinct operational and technological responses. CISOs should identify which threat actors are most relevant to them.
- *eCrime is the chief focus* – most organisations primarily need to defend against eCrime actors rather than nation-state threats. Luckily, eCrime actors can be defended against as they often use predictable techniques and aged vulnerabilities.
- *Operational cyber defence is crucial* – having strong awareness and compliance means little if the organisation can't detect and prevent intrusions. As the CISO, you must remember this.
- *Focus on getting the basics right*. Priorities should include implementing a basic technology stack (EDR, SIEM, etc.), ensuring visibility into the IT environment, deploying vulnerability scanning, enforcing MFA, and protecting privileged accounts.
- *Investment needs to be strategically placed* – CISOs should strategically allocate investments based on threat context rather than trying to achieve high maturity across all framework areas.

11

Being Brilliant at the Basics

Every week, a new buzzword captures the industry's attention, whether it's generative AI, quantum computing, or the latest automation breakthrough. As a CISO, staying informed on these trends is part of the job, but the real challenge is knowing what truly matters *right now*. When a breach hits, your ability to recover depends not on how many cutting-edge tools you've piloted, but instead, on whether your team has nailed the fundamentals.

That's why I keep coming back to the basics. They are the backbone of real-world resilience. Think about something as simple as asset inventory, for instance. If you don't know what you have, you can't protect it. If your **configuration management database (CMDB)** is incomplete, your risk picture is distorted. And if your backups aren't tested, they're just an illusion of safety.

Being brilliant at the basics isn't flashy. It's not headline-grabbing. But it's what separates the teams who survive from the ones who stumble.

When I explain this to non-technical audiences, I often use a football (soccer) analogy. The best midfielders aren't always in the highlight reels, but they control the game. Their consistency earns trust, and their precision creates space. And when pressure mounts, they hold the line.

Cybersecurity is no different. The teams that win aren't always the loudest, but they're the ones who do the right thing, every day, without shortcuts. They patch on time. They test their plans. They build trust through disciplined execution.

It is my pleasure to introduce **Sandro Bucchianeri, Group Chief Security Officer** at **National Australia Bank (NAB)**, where he leads one of the most complex and critical security portfolios in the Australian financial sector.

Sandro is a globally recognised cybersecurity executive with over 25 years of experience leading high-performing security functions across five continents. His career spans some of the world's most regulated and dynamic environments, including serving as Group CSO for Absa Group in South Africa, Chief Security Officer at the National Bank of Abu Dhabi in the UAE, and CISO at Investec PLC in London. In addition to his leadership roles, Sandro has advised global organisations through his consulting work, helping executive teams, boards, and security leaders build resilient strategies, uplift cyber maturity, and embed security as a business enabler.

A seasoned leader known for delivering impact through clarity, discipline, and cultural intelligence, Sandro brings a distinctive philosophy to cyber leadership – one that balances technical rigour with human connection. He is also deeply passionate about developing the next generation of cybersecurity talent. As the founder of the award-winning Absa Cybersecurity Academy, he created a platform to empower marginalised youth with career-ready skills, helping to unlock opportunities for those too often left behind.

Sandro believes that while culture can be shaped, it must first be understood and respected. As he often says, security is not just about controls; it's about people, trust, and building resilient systems from the ground up.

Brilliant at the basics: Leading cybersecurity with clarity, culture, and consistency

Sandro Bucchianeri

As a **Chief Security Officer (CSO)**, I've been blessed to work on five continents, and honestly the biggest lesson I've learned is probably going to disappoint anyone looking for some groundbreaking insight: just do the basics really, really well.

I get it – that sounds almost embarrassingly simple in a world where everyone's obsessing over the latest AI threat or zero-day exploit. But after years of working in banking environments where one screw-up can tank stock prices and have regulators breathing down your neck, I've seen the same pattern everywhere I've worked.

Whether I was dealing with the bureaucratic maze in D.C., trying to build trust with skeptical teams in Johannesburg, keeping up with London's breakneck pace, navigating cultural complexities in Abu Dhabi, or working with the laid-back-but-sharp Aussies in Melbourne, the story was always the same. The companies that actually survived the tough times weren't the ones with the fanciest security tools or the most elaborate incident response plans. They were the ones that had their fundamentals locked down tight.

Look, I used to think complexity meant sophistication. More tools, more processes, more acronyms – surely that meant better security, right? Wrong. Dead wrong. The best security teams I've worked with could explain their approach to a new hire in about 10 minutes, and that new hire could start contributing meaningfully within weeks, not months.

One of my favourite analogies comes from a story I read countless times to my son, Alexander, when he was a toddler: *The Three Little Pigs* – a classic children's fable with a timeless lesson. Build with straw or sticks, and the wolf will blow your house down. But take the time and effort to build with bricks, and you will be able to survive whatever comes your way.

This is a simple story that kids hear everywhere across the world. It's basically cybersecurity in a nutshell. We take shortcuts all the time – pile on tools without thinking about the foundation, skip some basic controls because they're not interesting. But sooner or later, something big hits. Ransomware, supply chain attack, someone clicks the wrong link. And suddenly, all those quick fixes don't matter because the whole thing falls apart. That's why I'm always telling my team the same thing: do it right the first time, even if it takes longer. Basics matter!

In cybersecurity, technical change is the easy part. Cultural change is the real frontier. And if you can't explain why something matters – if you can't frame it in a way that resonates – then all the policies and controls in the world won't save you. As a leader, your job isn't just to build secure systems. It's to inspire secure behaviour.

This chapter is my personal reflection of that philosophy, based on career lessons, scar tissue that is hard-earned through experience. It is about mastering the fundamentals, leading with empathy, and adapting with humility. And above all, it's about simplicity.

Simplicity is one of the most underrated strengths in cybersecurity. In a field filled with jargon, layers of controls, and complex architecture, clarity becomes a competitive advantage. Keeping things simple, whether it's your own messaging, your tech stack, or your metrics, makes it easier to scale, easier to govern, and easier to embed security into the business.

When people understand, they align. When systems are clear, they're more secure. So, my approach, always, has been to distil the complex down to what matters most. Because simple is not naive. Simple is disciplined. And simple gets it done. I'm not just talking here about technicalities, but also about culture.

In a world that constantly rewards speed and novelty, the CISO must focus on the basics, being the steward of consistency, clarity, and culture.

Develop your storytelling skills

Storytelling is a tool I've come to value just as much as technical precision. For many CISOs, storytelling is not a core competency, but for me, storytelling is a strategic skill. It's how I can bring people along for the journey with me. Whether I'm speaking or briefing to the board, my security engineers, business stakeholders, or frontline staff, I usually rely on storytelling to build bridges of understanding and, hopefully, trust.

When I walk into a boardroom full of executives who think security is just 'something IT handles', I can't lead with technical jargon. I need to paint them a picture they actually care about. For example, "Remember that competitor who lost 2 million customer records last year? They're still dealing with lawsuits. Their customer acquisition costs doubled. Want to know how that starts? Usually, with something as mundane as an unpatched server or a phishing email that someone clicked because they were rushing to catch a flight."

With my engineering teams, it's different. These are brilliant people who could reverse-engineer malware in their sleep, but sometimes they need to understand the 'why' behind the policies that might seem to slow them down. So, I tell them about the time I had to call a customer at 2 am to tell them their life savings might be at risk, or about the small business owner who almost lost everything because someone found a way past our defences.

And with business stakeholders who see security as the 'department of no'? I've learned to flip the script entirely. Instead of talking about all the things they can't do, I show them how solid security actually enables them to move faster, take bigger risks, and enter new markets, all because they know they've got a safety net that won't fail them (comparable to the brakes on an F1 car).

The frontline staff are probably my favourite to work with, though. These are the people who deal with real customers every day, who see the actual impact of what we do. When I explain to them that they're not just following some arbitrary policy – they're literally the last line of defence between some criminal and a family's mortgage payment – you can see something click. They start asking better questions, catching things they missed before.

After all these years and working across all these countries, I've realised that the combination of nailing the fundamentals and being able to connect with people on a human level isn't just nice to have – it's everything. Because, at the end of the day, security is about people protecting other people. And you can't do that if you can't first help them understand why it matters.

Build a strong security culture

In cybersecurity, culture starts with consistency. It is built into the daily habits, the small decisions, and the quiet moments when no one's watching.

I often compare it to physical fitness. You can't do one intense workout and expect to be healthy. You get there by showing up every day, putting in the work, even when it's boring. Security is the same. It's patching that server at 5 pm on a Friday. It's rotating credentials every quarter. It's reviewing logs that never flag anything...until they do. Consistency doesn't happen by accident in my experience; it happens by design.

As a CSO, my job is to create a culture where the basics aren't optional, where they're both per-formed and owned by the people doing the work. Here's how I've seen it come to life from my experience:

1. **Visible routines**: When the executive team joins tabletop exercises, when patch windows are non-negotiable, when updates are shared regularly, it sends a clear message: this matters!

2. **Recognition systems:** I make it a point to celebrate those who quietly uphold security standards. Sometimes it's an engineer who found a misconfiguration, sometimes it's a product manager who delayed a release to complete a threat model. Whatever it may be, I reward those who embrace the culture I have cultivated.

3. **Transparency:** When something goes wrong – and it always will – we focus on learning, not blame. Post-incident reviews should not be seen as witch hunts. They're feedback loops. This encourages openness, which fuels enterprise and team resilience.

As CSO, I have to role model this behaviour. What I mean is if I personally skip a risk review or wave through an exception, the message is clear: the rules are flexible. But if I lead by example, I encourage others to do the same.

> When security becomes habit, it becomes strength.

Embrace standardisation

Complexity is the enemy of security. I've seen firsthand that the more tools, exceptions, and configurations you allow, the harder it becomes to manage risk effectively, and the easier it becomes to miss something critical.

That's why I always advocate strongly for standardisation. I often tell my executive stakeholders, "You can have any colour of security you like – so long as it's blue."

Blue, to me, represents calm, trust, and consistency. It's about setting healthy boundaries rather than restricting innovation. Security doesn't need to be rigid, but it does need to be coherent.

When teams are given clear, pre-approved ways of working securely, they feel much more empowered. They don't need to go rogue or create shadow processes to get things done. Standardisation can give teams the freedom to move quickly, without fear or friction.

And just as importantly, it shifts us away from the stereotype of being a team that always says *no*. Rather than saying what can't be done, my cybersecurity team has options to offer, patterns, and frameworks that say, "Here's how you can do it – safely." This shift in tone changes everything. It turns security into a business partner, rather than a blocker. This is not easy, but the benefits are massive.

Here are just some of the benefits that standardisation unlocks:

- **Simpler operations**: Less time juggling tools, more time reducing risk
- **Faster response**: Clear playbooks and unified tooling when every second counts
- **Stronger ROI**: Reduced licensing costs, simplified training, and less complexity
- **Better governance**: Clearer reporting, auditing, and control validation

The advice I would give you here is that standardisation is not about always choosing the 'best' tool – it's about choosing tools that work well, work together, and are deployed consistently. Think about how a well-maintained fleet of reliable Toyota cars can be a better option than a garage of rarely used, mismatched sports cars.

In most environments, resources are already stretched and expectations are rising. Standardisation is a significant help. It creates trust, reduces friction, and allows innovation to flourish within a secure framework.

Lead with cultural sensitivity

As a CSO who has led teams across five continents, I've learned that security is never 'one size fits all.' What works in Melbourne may fall flat in Abu Dhabi. What resonates with a team based in London might alienate someone in Johannesburg. Cultural intelligence is akin to emotional intelligence, and it is essential to be successful as a leader.

Leading with cultural sensitivity as a leader means being present enough to listen, humble enough to adapt, and strategic enough to know when to push and when to pause. It also means recognising that leadership is about creating unity within diversity.

I've personally found that storytelling is a powerful bridge across cultures. In every setting, I come back to metaphors that resonate and work. One of my go-to lines is "When you cross the street, do you look both ways?" It's simple, universal, and instantly understandable.

Cultural awareness goes beyond communication, too, however. It also informs how we make decisions. In some cultures, top-down direction is expected. In others, consensus is considered to be king. In some organisations, you need formal rituals to embed change. In others, it's about relationship capital.

I've learned the hard way that a security control delivered with the wrong tone – even if technically perfect – can fail to land. That's why I moved away from the 'always saying no' model very early on in my career. Saying no without context creates resistance. Instead, as I mentioned earlier, I focus on offering secure alternatives that preserve speed and functionality. When people feel heard and respected, they're far more likely to partner with you.

And yes, threats differ by region. An ATM compromise in Australia may involve software manipulation. In South Africa, it might mean armed attackers with explosives. You can't apply the same level of urgency or risk framing in both cases. Context matters.

Language matters too. The way you speak about risk, resilience, and accountability should reflect the values of the culture you're operating in. The goal is to deliver your message in a way that makes people lean in, not tune out.

This is what culturally intelligent security leadership looks like. In our increasingly interconnected world, it's not a bonus. It's a baseline.

Communicate with simplicity and clarity

The ability to communicate with clarity is a core leadership skill. If you are not able to explain what matters, then you can't secure it.

Boards don't need to be experts in cybersecurity, but they do need to understand risk, and they're often overwhelmed with competing priorities. So, your job is to cut through the noise. To show them what matters, why it matters, and what action is needed – without technical jargon.

The test I use is simple: if I can't explain my strategy to my 11-year-old son, then I'm not ready to explain it to the board. My son, Alexander, is curious, and like most kids, he won't let me off the hook with vague answers. That discipline of simplifying without dumbing down has become one of my most valuable tools.

This goes beyond the boardrooms. Regardless of whether I'm talking to our frontline staff, engineers, regulators, or customers, the message must be clear, relatable, and real. People don't connect to metrics. They connect to meaning.

Don't idolise the board. Humanise it. Yes, they have impressive titles and credentials, but they're people first. They want to understand, and when you drop the buzzwords and speak plainly, you earn their trust.

I've also learned that trust is built outside the boardroom as much as inside it. To achieve this, I make time for one-on-one coffees. I ask questions. But most importantly, I always try to listen more than I talk. That is not always easy, but I've found the more I understand stakeholder concerns, the better I can try to frame cybersecurity in terms or language that they value and can grasp.

In the end, communication is what translates strategy into action, and simplicity is the engine of that translation. Strip away the noise. Focus on the signal. That's how you make security real and relevant.

Focus on the right controls

Not every cyber control is as important as the next; they are not created equal. And when the stakes are high, such as during a ransomware attack or a critical outage, your weakest link becomes your headline.

I've been through those moments. And I can tell you from experience: the most underrated control in the entire stack is backups. Not just any backups – tested, immutable, and recent backups. It's easy to say "We have backups." But unless you've restored from them under pressure, you don't really know how recent and complete they are.

Think of it like insurance. Everyone thinks they're covered – until they need to make a claim and realise that the fine print matters. Backups are the same. In a breach, if your last good backup is 72 hours old, you may have lost millions of transactions. If the backup is not immutable, it might be compromised. If it's not been tested, it might not even work.

That's why control validation is non-negotiable. I don't just want dashboards. I want evidence. I want to know that my controls are real – not theoretical.

In every environment I've led, I've focused on what I call control gravity – the idea that some controls hold the whole security posture together. These include the following:

- Identity and access governance
- Data classification and protection
- Privileged access management
- Endpoint protection and detection
- Backup and recovery
- Logging and monitoring
- Patch and configuration management

These are the bricks in your cybersecurity house. If they fail, your house collapses and the wolf gets in – no matter how beautiful your architecture looks on paper.

It's about having the right controls, but also, importantly, making sure of the following:

- They are applied consistently across the estate
- They are operating as intended
- They are positioned to protect what matters most

Your adversaries don't care how many controls you have. They care where the gap is. That's why a risk-based, tested, and disciplined approach is an essential basic.

> Controls are about building trust. Trust that your business can recover. Trust that you're prepared. Trust that your systems can take a punch and get back up.

Take feedback seriously

One of the most powerful traits a CISO – or any leader – can develop is the ability to truly take on feedback. Not just hearing it. Not just nodding along. But truly listening, processing, and acting.

It may sound simple, but in practice, it's hard. Our days are busy and full of meetings, and while we all say we want feedback and are theoretically open to it, feedback can be uncomfortable, confronting, or delivered without finesse. On the receiving end, it can be easy to get defensive, dismissive, or stuck.

Here's what I've learned: feedback is a gift. It's not always perfectly wrapped. It doesn't always come at the right time. But inside it, there's almost always something you can use to grow.

Working across 5 continents and more than 90 countries in my career, one thing has always held true – those who listen, adapt. And those who adapt, lead. For example, I've had colleagues say, "You don't listen to me." That can sting. But instead of arguing back, I've learned to pause and to reflect. And most importantly, to change. Because when people see that you're willing to act on their input, their trust in you multiplies.

Remember that feedback is not a threat, although it may sometimes feel that way. It's an advantage. It tells you where the blind spots are, it sharpens your judgement, and it deepens relationships. So, my advice to you is to keep your ears open. Always try to keep your own ego in check. And remember that growth comes from listening more than talking.

Build for resilience, not just compliance

Another key lesson I want to share with you is that compliance is not the destination you should be aiming for – it's merely a checkpoint. From my experience, true cybersecurity maturity is about building an organisation that can anticipate, absorb, adapt, and respond to threats in real time, rather than one that just passes audits.

Too often, I've seen organisations equate success with a clean audit or a ticked checklist. But those things – while necessary – aren't enough. Compliance is about satisfying requirements, while resilience is about surviving reality.

As a leader, I try to always coach my teams and business stakeholders to shift their mindset from "Are we compliant?" to "Are we resilient?" It is a subtle change, but being compliant doesn't mean you're safe. It just means you've met the minimum bar. And I'm sorry to say, attackers don't care about your audit rating.

Resilience means being ready. It means your people know what to do. Your systems can withstand disruption. Your data can be recovered. Your communication is clear. And your culture supports doing the right thing, especially under pressure.

That's why I've always prioritised the following:

- Scenario-based testing over policy documentation
- Continuous learning over one-time awareness activities
- Security by design over bolted-on controls
- Cultural change over checkbox compliance

You build resilience by embedding security into how the business operates – not just how the security team thinks. You do that by being visible, by being approachable, and by being consistent. Most importantly, you do that by showing the business that security is an enabler, not a blocker. Not the 'department of no', but the team that says "yes – *but safely, and here's how.*"

That's what world-class looks like. Resilience should not be considered a project. Instead, consider it a posture, one that is built, brick by brick, every single day.

From foundations to fluency

Getting the basics right is only the beginning.

The first stage of cybersecurity maturity is establishing strong foundations; the next is operational fluency: the ability to scale, adapt, and embed security across every layer of the organisation without creating friction. This is hard to achieve. From my own experience, fluency is what separates the teams that are constantly in firefighting mode from those that can anticipate, absorb, and adapt to change without chaos.

Note that fluency doesn't mean that you abandon the basics; it means you evolve them into habits, rituals, and architecture, and you begin to apply them with cultural intelligence across different teams, geographies, and maturity levels.

In my global consulting work with CISOs, boards, and security leaders, I've seen firsthand how the leap from foundational maturity to fluency is the true differentiator. The organisations that thrive are the ones where security is second nature. I've found that the same three pillars that guide my strategy – **visibility, coverage**, and **control effectiveness** – also serve as anchors during transformation. They just grow with you. Let me explain:

- **Visibility**: Visibility is about knowing where everything is in your environment. Mapping assets and accounts. But the fluency stage is when teams can answer questions such as "What changed yesterday?" without sending a dozen emails. It's when visibility becomes embedded into change management, **continuous integration** (CI)/**continuous delivery/ deployment** (CD) pipelines, and third-party onboarding. You move from discovering the environment to understanding its behaviour.

    That shift – from static maps to dynamic awareness – is where risk management becomes predictive.

- **Coverage**: Most organisations start with patchwork coverage. **Endpoint detection and response** (EDR) might be on some endpoints, logging might be incomplete, and **multifactor authentication** (MFA) might have 'temporary' exceptions. Fluency comes when coverage is enforced, measured, and automated on everything you know. Coverage becomes table stakes– an expectation, not a goal. And more importantly, teams begin asking questions such as "Where else should this control be?" instead of "Where is it missing?"

- **Control effectiveness**: Activating a control isn't the same as operating it effectively. Too often, controls are deployed and forgotten, generating alerts no one reads or blocking behaviours no one understands. Fluency is when every control has an owner, every alert has a playbook, and every dashboard drives action. It's about tuning noise-to-signal and shifting from passive monitoring to proactive detection.

As these three pillars mature, something else happens: security becomes less about enforcement and more about enablement.

When security teams have fluency, they stop being seen as blockers. They're no longer the team that says *no* to every idea. Instead, they become architects of safe execution. They offer choices, saying things like "Here are three secure ways to do this" instead of "You can't."

This shift also prevents the rise of shadow functions – those unofficial workarounds and rogue processes that emerge when the security path is too painful or unclear. When we offer flexibility within secure boundaries (what I call **shades of blue**), we give teams enough autonomy to innovate, while still protecting the business.

Ultimately, cybersecurity fluency is about cultural maturity. It's about embedding risk thinking into product teams, development squads, and frontline operations – not by force, but by design.

Security shouldn't be seen as a department; it should instead be viewed as a behaviour. Fluency is when that behaviour becomes second nature.

Conclusion — secure what matters most

Across different continents, industries, and crises, I've learned that world-class cybersecurity leadership is about knowing what matters most and protecting it with discipline, clarity, and purpose – building with bricks, not straw; doing the basics brilliantly, every day.

It's also about leading and communicating with clarity – whether to the board, an engineer, or a customer, as well as understanding that cybersecurity is a human challenge. Culture, not control, is your most powerful defence.

To every current and future CISO reading this, here is my advice: you won't always get it perfect, but if you stay grounded in the fundamentals and model the behaviours you want to see, you will earn trust. And trust is the currency of resilience.

In a world of noise, be the signal! Be the CISO that leads with simplicity, the steady hand that helps your organisation not just survive, but thrive.

Because cybersecurity isn't about saying "no" to everything. It's about saying "yes" to the right things – and doing them the right way.

This is what being brilliant at the basics truly means.

David's key takeaways — Being brilliant at the basics

Sandro's chapter is a powerful reminder that world-class cybersecurity leadership is built on clarity, consistency, and cultural fluency. His global experience, across five continents, offers a rich perspective for any CISO or cybersecurity leader operating globally and in diverse environments.

I can attest to the insights Sandro has shared in his chapter myself, and there are sobering lessons here in learning to operate effectively across different cultures. To engage the leaders in your teams, having a sensitivity to different styles makes a huge difference in how your direction is embraced by your staff. Your goal as a leader is to inspire them and not just tell them to follow your directions.

As a CISO and leader, Sandro's message for you is clear: excel at the basics and develop operational fluency. This is your competitive edge.

Here are the key takeaways from this chapter:

- *Master the fundamentals first.* Prioritise your core controls (such as patching, access management, privileged accounts, and backups) before chasing emerging tech. Being brilliant at the basics is the foundation of resilience.

- *Lead with cultural sensitivity and active listening.* Be sure to tailor your messages to be able to be understood by different cultures and organisational contexts. Relationships are built through presence, humility, and meaningful feedback loops.

- *Move away from answering any request with "No".* Actively address the perception of cybersecurity as the 'department of no', positioning it instead as a business partner and enabler. Do this by replacing rigid denials with secure alternatives, helping the business say "yes, safely" rather than "no".

- *Embrace standardisation.* This includes tools, playbooks, and processes that scale efficiently and reduce complexity across global teams. This makes your job much easier!

- *Validate and improve continuously.* Treat cybersecurity like a fitness discipline: sustained, routine effort trumps one-off sprints. Remember the example of backups; you don't know whether your backups really do the job until you suddenly need them, under pressure.

- *Focus on what matters most.* Some controls reduce risk more. Align your controls, investment, and governance to the actual risk, not theoretical coverage.

12

A CISO in Japan

In my career, I've been extremely fortunate to live for six years in Japan. I really do love Japan, and have had the privilege to live in Kobe when I was CIO at Eli Lilly and Tokyo when I was CIO at Metlife Japan.

Japan is a complex society with many quirks and unexpected characteristics. It's a delightful place to visit and travel through; you would be enchanted with the quality of life. There is an incredibly respectful culture, with customs such as physical bowing to management that would likely make most Westerners uncomfortable. Work, however, is tough, and I admire the Japanese salarymen for their stamina and absolute dedication to their career.

This is a country that has a high expectation of success – just watch any game of baseball and you will see!

In Japan, there has been a traditional expectation for career longevity, and staff have extreme loyalty to remain at firms for many years. Japan as a nation also has an aging population, thus there are fewer new graduates who can be attracted to start a new career in cybersecurity.

The CISO in Japan faces a challenge. In addition to Japan's geographical proximity to China, North Korea, and Russia (all renowned persistent threat actors), Japan also has US military bases within its territory in preparation for emergencies in East Asia, including Taiwan. Japanese technology is also a key part of many tech products and has been incorporated into military equipment in the US and elsewhere. CISOs must defend their enterprise when there are nation states that are antagonistic toward them.

Against this backdrop, they also have a severe cyber resource shortage. According to a survey by ICS2 in 2023 (`https://cybergovernancealliance.org/wp-content/uploads/2024/01/ISC2_Cybersecurity_Workforce_Study_2023-1.pdf`), there has been a shortfall in cyber professionals in Japan, with a deficit of approximately 110,000 professionals.

This is exacerbated by the inability to simply bring in foreign workers who have the language skills to easily provide support. Existing staff often are internal transfers who move into their roles merely because they have the multi-language skills needed. These staff may be bilingual; however, they may not have cyber experience or certifications.

It is my pleasure to introduce **Osamu Terai, Group CISO** of **Mizuho Financial Group**. Terai-san is an IT executive with strong international experience across technology and cloud. He has had a successful career at Nomura and Industrial Bank of Japan.

With more than 30 years of experience in the financial IT field, Terai-san will share his challenges as a CISO of Japanese traditional financial institutions and, further, share the structural and historical challenges of Japanese financial institutions behind them.

All CISO roles are difficult, but I'd argue that the challenges of CISOs in Japan are significant and among the most demanding globally. In this chapter, Terai-san will provide some great insights into a day in the life of a CISO in Japan. There is a common saying in Japan: "Ganbarimashou" (頑張りましょう). This means "Let's do our best"; it is commonly heard, and if I were a CISO in Japan, it is what I would want to do. However, expectations in Japanese society are always high. Theirs is a culture that expects perfection and "Kaizen" (改善), or the value of seeking excellence is what is sought.

The reality is that both co-exist for the CISO in Japan. You have the expectation of high craft and meticulous improvement, but then significant resource barriers and nation-state actors. This juxtaposition is particularly striking – Japanese culture demands the pursuit of perfection and continuous improvement, yet CISOs operate in an environment where perfect security is fundamentally impossible.

A CISO in Japan

Osamu Terai

To begin, I would first like to thank David for giving me the opportunity to contribute to this book. I have only been a CISO for a short time and have been in charge of cybersecurity for around four years, but I have tried to take every opportunity to absorb knowledge and take on good practices.

I met David at the FS-ISAC APAC Summit, one of the most engaging and interactive opportunities to get to know CISOs from other companies. Being able to interact with other CISOs at FS-ISAC events is very beneficial and important to me, not only because of the exposure to leading initiatives and ideas, but also because of the opportunity to establish personal connections with people such as David.

At the same time, I often perceive a gap (not only culturally, but in terms of knowledge and experience) between other companies and my bank and between other CISOs and myself.

When I was first asked to contribute to this book, I was hesitant, wondering whether I could provide any valuable insight to readers who are currently involved or interested in cybersecurity. However, when I spoke with David, he was in favor of including people with diverse experiences and backgrounds. So, although my account is short, I would like to introduce the issues I have struggled with and focused on in my life as a CISO so far, as well as give you an insight into the characteristics of Japan's corporate culture and IT environment.

The path to becoming a CISO in Japan

Why have I had such a short career as a CISO? I believe that this is symbolic of the **human resources** (**HR**) approach of Japanese companies, especially traditional financial institutions.

HR practices at Japan's legacy financial institutions have several characteristics, but I think the most well-known is the seniority system. This is a system in which promotions are essentially based on age. Within this system, a person must be of a certain age to be promoted to a senior position such as CISO. Recently, HR systems have been evolving so that people with the ability can be promoted more quickly regardless of age, but age is still a major factor in promotion.

Of course, to be a CISO at a large financial institution, one needs not only knowledge but also experience in emergency situations such as incident response, and the courage to approach senior leadership. It would therefore be impractical for an employee in their 20s to serve as CISO, no matter how knowledgeable that person is. What is typical in Japan, however, is that the appointment of a CISO is not only based on experience but also on the age balance between themselves and other leaders. Even if there is a CISO candidate in their 30s with outstanding knowledge and experience, it is not difficult to imagine that there would be concerns within the company about the age difference between this candidate and other C-suite members, as well as the other department heads who would work under the CISO.

Most traditional Japanese companies have, over a long period, built up practices to avoid disturbing the harmony of human relationships within the organization. I have never observed the appointment of a much younger CISO at those companies, and indeed, I may not see it happen in my career. Thus, when I meet CISOs from outside Japan who have been in their positions for more than 10 years, I do envy them. My key point is that Japan as a country is different, and operating here as a CISO reflects this difference.

Another characteristic of the HR systems of traditional Japanese financial institutions is the emphasis they have placed on developing 'generalists.' In my own case, I became a CISO after a career path that I imagine would not be typical in the West. After graduating from university, I worked for a bank's IT subsidiary, followed by an IT service provider, an IT consulting firm, and then a position as head of IT infrastructure at a securities firm.

Developing cyber talent

When I look at the careers of the cyber team members at the bank where I serve as CISO, those who join the banks as new graduates have a variety of internal work experience, but typically have less than four years of IT experience. When it comes to cybersecurity experience, they have even less. Before coming to the cyber department, some of these members were working in broader business roles – for example, in retail and corporate sales, sales and trading, overseas business planning, board coordination, compliance, and other areas.

At the time that these members were informed by their supervisors that they would be transferred to a department handling one of the bank's top risks, cybersecurity, some were highly motivated. There were members who joined the team with a genuine interest in cybersecurity, a field that is dynamic and growing. However, others were quite anxious about being thrown into a group of 'techies.'

There are three things I think that we as CISOs should do to ensure that such new members do not drop out and that they stay within the cybersecurity field.

First is to provide training to educate them and improve their skills. This does not mean simply presenting training programs on how IT systems are built and operate, what the vulnerabilities are, what it means to attack surfaces, how to defend against cyberattacks, how to detect cyberattacks, and what to do if a cyberattack is detected. While these are skills that need to be acquired by the new team members, it must be remembered that these same people were just recently in different roles, making asset management proposals to customers, for example. It is quite a challenge for them to make such a significant change in mindset.

We can compare this to using an igniter for a campfire. You can build a fire without one, but it is easier with the igniter. However, even if you can build a fire without an igniter, you must not stop fanning the flames and adding wood to the fire piece by piece until it is strong. This requires continuous effort on the part of each individual. If new organisational members cannot understand the cybersecurity and IT jargon that is often used in meetings, they may want to quit because they don't understand the job. This is like giving up on a campfire because you can't start it. To prevent this, an igniter (training) is needed to quickly reach the point where the fire will not go out (where staff feel comfortable).

Second is to convey the message that taking on a cybersecurity role is a good way to improve one's own broader business skills. This is particularly relevant for those working in a financial institution, such as a bank. It is a fact that banking operations are surprisingly siloed. Depending on the customers you serve and the tasks you are responsible for, there are specific departments you communicate with. Some departments naturally cover a broader scope – such as HR, internal communications, and compliance. In cybersecurity, you have to communicate with a much broader set of stakeholders on a regular basis.

> For example, when conducting a large-scale cyber exercise, the cybersecurity team must coordinate the exercise schedule, scenarios and logistics with a number of departments, such as crisis management, IT, operations, compliance, legal and risk management. If you look at people who are doing this well, we understand the ability to communicate effectively across functions and departments is critical to working in a cybersecurity team.

Third is to communicate the significance and purpose of cybersecurity and how it can impact operations, so that cybersecurity staff are aware and motivated to do such an important job.

Every banker understands how critical and important the banking and settlement processes are. However, they have a lower understanding of cybersecurity and how this is a prerequisite for the stable functioning of such a banking system.

Bankers naturally consider, for example, how credit and market risks will be affected if interest rates in Japan rise. But I think very few people understand, or at least try to understand, how information about, say, an active and powerful ransomware gang poses a risk to business. The role of cybersecurity staff in this context is to make everyone working for financial institutions understand that cyber risk does not refer to an act of God, but is one of the risks that should be taken into account in conducting their business (similar to credit risk and market risk), leading to autonomous control by the first **line of defense (LOD)**.

In addition, I would add that one of the attractions of cybersecurity work is the extremely important and unique activity of information exchange and sharing in the cybersecurity community. It is not enough to conduct closed activities only at one's own bank or organization. In Japan, there is a cybersecurity community called **Financial Services Information Sharing and Analysis Center Japan (Financial ISAC Japan)**, where people involved in cybersecurity at financial institutions share practical information in various areas, and there is FS-ISAC globally. However, there are not many places for information sharing at the CISO level.

Cybersecurity is often referred to as a 'non-competitive area', but I don't think there's any other non-competitive area where practices are shared and collaborated in such an organized way. Work in the corporate domain involves a lot of communication with people in the company, but participating in Financial ISAC Japan and FS-ISAC and being able to connect with people from other companies in the same industry, share concerns and practices, and develop friendly rivalries, is also very exciting and enjoyable for people in charge of cybersecurity

I genuinely believe that by working together, we can contribute to strengthening the cybersecurity of the community overall, as well as society as a whole. As a for-profit bank, the usual approach to social contribution is to contribute to the development of society by providing services to customers, but cybersecurity can contribute more directly by protecting the financial industry and customers from cyberattacks.

Cybersecurity roles constitute very meaningful and honorable work in this sense. We believe it is important to make people aware that the work we are undertaking has this critical impact.

The issue of risk acceptance

As a CISO, I have always found it difficult to deal with issues of risk acceptance. Running a bank involves a variety of risks that need to be taken into account. A bank that cannot manage risks will not succeed in the market, will have its license revoked by the authorities, or will simply fall out of favor with customers because it cannot provide reliable and trusted services.

The concepts of market risk and credit risk have a long history and are now recognized globally, including among financial authorities. The fact that the amount and control of risk are quantified in the original definitions of said risks is also an advantageous feature for their understanding globally. In these areas, historical data is abundant and can be trusted for accuracy. (Despite this, sometimes intense market crashes occur and impact institutions.)

In the case of cyber risk, the general practice of quantifying risk does not yet exist as far as I know. In fact, I know some CISOs who once tried but eventually gave up on quantification. This is a major factor that makes risk communication with the business difficult for CISOs. Executives and business departments understand the need for cyber countermeasures but struggle to prioritize other risks and investments for business strategy because it is difficult to quantify the amount of risk that cyber countermeasures will reduce.

In addition to business interruption risk, compliance risk, and legal risk, cyberattack risks include reputational risk. I think the news that a company has been hit by a cyberattack is more sensationalized to the public than it should be. And even though the company is a victim, an apology is required. This is especially true in Japan. And for a while, on social media, the news is exaggerated and distributed with information of uncertain authenticity. This creates a negative image of the company for a long time. What senior management doesn't want to see is the news that their company has been hit by a cyberattack.

What I noticed when I became the head of cybersecurity is that there are some senior executives who advocate a zero-tolerance approach to cyber risk and are extremely sensitive to the risk of cyberattacks. And then there are those key stakeholders who are willing to manage cyber risk rationally, without letting their fears guide their decisions, and instead adopt a more risk-based approach, which is based on a framework established by the company. Of course, the latter is the way to go, and this is what I recommend.

The problem a CISO faces is the judgment of what is acceptable risk. Personally, I feel that Japanese people are not good at risk-based approaches. The tolerance for loss and failure is extremely low in Japanese society. For example, most individuals tend to prefer savings to investments, which have the potential for loss. They see the downside more than the upside.

At the same time, in Japan, we have a culture of strong emphasis on the quality of product and services in order to meet the high demand from customers. Historically, we have enjoyed a strong manufacturing industry, which has produced high-quality products in response to customer demand. It is also well known that in Japan, some customers complain to the station staff when the train is only a few minutes late.

As a result, the management team will often adopt a zero-tolerance approach to risk (with the fear that customers will not tolerate service outages for any reason). I have seen this kind of situation many times, not only in cybersecurity but also in the field of IT system failures. This is because Japanese people are not very good at making risk-based choices. I feel this is the most difficult part of being a CISO at a Japanese financial institution.

Let's take an example – in Japan, it is generally not acceptable if management policy rules are not met. However, a typical question is whether it is acceptable to respond to gaps found in vulnerability assessments beyond the day limit set by the company policy.

If the rules cannot be met, the decision will be based on the criteria for risk acceptance, based on the likelihood and impact of an attack on the vulnerability. This seems logical, but how should the validity of the decision to accept or not accept the risk be verified in the end?

Unfortunately, I do not have a simple answer to this question. It is common to say that at the end of the day, it is a management decision, but what is that management decision based on?

My sense is that in many cases, they are making decisions based on their personal fears, as mentioned earlier. Often, senior management's decisions are conservative (without providing any rationale) because they will be held accountable in the event of a cyber incident.

At a traditional Japanese company and a financial institution that plays a role in managing critical infrastructure, this feeling is understandable, but it is also questionable whether we should allow ourselves to be influenced by the personal sensitivities and whims of senior management at any given time.

As a CISO, I try my best to provide input that allows senior management to make rational decisions without being influenced by their personal fears (I call them 'ghosts'). But that is easier said than done, and judging by the number of presentations and articles on the topic of what to report to the board of directors, I think CISOs around the world are struggling with the same issue. I'm not alone.

Governance meetings

In order to review the operational status of the cybersecurity risk management process, the financial institution I work for has set up several governance meetings attended by senior management and board members.

In order to be able to have a truly fruitful discussion at meetings like these, I think a CISO should address two things.

The first is to present the company's cyber risk in a way that senior management or board members can understand. Executives want to know where and how much of the cyberattack risk is associated with running businesses, how much of it is well controlled, and what and how much of the risk remains. All information should come down to this point of view.

A cybersecurity team's daily activities include defending against incessant external attacks and diagnosing vulnerabilities in internal systems. Cyber threats include state-sponsored actors, ransomware, and fraud over internet banking services. The challenge for a CISO is how well the CISO can translate those activities on the ground into business risks, which senior management wants to know about.

Another thing a CISO should do to improve the quality of discussions in governance meetings like this is to raise the level of cybersecurity knowledge among executives and board members. In order to discuss the risk of cyberattacks, basic knowledge of cyberattacks and cyber threat trends must be understood by management and board members.

Our cybersecurity team had been providing online training for management and board members once a year, but I thought this was insufficient. Thus, I decided to talk about cybersecurity at weekly meetings where most of the senior executives are present. Topics I covered included, for example, cyber incidents at other companies, trends in cybersecurity policies and regulations of Japanese and foreign governments, and descriptions of cyber threat actors. My talk on this lasts about five minutes, and executives, including the CEO, ask questions and make comments, if any.

I know it's not a systematic way of educating them, but by keeping them informed of the latest cybersecurity trends, I believe that cybersecurity has secured its place in the minds of executives. And that is becoming the foundation of meaningful discussion at governance meetings.

Challenges to IT/cybersecurity teams in Japanese organizations

One of the most difficult things to get across when I talk to CISOs and cybersecurity professionals who have never worked for Japanese banks is why it takes so long to implement a cybersecurity IT solution in Japanese banks. It certainly does take time, to the extent that I must admit it frustrates me too. Why is that? I think there are three reasons.

The first is that Japanese organizations don't have sufficient cybersecurity staff. Here are the results of a 2022 survey on this by NRI Secure Technologies, a Japanese cybersecurity consultancy and solution provider (`https://www.nri-secure.co.jp/news/2023/0201-2`):

Does your organization have sufficient number of cybersecurity staff?

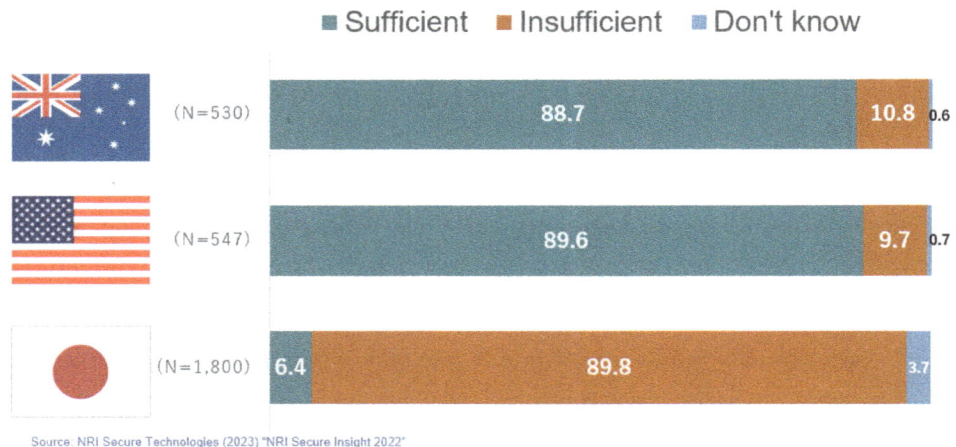

■ Sufficient   ■ Insufficient   ■ Don't know

(N=530)	88.7	10.8	0.6
(N=547)	89.6	9.7	0.7
(N=1,800)	6.4	89.8	3.7

Source: NRI Secure Technologies (2023) "NRI Secure Insight 2022"

Figure 12.1: Results of NRI Secure Technologies survey question on cybersecurity staffing numbers

Almost 90% of organizations surveyed in Australia and the US said, "Yes, we have sufficient cybersecurity staff." On the other hand, almost 90% of Japanese organizations said, "No, we don't have sufficient staff." What a difference!

In the same survey, there was another question asking about whether there is a CISO position in organizations. The result shows that almost 97% of organizations in both Australia and the US said, "Yes." But only 42% in Japan have CISOs in their organizations.

Given the significant shortage of cybersecurity team members in Japan, cybersecurity staff are usually very busy dealing with immediate threats, incidents, and regulatory-related tasks. Sometimes, they cannot secure time for future improvement.

The second reason for the length of time it takes to implement a cybersecurity solution in Japanese banks is that there are also very limited internal IT engineers in Japanese companies. Here is another interesting 2023 survey result by Japan's Ministry of Internal Affairs and Communications (https://www.soumu.go.jp/johotsusintokei/whitepaper/ja/r06/excel/f00350.xlsx):

Who takes IT development tasks in your organization? Internal engineers or external vendors?

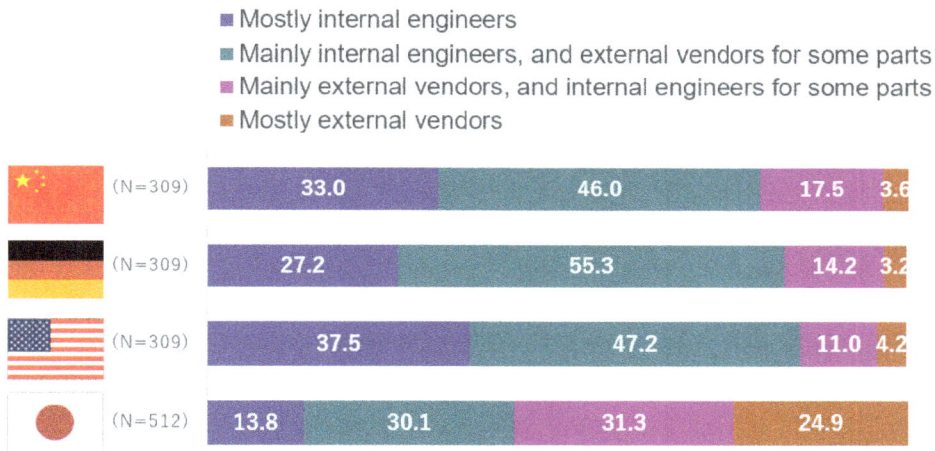

■ Mostly internal engineers
■ Mainly internal engineers, and external vendors for some parts
■ Mainly external vendors, and internal engineers for some parts
■ Mostly external vendors

	Mostly internal engineers	Mainly internal engineers, and external vendors for some parts	Mainly external vendors, and internal engineers for some parts	Mostly external vendors
(N=309)	33.0	46.0	17.5	3.6
(N=309)	27.2	55.3	14.2	3.2
(N=309)	37.5	47.2	11.0	4.2
(N=512)	13.8	30.1	31.3	24.9

Source: the Ministry of Internal Affairs and Communications (2023) 'Survey Research on Trends in Research and Development and Digital Application of the Latest Information and Communications Technology in Japan and Overseas'

Figure 12.2: Results of Japan's Ministry of Internal Affairs and Communications survey on IT development task distribution

The question in this survey is, "Who takes IT development tasks in your organization, internal engineers or external vendors?" There are four options given. The first two options mean that the organization has an internal capability for IT development. The last two options mean that the organization heavily depends on external vendors for IT development.

The results for the first three countries, China, Germany, and the US, show that around 80 to 85% of the organizations in these countries have the capability of IT development internally.

On the other hand, for Japan, it's limited to only 44%. More than half of Japanese organizations say they rely on external vendors, with one fourth of them saying they are fully dependent on external vendors for IT development.

What does this mean in the context of the implementation of cybersecurity solutions?

Implementing cybersecurity tools, or even doing a proof of concept of them, involves a number of hands-on tasks. However, for Japanese organizations, we have to ask external vendors to conduct these tasks. Of course, it comes with a cost.

Some Japanese financial institutions are trying to secure in-house engineering capability, as they feel that they cannot survive under these kinds of circumstances. That is a good development, and I would like to support and drive this direction.

The last challenge for Japanese financial institutions is about IT team structure. In the case of non-Japanese organizations, each technology stack and function that makes up an IT system is often a team of people with skills and experience in that area.

The good thing about this structure is that each area is managed horizontally by people with specialized knowledge, so standardization is naturally promoted. Also, many security products usually cover each area, and this structure makes it relatively easy to apply a tool across an organization. For example, you wouldn't deploy different certificate management tools in different application areas, but would implement just one single tool to cover all your IT systems.

On the other hand, in Japanese banks, especially in traditional and large Japanese banks, IT teams are often organized by business application area. Each team contains functions of IT infrastructure, security, and IT service management. It's a monolithic team by business application.

Here is a depiction of these two types of IT team structure:

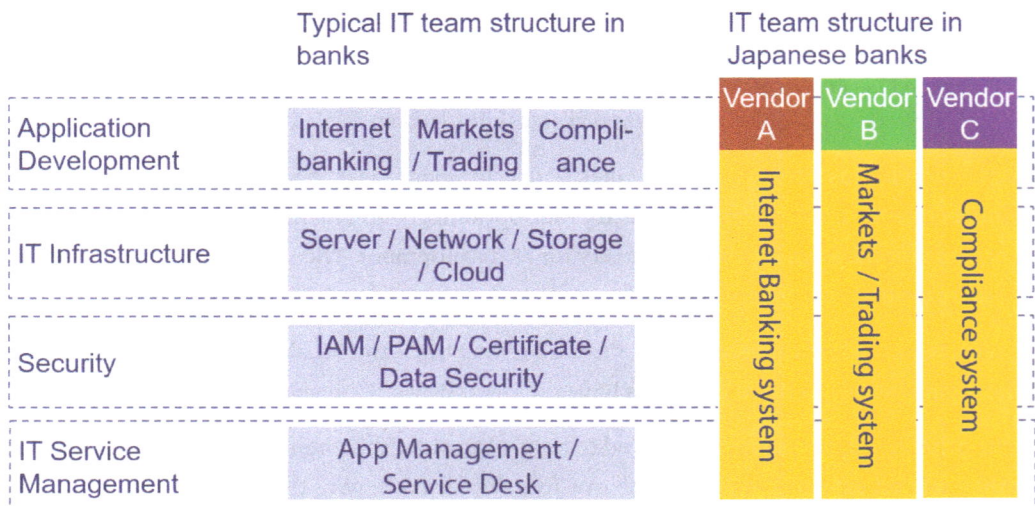

Figure 12.3: Two types of IT team structures

In the Japanese IT team structure, it is thought that the optimized and quickest decision-making and resource allocation are realized in the particular business area. However, from a whole organization perspective, it is an optimization in a limited area, which creates 'silos' within the organization.

This structure is not suitable for implementing a single tool to achieve a certain function and for having experts use it to cover the entire organization. For example, when deploying a certificate management tool for creating a crypto inventory for the whole organization, it is not clear who will take ownership and lead the deployment in this team structure.

It's not just about employees. Sometimes, quite often, different vendors support different business areas, as illustrated in *Figure 12.3*. This makes it difficult to coordinate enterprise-wide projects such as quantum-safe migration, which require holistic visibility and cross-functional teamwork.

These are the challenges that Japanese organizations, particularly financial institutions, have been facing. The CISO's role is to overcome these challenges by coping with the CIO and other senior executives, who are used to working in this way.

CIOs often constantly wonder how to make their IT organization more efficient. CISOs talk to CIOs about the need and usefulness of a horizontal organization, and we also think about the transformation approach together. In my case, for example, I proposed to the CIO the introduction of a mechanism for managing electronic certificates, which are currently managed on a system-by-system basis, in a common manner throughout the bank, and the establishment of a cross-cutting organization in line with this.

A call to action: Sharing information from Japan with the world

I would like to suggest that CISOs of Japanese companies make the effort to understand Japan's position in the global cybersecurity field and work together with others more globally.

Bordered by China, North Korea, and Russia, and only 111 km from Taiwan, Japan's geography has meant it has forged a relationship with each country that is unlike any other in the world. Japan finds itself in a complex mix of intimacy and vigilance in all aspects of these relationships, from politics and business to the family level.

From a cybersecurity perspective, those of us who know that hybrid warfare is used as a practical tactic know that in the event of a crisis in the region, Japan will undoubtedly be the target of cyberattacks. We also understand, with alarm, the risk of theft of sensitive information.

On the other hand, it is difficult to say that we have been able to share with CISOs in other parts of the world the cyber incidents occurring in Japan, the attack methods involved, and the activities of threat actors. Of course, I am aware that public organizations such as **Information-technology Promotion Agency (IPA)** and **Japan Computer Emergency Response Team Coordination Center (JPCERT/CC)** provide information in English, but as far as I know, there is not enough information sharing overseas by Japanese financial institutions and communities.

Now that machine translation has developed, it is technically possible for people from overseas to obtain and understand information transmitted in Japanese from Japan. However, there must be differences in the information gathering ability of those of us who live in Japan and use Japanese as our native language. Given Japan's unique geopolitical position, CISOs of Japanese companies should be more proactive in sharing information with other parts of the world.

My conclusion

Looking back on what I have written, I realize that I have focused on the barriers for Japanese financial institutions to promote cybersecurity measures. I don't mean to be negative; however, I often feel that such barriers have provided the CISOs of Japanese financial institutions with a uniquely challenging and rewarding experience. The HR systems of Japanese companies are deeply linked to long-standing employment practices and culture, and it will take a considerable amount of time to have the same flexibility as in other regions.

It is my duty to do as much as I can as a CISO within such constraints. For example, I am working on standardizing siloed system environments and operating systems. For instance, my bank has many internet gateways. Some are not managed by IT. We are working to consolidate those gateways into standardized gateways. This initiative has received support from executive management, and we believe it will effectively strengthen cybersecurity.

I have found this to be a very rewarding challenge for my career, from the viewpoint of not only enhancing cybersecurity but also promoting efforts to build an IT infrastructure for Mizuho Bank that is both secure and makes our business operations nimbler.

I remain very positive that it is a high priority on my agenda, and I believe that such a positive and challenging spirit is required of CISOs at Japanese companies. Because of the personnel system I mentioned earlier, not all of those in CISO roles in Japan were motivated to become CISOs themselves, but I would like Japanese CISOs to be more aware of the great work that CISOs do, not only to protect their companies and customers from cyberattacks, but also to contribute to the safety of society.

I have been working in the area of financial IT systems for almost 30 years, and I am quite confident in the knowledge I have built up. I hope my perspective is useful for aspiring CISOs, particularly those in Japan, when they consider their approach to cybersecurity.

David's key takeaways — A CISO in Japan

While there are some general lessons from this chapter for CISOs that aren't directly connected to Japan, for the global or regional CISO that has Japan as part of their accountability (or who may be working with teams in Japan), to truly own this, a greater understanding is required than an annual visit to Japan. From my own life experience, Japan has more complexity as a society than most places I have lived – cybersecurity accordingly reflects this reality.

There are subtle, unique lessons that a CISO must address to be able to protect this country effectively. And for many global enterprises, Japan remains a top 3 contributor to their revenue and growth opportunity.

My key learnings from this chapter include:

- *Japan has a career seniority system that means CISOs often must reach a certain age before appointment, regardless of technical expertise.* This cultural approach means many Japanese CISOs have shorter tenures compared to their international counterparts.
- *The overall cyber talent pool in Japanese companies is filled with 'generalist' resources, rather than specialists, who are internally transferred in from business roles such as sales or compliance, often with minimal technical background.* CISOs should provide training to these professionals to help them transform their mindset and develop the technical skills they need.
- *Japanese organizations are extremely risk-averse, and risk acceptance presents a challenge to CISOs.* The CISO must work to provide rational, data-driven risk assessments to combat decision-making based on personal fears rather than business logic.
- *Resource constraints in Japan are severe.* There is a deficit of more than 110,000 professionals. These limitations force cybersecurity teams to focus on immediate threats rather than strategic improvements, significantly slowing solution implementation of their roadmap.
- *Break down silos.* Silo challenges in Japanese banks are severe as IT teams are typically organized by business application area rather than technology stack, creating monolithic teams that resist enterprise-wide tool deployment. This structure makes it difficult to implement standardized security solutions across the enterprise and requires extensive coordination efforts.
- *Sharing threat intelligence is valuable.* Terai-san advocates for CISOs in Japan being more proactive in sharing threat intelligence and cyber incident information with international cybersecurity communities for the benefit of global efforts in cybersecurity.

If you are interested in reading this chapter in Japanese, you can download it here: https://github.com/PacktPublishing/A-Day-in-the-Life-of-a-CISO.

13

Navigating the C-Suite, Boards and DOPE Dynamics

There is not a day in the life of a CISO where the CISO does not have to work hard on navigating difficult and demanding stakeholders, including Executive Management and the board. At times, the CISO will have conflicting requirements from different executive stakeholders.

Both executives and boards are becoming more concerned and vocal about cybersecurity as they themselves are also starting to be held more accountable by various regulators. There have been instances where regulators have written to a board and strongly recommended that their Chief Information Officer (CIO) and CISO is replaced with a new incumbent. This trend will only continue, and as a result, the role of the CISO will become increasingly more difficult.

From my observations, most executives and boards do not understand cybersecurity, and even when there has been a push to add technology competency to the board matrix, this does not guarantee that the new board member understands cyber.

To complicate matters further, the CISO will often report to the CIO, and in that relationship alone, there can be a conflict of interest. Every CIO is rewarded for driving digital change and keeping the cloud/on-premise infrastructure operating 24x7. However, there can be a trade-off between operational efficiency and ensuring digital platforms are available with the requirements to patch critical vulnerabilities.

I've personally witnessed instances where a new CISO has inherited a strategy and budget but was prevented from being totally honest with the board about the cyber maturity of the organisation and the necessity for further budget to be allocated.

How the CISO navigates these obstacles can make or break their career.

In essence, the CISO should have a singular, uncompromising objective: to protect the enterprise from malicious actors. A capable CISO inevitably feels the weight of this responsibility, the burden to shield and defend. However, this duty must be balanced within the context of a functioning, profitable business. Excessive security-related friction can render the digital experience untenable, undermining both usability and operational effectiveness.

Consider how much pressure business executives place on the CIO and CISO to ensure the availability of secure systems; it is an incredible balancing act that is played out below the surface. The CISO will be held accountable to the Vulnerability Management Board Metrics, but at the same time, be subject to the business and their own IT colleagues not always cooperating with them on this effort.

How, then, can one, as a CISO, present themselves in an honest and positive fashion to the board when there are all these undertones and fissures that exist within each enterprise?

It is my pleasure to introduce **Shamane Tan, Chief Growth Officer** at **Sekuro**. She is a bestselling author, TEDx and Keynote speaker. As an industry expert, she has exposure to boards and CxOs that operate in this environment and will illustrate approaches to navigating relationships with stakeholders, including management and the board.

Navigating the C-suite, boards, and DOPE dynamics

Shamane Tan

In this chapter, I reimagine the dynamics of the corporate C-suite as a bustling schoolyard, where each executive plays a distinct role shaped by their function. The CEO takes the place of the school principal, focused on vision, leadership, and keeping everything running smoothly. The CFO becomes the math whiz, precise, logical, and focused on numbers. By using these familiar analogies, I offer CISOs a way to translate complex cyber topics into narratives that resonate with each leader's specific responsibilities. Understanding the motivations behind each role can help you frame conversations around what matters most to each executive, whether that's growth, compliance, risk, or operational stability.

Once those functional roles are clear, the next layer is understanding how each leader prefers to communicate. Here, I introduce the DOPE (Doves, Owls, Peacocks, and Eagles) personality model as a way to decode individual styles. For example, you might find that the Owl in the room values detailed data and well-structured logic, while the Peacock is drawn to big-picture storytelling and excitement. By recognizing these personality cues, CISOs can adjust not only what they say but how they say it, increasing the likelihood that their message will be heard and acted on.

Ultimately, this chapter equips CISOs to move beyond one-size-fits-all communication. By combining an understanding of executive roles with insight into personality styles, you can become more than technical advisors, instead becoming trusted partners who integrate cybersecurity into broader business conversations. It's not just about protecting the organization; it's about shaping a culture of shared responsibility, innovation, and resilience.

The schoolyard of the C-Suite

"I don't understand why he says it like this."

"I don't know how to get my message across to her."

"He just doesn't get me. I can't get through to him at all."

Sound familiar? These are the kinds of frustrations you'd overhear at corporate water coolers. If CISOs were back in school, the lunchroom conversations would likely echo the same sentiment. Boardrooms are the grown-up counterparts of homerooms, filled with different personalities.

The question isn't just, "How do we communicate better?" but rather, "How do we connect?"

Whether you're managing teams, collaborating with peers, or presenting to the board, the challenge is often less about budgets or resources and more about understanding people. To influence effectively, CISOs need to step into the shoes of their fellow executives and see the world through their lenses and speak their language.

In my LinkedIn course, *CISO Foundations: Influencing the Board and C-Suite*, which has drawn over 15,000 learners and aspiring CISOs, and in one of my books, *Building a Cyber Resilient Business: A Cyber Book for Executives and Boards*, I've delved deeply into this dynamic. One common critique I hear from board directors is this: "CISOs are excellent at their technical craft, but many still find it a challenge to think, act, and communicate like the rest of the business leaders."

Well, we're all on this mission to change that. To start with, let's explore how we can tailor our cyber risk messaging so that it resonates with our key players in the C-suite. Let's begin with the CEO.

Understanding the CEO — vision, strategy, and accountability

CEOs are the captains of the ship, responsible for leading the company toward sustainability, profitability, and expansion. Their workday is extremely diversified. Harvard research tracked 27 top-performing CEOs for over 60,000 hours and discovered that their time was divided into four important areas:

- 21% focuses on strategy,
- 25% on functional and business unit reviews,
- 25% on people and relationships, and
- 16% on organizational culture.

(Full article: 'How CEOs Manage Time', *Harvard Business Review*, July–August 2018. `https://hbr.org/2018/07/how-ceos-manage-time`)

What does this tell us? CEOs are genuinely concerned with the broad picture: strategy, alignment, people, and trust.

In the framework of the schoolyard, the CEO serves as the principal. They set the school's vision, ensure the playground is safe and fun, and balance the needs of stakeholders (students, parents, and teachers). The principal does not oversee every dodgeball game or snack transaction, but they are held accountable when something goes wrong, particularly during severe situations, such as a school-wide emergency.

Similarly, CEOs are held accountable to their boards and shareholders, and increasingly, they're thrust into the spotlight during cyber crises. A CEO's capacity to manage the firm through uncertainties, including data breaches, is being scrutinized more than ever before. This presents a significant opportunity for CISOs to demonstrate value.

Here are some key strategies to engage the CEO:

- **Focus on business-critical outcomes:** Position cybersecurity as essential to protecting revenue, brand reputation, and customer trust. For example: "A ransomware attack could disrupt core business operations, leading to service outages that erode customer confidence and damage our market reputation." Emphasize that cybersecurity is not just an IT issue, but a business continuity and growth enabler.

- **Leverage analogies:** Use relatable comparisons to make cybersecurity seem more intuitive. A well-known example compares cybersecurity to the brakes on a race car. Brakes do not just slow the car down; they give the driver the confidence to go faster. In the same way, strong cybersecurity does not hold the business back. It provides it with the confidence to grow, innovate, and take strategic risks, with greater control.

- **Link cyber risk to business goals**: CEOs should understand that cyber events are not an 'if' but a 'when', and even more, they must plan as though a breach has already happened. A CISO who aligns their cyber resilience strategy with the CEO's strategic priorities becomes an invaluable counsel. For example: "Investing in cybersecurity not only supports our digital transformation efforts and enables expansion, but ensures we can operate through disruption as if compromise is already part of our reality. It protects shareholder value by safeguarding reputation, ensuring service continuity, and preventing costly disruptions that would otherwise erode market confidence."

While the CEO is focused on the big picture, another key player zeroes in on the financials, the Chief Financial Officer (CFO).

Engaging the CFO — numbers, risk, and investments

The CFOs are the organization's financial architects. They monitor cash flow, assess financial health, and set budgets. They perceive the world through numbers, and cyber risk is no exception.

If they were back in school, your CFO would be like a math whiz who carefully counts every marble and makes the smartest trades during playtime, always focused on maximizing their winnings.

A smart math whiz won't just collect marbles; they'll also invest in a sturdy marble pouch or container, because no matter how many marbles they win, if they don't secure them, they risk losing everything to theft or an accident.

Similarly, cybersecurity is not just about playing the game well (business growth); it's about making sure your winnings (data, finances, and operations) are protected. Without it, a single breach could be like losing your entire marble collection, leaving you with nothing left to trade, play, or build with. Investing in security isn't just an abstract expense, it is like securing your marbles. It ensures you can keep playing the long game and growing without unnecessary risk.

Key strategies to engage the CFO include:

- **Quantify the cost of inaction:** Make cybersecurity risks tangible by linking cyber incidents such as data breaches or ransomware attacks to specific financial business impacts, including lost revenue, regulatory fines, and reduced growth due to reputational damage. In one case I know of, a CISO framed a threat by presenting dollar estimates for potential operational downtime and brand damage during a simulated breach scenario. The result was that a skeptical CFO approved the requested budget within days after seeing the financial exposure laid out in business terms.

- **Position cybersecurity as a strategic investment:** One way to do this is by framing cybersecurity as similar to an insurance premium. It is an upfront cost that protects the organization from significantly larger financial losses in the future. Use risk quantification models such as the FAIR methodology to show how potential losses from cyber incidents compare to the cost of preventive measures. This will make the return on investment (ROI) more tangible and easier to evaluate. In one instance I'm aware of, a CISO used a side-by-side analysis to show how strengthening enterprise-wide resilience strategies could prevent multimillion-dollar losses. Once the CFO saw the figures lined up, the conversation shifted from "Is this worth spending money on?" to "How do we invest smarter?"

- **Use metrics that matter:** With your metrics, focus on tangible outcomes, such as reduced downtime or minimized financial exposure. One CISO I worked with transitioned from reporting technical stats such as patch counts to business-focused outcomes such as reduced recovery time and avoided financial loss. That pivot earned them not just attention, but a recurring seat in the CFO's quarterly reviews.

In *Building a Cyber Resilient Business*, I interviewed CFOs who emphasized the importance of integrating cybersecurity with enterprise risk management (ERM). They wanted clarity on how cyber risks stack up against other risks, and how cybersecurity investments align with business goals. Speaking their language, data and ROI, is the quickest path to gaining their buy-in.

In his roles as CIO, the lead author of this book, David Gee, found it particularly effective to engage CFOs by bringing them into strategic trade-off conversations and ensuring they understood the broader business benefits of the strategy roadmap, including how it supports risk buydown.

Aligning with the CRO — anticipation and preparedness

The Chief Risk Officer (CRO) is the organization's risk sentinel. Their role is to anticipate risks, prepare responses, and prioritize mitigation strategies. Cyber risk is one of many concerns on their radar, but its rising prominence demands collaboration.

Again, if you were back at school, the CRO would be the vigilant playground monitor, the one walking the perimeter, scanning for hazards, and making sure everyone follows the rules. Whether it's spotting a broken swing or intercepting a brewing dodgeball ambush, their role is to ensure that everyone can play safely and knows when to step aside or take cover.

Key strategies for engaging the CRO include:

- **Frame cybersecurity as the CRO's best friend**: show them how your cyber defenses extend their vision, ensuring they aren't blindsided by digital dodgeballs. For example, 'Our heatmap of cyber risks acts like binoculars for spotting threats early.'
- **Integrate cyber risk into ERM:** Understand how your CROs prioritize cyber risk within the broader risk landscape and how they are ensuring cyber risk is integrated into their ERM strategy. Are current metrics focused more on incidents and attacks, or on the maturity of internal controls and mitigation actions? Make the connection clear between cybersecurity and the organization's overall risk frameworks. For example, "Cyber incidents impact operational, reputational, and financial risks, making them central to ERM."

- **Provide predictive insights:** In my discussions with CROs, many emphasized the importance of looking beyond historical data to predictive modeling, which supports faster decision-making and sharper prioritization in high-stakes moments. To do this, collaborate with the CRO on identifying shared strategies, trend indicators, and forward-looking data that help anticipate emerging threats in a broader risk context.

- **Collaborate on KPIs that matter:** Work with the CRO to co-develop meaningful KPIs that reflect the organization's cyber risk posture and maturity. These should go beyond technical indicators to include metrics on control effectiveness, risk response readiness, and alignment with the organization's enterprise risk appetite. When cybersecurity KPIs are integrated into the broader risk dashboard, they reinforce shared accountability and strengthen executive buy-in.

Working closely with your CROs can achieve meaningful business outcomes. The perspectives of the CRO can help you expand your viewpoint as well, and having them as your advocate can help the business perceive cyber risk more seriously too.

Partnering with the CIO — bridges and boundaries

The CIO plays a critical role in connecting technology strategy with broader business goals. While their primary focus is on driving IT innovation and operational efficiency, cybersecurity often sits within their domain, or at least near it. This overlap can create both opportunities for collaboration and tension with the CISO.

In many organizations, the CIO holds more influence than the CISO and often speaks on behalf of cybersecurity at the executive level. While this may streamline communication, it can also dilute or reframe the security message, especially when it reaches the board. This is a reality that needs to be acknowledged if we want to establish healthy boundaries and ensure that cybersecurity receives the distinct voice and visibility it deserves.

If your CIO were a kid in school, they'd be creative, bold, and always pushing boundaries, the one inventing the most intricate playground games and obstacle courses. But even the most imaginative designs need guardrails. A strong partnership between CIO and CISO ensures that innovation and safety go hand in hand.

Here are some key strategies for engaging the CIO:

- **Respect differences**: Recognize that IT and cybersecurity are distinct yet deeply interconnected disciplines. The CIO is responsible for building and maintaining the organization's digital infrastructure; the 'jungle gym' of IT systems. Position cybersecurity as the safety padding underneath it, designed to ensure safe, sustainable operation. In one organization I worked with, I saw the turning point come when the CISO acknowledged the CIO's technical vision and framed security as a shared enabler rather than a constraint. That shift alone moved the relationship from tension to partnership.

- **Frame security as a business strength:** Use analogies to make your point more intuitive. For instance: "Just as a swing set needs secure bolts, cybersecurity allows our digital playground to operate without fear of collapse." One CIO I partnered with once said, "The only thing worse than a failed system is one that was secure but unusable." That comment stuck with me. It became a guiding principle in our conversations: security should never break the experience; it should quietly strengthen it.

- **Build trust through collaboration:** Work closely with the CIO on shared initiatives such as secure cloud migrations, system upgrades, or endpoint strategies. Find common ground in balancing usability and protection. In digitally progressive organizations, I've seen CIO-CISO relationships flourish when the two leaders co-created joint KPIs and presented a united front to the board. It's like how kids bond by creating a game together on the playground. They co-own the rules, the space, and the outcome.

Organizations where CIOs and CISOs have established a great partnership often see accelerated timelines for digital transformation and better security outcomes – a win-win for both parties.

Influencing the board – clarity, context, and collaboration

Going back to our school analogy, the board is responsible for the school's general direction and governance, including holding the principal (CEO) accountable. They care about the school's overall success, including keeping it competitive and avoiding controversies. The board isn't concerned with the daily drama of the students' playtime, but they do want evidence that the playground is safe, effective, and contributes to the school's reputation.

Likewise, our boards are responsible for organizational oversight, including cyber risk. They require succinct, practical insights to make informed decisions, not technical jargon or endless data.

Key strategies for engaging the board include:

- **Simplify matters**:
  - Explain to the board how cyber risk impacts other organizational areas, such as financial stability and reputation. Board members don't need every technical detail. What they need is clarity on how cybersecurity risk ties directly to core organizational concerns, such as financial stability, operational continuity, brand reputation, and stakeholder trust.
  - Focus on big-picture impacts and frame cybersecurity in terms of outcomes they care about. For example, instead of diving into patch management or threat detection tools, share high-level updates such as "By reducing ransomware-related downtime by 30% and improving response capabilities, we've increased our resilience to major disruptions. Our simulations show faster recovery times, which means less disruption to business continuity."

    One CISO I observed began their board presentation by sharing how a recent cybersecurity initiative helped prevent a third-party incident from escalating into a customer-facing breach. The board immediately paid attention because the outcome reinforced their responsibility for protecting stakeholder trust and avoiding reputational damage. Framing it this way positioned cybersecurity as a strategic safeguard, not just a technical function.

  - Respect the board's expertise but meet them where they are. A standout observation from my conversations with board directors is that while they are highly capable and strategic in their own domains, many feel alienated by overly technical CISO presentations. One board member once said to me, "If a CISO can't explain what they're doing without sounding like a tech manual, how do we know they're leading with the business in mind?" This tells us that the board doesn't want to be overwhelmed with jargon or made to feel out of their depth. The most effective CISOs are those who can translate complexity into decision-ready insight clearly, concisely, and confidently.

- During a board presentation, keep updates short but impactful – for example, by using a three-minute approach (sometimes known as a 'three-minute drill')

  Some CISOs prefer to use a three-slide approach:

  - ⬚ Slide 1: Current cyber risks and their business impact.
  - ⬚ Slide 2: Key actions taken and their measurable outcomes.
  - ⬚ Slide 3: Strategic priorities and required resources for the next year.

- **Highlight successes**:

  - It's important not only to show why cybersecurity matters, but to demonstrate that mitigation efforts are working. Share measurable outcomes that reflect reduced exposure, improved resilience, or operational gains.
  - Board members want to see progress over time and understand how cyber investments are delivering value. For example: "Our recent efforts reduced vulnerability exposure by 40%, helping ensure uninterrupted operations during peak customer periods." These results give confidence that the organization is not just reacting to threats but maturing its security posture with strategic intent.

- **Encourage ownership**:

  - The board plays a key role in governing cyber risk, and that responsibility extends beyond the CISO. It includes every C-suite leader, from operations to finance to legal. Help the board see that cybersecurity is a collective responsibility, not a siloed function. Returning to our earlier analogy, keeping the playground safe isn't just the principal's job. It also involves support from, for example, the parent-teacher association and teachers, and needs the cooperation of students. Likewise, organizational cyber resilience relies on shared awareness, decision-making, and accountability across the leadership team.
  - Encourage collaboration by recommending participation in industry-wide information-sharing initiatives such as Information Sharing and Analysis Centers (ISACs). These platforms help organizations stay ahead of emerging threats and learn from sector-wide incidents, which will strengthen their overall cyber posture.
  - You could also encourage board directors to boost their oversight role by participating in cybersecurity governance programs offered by director institutes and board associations. These initiatives are designed to equip boards with the knowledge and confidence to navigate cyber risks as part of their broader fiduciary responsibilities.

These strategies will help the board in prioritizing expenditures on mitigation efforts, understanding the actual return on investments and recognizing the value that you, as the CISO, bring to the organization when you develop programs and provide tangible insights into which initiatives are successful or not.

It's also worth assessing whether your board believes they're investing appropriately in cybersecurity. Do they believe that they are well equipped in protecting their crown jewels? If not, consider how this can be improved. Does the board understand their exposure to risks? Have all the necessary risk transfer options been considered? It is important for organizations to keep up with current affairs and be prepared for regulatory changes. How are they maintaining foresight and factoring in future economic drivers and digital transformation impacts on cyber risk?

If there are any tough questions directed at you from the board, stay calm, answer confidently, and redirect the focus to facts. Another effective approach is to bring the conversation back to the fundamentals. In cybersecurity, this often means anchoring discussions in a consistent framework such as an Information Security Management System (ISMS), the NIST Cybersecurity Framework, or another widely accepted standard. While the external environment continues to evolve, these frameworks offer a stable point of reference that helps the board make sense of complexity and also helps to build their confidence in the organization's approach to managing risk.

The art of connection

Influencing the C-suite is about relationships, as well as clear and simple communication. Each executive contributes a unique perspective, shaped by their responsibilities. Good CISOs adapt their messaging to resonate with these unique viewpoints.

As I've always shared in my keynote speeches, it's never just about business. It's always personal. Our goal is to take the journey with our stakeholders, evolving from a technical advisor into a truly trusted partner.

When CISOs align cybersecurity with their peers' goals and/or incentives, they unlock greater potential for collaboration. This is also when transformation happens.

In this final segment of the chapter, I will share a simple but very powerful way of understanding the different personalities of our stakeholders better so that we can communicate more effectively with them.

Decoding executive personalities

Understanding the motivations of your C-suite stakeholders is vital, but to truly connect, you need to go deeper, to the core of how they think, act, and communicate. Over the years, I've worked with diverse personalities and founded communities of more than 4,000 cyber leaders. Along the way, I've developed a knack for stakeholder management, recognizing that successful communication is as much about personality alignment as it is about content.

This is where personality frameworks come into play. Tools such as the Myers-Briggs Type Indicator, the Enneagram, or the dominance, influence, steadiness, conscientiousness (DISC) assessment are well-known; however, the DOPE Personality Model is my personal favorite due to its simplicity and applicability.

The DOPE model was created by Richard M. Stephenson (`https://richardstep.com/dope-personality-type-quiz/`) to categorize personalities into four easy-to-remember bird types: **Doves, Owls, Peacocks,** and **Eagles**. Each bird represents a unique feature that influences communication preferences and decision-making styles.

Let's have a look at the DOPE birds.

The Dove: the harmonizer

Doves are empathetic, compassionate, and people oriented. They thrive in harmonious and collaborative surroundings, yet they tend to avoid conflict and risk-taking.

Common traits: Loyal, team players, prefer consensus over conflict.

How to engage them: Emphasize teamwork, shared goals, and the significance of collaboration. Avoid using forceful or overly direct words, which may make them uncomfortable. Speak to their desire for togetherness and alignment.

As an example, in the event of a breach, a dove may respond positively to a statement such as "I understand this situation is stressful for everyone. We've isolated the affected systems to minimize disruption to the team's work. To prevent this in the future, I recommend rolling out training programs that will empower employees to recognize threats without feeling overwhelmed." Such an approach is consistent with their desire for unity and a harmonious work atmosphere.

The Eagle: the driver

Eagles are brave, decisive, and results-focused. They excel in high-pressure situations and thrive on challenges, but their direct nature can sometimes come across as abrupt or abrasive. Eagles respect efficiency and expect swift action.

Common traits: Confident, competitive, direct.

How to engage them: Use concise, result-oriented language that focuses on outcomes and impact. Skip unnecessary details and provide high-level takeaways that appeal to their need for quick, effective decision-making.

An Eagle might respond to a breach with urgency and demand immediate fixes, expecting action plans and timelines to be clear and efficient. They will likely take to clear and result-oriented action statements such as, "We've isolated the affected systems to prevent further damage, and the team is deploying a patch that will neutralize the threat within the next two hours. Meanwhile, here's a step-by-step timeline for full containment and recovery over the next 24 hours."

The Owl: the analyst

Owls are logical, methodical, and detail oriented. They excel in environments that prioritize structure, evidence, and well-supported arguments. They are risk averse by nature and make cautious and meticulous decisions.

Common traits: Analytical, perfectionist, focused on facts and data.

How to engage them: Provide well-structured, evidence-based arguments backed up by data and logical reasoning. They favor precision and clarity, so avoid vague or highly emotional appeals.

An owl may require detailed documentation before agreeing to the next steps. If you are dealing with an incident, they will likely want a thorough analysis, such as "We've identified the breach's origin: a phishing email that compromised a user's credentials. Our preliminary analysis shows lateral movement in the network, targeting the finance database. The affected systems have been isolated, and a patch to neutralize the threat is being deployed."

Provide data-backed justification for solutions you plan to implement, and be sure to share a comprehensive plan with them to gain their buy-in. This will speak to their analytical mindset and data-driven approach.

The Peacock: the motivator

Peacocks exude charisma, enthusiasm, and optimism. They thrive on recognition, creativity, and engaging narratives. They are often the life of the room, bringing energy and excitement to discussions.

Common traits: Energetic, outgoing, creative.

How to engage them: Use inspiring stories, emphasize success, and maintain a dynamic, upbeat tone. Avoid overly dry or detail-heavy discussions that might lose their attention. Instead, connect with their desire for recognition and innovative ideas.

For example, a peacock might respond enthusiastically to a statement such as "This cybersecurity program is a game-changer – it positions us as industry leaders in innovation and trust, setting a new standard for others to follow." This approach connects with their need for recognition as well as their enthusiasm for daring new ideas.

Adapting your communication to improve alignment

Tailoring your message to your audience is a strategic lever. The more you understand how different executives prefer to receive information, the more effectively you can influence outcomes. The DOPE framework provides a useful lens for this.

The following table offers quick-reference suggestions on how to adapt your communication style to each archetype, helping you align more closely with their priorities and decision-making preferences:

Trait	Dove	Owl	Peacock	Eagle
Primary Focus	Team harmony and minimizing disruption.	Logical analysis and understanding root causes.	Innovation, communication, and big-picture vision.	Quick decision-making and achieving results.
Communication Style	Collaborative and empathetic.	Detailed, data-driven, and logical.	Enthusiastic and visionary.	Direct, concise, and action oriented.
Response to Breach	Concerned about people's impact and team well-being. Wants to ensure minimal stress for employees.	Asks for comprehensive details about what happened and why. Prioritizes data and root cause.	Wants to discuss reputation management and how to position the company as resilient and innovative.	Demands immediate fixes and clear timelines for resolution.
Preferred Action Plan	Collaborative, focusing on minimizing tension within teams.	Thorough and methodical, based on evidence and analysis.	Optimistic, emphasizing future opportunities.	Fast and results-driven, emphasizing speed and efficiency.
Strengths	Nurturing a team-first environment; ensuring policies don't overwhelm employees.	Deep dive into systems, forensics, and precise execution.	Energizing stakeholders; gaining buy-in for new initiatives.	Leading during crises; driving action and accountability.
Challenges	May avoid confrontation or delay decisions to maintain harmony.	Can overanalyze and delay actions during critical moments.	Might focus on flashy solutions over practical ones.	May overlook details or team concerns in their drive for results.

Although most people have a dominant bird type, most also exhibit characteristics of two bird types. Understanding these blends, coupled with your own dominant bird type, can help you tailor your communication style to connect with others, create trust, and develop meaningful collaboration.

Aligning cybersecurity with the C-suite — a recap

Throughout this chapter, we've explored how to tailor cybersecurity messaging to key players in the C-suite, from the CEO to the CFO, the CRO, the CIO, and the board. Each role brings unique perspectives, priorities, and communication preferences.

The DOPE Personality Model offers another layer to this insight, enabling you to adapt your messaging further, not only to roles but also to individual characteristics. By aligning with each executive's personality – whether through empathy for Doves, data for Owls, results for Eagles, and so on – you can turn challenges into opportunities for connection.

Ultimately, the role of the CISO is not just to secure the organization but to bridge the gap between technical expertise and strategic leadership. When CISOs connect with their peers on a personal level, tailoring their language, analogies, and metrics to resonate with different perspectives, they elevate their influence from technical advisors to trusted partners.

In the C-suite schoolyard, this ability to connect, influence, and lead is the key to creating a safe, innovative, and collaborative environment. In this environment, every stakeholder is empowered to contribute to a resilient future, one that is defined by trust.

David's key takeaways — Navigating the C-Suite, boards and DOPE dynamics

Shamane has shared an intriguing account of how to navigate powerful stakeholders in this chapter, including executive management and the board. As a CISO, CIO and Risk Executive, I've personally spent many hours in the boardroom working with different personalities across many companies. Successfully navigating this dynamic is complex; this is why Shamane's playbook here is so valuable. The modern CISO must be great at this, and their own career survival is often dependent on developing subtle skills in the boardroom. Just being good is not going to be enough.

Here are the key points from Shamane's chapter:

- *Use personas for board engagement.* As a CISO engaging with board members, assigning different personas based on each stakeholder's background and priorities, and tailoring your communication to these, can significantly improve your effectiveness and security program success.

- *Make the effort to align cybersecurity with the business.* The goal for CISOs is to become trusted partners. You can do this by aligning your cybersecurity programs with the overall business goals and values.

- *Speak the language of the board.* Board members will trust recommendations more when presented in familiar business terms rather than technical jargon. Speaking their language demonstrates you understand their priorities and helps you get the buy-in you need from them, transforming you from a technical specialist into a trusted business advisor.

- *Align security initiatives with individual board member agendas.* Each board member typically champions different priorities, such as growth, efficiency, or compliance. When you align security initiatives with their individual agendas, you convert potential sceptics into advocates who could then champion your security program.

14
Systems Thinking for CISOs

A day in the life of a CISO invariably feels like a series of firefighting activities. You have many issues and incidents to deal with, and these are never-ending. It brings to mind the analogy of drinking from the firehose, and there is rarely any appreciation shown for this effort.

How, then, does the CISO act in a way that is more strategic and considers the bigger picture? One such approach is to consider **systems thinking**.

Systems thinking promotes a culture of continuous learning and adaptation. By regularly analyzing the interactions and performance of the security system, CISOs can identify improvement opportunities, refine strategies, and stay ahead of emerging threats.

The systems thinking approach requires a shift in mindset from a reductionist, siloed approach to a more integrated, holistic perspective. For the CISO, this means developing skills in systems analysis, understanding complex interactions, and fostering a culture of collaborative, strategic thinking about cybersecurity.

The truth is that you will be shifting between the normal chaos of the day and trying to step back to look at the bigger picture. This is not an easy thing to achieve, and often the short-term urgent tasks will overtake the more long-term priority items.

With that, it is my pleasure to introduce **Phoram Mehta**, vice president and **head of international cyber risk** at **PayPal**. During his long career with the company, commencing as principal information security architect, he has also held the APAC CISO role.

Phoram is a strong advocate for applying systems thinking and believes that it provides a holistic and strategic approach to managing cybersecurity challenges.

Systems thinking for the CISO

Phoram Mehta

This chapter includes frameworks and practices on systems thinking, which I personally believe can be applied in my role as a security leader. Hopefully, you will also gain some insights and ideas to explore in your own role as CISO.

As our field continues to get more complex by the day, and the number of threats, security requirements, and constraints also continues to rise, one must wonder whether a fundamental shift in how we approach enterprise cybersecurity is required.

While still small, an increasing group of experienced leaders believe that systems thinking may have some answers. I am sure that these thoughts and the sharing of my experience in this chapter, along with all the other sharing by David and fellow security leaders in this book, will provoke further discussions and new approaches to security management challenges faced by those responsible for managing cyber risk.

But first, allow me to provide some background for this approach and where it came from.

The evolution of problem-solving

The unique ability of our species to solve problems is what has enabled us to maintain our top position in the food chain, discover fascinating laws of physics, and build systems that enable us to live a life full of conveniences and comfort.

Every major era of problem-solving has required some foundational understanding and methodology to analyze the problem and then figure out one or more possible solutions.

From Industrial Revolution to digital transformation

The Industrial Revolution marked a pivotal moment in human history, introducing a systematic approach to solving complex problems based on the reductionist theory first proposed by René Descartes in *Discourse on the Method of Rightly Conducting One's Reason and of Seeking Truth in the Sciences* (1637). This approach was elegantly simple: break down seemingly insurmountable challenges into smaller, manageable components, solve them individually, and then reconstruct the solution. This simple methodology transformed manufacturing, engineering, and countless other fields throughout the 19th and 20th centuries.

This approach gave birth to assembly lines, standardized processes, and the very foundation of modern manufacturing. Henry Ford's revolutionary production line for the Model T wasn't just about building cars faster; it was about breaking down a complex process into its constituent parts, optimizing each step, and creating a repeatable system that could scale efficiently.

As we venture deeper into the 21st century, we're discovering that digital transformation requires a different perspective, however. The complexity of modern systems isn't just in their components, but in the intricate web of interactions between these components, their operators, and their environment.

The digital acceleration

I've experienced a constant in my career, and that is that the velocity of digital change continues to accelerate. I'm certain that this trend will continue to be a factor that we all have to learn to deal with.

When you think about today's business landscape, it is now almost entirely digital. Operations that once took days or weeks are now executed in seconds. For example:

- Financial transactions that required physical paperwork and multiple bank visits now occur instantly through digital platforms
- Car assembly, while still physical in nature, is orchestrated by sophisticated digital systems that coordinate thousands of components and processes in real time
- Supply chain management has evolved from manual tracking and phone calls to automated systems that optimize routes and inventory in milliseconds

This acceleration has brought unprecedented efficiency, but it has also introduced new complexities. In our rush to embrace digital transformation, we sometimes forget a crucial fact: these systems, no matter how automated, are ultimately socio-technical in nature. They are designed, operated, maintained, and used by people. This human element introduces variables that cannot be reduced to simple components and reassembled.

The case for holistic thinking in modern systems

The limitations of reductionist thinking become apparent when we consider modern digital systems. Breaking down a problem into its smallest components might help us understand individual elements, but it can blind us to the crucial interactions between these elements. In a socio-technical system, these interactions often matter more than the individual components themselves.

Consider a modern banking system:

- The technology stack might be flawless
- The security protocols might be state-of-the-art
- The user interface might be intuitive

Yet, if the interactions between these components and their human operators aren't carefully considered, the system remains vulnerable. A perfectly secure system can be compromised by social engineering, while a technically vulnerable system might remain safe due to strong human oversight and robust processes.

Systems thinking – a framework for complex challenges

In my experience, systems thinking offers a more comprehensive approach compared with the conventional reductionist method to understanding and managing modern digital environments. It acknowledges that systems are dynamic entities that constantly evolve based on:

- The behavior and decisions of their operators
- Changes in the external environment
- Modifications to individual components
- The complex interactions between all these elements

This approach is particularly relevant in cybersecurity, where the traditional perimeter-based security model has given way to a more fluid and dynamic understanding of organizational security. The modern security perimeter is no longer a fixed boundary; it is a constantly shifting area that, in addition to the enterprise network, also includes:

- Cloud services and applications
- Remote work environments
- Mobile devices
- Internet of Things (IoT) systems
- Third-party vendors and partners

To break this down further, key factors somewhat unique to our industry that make systems thinking an ideal candidate for cybersecurity are:

- Dynamic threat landscape:
    - Adversaries constantly evolve their techniques
    - New vulnerabilities emerge regularly
    - Attack surfaces expand with technological advancement

- Complex interconnections:

  - Systems interact with multiple stakeholders

  - Security measures affect business processes

  - Technical solutions impact user behavior

- Rapid technological evolution:

  - Emerging technologies create new opportunities and risks

  - Innovation requires constant adaptation of security measures

  - Integration of legacy and modern systems present unique challenges

For these reasons, the cybersecurity industry uniquely exemplifies why adapting a systems thinking approach is crucial in the modern digital age.

Systems thinking principles in an enterprise cyber system

The interconnected nature of organizations these days requires a holistic approach to domains such as risk management. Like pain in the body, risk may originate in localized areas but can have wide-ranging effects and can be quite debilitating. I truly believe systems thinking provides a framework that CISOs can use to develop security programs that mirror the complexity and adaptability of natural systems such as the human body.

Let's explore how each systems thinking component applies to cybersecurity:

- **Interconnectedness**: *"Our lives, our fortunes and our sacred honor."* This line from the United States Declaration of Independence is a reminder of the commitment the signers were prepared to make for the cause of American independence. It's also an acknowledgment of the interconnectedness they felt between each other in their vision of the future for the new enterprise.

  It is time that CISOs truly embrace a similar mindset. For decades, security organizations have been trying to implement solutions without achieving the desired results, and the most they have been able to do about behavior change is print posters that read "Security is everyone's business."

CISOs should strive to understand how everything inside an organization is interconnected and build programs with the following attributes:

- Recognition that security measures affect all aspects of business operations. From the 92 million records lost in the 2004 AOL data breach (`https://www.nytimes.com/2004/06/23/technology/aol-engineer-sold-92-million-names-to-spammer-us-says.html`) to today, security programs and the role of a CISO have changed drastically. Hence, it is no longer enough for our programs to be focused only on the technical aspects of cybersecurity.

- An understanding of how changes in one area impact others. Adoption of a RAG solution to create a customer-facing AI experience, for example, won't just affect security, but it will have implications on privacy, legal, ethics, product, operations, and many other areas.

- Consideration of both direct and indirect effects of security decisions. For instance, blocking access to certain public websites, external storage devices, and other security restrictions while closing data leakage options may also result in employees trying to find workarounds, such as installing certain software that possesses data transfer capability, deploying shadow cloud instances that are unsanctioned and can indirectly lead to creating new risks for the organization.

- **Synthesis**: To truly know the system, one has to understand the whole and the parts at the same time:

  - Look at the whole system rather than individual parts. For instance, when a bug bounty program was introduced in one of the firms I worked at, it did eventually change the entire product lifecycle and helped security champions integrated with product teams to share live examples from the bug bounty submissions and explain do's and don'ts clearly.

  - Understand how different security measures work together. A layered security strategy requires that we understand the role that controls at each layer play to ultimately form an effective overall defense.

  - Identify patterns and relationships in security incidents. I'm referring here to post-incident analysis to specifically understand the patterns where a layered strategy may not be effective under certain circumstances.

- **Feedback loops:** This refers to implementing continuous monitoring and improvement. In an assume-breach mindset, which many security functions have come to adopt, lessons learned are equally, if not more, important than any plans to detect and prevent security incidents.

  In 2011, when Dmitri Alperovitch (CrowdStrike co-founder) talked about two types of companies, those that are breached and those that don't know that they are breached, the industry was not quite ready to accept the grim future ahead. Today, most large enterprises have at last accepted this and prioritized cyber resilience as part of the security program. Continuous improvement is a key part of this, including:

  - Learning from security incidents and near-misses. Consider establishing a learning loop, outside of the incident response and reporting playbook, to investigate every incident and adverse event for the sheer purpose of collecting feedback on errors, misconfigurations, or other gaps that should be remediated and prevented in the future.
  - Adjusting security measures based on operational feedback. With security budgets rising, CISOs are being asked to help find ways to optimize their spending. Feedback loops are a good way to evaluate the effectiveness of specific investments made and make appropriate changes.

- **Causality:** This refers to understanding the root causes of security incidents:
  - Identify systemic vulnerabilities. It has often been the case that incidents with the biggest impact are not due to a zero-day or sophisticated attack vector. Systemic issues in an organization have an interesting way of claiming their day in the limelight too, and often are only identified when proper due diligence is performed. Even regulations in certain jurisdictions have started requiring organizations to establish processes to identify systemic material weaknesses. This typically occurs when the risk acceptance process is entirely dependent on a single metric, such as severity. Taking the time to understand whether the organization has vulnerabilities that never seem to get remediated can help identify causes of potential systemic issues.

- Recognize patterns in security breaches. Correlation doesn't always equate to causality, but it can be a good starting point to identify repeated behavior that contributes in some way to incidents or breaches. For example, weak **multi-factor authentication (MFA)** could be the cause of many incidents, but the fact that most checks and audits are passing could lead the CISO to believe that the presence of MFA, no matter how weak, cannot possibly be the cause of those incidents.

- **Systems structure**: This primarily refers to designing security architectures that support business objectives.

In today's world, every company has either already undergone or is in the process of undergoing digital transformation. Cyber risks are now as important, if not more so, than traditional risk domains within operational aspects of an enterprise strategy. It is therefore critical that system design takes security into consideration as early in the process as possible. This includes:

- Building in redundancy and resilience. This is a more recent concern for CISOs. Since the 2024 CrowdStrike outage incident, CISOs are not only being increasingly put in charge of cyber resilience, but as regulations such as DORA (European Union), CPS 230 (Australia), and so on require a focus on operational risk, including cyber, security programs now need to prioritize availability as much as confidentiality and integrity.

- Creating adaptive security frameworks. The history of data breaches around the world has shown us that point-in-time assessments have limited value. Seeing how rapidly technology stacks, third-party dependencies, and expectations change, it is important to adapt a security framework that is equally dynamic to allow CISOs to communicate risks, investment asks, and decision-making requests in a terminology that is well understood and consistent across business units.

- **Dynamic equilibrium**: This refers to maintaining a balanced state. In the context of cybersecurity, it includes:

- Protecting the enterprise while enabling business growth. For the longest time, the primary trade-offs CISOs and security teams focused their entire attention on were protection versus convenience. This equation has now changed to protection versus enablement. Businesses are actively leveraging strong security as a differentiator and expect CISOs to support key growth initiatives without compromising regulatory compliance.

- Balancing security, compliance, and risk management requirements with operational needs. This is extremely important for security programs and the key difference between mature programs and those driven primarily by compliance or doing the bare minimum.

- Adapting to changing threat and regulatory landscapes. Whatever hopes harmonization of USB-C as a phone charging standard offered to the world, for example, quickly dissipated when it came to the desire to harmonize cyber risk regulatory requirements. Hence, the onus is on CISOs to build an intelligence layer that enables dynamic equilibrium between foundational cyber hygiene and disparate requirements between national, sectoral, regional, and global regulatory landscapes. This is similar to the rapid evolution of threats and the need to build agility as a capability to respond and, ideally, prevent new attack vectors.

That's more than a mouthful, I agree. If you are still reading and somewhat aligned, or at least intrigued, let's push for another mindset shift – the primary objective of the CISO and thereby the security team is no longer to prevent every single attack, or even to achieve compliance with the strictest of regulatory requirements. It is without a doubt to enable the business to leverage technology advancements, partnerships, and other avenues made possible through innovation, while managing the risk of a cyber incident, attack, or requirement from regulators, partners, customers and other key stakeholders.

Designing an enterprise cybersecurity program with a systems thinking approach

My view is that a truly resilient system must meet the following foundational expectations:

- Maintains essential functions during disruptions
- Recovers quickly from security incidents
- Learns and adapts from experiences
- Evolves to meet new challenges

This requires **comprehensive cyber resilience**:

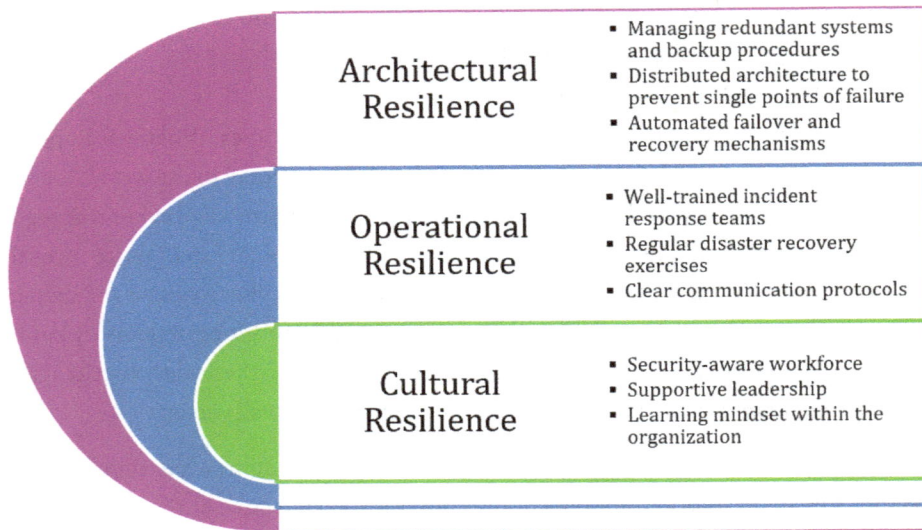

Architectural Resilience	• Managing redundant systems and backup procedures • Distributed architecture to prevent single points of failure • Automated failover and recovery mechanisms
Operational Resilience	• Well-trained incident response teams • Regular disaster recovery exercises • Clear communication protocols
Cultural Resilience	• Security-aware workforce • Supportive leadership • Learning mindset within the organization

Figure 14.1: Comprehensive cyber resilience

As shown in the preceding figure, comprehensive cyber resilience requires thinking beyond a singular technology infrastructure or even a data center. It requires a deep understanding and interconnectedness between foundational elements, starting with people and the company culture, then strong operational hygiene through mature processes, and finally, a flexible architecture that can meet changing business needs.

A system should also focus (at least equally) on collecting metrics to make sure the feedback loops are monitoring for any anomalous behavior in the system so that the operators can react in a timely manner, as well as ensuring that the cybersecurity program in place is effective.

Traditional security metrics often focus on technical indicators:

- Number of incidents
- Time to detect
- Patch compliance rates

However, a systems thinking approach requires more comprehensive measurement, encompassing business impact metrics, adaptation metrics, and cultural metrics. For example:

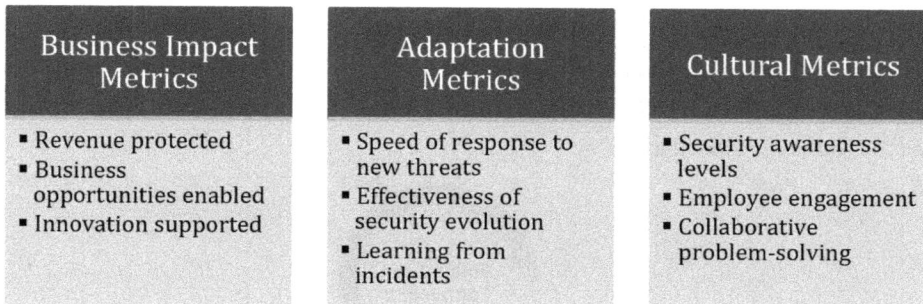

Business Impact Metrics	Adaptation Metrics	Cultural Metrics
• Revenue protected • Business opportunities enabled • Innovation supported	• Speed of response to new threats • Effectiveness of security evolution • Learning from incidents	• Security awareness levels • Employee engagement • Collaborative problem-solving

Figure 14.2: Examples of relevant metrics

As organizations continue their digital transformation journey, the security function must also evolve to meet new challenges. This evolution requires continuous upskilling, cultural transformation, mindset shifts, and practicing innovation:

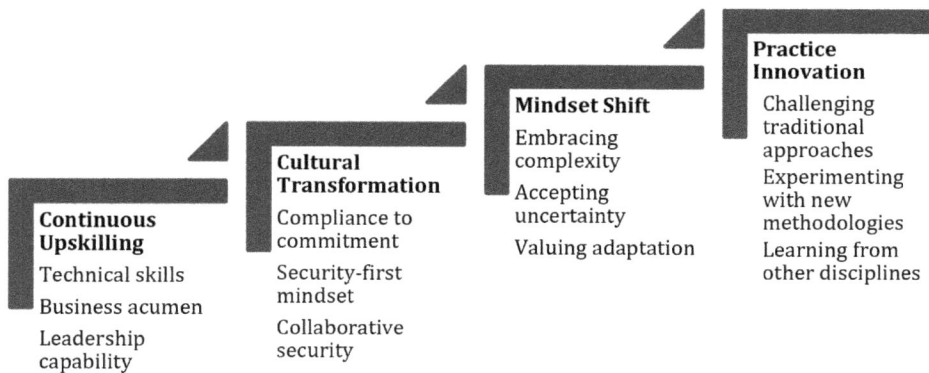

Practice Innovation

Challenging traditional approaches

Experimenting with new methodologies

Learning from other disciplines

Mindset Shift

Embracing complexity

Accepting uncertainty

Valuing adaptation

Cultural Transformation

Compliance to commitment

Security-first mindset

Collaborative security

Continuous Upskilling

Technical skills

Business acumen

Leadership capability

Figure 14.3: Evolution of a cyber team

As technologies, business models, and other aspects of an enterprise system continue to change, CISOs should make an effort to effect change in areas in their control, such as those I have discussed here.

Embracing systems thinking in cybersecurity

To recap the case for applying systems thinking to cybersecurity, the journey from the Industrial Revolution to today's digital age has taught us valuable lessons about problem-solving and system management, and while breaking down complex problems into smaller components remains useful, modern cybersecurity challenges require a more holistic approach. Systems thinking provides the framework needed to:

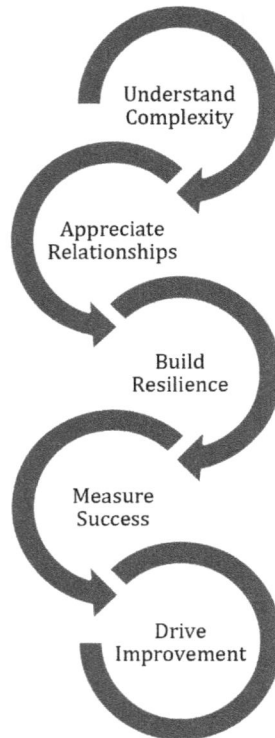

Figure 14.4: The value of systems thinking

As we look to the future, successful cybersecurity leaders will be those who can:

- Think systemically about security challenges
- Build adaptive and resilient security programs
- Foster a culture of continuous learning and improvement
- Balance security requirements with business needs
- Embrace innovation while managing risk

The path forward requires us to challenge our assumptions, update our practices, and continuously evolve our approach to security. By embracing systems thinking, we can build security programs that not only protect our organizations today but also adapt and grow to meet the challenges of tomorrow.

Practical applications and strategic implementation of systems thinking by CISOs

This section presents a playbook for CISOs to put the concepts introduced throughout this chapter into practice.

Note that it is not necessary or recommended to apply everything at once. Organizations, depending on the culture, technology, and security program journey, as well as competing business priorities, may directly benefit from or reject changes at fundamental levels. CISOs and other leaders should make sure that they have first spent enough time discussing systems thinking with their team and identifying areas that seem like the right fit to devise a plan for rolling it out within the enterprise.

The following subsections will help CISOs consider key components of systems thinking to prioritize and implement, and also to assess and make appropriate adjustments as they proceed.

Holistic risk management

Systems thinking revolutionizes how CISOs approach risk management by encouraging them to view enterprise infrastructure as an interconnected network. This perspective can reveal critical insights that might be missed when examining security elements in isolation.

In practice, this means understanding that a vulnerability in one system could have cascading effects throughout the organization. For example, a seemingly minor weakness in an HR portal might provide attackers with the foothold needed to access more critical systems. By mapping interconnections like these, CISOs can:

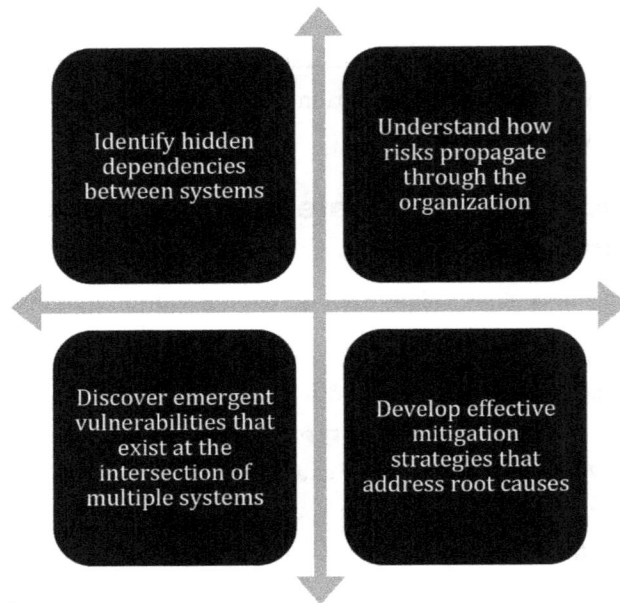

Figure 14.5: Benefits of mapping interconnections in risk management

A systems-based risk management approach also considers the temporal aspect of risk. I remember times when it was extremely hard to zoom out from the day-to-day operational matters enough to realize how the organization and infrastructure, as well as the interactions between them, were changing. Rather than viewing risks as static entities, this approach recognizes that they evolve over time through:

- Changes in the threat landscape
- Evolution of business processes
- Introduction of new technologies
- Shifts in organizational structure

This dynamic view enables more effective risk prioritization and resource allocation. Instead of focusing solely on individual risk scores, CISOs can consider:

- Risk velocity (how quickly a risk can materialize)
- Risk interconnectedness (how one risk might trigger others)
- Risk persistence (how long a risk might remain relevant)
- Risk adaptability (how risks might evolve in response to controls)

Adaptive security strategy

An adaptive security strategy built on systems thinking principles enables organizations to respond effectively to changing threats while maintaining operational efficiency. This approach recognizes that security cannot be static in a dynamic environment. As a leader, this, in my opinion, is much more important than understanding the details of every incident and feeling like one is in control of point-in-time threats.

Key elements of an adaptive security strategy include:

- Continuous assessment
- Flexible controls
- Mechanisms for learning from past successes and failures

Here are some examples for each of these elements:

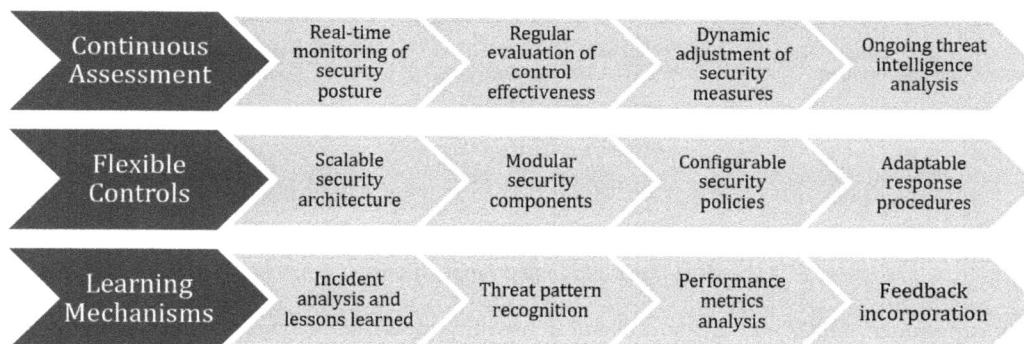

Continuous Assessment	Real-time monitoring of security posture	Regular evaluation of control effectiveness	Dynamic adjustment of security measures	Ongoing threat intelligence analysis
Flexible Controls	Scalable security architecture	Modular security components	Configurable security policies	Adaptable response procedures
Learning Mechanisms	Incident analysis and lessons learned	Threat pattern recognition	Performance metrics analysis	Feedback incorporation

Figure 14.6: Key elements of an adaptive security strategy

The adaptive strategy must also account for:

- Emerging technologies and their security implications
- Changes in business processes and requirements
- Evolution of regulatory requirements
- Shifts in organizational structure

Shared responsibilities

Systems thinking naturally leads to the breakdown of organizational silos by highlighting the interconnected nature of security challenges. This integration is crucial for effective security management. With increasing dependency on cloud, **software as a service (SaaS)**, and other partners, it is important for CISOs to adopt and promote a shared responsibility model. Even internally within an organization, a CISO should understand and map various dependencies for tech risk, resilience, cybersecurity, and other protection as well as enablement objectives. As security continues its journey from the basement to the boardroom, the scope of responsibilities, and thereby the impact, of CISOs also evolves.

Practical approaches to breaking down silos include:

- Creating cross-functional teams
- Developing integrated processes
- Leveraging communication channels

Here are some examples of what this could look like:

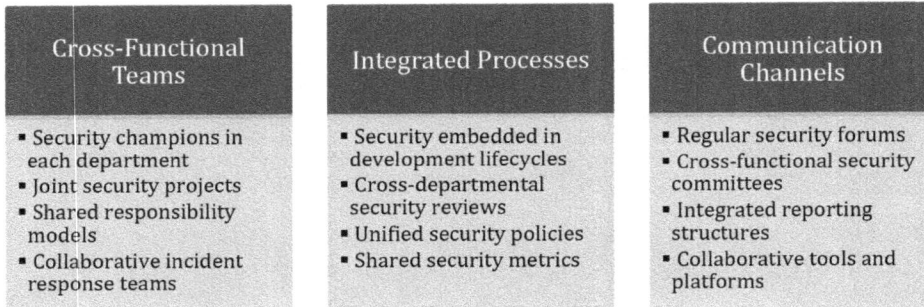

Cross-Functional Teams	Integrated Processes	Communication Channels
▪ Security champions in each department ▪ Joint security projects ▪ Shared responsibility models ▪ Collaborative incident response teams	▪ Security embedded in development lifecycles ▪ Cross-departmental security reviews ▪ Unified security policies ▪ Shared security metrics	▪ Regular security forums ▪ Cross-functional security committees ▪ Integrated reporting structures ▪ Collaborative tools and platforms

Figure 14.7: Breaking down silos and promoting shared responsibilities

In my experience, CISOs who are successful in breaking down silos achieve one or more of the following benefits:

- Improved operational efficiency
- Enhanced innovation capability
- Better resource utilization
- Stronger organizational resilience

Integrating feedback into the security lifecycle

Feedback loops are crucial mechanisms for maintaining and improving security posture. Systems thinking helps identify and leverage these loops effectively. On multiple occasions in my career, I have seen leaders who are not sure whether things are moving in the right direction due to a lack of strong feedback loops.

Here are some suggestions on the types of security feedback loops to consider building:

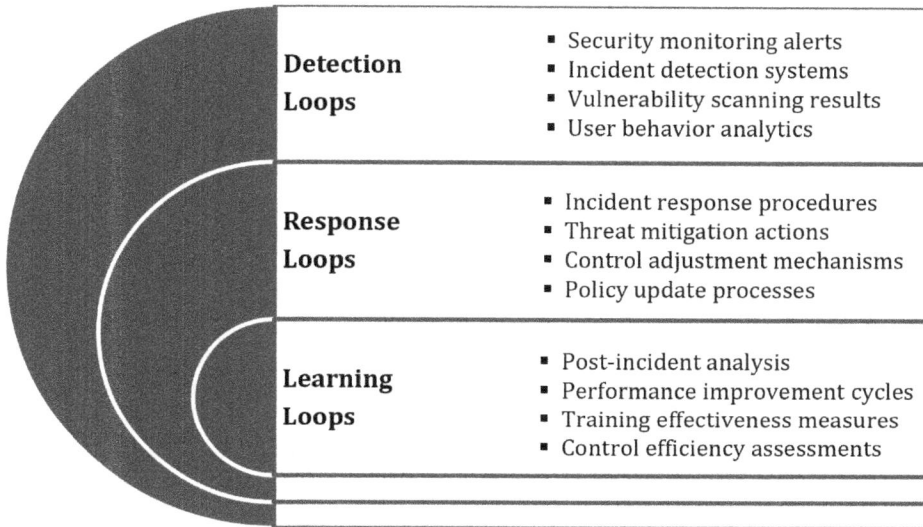

Detection Loops	■ Security monitoring alerts ■ Incident detection systems ■ Vulnerability scanning results ■ User behavior analytics
Response Loops	■ Incident response procedures ■ Threat mitigation actions ■ Control adjustment mechanisms ■ Policy update processes
Learning Loops	■ Post-incident analysis ■ Performance improvement cycles ■ Training effectiveness measures ■ Control efficiency assessments

Figure 14.8: Feedback loops to consider

Understanding and implementing these loops enables:

- Faster threat detection and response
- More effective security controls
- Better resource allocation
- Continuous improvement

Strategic planning

Systems thinking supports long-term strategic planning by providing a framework for understanding how security needs will evolve over time.

Key elements of long-term security planning include:

- Technology evolution
- Capability development
- Resource planning

Here are some examples of what this may mean:

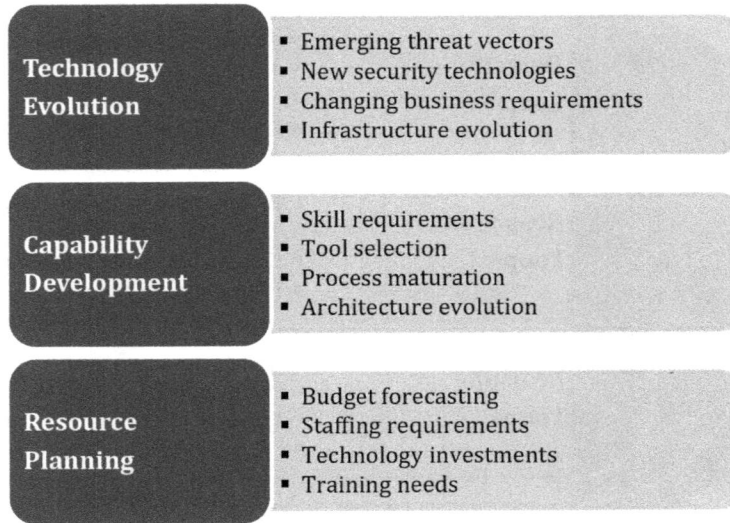

Technology Evolution
- Emerging threat vectors
- New security technologies
- Changing business requirements
- Infrastructure evolution

Capability Development
- Skill requirements
- Tool selection
- Process maturation
- Architecture evolution

Resource Planning
- Budget forecasting
- Staffing requirements
- Technology investments
- Training needs

Figure 14.9: Approach to long-term strategic planning

This long-term view enables:

- Better alignment with business strategy
- More efficient resource allocation
- Improved risk management
- Greater organizational resilience

Culture and insider threat management

Systems thinking recognizes that human behavior and organizational culture are fundamental to security effectiveness.

The meaning of trust continues to evolve outside and within an organization. Hence, it is imperative to ensure that the culture and behavior align with the security philosophy.

Key areas to focus on when assessing the overall state of enterprise insider threat and managing it include:

- Policy design
- Behavior analysis
- Cultural development

This may look like this:

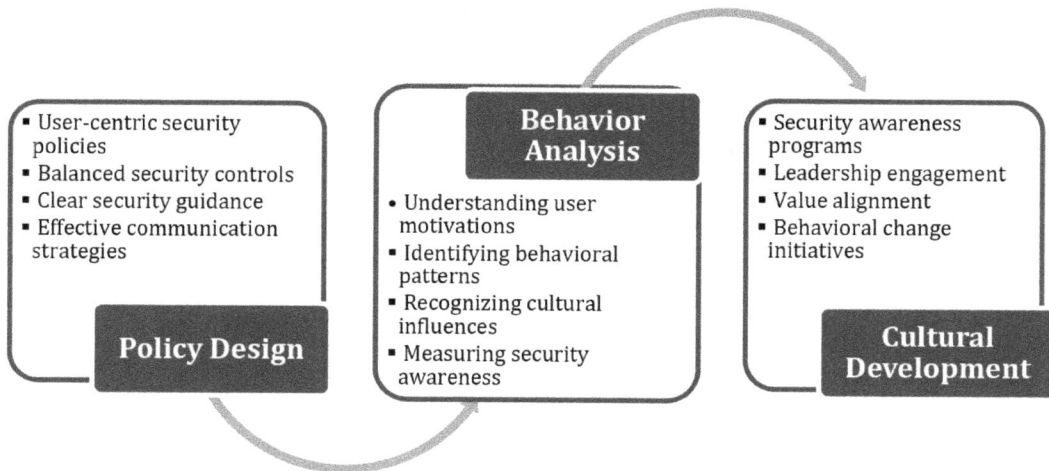

Figure 14.10: Taking a human-centric approach

This human-centric approach leads to:

- Better security compliance
- Stronger security culture
- More effective controls
- Reduced security incidents

Resource optimization

Systems thinking enables more efficient resource allocation by providing a comprehensive view of security needs and impacts.

A CISO spends a considerable amount of their time trying to optimize protection against cost. Employing some of these tactics from systems thinking will help ensure a sustainable budget while achieving key results.

To optimize resources, key areas of focus include:

- Resource allocation strategy
- Performance monitoring
- Resource analysis

Here are a few examples of these:

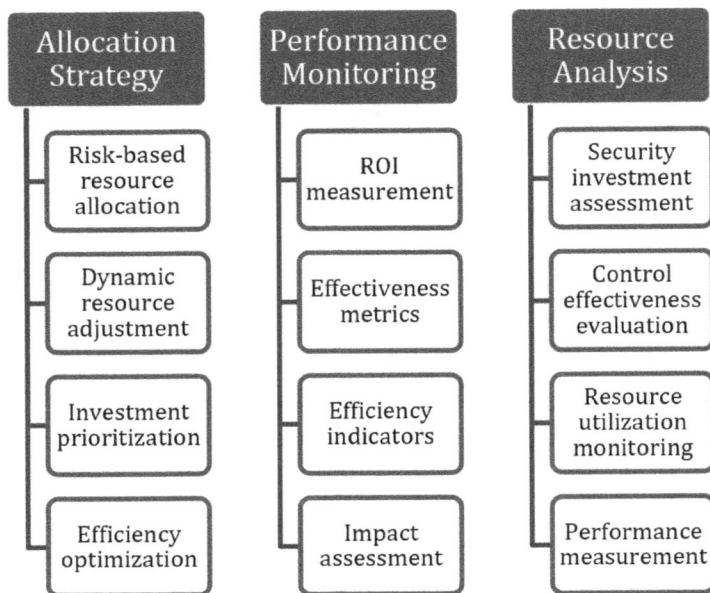

Allocation Strategy	Performance Monitoring	Resource Analysis
Risk-based resource allocation	ROI measurement	Security investment assessment
Dynamic resource adjustment	Effectiveness metrics	Control effectiveness evaluation
Investment prioritization	Efficiency indicators	Resource utilization monitoring
Efficiency optimization	Impact assessment	Performance measurement

Figure 14.11: Resource optimization approach

This approach ensures:

- Optimal resource utilization
- Better security outcomes
- Improved cost efficiency
- Greater organizational value

Alignment with business objectives

Ultimately, the reason the CISO and the security function exist is to support business objectives. It is therefore critical that the CISO invests appropriate time and effort into making sure the security function understands this link and ensuring strong alignment with the overall business strategy and objectives.

This, I believe, has been the most important change – two to three decades ago, security functions were being run by business leaders due to the need for management experience at the cost of technical skills, but today we need leaders who are technically adept. To be a good CISO, however, you also need a strong understanding of business objectives and the ability to apply integrated approaches such as systems thinking to lead an effective security program.

Key areas to focus on aligning with business objectives are:

- Strategic integration
- Value creation
- Performance measurement

Here are some examples to help you:

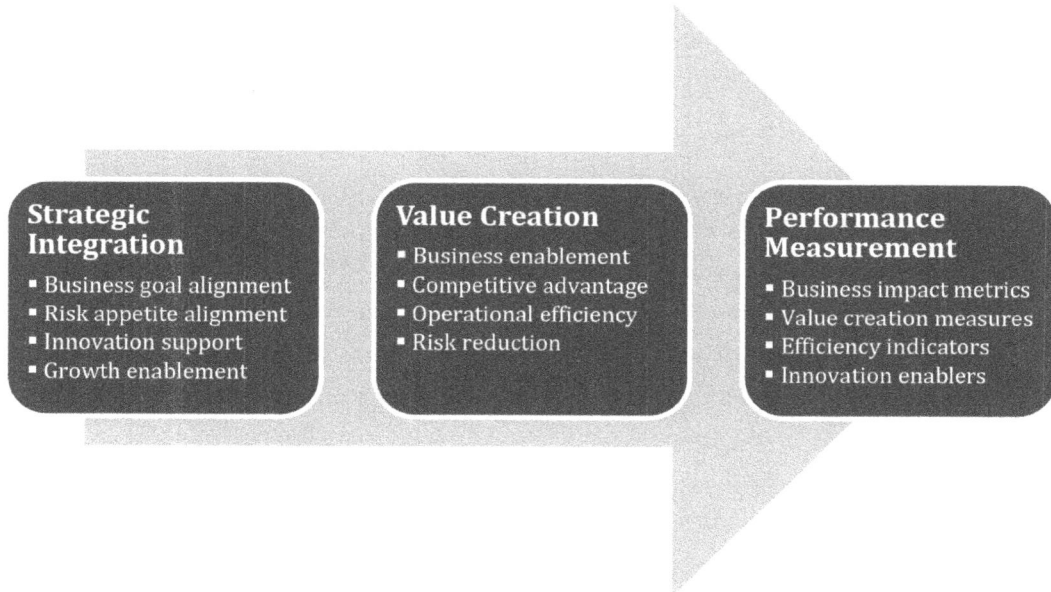

Figure 14.12: Aligning with business objectives

This alignment ensures:

- Better business support
- Improved security effectiveness
- Greater organizational value
- Enhanced stakeholder support

Summary

Systems thinking transforms cybersecurity from a technical function into a strategic business enabler. The comprehensive approach it offers ensures that security not only protects the organization but also supports its growth and innovation while optimizing resource utilization and maintaining resilience in the face of ever-changing threats.

David's key takeaways — Systems thinking for CISOs

Systems thinking is particularly valuable for CISOs because it addresses the interconnected nature of modern cybersecurity and how it fits into organizations. It is too easy to be drawn into narrow thinking and not to see cyber as a broader organizational problem to address.

As CISOs, we observe that vulnerabilities can exist across technology, processes, and human behavior in ways that traditional component-by-component analysis will perhaps overlook. A CISO who builds defense across these areas that can evolve with dynamic threats will be more successful, and systems thinking can help with that.

Key takeaways from this chapter include:

- *Traditional approaches that break problems into isolated components are insufficient for modern cybersecurity challenges.* CISOs must adopt a more holistic view that considers the interconnected nature of technology, people, and processes within the organization.

- *The CISO must enable business growth while managing risk.* With this approach, cybersecurity becomes a strategic enabler rather than just a protective function for the business.

- *Build adaptive programs* that focus on creating security frameworks that can evolve with changing threats, recover quickly from incidents, and learn from experiences.

- *Break down organizational silos.* Successful CISOs promote shared responsibility models that highlight the interconnected nature of cybersecurity in the organization.

- *Cyber metrics must consider measurement beyond traditional indicators.* In addition to, or even instead of, purely considering metrics such as incident counts and patch compliance, focus on business impact metrics, cultural metrics, and adaptation metrics that demonstrate the security program's true value to the organization.

- *CISOs need a diverse skillset.* This includes strong technical skills combined with a deep understanding of business objectives, strategic thinking capabilities, and the ability to communicate security concepts through the business context to gain stakeholder support and alignment.

15

The CISO as a Change Agent

The typical CISO would not see their brand as being a change agent. They have traditionally come from information security roles with a strong technology background. Their career has likely grown through network security, systems administration, or perhaps from security engineering roles. This training and experience would have provided them with detailed skills at a technical level. CISOs with backgrounds like this will understand the configuration of cyber controls and how these layers operate.

As cybersecurity has become more mainstream, the demands on the CISO have changed. The kind of knowledge that CISOs coming through traditional routes will have gained is valuable; however, the requirements of the contemporary CISO have morphed.

The profile of the CISO that recruiters are now searching for has the technical skills, but they also have much more. There are some new expectations that are more aligned with driving change.

New CISOs will therefore have to develop a cyber strategy that is aligned with and enables the business IT strategy. All business leaders want to drive their customer experience, and the 'friction' that cybersecurity creates is generally unwelcome.

The new CISO must think strategically about cyber and, in doing so, build strong stakeholder engagement. This will require them to evaluate risks holistically rather than in a siloed manner. From my experience the CISO will have to speak business language and be able to articulate commercial risk reduction that does not require any translation.

Jargon and techy talk must give way to the CISO being seen as a change agent. This will be with the goal of reducing risk and involve driving change through transformation projects and regulatory remediation.

It is my pleasure to introduce **Fal Ghancha, CISO** at **Jio Blackrock**. He manages cybersecurity for this company, which is a joint venture between Jio Financial Services Limited (JFS) and BlackRock, the world's largest asset manager. Fal has a deep history in cybersecurity and has also served as CISO for Aegon Life and DSP Mutual Fund in Mumbai.

As I am myself a person who identifies as a change agent, I love the energy, pace, and challenge of transformation. This is not tiring, but just the opposite; it just makes me excited to go to work. Let's hear from Fal on this topic.

My journey to becoming a change agent

Fal Ghancha

Throughout my career, I have driven critical technology projects that have transformed cybersecurity postures and redefined operational resilience. From establishing a comprehensive cybersecurity operations center (SOC) to deploying advanced data leakage prevention (DLP) systems, my efforts have centralised threat detection, mitigated risks, and enhanced data protection capabilities. My rollout of web application firewalls (WAFs) and implementation of a robust application security framework have further fortified digital ecosystems against threats. As these examples demonstrate, I am highly committed to proactive safeguarding of organisational assets.

In industrial environments, I led the segregation of supervisory control and data acquisition (SCADA) networks to secure operational technology systems, ensuring that industrial systems remained isolated from external vulnerabilities while integrated with broader IT frameworks. This initiative, alongside projects such as identity and access management (IAM), business impact analysis, and cyber defence centres, strengthened my ability to balance security imperatives with business continuity. Each project required not only technical proficiency but also the capacity to align cross-functional teams and embed security into core processes.

These experiences have cemented my role as a change agent in the cybersecurity domain. By fostering a culture of accountability, transparency, and innovation, I have enabled organisations to adapt to ever-evolving cyber threats. My strategic approach to blending technology, governance, and human-centric practices ensures that cybersecurity becomes a dynamic and integral part of every business decision.

As I reflect on my journey to becoming a change agent, I am reminded of my humble beginnings in the quaint village of Anjar. In those formative years, the concept of cybersecurity was rudimentary at best, confined to username-password combinations and the occasional thrill of a 56 kbps dial-up connection – a luxury that allowed me glimpses of grainy images on websites such as Glamsham.com, a nostalgic hub for Bollywood enthusiasts. The world of multi-factor authentication and sophisticated security tools was yet to unfold, leaving a vast, uncharted frontier for exploration.

It was during this era, devoid of the jazzy, modern-day security frameworks, that my fascination for the digital realm took root. The simple act of hacking usernames, deciphering modem codes, and uncovering vulnerabilities sparked a sense of excitement and curiosity within me that would later define my career. Those early experiments were the foundation of my lifelong passion for understanding, protecting, and navigating the intricacies of the digital world.

Two decades and countless adventures later, I find myself penning this narrative, a testament to a journey marked by relentless curiosity, adaptation, and an unwavering commitment to the field of cybersecurity. From those modest beginnings to the sophisticated, multi-dimensional challenges of today, the path has been nothing short of extraordinary.

In this chapter, I will share my journey to becoming a change agent within my role as a CISO with you, starting by giving you a glimpse into a day in my life as a CISO.

How my day as a CISO goes

Mumbai, the beating heart of India's financial ecosystem, thrives as a global hub where billions flow daily through its veins. From bustling Dalal Street to high-tech payment systems, the city orchestrates financial trades on a monumental scale. Mumbai wakes before the sun, and most days, so do I.

Waking early is a habit I've picked up over the years, not entirely by choice. In this city, where the pulse of the financial industry never stops, being a CISO often means living on borrowed time. Something's always happening, and it's rarely predictable.

Today starts with a faint buzz on my phone at 5:42 am. It's not the alarm I set for 6 – it's an alert from the security operations center (SOC). A phishing campaign is targeting one of our digital platform support partners. Great. I haven't even had my chai yet. I tap out a few quick instructions to my team before dragging myself to the kitchen, promising myself I'll enjoy this cup no matter what.

Sipping my tea, I can't help but reflect on how different this is from my early days in manufacturing. Back then, cybersecurity meant securing operational technology – clunky legacy systems that nobody had touched in decades. It was frustrating and fascinating, like trying to upgrade an old Ambassador car with Tesla software.

Finance, though? It's a battlefield. Here in Mumbai, the stakes are colossal. A breach isn't just a hit to the bottom line; it's a blow to trust – the one thing you can't buy back. Every attack feels personal, every weak link a potential disaster. And yet, there's something exhilarating about it. The urgency. The stakes. The adrenaline.

Fires to put out

Lunch doesn't happen. It turns out the phishing attack from this morning is worse than we thought. Several employees at a partner of ours clicked on malicious links, exposing sensitive systems. I'm on calls for the next two hours, coordinating containment measures. My SOC team is stretched thin, and I can sense their frustration. I try to stay calm, but it's hard not to snap when I'm explaining the same thing for the third time to someone clearly not paying attention.

By 3 pm, we've contained the issue. Barely. I grab a protein bar and make a mental note: we need to schedule another round of phishing simulations, and maybe also rethink some of our partnerships.

The human side of security

At 5 pm, I'm back in the SOC, sitting with a SOC analyst who's walking me through their response to the incident. They're nervous, stumbling over words, and I'm too tired to pretend I didn't notice the mistake they made during escalation. But instead of pointing it out directly, I ask them to explain their reasoning. As they do, they catch the error themselves. It's a small teaching moment, but these moments matter. I've learned over the years that building a strong team isn't about perfection; it's about resilience and growth.

It's moments like these that remind me why I value humility and understanding in leadership. I've learned that, sometimes, the greatest growth comes not from telling someone what they did wrong, but from creating the space for them to discover it on their own.

The city that never sleeps

By 8 pm, I'm finally at my desk, reviewing reports. The SOC is quiet for now, but I know better than to trust the calm. Mumbai's financial arteries never rest, and neither do the threats. I spot a typo in one of the reports and groan. It's a minor thing, but it bothers me. Before I can stop myself, I'm correcting it. "You're a CISO, not an editor," I mutter, shaking my head.

Before shutting down for the night, I take one last look at the dashboard. Everything's green. For now. I know it won't last. Tomorrow will bring new fires to put out, new threats to counter, and new ways to adapt. That's the nature of the job. It's exhausting but also oddly fulfilling.

Managing the stress that comes with this responsibility hasn't always been easy; it's something I've had to learn, often the hard way. Over time, I've come to see pressure not as a burden but as a constant companion that sharpens my focus and fuels my drive. In moments like this, when the quiet gives me space to reflect, I'm reminded why I do what I do. It goes beyond protecting systems; it's also about finding purpose, embracing resilience, and knowing that each step I take contributes to something bigger than myself. That realisation keeps me steady, even in the face of uncertainty.

As I step outside into the humid Mumbai night, the city hums around me – a chaotic, relentless symphony. I take a deep breath, letting the sea breeze remind me why I do this. Because here, at the intersection of chaos and opportunity, is where I thrive. This is where I can drive change.

Being a change agent

The role of a CISO often feels like that of a change agent. It may be thought that the biggest challenge as a CISO is building defences. It's not. It's actually changing mindsets.

Years ago, during my early days in finance, I remember walking into a boardroom where cybersecurity wasn't even on the agenda. Back then, it was an IT problem, something to be patched and forgotten. Convincing leadership that cybersecurity is a business enabler – not just an expense – was like pushing a boulder uphill.

I started small, focusing on quick wins. One of the first changes I implemented was a dashboard, which I famously call a 'spider dashboard,' that visualized risks in a way even non-technical leaders could grasp.

When they saw the number of threats intercepted daily, the lightbulb moment happened for them. Slowly, they began to see security as an investment. Over time, those small wins snowballed. Today, I'm proud to say our security strategy is woven into every major business decision.

Over the years, I've worked to break down silos between technology, compliance, and business units on the ground. In one memorable project, we revamped a CRM system's security (where millions of customers' information was stored). This was a daunting task, given the legacy tech involved. It took months of collaboration, late nights, and a lot of frustration, but when the new system went live, it was a turning point. For the first time, teams across departments saw cybersecurity as something that empowered them, rather than something that hindered them.

The CISO as a change agent and James Bond

When you think of a CISO, you might picture someone buried in spreadsheets or obsessing over compliance manuals. What you might not realize is just how much the role has in common with James Bond – the suave, world-saving agent with a penchant for the dramatic.

Sure, the stakes and settings are different, but the essence of the roles is strikingly similar: like Bond, the CISO is also an agent protecting what matters most, often without fanfare.

Missions: safeguarding in a world of high stakes

James Bond saves the world from catastrophic threats – rogue nuclear weapons, deadly viruses, or tech-savvy villains with global domination in mind. For a CISO, the battles may not make headlines, but they are no less consequential. A CISO's mission is to shield organisations from cyber threats that could grind operations to a halt, tarnish reputations, and wreak financial havoc.

Whether it's setting up a cyber defence centre or thwarting a phishing campaign targeting key stakeholders, the stakes for a CISO are also immense. A failure in Bond's world could cost lives; in mine, it could expose millions of records, undermine trust, and disrupt critical services. Both roles demand unshakable focus and the ability to think on your feet.

To manage this, I rely on staying practical and breaking large challenges into smaller, actionable tasks, taking one step at a time. For my team, I encourage open conversations and foster a sense of togetherness, ensuring they feel supported in their roles. Together, we tackle the strains of this demanding work, drawing strength from each other and finding motivation in every small win we achieve.

The arsenal: tools for defense and offense

Bond has Q, his ever-reliable gadget guru, equipping him with everything from exploding pens to biometric trackers. My arsenal is less flashy but no less effective: firewalls, intrusion detection systems, WAFs, and advanced threat intelligence platforms.

In a previous stint as a CISO, I championed SOCs as well as tools such as IAM and DLP systems.

The star of my toolkit is the spider graph dashboard I mentioned earlier – a visual powerhouse that elaborates on an organisation's cybersecurity status, tracks mitigation progress, and aligns defenses with business objectives.

While Bond's gadgets dazzle on screen, my tools work quietly in the background, keeping the organisation secure.

In the shadows, quietly making a difference

Bond's triumphs are classified, his heroics often unsung. A CISO's victories are similarly invisible. When I stop a ransomware attack in its tracks or neutralize a zero-day vulnerability, there's no red carpet or standing ovation. Systems run smoothly, employees remain productive, and customers stay oblivious to the threats lurking in the shadows.

But when things go awry? That's when the spotlight finds us. A breach – like Bond's villains' grand schemes – grabs attention and demands decisive action. I've been in those pressure-cooker moments, leading response teams to stabilise operations and mitigate fallout, all while staying calm under scrutiny.

I'm content without receiving credit, as my true satisfaction comes from knowing I've safeguarded the organisation from harm. Of course, recognition would be nice, but I learned early in my career that what truly matters is your own sense of judgement and the quiet confidence that comes from reflecting on the impact of your actions.

Allies and adversaries

James Bond battles larger-than-life villains and navigates murky alliances. My adversaries are no less formidable: state-sponsored hackers, organised cybercriminals, and even internal threats.

Building strong alliances as a CISO is crucial, whether it's with regulatory bodies such as the Securities and Exchange Board of India (SEBI), internal stakeholders, or cross-functional teams. Throughout my career, I've collaborated with business leaders to align cybersecurity strategies with organisational goals. Much like Bond relies on M and his trusted allies, I've built networks of support, industry communities that ensure resilience against developing threats.

Building a CISO community is deeply personal to me because it reflects the journey I've had in cybersecurity – starting from my early days exploring the basics to leading large-scale projects. Along the way, I've learnt the immense value of shared knowledge and mentorship from those who have faced similar challenges. By coming together as a community, we not only strengthen our collective defences but also guide the next generation of leaders, helping them navigate the complexities of projects. For me, it's about ensuring that the lessons I've learned through experience – both successes and failures – are passed on, empowering others to grow. It's about building a legacy of collaboration, resilience, and mentorship for the future.

The people factor

We know that James Bond relies on charm and wit to sway allies and outsmart foes. For a CISO, the human element is just as vital. Technology can only go so far without engaged, informed people behind it. Training employees to spot phishing attempts, embedding cybersecurity into the organisational culture, and working with trustees and boards to prioritise security are as important as any tool.

For instance, during my manufacturing industry stint, I led the segregation of SCADA networks to protect industrial systems. This required collaboration across technology teams, original equipment manufacturer (OEM) providers, and business stakeholders. It's a reminder that even the most sophisticated solutions need human co-operation to succeed.

In my role, I've been dedicated to embedding a strong cyber culture within the enterprise, fostering awareness, accountability, and collaboration across all levels to ensure that cybersecurity becomes an integral part of every employee's mindset and daily operations.

Shared purpose: guardianship

At their core, both James Bond and a CISO are guardians. Bond protects the world from chaos; I safeguard an organisation's digital heartbeat, ensuring that operations continue seamlessly and trust remains intact. Our victories, while often invisible, are no less significant – whether it's neutralising a global threat or averting a data breach.

So, while I'll probably never drive an Aston Martin or wear a tuxedo to work, I understand the weight of the mission. Like Bond, I know this: to protect, adapt, and endure in an ever-changing world isn't just a job – it's a calling.

My passion for this guardianship position comes through within my own team and also through co-operation across the industry with fellow CISO colleagues. Relationships with other CISOs allow me to remain grounded and have some candid dialogue with others who are going through the same challenges.

Building a culture of resilience

Cybersecurity transcends the realm of mere technical implementation; it is a symbiotic blend of strategy, governance, and human-centric practices. Over the years, in my capacity as a CISO, I have orchestrated a paradigm shift, laying the groundwork for a cyber-aware, transparent, and security-first organisation.

My journey has underscored one immutable truth: technology may underpin the framework, but it is people and processes that fortify the edifice.

Cultivating a cyber-aware ethos

When I assumed the mantle of CISO, my primary objective was to embed cybersecurity into the organisation's ethos. It was imperative to foster a collective sense of responsibility across hierarchies. To this end, I spearheaded an immersive suite of awareness programmes: live phishing simulations, nuanced workshops tailored to diverse teams, and executive-level briefings that connected cybersecurity to business imperatives.

These initiatives dismantled the long-standing perception of cybersecurity as an esoteric, IT-driven function. Employees began to perceive themselves as custodians of digital resilience. Gradually, the organization evolved into a collaborative ecosystem where every stakeholder, irrespective of their role, contributed to fortifying our defences. For instance, during my previous CISO stint, our structured approach to cyber-awareness programs led to measurable reductions in phishing susceptibility, reinforcing a culture of vigilance.

Bridging silos with transparency

Transparency is the bedrock of trust, and trust is indispensable for effective collaboration. Recognising this, I pioneered the adoption of a sophisticated spider graph dashboard, as I mentioned earlier – a visual tour de force that demystified our cybersecurity landscape. This dashboard encapsulated the following:

- Real-time vulnerability mapping across operational silos
- Progress tracking of mitigation initiatives
- A dynamic portrayal of our cybersecurity maturity trajectory
- Detailed threat analysis, including sources, vectors, and severity rankings
- Compliance metrics to align with regulatory frameworks and benchmarks

The spider graph became a linchpin in democratising cybersecurity insights. It was accessible to every echelon, from frontline managers to the boardroom. By transforming technical data into actionable intelligence, the dashboard empowered informed decision-making and cultivated a shared sense of achievement as milestones were realised. For example, during the implementation of the cyber defense center (SOC++), the spider graph dashboard helped track live threat responses, showcasing actionable metrics to both operational teams and executive leadership.

Developing our cybersecurity maturity

A key inflection point in our journey was the conceptualisation and operationalisation of a cybersecurity maturity roadmap. This meticulous blueprint delineated our strategic goals into actionable phases, enabling structured and measurable progression. My spider graph dashboard played a pivotal role in monitoring our advancement, spotlighting gaps, and recalibrating priorities.

This iterative approach facilitated our ascent through maturity levels. From implementing cutting-edge solutions such as IAM systems to launching the Application Security Framework for our web platforms, every milestone was a testament to our commitment to excellence.

These projects strengthened our technical architecture and underscored our emphasis on safeguarding sensitive customer data and ensuring operational continuity.

Redefining our approach to data governance

In today's hyper-connected ecosystem, data is the lifeblood of an organisation. However, safeguarding data necessitates more than regulatory adherence; it requires an intrinsic culture of care and stewardship.

I architected and championed information barrier policies that redefined our approach to data governance. These policies delineated stringent protocols for data access, usage, and dissemination. They were fortified by robust access controls, role-based permissions, and periodic audits.

Beyond compliance, these policies helped cultivate a conscientious workforce that internalised the sanctity of data protection. Employees no longer viewed these measures as restrictive mandates but as pivotal facilitators of trust and reputation. Essentially, they helped create a secure culture where staff understood how they needed to operate safely.

The outcome: a vanguard of cyber resilience

Reflecting on this transformative journey, I take immense pride in the cultural metamorphosis we achieved. Cybersecurity is no longer an ancillary concern, but a strategic imperative integrated into our organisational DNA. Employees now exhibit a proactive vigilance, leadership enjoys unparalleled visibility, and our stakeholders rest assured in the knowledge that their interests are safeguarded.

My spider graph dashboard, cybersecurity maturity map, and information barrier policies have transcended their functional roles to become emblematic of our ethos. They symbolise a collective commitment to resilience, highlighting the power of collaboration, transparency, and foresight.

A continuing evolution

Building a cyber-resilient organisation is neither a finite project nor a solitary endeavour; it is an evolving journey necessitating continuous recalibration.

As a CISO, my role transcends operational oversight. I am a change agent, a cultural ambassador, and a strategic advisor. If there is one enduring lesson from my odyssey, it is this: the most formidable defence lies not in technology alone but in the symbiotic confluence of people, processes, and purpose.

Through these collective efforts, the organisation has been empowered to combat the relentless challenges of ever-evolving threats. By establishing a culture of transparency, fostering collaboration, and embedding cybersecurity into the core of its operations, we have created a robust framework capable of withstanding adversities. Together, we are not just reacting to threats but proactively shaping a future where resilience is our strongest asset.

David's key takeaways — The CISO as a change agent

A great CISO is also a great change agent. For me, the modern CISO *must* act in this manner. In the past, it was okay for the CISO to just be the technical leader, but that is no longer enough. There is an expectation from the board and management that the transformation uplift that the CISO is responsible for can be made in a manner that disrupts the business the least but reduces the risk the most.

It would be fair to say that many CISOs are not exceptional at being a change agent, and this is a developmental area to work on. The CIO has also had to grow this competency to be able to deliver digital change to their stakeholders. I myself was a transformational CIO and transitioned into a CISO role from there. In doing so, I continued to see my role as driving change. In my case, HSBC was undertaking a $1B cyber uplift, and organisational change impact was paramount to this success.

Fal's sharing of his story and advice in this chapter is very important for this reason: that the CISO is now expected to be a change agent, and that it is no longer okay to be ineffective at this. This does not come without personal risk, as being a change agent is hard, and as a CISO, you already have a difficult role. I'd argue that while this will make you uncomfortable, there are clear benefits for you in embracing this.

Here are the key points from Fal's chapter:

- *The CISO role has evolved from a purely technical position to one requiring strategic business alignment*, with modern CISOs needing to balance technical expertise with change management and business communication skills.

- *CISOs must act as cultural transformers*, working to change organisational mindsets from viewing cybersecurity as just an IT expense to seeing it as a critical business enabler and strategic investment.

- *The CISO role requires building strong stakeholder relationships and breaking down silos between technology, compliance, and business units*, while communicating complex security concepts in business-friendly language.

- *Modern CISOs need to balance technical implementation with human-centric practices*, focusing on building a cyber-aware culture through training, awareness programmes, and transparent communication.

- *Successful CISOs must manage stress and pressure while building resilient teams.* Focusing on mentorship can help with this, as can focusing on creating teaching moments that encourage growth and learning from mistakes.

- *CISOs are guardians of their organisations.* Like a guardian (or James Bond), CISOs work behind the scenes to protect organisations from threats while building alliances across the industry and fostering a community of security professionals.

16

Alternative Career Paths to Consider

When I think about a good analogy for the career of a CISO, I think about the **firefighter** and the **architect** analogy. In this context, a firefighter CISO spends their time extinguishing threats and responding rapidly to new incidents. The bushfires in Australia can be particularly volatile, and this is akin to what we are seeing in the business landscape today.

On the other hand, an architect CISO takes a step back and looks at the overall picture with regard to the cyber risk profile. This CISO will be focused on security by design principles and setting strategic direction for the enterprise to follow.

The average tenure of a CISO tends to be about 24 months (2 years). There are many reasons why this is the case, but it is sufficient to acknowledge that these are difficult roles with a great degree of responsibility and pressure. Every CISO must embrace the fact that their career may not be long-term, and in that regard, have the courage to do what is required without having the assurance of knowing that their own tenure is secured.

Given this outlook, the CISO must always have one eye on the threats and one eye on their stakeholders to keep them happy – they must be both firefighter and architect. A CISO's mythical third eye, the so-called *ajna chakra*, might also be trained on their future career. Note that this chakra is thought to be related to intuition, wisdom, and insight beyond the physical world.

Although there is a shortage of cyber resources globally, that does not mean that the CISO will always get a new role immediately, nor do they always want to jump back on the front line. Fatigue and stress may make some other alternative positions more attractive to consider.

One individual who has navigated these varied paths with notable success is **Abbas Kudrati, Chief Identity Security Advisor (APAC)** at **Silverfort**, and formerly Chief Security, Risk, and Compliance Advisor at Microsoft. Abbas brings a unique blend of academic, advisory, and practitioner experience and has authored six books in the domains of cloud, cybersecurity, and risk management. His perspective on alternative CISO career paths is both practical and visionary.

It is my privilege to ask Abbas to share his thoughts on alternative CISO career paths and why these should be considered viable options.

Alternative career paths for CISOs to consider

Abbas Kudrati

The role of CISO is demanding, requiring a combination of technical knowledge, strategic thinking, and leadership skills. As cybersecurity threats continue to evolve, CISOs are constantly on the frontline, protecting their organisations from breaches and ensuring strong security postures. While many CISOs find great satisfaction in their positions, after years of service in this high-pressure role, some CISOs might seek new challenges or a change in pace.

Fortunately, the skills and experience acquired as a CISO open numerous doors to alternative career opportunities. This chapter explores these alternatives, helping you understand options you may wish to consider and, therefore, make informed career decisions.

Alternative roles for CISOs

Throughout my career, I've had the privilege of serving in roles that span the full spectrum of cybersecurity leadership – from enterprise CISO positions to academic appointments, board advisory roles, and, most recently, as Chief Identity Security Advisor for Silverfort. This journey has not only broadened my understanding of cybersecurity as a discipline but also deepened my appreciation for its role in enabling trust, resilience, and competitive advantage at the highest levels of business.

Like many senior security leaders, I've come to recognise that the CISO role, while mission-critical, is not always a long-term destination. The demands of the position, coupled with its evolving scope and complexity, often prompt seasoned professionals to consider alternative paths – ones that leverage their expertise in different, yet equally impactful ways. In today's environment, where cyber risk is a board-level issue, there is a growing demand for experienced CISOs who can operate as strategic advisors, technology evangelists, and transformation leaders.

In this section, I outline six career paths that I believe are particularly well-suited for CISOs exploring their next move. These roles were selected not only for their alignment with the skills and leadership qualities most CISOs already possess, but also for their strategic relevance within the broader business and risk ecosystem.

For each role, I provide a high-level overview, a summary of key responsibilities, insight into the required skills and qualifications, and a view of where the role typically resides – be it in technology firms, consulting environments, or boardrooms. I have also touched on my own experience in those roles I have held. The goal is to equip you with a clear understanding of the options available and to help you think beyond the operational demands of the CISO role towards opportunities that allow for continued leadership, influence, and contribution at the executive level.

Field CISO

Field CISOs act as senior cybersecurity experts for a specific region or industry, representing the company's security solutions to customers and partners.

The role involves a mix of technical expertise, customer interaction, and strategic influence.

Serving as a field CISO has been one of the most dynamic and intellectually rewarding phases of my career. Unlike my prior roles as an enterprise CISO, where I was deeply embedded in the internal rhythms of a single organisation, the field CISO position demanded a broader lens – representing cybersecurity solutions across multiple clients, verticals, and regulatory contexts.

One particularly memorable engagement for me in this role involved working with a healthcare provider struggling to adopt Zero Trust principles amidst a patchwork of legacy systems. As a field CISO, I had to step in as a translator between their internal stakeholders, regulatory constraints, and the capabilities of our platform. The credibility I brought from my own operational experience was crucial in building trust and shaping pragmatic, phased adoption plans.

What I learned most from this role is how to engage in 'strategic storytelling' – connecting technology capabilities to business imperatives in a way that resonates with both technical teams and senior executives. It also deepened my appreciation for the diversity of cybersecurity challenges across industries and geographies and reinforced the importance of empathy in advisory work. The field CISO role sits at the nexus of innovation, influence, and execution, and success here requires as much emotional intelligence as it does technical acumen.

Typical field CISO responsibilities include the following:

- **Customer engagement**: Collaborating closely with customers to understand their security needs and challenges
- **Solution advocacy**: Advocating for the company's cybersecurity solutions, demonstrating how they address customer needs
- **Thought leadership**: Providing thought leadership by participating in industry events, webinars, and conferences

- **Advisory services**: Offering advisory services to customers, helping them optimise their security strategies

- **Creating a feedback loop**: Gathering feedback from customers and relaying it to the product development team to enhance security solutions

Skills and qualifications that field CISOs are likely to need include the following:

- Strong customer relationship management skills

- In-depth knowledge of cybersecurity products and services

- Excellent presentation and public speaking abilities

- Understanding of the specific industry or region they serve

- Extensive experience in a senior cybersecurity role

- Relevant cybersecurity and industry-specific certifications

Field CISOs are often employed by cybersecurity vendors or large IT service providers. The role offers you the chance to collaborate closely with customers, helping them solve complex security problems while representing innovative security solutions. It also provides you with further opportunities for public speaking and industry recognition.

Virtual CISO (fractional CISO)

A **virtual CISO** (vCISO) provides cybersecurity leadership and expertise to organisations on a part-time or contract basis.

This role is ideal for small to mid-sized organisations that require the strategic guidance of a CISO but cannot afford a full-time position.

My transition into vCISO roles was both a personal and professional pivot, allowing me to remain deeply engaged in strategic security leadership while gaining flexibility in how and where I worked. As a vCISO, I've supported multiple organisations simultaneously, each at different levels of cyber maturity. This diversity has kept my perspective sharp and solutions context-aware.

I vividly recall working with a fast-growing fintech start-up that had no formal security leadership in place. In just six months, we moved from ad-hoc practices to a structured cyber risk framework aligned with ISO 27001, enabling us to secure funding and customer trust. The ability to embed myself within their leadership team – even part-time – and guide them through this transformation was incredibly fulfilling.

Compared to traditional CISO roles, the vCISO path demands greater agility, self-management, and the ability to rapidly understand new business models and cultures. It also taught me how to operate with greater efficiency, prioritizing high-impact initiatives and aligning quickly with executive agendas. For senior professionals looking to apply their expertise in a more flexible and consultative format, the vCISO role offers both challenge and purpose.

Typical vCISO responsibilities include the following:

- **Strategic planning**: Developing and implementing cybersecurity strategies aligned with the organisation's goals
- **Risk assessment**: Conducting regular risk assessments to identify and mitigate potential security threats
- **Policy development**: Creating and enforcing cybersecurity policies and procedures
- **Compliance**: Ensuring that the organisation complies with relevant regulations and standards
- **Incident response**: Developing and managing incident response plans to manage security breaches
- **Training**: Conducting training sessions to raise cybersecurity awareness among employees

Skills and qualifications that vCISOs are likely to need include the following:

- The ability to be flexible and manage multiple clients and adapt to different organisational cultures
- Comprehensive understanding of cybersecurity best practices and technologies
- Excellent communication skills to effectively interact with various stakeholders
- Extensive experience in a senior cybersecurity role
- Relevant certifications such as CISSP, CISM, or CISA

vCISOs typically work as independent contractors or through cybersecurity firms.

The role offers you flexibility and the opportunity to work with a diverse range of organisations, providing strategic cybersecurity guidance without the demands of a full-time position.

CISO advisor

A CISO advisor provides specialized advice and mentorship to CISOs, helping them navigate complex cybersecurity challenges and improve their leadership skills.

This role is often suited for seasoned cybersecurity professionals who have had extensive experience as a CISO.

After spending years in the operational hot seat, stepping into the role of a CISO advisor felt both natural and deeply rewarding for me. In this capacity, I've had the privilege of mentoring and coaching senior security leaders – helping them navigate high-stakes decisions, develop board-ready communication strategies, and build influence across the business.

One particularly impactful engagement involved coaching a first-time CISO at a multinational logistics company. They were technically brilliant but struggled with stakeholder alignment and board engagement. Through structured sessions, scenario-based role play, and executive narrative development, we helped turn the tide – not just improving their performance, but also reinforcing their confidence and leadership presence.

The CISO advisor role allows you to operate with a long-term view – focusing not just on fixing issues, but on growing people. It has reminded me that leadership in cybersecurity isn't only about technology or controls; it's also about mindset, influence, and developing resilience in others. For experienced CISOs who want to give back while staying intellectually engaged, this role offers a unique opportunity to shape the profession at a systemic level.

Typical CISO advisor responsibilities include the following:

- **Mentorship**: Providing mentorship and guidance to current CISOs
- **Strategic advice**: Offering strategic advice on cybersecurity strategies and policies
- **Problem-solving**: Assisting in resolving complex cybersecurity issues
- **Industry trends**: Keeping CISOs informed about the latest trends and developments in cybersecurity
- **Networking**: Facilitating networking opportunities for CISOs to connect with peers and industry experts

Skills and qualifications that CISO advisors are likely to need include the following:

- Extensive experience as a CISO or in a senior cybersecurity role
- Ability to provide high-level strategic advice
- Excellent communication and interpersonal skills
- Proven leadership and mentorship abilities
- Advanced cybersecurity certifications and industry recognition

CISO advisors can work independently or through consultancy firms. This role provides you with the opportunity to influence the next generation of cybersecurity leaders and stay engaged with the evolving cybersecurity landscape, beyond your tenure as a CISO.

Field CTO

A field **Chief Technology Officer (CTO)** serves as a technical ambassador for a company, focusing on promoting and implementing advanced technology solutions for clients. This role blends technical expertise with strategic insight, requiring a deep understanding of both the technology and business aspects of cybersecurity.

Typical field CTO responsibilities include the following:

- **Technical leadership**: Providing leadership and vision to clients, guiding them through technology adoption and implementation
- **Solution design**: Designing and architecting technology solutions that meet client needs and align with their strategic goals
- **Innovation**: Promoting innovation by identifying emerging technologies and integrating them into client solutions
- **Stakeholder engagement**: Engaging with senior stakeholders to understand their business challenges and provide appropriate technology solutions
- **Product development feedback**: Collaborating with internal product teams to provide feedback on market needs and product enhancements

Skills and qualifications that field CTOs are likely to need include the following:

- Extensive knowledge of current and emerging technologies
- Ability to align technology solutions with business objectives
- Strong ability to communicate technical concepts to both technical and non-technical audiences

- Proven leadership skills in driving technology adoption and innovation
- Relevant technical certifications and advanced degrees in technology or business

Field CTOs are typically employed by technology vendors, consulting firms, and large enterprises. Their roles are different to more enterprise-based CTOs, in that the role offers a unique blend of technology and business, providing you with opportunities to influence technology strategies at an elevated level and drive innovation across multiple organisations.

Chief Cybersecurity Advisor

A **Chief Cybersecurity Advisor (CCA)** provides strategic guidance and advisory services to organisations on their cybersecurity strategies and policies. This role typically involves collaborating with multiple clients, offering expert advice on how to enhance their security posture, manage risks, and comply with regulations.

During my time as a CCA, first at Microsoft and now at Silverfort, I experienced a notable shift in focus compared to my earlier roles as a CISO. As a CISO, much of my time was spent deep in operational execution: managing incidents, responding to regulators, and working through immediate business risks.

In contrast, the CCA role allowed me to operate more broadly and proactively. Rather than focusing solely on one organisation, I engaged with CISOs, CIOs, and boards across a wide range of industries. I was advising not just on today's threats, but on how to design cyber resilience into the business model itself.

I've found that one of the most rewarding aspects of this role has been the ability to shape strategic direction at scale. I remember consulting with a large financial institution undergoing a digital transformation. They were grappling with identity sprawl, legacy systems, and compliance pressures. Rather than prescribing a solution, my role was to help the executive leadership reframe the problem, to see identity not as a constraint, but as a core facilitator of trust and agility. That shift in mindset ultimately helped unlock both innovation and stronger controls.

This role taught me to see cybersecurity as more than a defensive discipline. I now see it also as a lever for strategic differentiation. Furthermore, it honed my ability to influence at the executive and board level, where success depends less on technical depth and more on framing cyber risk in the language of business outcomes.

Typical CCA responsibilities include the following:

- **Strategic planning**: Developing and refining cybersecurity strategies tailored to the unique needs of each client
- **Risk management**: Identifying and assessing potential security risks and developing mitigation strategies
- **Policy development**: Assisting in creating and implementing cybersecurity policies and procedures
- **Compliance**: Ensuring that clients adhere to relevant cybersecurity regulations and standards
- **Training and awareness**: Conducting training sessions and awareness programs to educate employees about cybersecurity best practices
- **Incident response**: Providing guidance on incident response planning and management

Skills and qualifications that CCAs are likely to need include the following:

- A deep understanding of cybersecurity technologies and trends
- The ability to develop long-term security strategies
- Excellent communication skills to convey complex security concepts to non-technical stakeholders
- Previous experience in consulting or advisory roles (advantageous)
- Relevant certifications such as CISSP, CISM, or CISA

A CCA often works for cybersecurity consulting firms or as an independent consultant. This role provides the opportunity for you to work with a variety of organisations, from small businesses to large enterprises, across different industries. This diversity can be intellectually stimulating and offers a broader perspective on cybersecurity challenges and solutions than just being a CISO.

Cybersecurity consultant/contractor

Cybersecurity consultants or contractors offer specialized expertise to organisations on a temporary or project basis.

This role involves conducting security assessments, developing security strategies, and assisting with specific cybersecurity projects.

Returning to consulting after holding in-house leadership roles gave me a fresh perspective on the unique value consultants can bring. As a cybersecurity consultant, I've been able to apply hard-earned experience to a diverse range of organisations – each with its own culture, risk appetite, and maturity level. The tempo is different, but the impact can be just as significant.

I recall leading a consulting engagement for a regional bank that had just failed a major audit. They needed both rapid remediation and a long-term roadmap that would satisfy regulators and internal audit. By working closely with their CIO and security team, we established an accelerated risk reduction program while laying the foundation for a sustainable security governance model. What might have taken years internally, we achieved in under six months.

Consulting has honed my ability to assess environments quickly, ask the right questions, and deliver focused outcomes. It's also reinforced the importance of balancing best practices with pragmatism. For CISOs seeking variety, intellectual stimulation, and the chance to drive measurable change across sectors, a consulting career can be both energizing and high-impact.

Typical consultant responsibilities include the following:

- **Security assessments**: Conducting comprehensive security assessments to identify vulnerabilities
- **Strategy development**: Developing and implementing cybersecurity strategies
- **Compliance**: Assisting organisations in achieving and maintaining compliance with relevant regulations
- **Project management**: Managing cybersecurity projects, ensuring timely and effective completion
- **Training**: Providing training and awareness programs to improve the organisation's security posture

Skills and qualifications that cybersecurity consultants or contractors are likely to need include the following:

- Deep knowledge of cybersecurity principles and best practices
- Ability to adapt to different organisational environments and needs
- Persuasive communication skills to work effectively with various stakeholders
- Proven experience in cybersecurity roles
- Relevant certifications such as CISSP, CISM, or CISA

Cybersecurity consultants and contractors can work independently or through consultancy firms.

This role offers you flexibility, as well as diversity in projects and the opportunity to provide high-impact solutions to various organisations.

My conclusion

Transitioning from the role of a CISO to an alternative role or career path can be a fulfilling and rewarding experience. The skills and knowledge you acquire as a CISO are highly transferable and valued across various roles in the cybersecurity industry and beyond.

Whether it is becoming a field CISO, a vCISO, a CISO advisor, a field CTO, a CCA, or exploring other consultant or contractor roles, CISOs have a wealth of opportunities to continue making a significant impact in the world of cybersecurity.

By carefully considering your interests, strengths, and career goals, you can successfully navigate your next career move or a change to your career path and continue to thrive beyond your role as a CISO.

David's key takeaways – Alternative career paths to consider

In this chapter, Abbas has shared a number of roles that can follow on well from the CISO role, offering alternatives to consider as you evaluate options for your career path and contemplate developing new skills, knowledge, experience, and behaviours.

The role of the CISO is extremely challenging – it can feel like a long-distance sprint. There are many times that you will, as CISO, by default inherit the accountability of a peer who has not stepped up to their role. I've seen many CISOs take on tasks that the CTO, **Chief Data Officer (CDO)**, and CIO should own. You may be used to taking on these hard yards, but for many, this is very stressful and impacts career longevity.

For this reason, Abbas's chapter is highly valuable, providing much for the CISO to consider. Even if you choose to take on such alternate roles in the short term, this can be a wonderful new learning experience.

The key points from Abbas's chapter include the following:

- *The CISO role isn't for everyone.* There are similar alternatives that can provide a challenge and the opportunity to build on the transferable skills you have developed as a CISO.
- *The field CISO role offers an excellent career path for technical professionals who want to combine deep technology expertise with strategic business impact*, to guide clients through advanced technology adoption at an executive level across multiple organisations.
- *The vCISO role has emerged as a flexible option for CISOs*, allowing professionals to provide part-time or contractual CISO services to organisations that cannot afford full-time security leadership.
- *The CISO advisor role offers experienced security leaders the opportunity to mentor and guide current CISOs*, focusing on strategic guidance and professional development.
- *The field CTO role is an option for CISOs interested in becoming technical ambassadors,* while developing their strategic business skills.
- *The CCA role is another that presents CISOs with the opportunity to work within a broader remit and with a variety of organisations*, providing strategic guidance and advice on cybersecurity strategies and policies.
- *Consulting and contracting roles also provide opportunities for CISOs to work on specific projects across multiple organisations*, with more flexibility.

17

So, You Got Fired

The role of the CISO is one lived on the precipice of chaos. From their vantage point, the CISO is in a position to see most of the faults and gaps that the enterprise faces. These truths may be candidly conveyed to the security team, yet the message presented to senior management and the board is often more tempered, perhaps an instinctive act of self-preservation, likely a result of the unforgiving demands of the role.

Indeed, the demands of the position leave little room for rest. Annual leave is often curtailed, and personal time is frequently disrupted by incidents or near misses. Even when the security team performs at its peak, it is usually only the CISO who recognises the sacrifices involved. Recognition and celebration are rare (and thus, never unwelcome). Thriving in such a position demands extraordinary resilience, persistence, and what might be considered by some as superhuman capabilities.

When a serious incident occurs, the CISO often becomes the scapegoat. Many executives and board members lack a deep understanding of cybersecurity, and earlier warnings about insufficient budgets or resources are seldom recalled in the aftermath of a breach. Regulators, too, may demonstrate limited comprehension of the realities of the role, at times calling for the removal of both the CISO and CIO when outcomes reflect poorly on the organisation. In such an environment, the question naturally arises: who would willingly choose to become a CISO?

It is against this backdrop that the next generation of leaders is shaped. Aspiring CISOs, observing the fate of their predecessors, may be understandably apprehensive. Yet, there is another way to view this reality. Each difficult episode offers lessons. Success can emerge from failure if one is willing to examine the experience, internalise its lessons, and adapt accordingly. The CISO's path is not an easy one, but it remains a path of critical importance, demanding both courage and the capacity for continual growth.

So, if one does find oneself in the unenviable position of having lost their job as CISO, how does one reframe the experience as a pivot point for strategic career repositioning, rather than a failure? Scenarios like this require you to evaluate your own parachute and plot your own next steps.

Allow me to introduce you to **Dr Matthew Ryan**, a former colleague of mine at Macquarie Group, and now **Head of Cyber, Data and AI Risk** at **NAB**. Matt has worked at several highly regarded banks and for APRA, the Australian Regulator. He has a passion for cybersecurity and a strong desire to climb the ladder to senior roles. He always impressed me with his deep thinking and ability to plough through the work of three leaders.

Matthew also has an extensive career in the Australian Navy and is pursuing his second PhD in cyber economics (his first was in cybersecurity, with a focus on ransomware).

This chapter from Matt is a timely one, as, while the book so far has explored the careers of many CISOs around the world and from many sectors, wherein many have talked about survival skills and learning valuable life lessons, no one else has addressed directly how to respond to being fired or restructured out of an organisation. I applaud Matt's courage in taking on such a sensitive topic.

Losing one's job is never easy, and we must always try to understand our own shortcomings in such scenarios and distinguish the actual reality of difficult situations from our own (probably distorted) reality. Considering what could have been done differently is equally valuable.

The courage to reflect on one's own career and make a decision to shift is always a key milestone that every leader will face at some point. In my book *The Aspiring CIO and CISO*, I talk about career management being akin to an elevator – sometimes it goes up, and other times down. But the elevator can also get stuck on a floor, or you might choose to press the *Close door* button as you don't desire to take a move right at that moment.

Over to you now, Matt!

So, you got fired — congratulations!

Dr Matthew Ryan

It sounds absurd, even perverse, to offer kudos at a time like this. Yet for many mid-career cyber-security and technology leaders, an abrupt exit does not always have to be a shameful ending; it may even be considered by some to be a rite of passage. In the moment, of course, it never feels that way. The day you lose your position, whether you were gently nudged to 'resign' or outright shown the door, can feel like a personal cataclysm.

Your confidence is shaken, your professional identity thrown into question. But as counterintuitive as it seems, this unwanted turning point often becomes the very crucible that forges stronger leaders. This chapter explores that emotional journey: the soaring highs and crushing lows of leadership, the inevitability of failure, and the resilience that pulls you through to the other side. It draws on my personal experience of working with and being mentored by CIOs, CISOs, and other senior executives who have ridden this rollercoaster and lived to tell the tale with a wry smile. It won't promise a fairy-tale ending, but it will illuminate the value, perhaps even the necessity, of a time, if it comes, when who and what we know unravels.

The characters in this chapter are fictional, but only just. They're stitched together from the war stories, coffee-fuelled confessions, and 'off-the-record' chats with real CIOs and CISOs. If they seem familiar, it's because they are. These aren't heroic tales of flawless leadership; they're stories of ambition, burnout, the occasional career faceplant, and the outcomes of unfortunate incidents. Welcome to the reality of life at the top, where the pressure is high, the Wi-Fi is unreliable, and your tenure might end before your coffee gets cold.

Bob's story

On a grey Wednesday afternoon, one CISO (let's call him Bob) sat in a glass-walled conference room facing the CEO and head of HR. The meeting invitation had been cryptic, last-minute, and in an unusual location. Bob's stomach was already churning; in our world, a surprise meeting often means change is about to occur. Sure enough, as the CEO gravely thanked him for his service, Bob felt the blood drain from his face. A data breach the month before had put the company in a tough spot, and someone had to carry the blame. The irony was not lost on him; for years, he'd preached to his team that breaches are inevitable ("not if, but when," he would say), yet he hadn't applied the same maxim to his own job security. He was being escorted out for the very thing he'd spent his career preparing to handle. In that surreal moment, as he handed over his badge and laptop, Bob realised this was the precipitous end of a chapter he'd once imagined would last much longer.

Back at home that evening, Bob sat on his couch in a daze, replaying the brief conversation a hundred times over. Could he have argued his case better? Should he have fought harder to stay? The truth was, once the decision was made, there was no boardroom debate that could unfire him. The sooner he accepted it, the sooner he could move on. It took a few sleepless nights and long walks for the fog of disbelief to begin lifting. Only then did the kaleidoscope of emotions come into focus: the sting of public failure, anger at how things had been handled, and oddly, a tinge of relief that the stressful saga was over. Today it was a breach; tomorrow it could have been something else. In the high-wire act of leadership, a fall is almost always inevitable, one way or another. This was Bob's fall. Now he had to figure out how to climb back up.

For Bob, making peace with this abrupt ending was the hardest step. A mentor had once told him, "When it's over, it's over, don't waste your energy fighting a decision that's already made." Sage advice, but bitter medicine. Still, he knew that stewing in resentment would only delay his comeback. So, he forced himself to confront a new reality: for the first time in years, he wasn't responsible for protecting anything except his own sanity. In the weeks that followed, an unexpected silence descended. Bob's phone, once vibrating incessantly with vendor calls and meeting requests, had gone eerily quiet. He had been a regular on the conference circuit, always invited to panels and roundtables, but suddenly those invitations were drying up. It dawned on him that many people who'd courted his time weren't interested in *him*, but in his title and association with his prior firm.

Without the three-letter acronym trailing his name, Bob was quietly dropped from the industry A-list. It was a humbling reality check. He thought back to the mountain of business cards he'd collected at conferences, and the flood of LinkedIn compliments he'd once received. Now, only a small circle of genuine friends and colleagues bothered to check in. The cybersecurity world, as it turns out, is both tiny and fickle. A place with a long memory for missteps and a short one for friendships. As an ex-CIO dryly told him over coffee, "You'll be amazed how many people you called 'mate' yesterday won't return your calls today." And sure enough, Bob found himself sorting through the silence, identifying who had been around for the logo on his badge and who was in his corner.

The hardest part wasn't just losing the job; it was seeing those he'd spent years in the trenches with now keeping a safe, almost clinical distance. Midnight war-room pizzas, in-jokes over failed changes, shared victories, and long nights, all of it vanished with his corporate phone and email account. There's a quiet sting in that kind of disappearance, and an added layer of awkwardness when you bump into former colleagues. There will always be doubts on both parties' side: what really went down, and why did you really get fired?

It was as if his professional fall from grace had become socially transmissible; people kept their distance as if his emails now carried malware. Swallowing his pride, Bob cautiously dipped a toe into the job market. That, too, proved to be an emotional minefield. Rewriting his resume felt like reliving every moment he'd rather forget, and reaching out to old contacts carried the awkward subtext of "I'm available, please notice." He quickly learned that at his level, the playing field isn't just small, it's practically a closed loop. After years of climbing the cybersecurity ladder in the finance sector, there were only so many CISO roles to aim for, and a surprising number were now occupied by people he'd once sparred with: that candidate he passed over for his deputy role two years ago, now the hiring executive. The security manager he butted heads with a decade back, currently gatekeeping at another top-tier bank. One interview barely made it past introductions before quietly imploding under the weight of old office politics. In the rarefied air of cybersecurity leadership, every burnt bridge has a long memory and a habit of reappearing just when you need to cross it. Bob was now grappling with the consequences of wars he thought he'd already won or at least outlived.

With traditional job boards yielding little more than generic rejections, Bob refocused on his personal network. He realised he had been so consumed by his last role that he hadn't nurtured many relationships outside of it. Now was payback time for that oversight. He began sending messages to old acquaintances, ex-colleagues, peers in the industry, and that vendor-turned-friend who had moved on to a new company. It was humbling to ask for leads and advice, but to his surprise, a few doors opened this way. A friend of a friend knew a start-up that needed a seasoned hand to build their security program. A former teammate suggested a contract consulting gig to keep him busy (and pay the bills) while he looked for a more permanent role. None of these opportunities came from the online listings he obsessively refreshed each morning; they came from people.

The experience drove home a lesson he'd known intellectually but never truly *felt* until now: in this game, your network is your lifeline. As weeks turned into a couple of months, Bob also confronted the uncomfortable gift of free time. At first, he didn't know what to do with himself on Monday mornings besides trawl LinkedIn. The unstructured days felt alien after years of back-to-back meetings. Whether the time on the bench stems from getting fired, being restructured, or being on gardening leave, you need to find mental and physical stimulation to help you get through this period, as Bob learned.

> Reflecting on my own personal experience of transitioning careers and being benched, **Brazilian Jiu-Jitsu (BJJ)** always provided me an outlet, because it gave me a purpose. When someone is trying to strangle you, you can't ruminate on a missed promotion, failed stakeholder relationship, or board presentation gone wrong; you're forced to be fully present, or your survival is about to be in danger. The combination of problem-solving, physical exertion, and the camaraderie of BJJ became my sanctuary. It offers an opportunity to leave your personal troubles at the door and focus on the task at hand: surviving, then winning.

The discipline of martial arts – tapping out when necessary, learning from each defeat, showing up again (and again) – mirrors the resilience we all need in our professional life, especially if we want to survive at the top. Bit by bit, you will be able to turn your involuntary sabbatical into an opportunity to sharpen the edges that had grown dull while you were firefighting daily crises, albeit through increasingly passive-aggressive email threads. Use the time you have available well: take a holiday, take the time to read, reflect on how you can become better, and even take an online course to brush up on that cloud security you never had time to study before.

For many, there will be a fork-in-the-road moment that a lot of ex-executives know all too well. A former colleague put in a good word for Bob at a mid-sized company that was looking for a security director. It wasn't a CISO role, more like a deputy position two rungs down from the C-suite, but it was a solid job at a stable company. At the same time, Bob had a few irons in the fire for another shot at a top role, including slow-moving conversations with a big tech company that hinted at a CISO opening on the horizon. The dilemma was classic: grab the sure thing now, even if it felt like a step backwards, or hold out for a shot at the top again, which might or might not materialise.

Bob's savings weren't bottomless, and the emotional drain of job hunting was starting to feel like a second unpaid job. Pride tugged him towards holding out; pragmatism whispered that a steady paycheck beats philosophical purity. Bob wrestled with the decision, knowing full well that neither option came with guarantees or inner peace. Eventually, he chose sanity over status and took the security director role. In the end, trading a corner office dream for stability and a clean slate wasn't a failure; it was a different kind of strength, the kind that comes with swallowing your ego and getting back in the game.

In truth, many of Bob's peers were making similar moves, sidestepping to lower positions or consulting gigs, or leaping to adjacent fields, anything to stay in the game and keep their skills sharp while waiting for the next big opportunity. He knew of one former CIO who spent nearly two years chasing that next big title, draining her savings and spirit before finally landing a role that, from the outside, made the struggle seem worth it. Bob wasn't sure he had the appetite for that kind of gamble.

Alice's story

Bob's story, while unique in its details, was far from an isolated case. Consider Alice, a seasoned CIO at a fast-growing tech company. She had been poached from a comfortable role to lead a start-up through an ambitious growth spurt and digital transformation.

For two years, Alice poured her life into the job: long nights of strategising, firefighting outages at dawn, mentoring a young IT team. Under her leadership, the company modernised its infrastructure and rolled out a successful new app that wowed the board. By all visible measures, she was succeeding.

Yet, in the very meetings where she presented record uptimes and very positive security metrics, she felt an undercurrent of tension with the new CEO. She was brought in by investors to shake things up, and shake she did.

Philosophically, Alice and the CEO were oil and water: her careful and long-term planning-based approach clashed with the CEO's appetite for high-risk, high-speed pivots. The strain began to show in tense boardroom exchanges and terse email threads. Still, Alice was caught off guard when, one Friday just after lunch, she was asked to 'step down.' The official line was that the company needed a different kind of leader for its next chapter. In truth, it felt like a polite way of telling her she wasn't wanted anymore.

Alice packed up her office in a haze of disbelief. Walking to her car with a banker's box full of hard drives and award plaques, she tried to process what had just happened. How could delivering stellar results and working herself to exhaustion still end like this? That evening, she sat at her kitchen table far earlier than her family was used to. Her teenage son raised an eyebrow and asked, "Mum, why are you home for dinner on a Friday?" It was meant in jest, but the question stung;

it drove home how absent she had been. Alice mustered a wry smile and replied, "Apparently, I have some free time now." Saying it out loud made it real. After her family went to bed, a wave of emotions hit her like whiplash: pride in what she'd achieved, anger at the CEO's cavalier decision, embarrassment (despite the platitudes, being asked to leave felt like failure), and a strange, guilty sense of relief. The job had consumed her. Maybe, just maybe, this was an unplanned chance to reclaim a piece of herself.

Word of Alice's departure spread quietly through her professional circles. Unlike Bob, Alice had always been a consummate networker; she made a point to mentor junior colleagues, stay in touch with former teammates, and speak at industry events. That groundwork paid off. Within a few weeks, a couple of board members from companies she'd advised in the past reached out, as did an old boss who offered her a short-term advisory project to tide her over.

It was comforting to discover that her reputation stood on its own, beyond the logo on her last business card. Still, she wasn't in a rush to jump into another high-pressure role. Instead, for the first time in her career, Alice hit the pause button. She accepted her former boss's offer but only as a part-time consultant. For the rest of her days, she gave herself permission to slow down. She attended her daughter's soccer games without checking her email on the sidelines. She booked a yoga retreat that she'd daydreamed about during stressful product launches. In the gentle rhythm of these weeks, she found space to rediscover passions that had lain dormant. An old sketchbook on her shelf beckoned; she began drawing again, surprised at how the pencil in her hand felt more freeing some days than a keyboard.

Little by little, Alice's perspective shifted. The initial sting of her exit softened into a cautious optimism about the future. She realised she didn't have to chase the exact same brass ring as before. In fact, she felt a burgeoning desire to apply her skills in a way that aligned better with her values, even if that meant a less glamorous title or a smaller organisation. After a few months, as her confidence rebounded, she began entertaining conversations about new roles.

One day, a former industry peer floated an idea: would Alice consider co-founding a boutique consultancy to advise start-ups and boards on IT strategy? The idea excited her. It wasn't the traditional next step of landing another CIO gig, but it blended her expertise with the autonomy she craved. By the time she signed her first client contract, Alice understood that her forced exit had ironically given her the push she needed to reinvent herself. She was still very much in the game, just playing it by a different set of rules that she herself got to write.

The cycles of leadership: falling, rising, and the art of resilience

There's a rhythm to these leadership journeys, an emotional cycle that repeats in different forms. A moment of triumph is often followed by a setback; a peak is inevitably followed by a valley. It's almost ritualistic. In cybersecurity, we often say every breach follows a pattern: detect, respond, recover, learn. Career upheavals are not so different. First comes the shock and denial (*Did that really just happen to me?*), then the frantic response (*What do I do now?*), the slow recovery (rebuilding confidence and direction), and finally, the retrospection (*What did I learn? How will I do things differently?*). Names and circumstances vary; Bob, Alice, and countless others have worn these shoes, but ultimately, the pattern of rise, fall, and rise again is strikingly consistent. It's practically a rite of passage at the top. No one emerges from a long career in cybersecurity and tech leadership without a few scars and stories.

If there's one secret shared in hushed tones among veteran CIOs and CISOs over late-night whiskies at conferences, it's that failure is not the opposite of success; it's part of the journey. You will slip. You will be humbled. You might even get the proverbial rug pulled out from under you at the height of your game. That doesn't mean you weren't good enough; often, it means you tackled hard problems, made tough calls, and sometimes life (or corporate politics) had other plans. As one battle-weary CISO joked, "I've earned my black belt in boardroom brawling, and all it taught me is how to fall gracefully." Behind the humour lies truth: resilience isn't just a buzzword, it's a necessity. It's the quiet, dogged determination to keep moving forward, even when you're bruised and uncertain.

In the end, what separates those who stagnate from those who soar isn't avoiding failure; it's learning to embrace it, learn from it, and adapt to it. The emotional cycles of leadership, as tumultuous as they are, have a way of refining true professionals into wiser, more empathetic versions of themselves. Today's humiliation can become tomorrow's anecdote, even a badge of honour. The CIO who got ousted after an **enterprise resource planning (ERP)** go-live disaster might later chuckle about it on a panel, recounting how that fall pushed him to become a better communicator. The CISO who walked out with a cardboard box might use that experience to mentor the next generation on handling crises with grace. These scars are proof of having dared greatly.

For the mid-career reader wrestling with their own crossroads, whether you've been recently 'congratulated', feel stuck on a plateau, or are bracing for the next big challenge, remember that you're in good company. The path to the summit is rarely a straight line. It winds through dark forests of doubt and across plateaus of hard-won calm. You'll lose your footing at times, but each stumble teaches you how to climb better, how to bounce back faster. One day, you may even look back and feel a strange gratitude for the twists in your journey. After all, without them, you wouldn't have the steel in your spine or the stories in your pocket.

In the grand saga of a career, a chapter of failure and reinvention isn't the end of the book; often, it's where the story truly gets interesting.

David's key takeaways — So, you got fired

I love this chapter for many reasons; it is both direct and very realistic. Many are willing to talk about lessons learnt, but not to directly address the consequences of being fired and dealing with this scenario. Dr Matt Ryan has shone a light into a dark corner that many don't want to speak about.

From my own experience, being fired is incredibly humbling. We, as leaders, need to learn from such adverse circumstances. If and when this happens, it can be one of the best lessons that you ever receive. This is black and white in terms of personal impact; regardless of whether you agree or not with the situation, you will likely feel immediately uncomfortable and will usually want to get back into a new role as soon as possible. But this unease is what must drive your reflection and learning. Embracing these learnings will make you a better leader and CISO.

The key learnings from Matt's chapter include the following:

- *Abrupt job losses are common career experiences that, while initially devastating, can become transformative growth opportunities.* Your attitude to accepting this and reflecting is key to learning.

- *Leaders often experience a predictable pattern when terminated*, from shock/denial to response (immediate actions), recovery (rebuilding confidence), and retrospection (learning and adaptation).

- *Job loss leads to a network reality check.* The strength of your network can become amplified, and you will treasure professional relationships that are genuinely meaningful (versus those based solely on position and title; unfortunately, many industry 'friends' will disappear when the corporate email is deactivated).

- *Networking and maintaining positive relationships are crucial for future opportunities.* The senior leadership job market is a small ecosystem where past conflicts can resurface.

- *Forced exits often lead to valuable personal reassessment,* allowing you to reconnect with neglected aspects of your life and reconsider what success truly means to you.

- *Take the time to smell the roses.* Many executives find that stepping down the career ladder temporarily, exploring consulting, or pursuing entrepreneurial ventures can actually lead to more fulfilling careers better aligned with personal values.

- *Resilience is the ultimate skill.* Your ability to embrace failure, learn from it, and adapt distinguishes those who thrive long-term.

Part 3

Advanced CISO Toolkit

Your development journey continues in this part of the book with advanced skills you may not yet have mastered. These are subtle lessons that can transform CISO effectiveness, including on post-breach recovery, cybersecurity strategic planning, and talent development, while learning about proven dos and don'ts from seasoned practitioners. These chapters also include tips on helping you navigate critical vulnerability management and consider how to handle AI's promise and challenge as a CISO. These expert insights can help you unlock complex organisational challenges, build high-performing teams, and drive enterprise resilience through strategic thinking.

This part has the following chapters:

- *Chapter 18, Rebuilding After a Breach*
- *Chapter 19, Cyber Strategy That Makes A Difference*
- *Chapter 20, Dos and Don'ts for CISOs*
- *Chapter 21, Developing Cyber Talent*
- *Chapter 22, Managing Critical Vulnerabilities*
- *Chapter 23, AI: The Promise and Challenge*

Unlock this book's exclusive benefits now

UNLOCK NOW

Scan this QR code or go to `https://packtpub.com/unlock`,
then search this book by name.

Note: Have your purchase invoice ready before you start.

18

Rebuilding after a Breach

The average CISO has likely not experienced needing to rebuild after a serious incident – this is a story that is not often told. As a CISO, your job is typically protecting the enterprise and spending much of the day remediating known gaps.

This chapter is about the one that got away. Your enterprise was breached, and your job is to start again. There are very few CISOs who would want to talk about this topic; indeed, many have been fired because of a major incident.

When bad things happen, the first focused actions are to restore operations. This process itself is not the end, but in many ways the beginning. A cyber 'restore' is purely data restoration to your current platforms. The board and management will be concerned about how customer and stakeholder confidence is regained and that the business can resume.

In some cases, the embarrassing series of events that a breach can result in can have a real negative impact in terms of reputation damage. For these situations, just a restore is not enough; a restoration will require a rebuild too.

A rebuild is a large-scale transformation exercise. It is effectively 'rebuilding from the ashes', and every prior foundation should be evaluated and, when required, re-laid.

This competency is not one that most CISOs possess. You may have been asked to carry out large-scale projects before, but rebuilding is different, as the pressure on you varies greatly.

There are hard choices to make in terms of this change, and this is across the *people* and culture that allowed this breach to occur. This is not just within the cyber and technology teams but, perhaps more broadly, in the risk culture of the business that helped facilitate this event.

There will surely be *process* improvements that will be required, as well as *technology* remediation. A true cyber transformation requires a rethink to understand both how the breach occurred and how the defences would be redesigned to harden the capability.

While this is happening, there will continue to be pressure from management and boards on the progress of the rebuild. The concern will be around understanding how it reduces risk and whether this can be quantified. There will be many stakeholders who are concerned that this is quickly addressed.

Here, I'll introduce **Daryl Pereira, Director** and **APAC Head of Office of the CISO** at **Google Cloud**. He has extensive experience across different industries and geographies.

Daryl was previously the founding partner of the Cyber Consulting practice at KPMG Singapore and led the cyber practice across the ASEAN region; prior to that, he held global IT leadership roles at Deutsche Bank and Westpac Bank, and started his IT career working with the Federal Government of Australia. He is active in the industry and is an Adjunct Lecturer at the University of Canberra and Singapore Management University, and was formerly the President of ISACA Singapore. He is currently Governor at the Institute of Internal Auditors.

It will be fascinating to get inside Daryl's mind as he tackled such a rebuild, and understand how he did this and what lessons he learnt in doing so.

Redesigning the cyber strategy after a major breach

Daryl Pereira

Imagine my surprise when I was asked to step in to help redesign the cyber defence in a large organisation that had been recently breached by a skilled adversary, purported to be a nation state.

At the time, not much was known about how much investment had been put into cybersecurity, or how well trained the technology team was, or whether the business leaders understood and supported the cultural and organisational changes needed to bring about a permanent uplift to their organisation's cyber posture. Nonetheless, the challenge to make a difference to this organisation for the sake of the many stakeholders and the huge number of customers (numbering in the millions) who had been affected by the breach proved compelling. Given the complexity of the case, the immense size of the organisation and the media attention, I knew this would not be an easy task to take on, nor would it require any less than my full-time dedication for two years, plus even more time for the rollout and implementation. Steadying my nerves, I said to the stressed CISO caller, "Yes, I will do this. I want to help!"

I was given a mandate by the chairman of the board to work directly with the C-suite, to help them identify, design and implement core functions, processes and architectures needed to give them a better chance to resist the next attack.

Over the next few pages, I will walk you through the thinking, methods and processes that went into my redesign of the cybersecurity defence at this organisation, a project that would indeed prove to take two years of close supervision, as well as another three years of implementation.

My starting point — understanding the nature of the breach

The breach unfolded with stark clarity, as the detailed incident report resting before me attested. The digital forensics team had meticulously pieced together the attacker's journey, pinpointing the initial point of compromise: an overlooked and unprotected desktop. This rogue machine, absent from their inventory and therefore outside the scope of their monitoring systems, represented a glaring gap in the cyber defences. Its antiquated operating system, long since abandoned by vendor security updates, had presented an open invitation to malicious actors exploiting well-documented vulnerabilities.

The attackers' methodology was classic, yet effective: a carefully crafted phishing email designed to entice the unwary user, serving as the delivery mechanism for an insidious payload. Once executed, the malware established a foothold, deploying keyloggers to capture privileged credentials and, more alarmingly, rootkits that burrowed deep into the system, creating clandestine backdoor access points. This initial compromise was merely the first domino.

Operating with calculated patience, the attackers employed sophisticated evasion techniques to remain undetected by the existing intrusion detection systems. Time became their ally. They moved laterally through the network, exploiting trusted relationships and unpatched vulnerabilities in other connected systems. Over the weeks, their access broadened, creeping across network segments until they had achieved a terrifying level of control and the keys to the entire organisation's IT infrastructure lay within their grasp.

The incident report painted a grim picture of a security failure rooted in overlooked assets and insufficient vigilance, a stark reminder of the persistent and evolving threats we face.

Addressing the root causes

After reading the initial cyber forensics report of what occurred during the breach and the likely root causes, I focused on examining the root causes in more detail. My first task was to understand how the IT and security teams had responded during the breach, specifically to know how these teams worked with the business and other stakeholders to arrest the breach and regain control.

I found that several core functions needed attention.

Dedicated CISO versus CIO with security responsibilities

The absence of a CISO or a comparable high-ranking cybersecurity executive within the organisation signified a critical gap in its security framework. At the time, the highest cybersecurity authority resided in the IT security manager, who operated under the head of IT networks, ultimately reporting to the **Chief Information Officer** (**CIO**). This hierarchical structure reflected a historical perspective where senior management did not differentiate between general IT functions and the specialised domain of cybersecurity, effectively treating them as one and the same.

This lack of dedicated, top-level cybersecurity leadership can expose an organisation to significant risks, hindering the development and implementation of a proactive security strategy aligned with evolving threats and industry best practices. The absence of a CISO also limits an organisation's ability to effectively communicate cybersecurity risks to the executive level and integrate security considerations into strategic business decisions.

Central CISO team versus business-embedded CISO team

The organisation operated with a decentralised business model, comprising four separate entities, each with its own CEO, dedicated management structure and geographically dispersed operational centres. Despite this autonomy at the business level, a strategic decision had been made to centralise all IT functions and processes under a single, overarching IT organisation. This consolidation meant that while each individual business unit retained a CIO and a localised IT team, these personnel ultimately reported to the central CIO.

This structure facilitated interaction and alignment between the embedded IT teams and their respective business leadership; however, it extended to the cybersecurity domain too, where the CISO function was predominantly managed at the central level. In each of the four business-specific IT teams, the security presence was minimal, typically consisting of a limited number of security staff and one IT security manager, all under the direction of the central CIO. This resulted in a dichotomy where business-specific IT operations were locally managed, but cybersecurity oversight and implementation were largely dictated and controlled from a central point.

CEO and business leader buy-in with cyber strategy

At the time of the breach, there was limited CEO and board oversight of the cyber strategy, or governance over cyber risk management programs.

Skipping CEO and business leadership involvement in the cyber strategy is a risky move. Business leaders bring key insights on risk, operations and budgets that are crucial for a good strategy. Their absence can lead to a strategy that's too tech-focused and doesn't tackle real business risks or support the company's goals. Without them, the strategy might also miss out on vital resources and attention and not fit with overall planning. Plus, no business leaders involved means less accountability and makes enforcing security policies harder, potentially causing divisions and weakening the company's security, making it more vulnerable to threats.

IT management's protection, monitoring and response capabilities

The IT department lacked a mature and well-defined process for proactively protecting and monitoring its environment to detect potential security threats. The post-mortem of the cyberattack revealed that the attackers had gained control over a period of a few months and were in the network for several months before being discovered.

Beyond traditional protection controls such as password policies and user administration, a critical gap existed in the organisation's security posture. Specifically, there was an absence of identity and access management systems, where the use of shared privileged accounts and weak controls over authentication and privileged access had become the norm. In addition, data security controls over data confidentiality, integrity and availability were managed with weak and inconsistent policies and data encryption had not been implemented to protect the most valuable data/'crown jewels', as data classification had not been done. Most concerning was the lack of system inventory, resulting in a patchwork of security coverage with multiple unmanaged systems found to be outside the visibility of the IT team. The security architecture was insufficient for protecting digital assets and was a significant gap in the organisation's security.

In terms of threat monitoring, beyond the deployment of standard **Security Information and Event Management (SIEM)** tools, there was no comprehensive and resilient security monitoring. Processes designed for the early detection of malicious activities, continuous monitoring of system behaviour and efficient triage of any identified **Indicators of Compromise (IOCs)** or **Indicators of Attack (IOAs)** had not been implemented effectively. Furthermore, the organisation lacked adequate mechanisms for identifying and responding to unusual or anomalous user behaviour (which could signify insider threats or compromised accounts). This deficiency in proactive threat detection and monitoring capabilities left the organisation vulnerable to advanced persistent threats and other sophisticated cyberattacks that could potentially bypass traditional security controls. The reliance solely on SIEM tools without supplementary layers of detection and analysis created a significant blind spot in the organisation's overall security defences.

A 'refreshed' cyber security strategy

The organisation needed a new way to look at cybersecurity, something that was universally accepted as a standard and could form the foundation for building the new cybersecurity strategy.

I consider cybersecurity frameworks as a good starting point for organisations that need to uplift their approach to cybersecurity. Not only do you get a breadth of cyber topics that need to be covered, but you also get guidance through a comprehensive suite of controls and processes that would form the backbone of a good cyber defence. But for this scenario, something more was needed to connect the cyber framework to the business processes, business strategy, enterprise risk management and human-centric aspects of cybersecurity.

What we needed was a fusion of a cybersecurity framework with a cyber strategy framework. I borrowed from the NIST **Cybersecurity Framework (CSF)** and a cyber maturity framework compiled by a Big 4 firm. The fusion of these would then form the basis of a cybersecurity strategy for this organisation.

In this section, I will take you through how to design your own refreshed cybersecurity strategy that will be the optimal blend of business and technology.

Starting to shape a cybersecurity strategy

Shaping a cybersecurity strategy can be challenging with the multitude of stakeholders, business objectives, resource constraints, overlapping or disparate business and technology processes and a mix of legacy and emerging technology involved, each with its own risks.

There are many ways to design a cybersecurity strategy. My preference is to use a proxy by, as I've mentioned, conducting a cyber maturity assessment using a holistic cybersecurity framework that acknowledges the need for business objectives to be blended with IT imperatives, while allowing for operational and technology risks. This framework must be grounded by standards or de facto standards that have received industry-wide support, which then lends a credibility factor that can withstand C-suite, regulator and auditor scrutiny.

Where do you start with something like this? I'd suggest reviewing the organisation's business strategy and understanding how the IT strategy intersects with that business strategy. The resulting intersections of business needs and the supporting IT infrastructure (including data, systems, hardware, people, etc.) can form the basis of a cybersecurity strategy. To build on this, the following steps can be taken.

Stratify cyber risks

An organisation's cybersecurity strategy begins with a thorough classification of its cyber risks. This crucial step involves taking a multifaceted approach, starting with direct engagement with business leaders across various departments – CISOs should conduct detailed interviews to gain insights into each business unit's objectives, operational processes and reliance on technology and data. Simultaneously, a comprehensive review of the company's overarching business strategies and goals is essential to establish the organisation's overall risk tolerance. This understanding of risk appetite, as it relates to achieving business objectives and maintaining operational efficiency, forms the foundation for effective cybersecurity planning.

Identifying where cyber risks are most concentrated is a key outcome of this initial assessment. Business units that are integral to both current and future business operations, particularly those heavily dependent on technological infrastructure and data management, will inherently present a higher concentration of potential cyber threats.

It's important to recognise that the specific nature and distribution of these risks will vary significantly from one organisation to another. For example, an organisation that maintains its data and applications within its own physical infrastructure will face a different set of cybersecurity challenges and require different mitigation strategies compared to an organisation that primarily utilises cloud-based services for data storage and processing.

Increasingly, we are seeing that cloud-based IT environments are surpassing the cybersecurity resiliency of on-premises IT environments, as cloud service providers are able to embed security as part of the core design of the IT infrastructure and IT applications based on 'secure-by-design' and 'secure-by-default' principles.

The interconnectedness of systems, the sensitivity of the data handled and the potential impact of a security breach on business continuity and reputation will all contribute to the unique risk profile of each organisation. Therefore, a tailored approach to risk classification, based on a deep understanding of the business context, is paramount for developing an effective and relevant cybersecurity strategy.

Identify the 'crown jewels'

Essentially, a solid cybersecurity strategy for any business focuses on shielding its most important tech stuff. This means spotting the cyberattacks that could really mess things up for the key business functions, such as finance, orders, development, production and crunching data. Since all of these rely on tech, the main goal is to keep that tech running smoothly and keep it secure.

To do this right, companies need to really look at their sensitive information, the systems they use for it and all the underlying tech that makes everything work. This whole mix of data, software and hardware comprises the 'crown jewels' that must be protected at all costs, and is really the heart of the business. By focusing on these crucial areas, security teams can tackle the biggest risks and keep things going even when cyber threats pop up.

Adopt a cybersecurity standard

As mentioned earlier, to withstand external scrutiny, there is a need to ground your cybersecurity strategy and framework in established or authoritative cybersecurity standards or de facto standards. As there are basically only two such global cybersecurity standards, namely the U.S. **National Institute of Standards and Technology's (NIST's)** CSF and ISO/IEC 27001 information security management systems, CISOs are well placed to adopt either of these to define the control objectives for their cyber maturity uplift program.

NIST as a baseline for a cyber strategy

To redesign the cybersecurity strategy and defence capabilities in my organisation, I needed something that could provide the granularity of technology-focused controls to be implemented; not a checklist approach, but one based on assessed cyber risks. At the same time, I needed to go beyond the traditional technology controls and take a more holistic view of operational and people-related risks that intersect with cybersecurity.

As I mentioned earlier, I decided to use a combination of NIST CSF and the before-mentioned cyber maturity framework. NIST was chosen because it offers varying maturity levels, which allows the flexibility to specify controls based on the risk and the desired level of organisational maturity. Wrapping NIST in the overarching cyber maturity framework, consisting of six cyber domains, allowed closer integration with organisational and operational processes, and the opportunity to demonstrate to business leaders that the new cybersecurity strategy was business-aligned – thereby making it that bit easier to obtain C-suite and board buy-in.

NIST primer

The NIST framework distinguishes itself by organising essential cybersecurity elements into these domains: Identify, Protect, Detect, Respond, and Recover.

These encompass a cybersecurity lifecycle, providing a valuable structure for communicating technical controls to non-technical audiences such as business leaders and boards of directors.

Designing a refreshed strategy

When starting out with fixing a cybersecurity defence that has not performed to expectations, we need to acknowledge that security risks come not just from technology, but also from the people and processes of the organisation. With that as an underpinning concept, the next step to developing a new cybersecurity strategy is to identify the processes, people and technology aspects that will form a strong backbone for the strategy.

Specifically, there are six organisational domains that a cybersecurity strategy should cover.

Leadership and governance

Within this domain, I looked to implement structural changes and reporting lines that demonstrated due diligence, ownership and effective risk management.

Cyber governance starts with understanding:

- How business and IT management have defined their ownership of the cyber risk program
- The governance structure into which the CISO reports (for example, cyber committees, IT committees or risk committees)
- CISO team structure and accountability lines into business leadership
- Responsibility on the business leadership side for cyber risk in each business function

> Typically, we see an embedded **Business Information Security Officer (BISO)** type role sitting in the business lines representing the business line's interests, and working as a counterpart to the central CISO team that is responsible for the whole of the organisation's security policy, standards and architecture implementation.

As a key part of governance, I defined and identified the organisation's 'crown jewels', also known as sensitive data assets. Data classification must be a joint exercise with the business specifying the criticality of the data to business operations, while IT/CISOs define the controls needed to secure the different data types.

Another area of governance that can be overlooked is third-party supplier relationships. I worked with counterparts in the business lines to identify external relationships and dependencies. Outside of traditional vendor risk management, care should be taken in regard to other third parties upon which the organisation relies for the supply of services, people or technology.

Do we know and have we assessed the organisation's current cybersecurity capabilities? A good cybersecurity strategy identifies where investment is needed in terms of people, processes and technology, based on the security objectives, risk prioritisation and control gaps identified during the cyber maturity assessment.

Finally, I needed to understand how educated the board and executive management were on current cybersecurity concerns and cyber risk management solutions. Regular cybersecurity threat landscape updates, which are pertinent to the organisation's business, should be part of the CISO's board engagement. Hiring an external subject matter expert to assist with board education can also be valuable and provide fresh perspectives and wider industry viewpoints than would be possible if educational efforts were undertaken only by internal resources.

Human factors

In this second domain, I recognised that human factor risk continues to be one of the top exploited weaknesses in any cyber defence. The prevalence of 'social engineering' based attacks has grown over the years to become the preferred means of cyberattack in over 50% of successful breaches, according to various industry reports (for example, Verizon's 2024 Data Breach Investigations Report: `https://www.verizon.com/business/resources/reports/2024-dbir-data-breach-investigations-report.pdf`).

In order to manage human factor risks, I first worked on integrating a strong cybersecurity culture that empowered and ensured the right people were in key jobs, and had the right skills and knowledge to make the right decisions. I also ensured that cultural expectations were defined, and supported these by running curated and company-tailored training and awareness programs to help uplift staff awareness. Tailored training provided to front-line customer-facing staff should be different from the training provided to IT security staff and business leaders.

Another important measure for this domain is the organisation guarding against insider risk by having all staff with access to sensitive systems or 'crown jewel' data go through an intensive personnel screening or security vetting process.

Finally, any good implementation of human factors risk management requires the CISO to review how the organisation has defined talent management for cybersecurity roles and non-security technology-related roles. Each role should have its own learning path and defined credentials to support the individual's learning journey and levelling up of cybersecurity knowledge. For example, in my refreshed strategy, I ensured that IT personnel do not perform both IT and cybersecurity tasks without adequate security training, as these are now two clearly delineated roles that often have complementary but incompatible security control responsibilities.

Information risk management

In this third domain, my focus turned to understanding the risk management methodology of the organisation. Often, this entails working with the **Chief Risk Officer** (**CRO**) team to integrate the cybersecurity risk approach into the overarching organisational/enterprise-wide risk management framework. Cyber risks are, after all, seen by most CROs as a subset of the comprehensive enterprise risk framework.

A key starting point is to understand how the organisation identifies and communicates risk appetite and risk tolerance. This will set the baseline for categorising cyber risks into 'must fix now' versus 'can fix later' versus 'nice to have' categories. From this point, I was then able to review how each identified cyber risk was linked to each 'crown jewel' digital asset, before assessing the effectiveness of the risk mitigation or risk avoidance plans by undertaking a controls mapping process (the mapping goes from crown jewel -> cyber risk -> controls). I then defined the metrics used to measure risk, as well as the correct and continuous operation of the assigned controls.

Finally, to cap off this domain, it is imperative to include third-party supplier accreditation as a topic for risk and controls management. Third-party providers can include such things as the supply of IT systems, procurement of hardware, software design and coding and managed IT services such as security operations centres or IT helpdesks.

Business continuity and crisis management

Within this fourth domain, I looked into whether the organisation was prepared for another security event and how it could prevent or minimise the impact of a cyberattack through successful crisis and stakeholder management.

In many organisations, the **Business Continuity Plan** (**BCP**) covers various scenarios for business operation interruptions, with the usual suspects such as flood, fire, earthquake and physical intrusion/robbery covered well. However, I realised that the BCP in this organisation did not extend to cover cyber risk-related scenarios, such as malware, social engineering, **Denial-of-Service** (**DoS**), and supply chain attacks.

A good BCP that has been tailored for cyberattack scenarios will typically outline how management will manage cyber incidents, as well as how to perform an analysis of operational risks and financial requirements that may occur due to an attack. For each different cyberattack scenario, there must be a tailored and tested BCP that caters for a joint business and IT strategy to respond and recover. For example, a ransomware attack will require a response focused on cyber forensics to determine what data has been exfiltrated and the extent of control the attackers have within your IT environment, as well as ensuring offline back-ups are clean and restorable, while looking to regain control of your IT systems and data. On the other hand, the response to a DoS attack, where key IT systems and infrastructure are taken down by attackers, would be more focused on minimising operational downtime by blocking the initial attack, side-stepping by changing IP/URL addresses to avoid further IT infrastructure overload and adding layers of protection to network appliances.

It was crucial for me to review how resources were assigned and how they were trained to execute these BCPs. I did this by running mock scenarios. A written plan can only do so much, as without training and testing your personnel in their respective BCP roles and responsibilities, the plan may not be actionable and critical dependencies for different response tasks may go undiscovered.

> By assessing cyber-incident response capabilities, CISOs can help the organisation determine whether it might be more advantageous to retain a third-party provider with proven expertise in incident response.

One final key topic in this domain is the need for a good **Crisis Management Plan (CMP)**. A CMP is worth its weight in gold during a cyberattack, when all the different management teams are scrambling and possibly tripping over each other to execute their respective BCPs. I had to ensure that the CMP allowed for the CISO team to integrate with other business teams in decision-making processes involving corporate communications to regulators and customers, as well as internal stakeholders such as employees and management.

A good CMP can help prevent reputational damage in a crisis by planning when and how each team (and prior agreement on whether it is a business leader, IT leader or cyber leader) should handle queries from the media, regulators, the board, employees and other stakeholders.

Technology and operations

This domain is the one many CISOs find the most comfortable as it focuses on well-tested and familiar IT security and IT controls. Accordingly, I will not delve too deeply into this domain, as most CISOs will already be well versed in security protection tools, processes and operations.

One question to keep in mind for this domain is how control measures are implemented to address identified risks and minimise the impact of a cyberattack. I have used both NIST CSF and ISO 27001 as a baseline in previous organisations to help guide me in the design of appropriate security controls, based on the organisation's maturity level. In the case I am discussing in this chapter, I decided to adopt the NIST CSF as we were starting from a moderately low base of cyber resilience, which needed a multi-year program to uplift to a more acceptable level.

> The NIST CSF caters for varying starting and ending levels of cyber maturity based on the desired 'end state', and guides the CISO and management in progressing upwards, through four stages, namely, Partial (Tier 1), Risk-Informed (Tier 2), Repeatable (Tier 3) and Adaptive (Tier 4).

The first place I started was by looking at how technology (e.g., IT, OT, engineering operations) and security management have catalogued all relevant cybersecurity control objectives specified by policies and standards, and then linked those control objectives to the actual IT/cybersecurity controls that currently existed within the organisation. Where a gap was found between a control objective and the actual controls implemented, this then became a control gap that was documented for further review, risk assessment and risk ranking. Eventually, a new control would be designed, tested and deployed to mitigate any risk exposure due to this control gap.

When reviewing technology and operations controls, it is important to include controls spanning traditional IT topics such as IT inventory, secure software development lifecycle, patch management, IT production management and privacy. It is also important to extend this review to adjacent topics such as data governance, third parties and outsourcing, business continuity and regulatory requirements when assessing this domain.

As part of a good NIST-based cybersecurity defence, one area I paid special attention to is the 'Protect' function. I conducted a full review and then redesign of each control against the typical topics, such as identity, multi-factor authentication and access control, privileged access management, data security/encryption, information protection processes and protective technology. This was backed up by new controls over security patch management and security architecture redesign covering the IT infrastructure, operating system and application software layers. However, I was cognisant that one of the root causes of the scale of the cyberattack was the organisation's then-current inability to detect cyberattacks or malicious activity in a timely manner, with the attack going undiscovered for several months. This meant a full redesign and implementation of continuous monitoring systems and threat and vulnerability management, as well as implementing structured processes for anomaly detection, all of which are crucial to discovering and analysing potential pathways for cyberattacks in a timely manner.

Finally, I took great care to integrate the new CISO team and operations with the broader IT service management activities to ensure that no team was running in operational silos. Any silos reduce the operational effectiveness of key controls, where it is common for such controls to span across the responsibilities of various IT teams or cybersecurity teams. A tight bond with the IT team, together with clearly documented roles and responsibilities, is crucial to securing this fifth domain.

Legal and compliance

The final domain of a cybersecurity maturity uplift program is every CISO's favourite topic. While we must all live in a world that is determined by relevant regulatory and international certification standards for our respective industries, it is important to remember that as CISOs, we should always use regulatory compliance as a baseline of essential security controls and processes. By this, I mean that regulatory compliance is not the high watermark I would want to aim for when it comes to building up my organisation's cyber maturity. Instead, IT/cyber regulatory compliance forms a good baseline or foundation from which we can draw inspiration or comfort that we are doing the essentials. A risk-focused CISO knows, however, that we must go beyond regulatory requirements to identify additional controls, technology, people and processes that need to be deployed based on the identified risks in the information risk management domain. Hence, a risk-based approach that builds on top of legal and regulatory requirements was what I sought to implement.

To crystallise this new way of thinking, I had to seek support from the board and CEO to formalise cybersecurity as a recurring item for the audit committee and the risk committee, as well as the IT management committee. This allowed me to raise the importance of cybersecurity as an ongoing 'business risk', not just an 'IT risk' as it was perceived at the time. This also allowed the business leaders and directors on the risk committee to gain a view of much-needed investments to bolster the cyber defences, be it more management oversight and support, more specialised cyber professionals, better integration of cybersecurity into other operational processes or simply better security technology.

Cyber security goes beyond IT security

As I worked through the project to uplift the cybersecurity defence, assessing the key areas for cybersecurity investment and building a new cyber strategy, one principle kept recurring time and time again – that CISOs need to also be business savvy.

During various conversations with the group CEO and the line-of-business CEOs, it became apparent that to be successful, any cybersecurity strategy would need their buy-in. This buy-in would need to be built on a precise understanding of their business objectives and must address business risks arising from their push towards digital transformation, the realities of remote work and increased cyberattacks targeting their expanding digital infrastructure. I also saw great benefit in engaging early with the risk owners (i.e., business process and business system owners) because I could facilitate and work with them from the start to address the cyber risk that they now agreed would impact business operations, rather than just IT.

Previously, cybersecurity was seen as a subset of IT and under the purview of only the CIO. But now, with the uplift of management awareness, boardroom support and buy-in from management, the CISO was seen as a business enabler, allowing the organisation to embrace new ways of digital transformation in a safe and responsible manner. This was the biggest change in the cyber culture in the organisation, and it allowed me to facilitate collaboration across the different business lines and the IT department.

I would also stress that a 'cyber resilience by design' approach is crucial and requires security controls to be integrated from the initial planning stages rather than being an afterthought.

CISOs have to drive a comprehensive transformation. This begins with fostering a culture where cyber risk awareness becomes part of every employee's mindset and decision-making process. This cultural shift must be supported by embedding dedicated security experts directly within project teams. This is especially the case for strategic initiatives involving critical digital assets and significant IT investments. These embedded experts ensure that security considerations are woven into every phase of implementation and help to prevent costly security gaps.

Effective security-by-design controls and architecture are built through strategic investment in people first, processes second, and technology third. Unfortunately, the most advanced security tools are only as effective as the skilled professionals who implement them and with well-defined processes that govern their use.

Cybersecurity is a team sport, and your own success as a CISO requires coordination between business units, IT departments and cybersecurity teams. As a CISO, you need to be prepared to break down silos and drive an integrated approach – that is where security becomes everyone's responsibility.

Finally, I leave you with this advice: CISOs should educate the board and C-suite on the latest cyber challenges, and continually test their organisation's cyber resiliency through red-teaming, bug bounties and table-top cyber crisis exercises with senior management. This will not only ensure that cyber crisis management teams are prepared for high-pressure situations, but also ensure the moving target that we deal with in this profession remains relevant and visible.

In this reality of exponential growth of cyberattacks, a strong relationship with senior management, a risk-based cybersecurity strategy, program and culture and an 'assumed breach' mindset are essential. This proactive approach is driven by the CISO and helps to ensure everyone, across all business units, anticipates and prepares for cyberattacks. This is the key to building a cyber-resilient organisation.

David's key takeaways — Rebuilding after a breach

Daryl has had the career privilege to take an architected 10,000 foot persepctive to redesign cyber defences that have failed. This requires both a strategic mindset and an ability to zoom into the fine details.

For most of us who have been a CISO, this is not a task that we have likely ever completed. Indeed, this is a task that I would never wish upon anyone. However, if this does occur, then taking the lived experience of Daryl and his peers can help you be successful.

Key points learned in this chapter include:

- *Redesigning cybersecurity defence takes time*, particularly if you are working for a large organisation, and following a significant breach. For Daryl, this meant at least two years of full-time dedication plus three years of implementation.

- *Your inventory accuracy matters*. The breach Daryl refers to in this chapter originated from an overlooked desktop outside the inventory scope, with attackers using phishing and malware to establish access, eventually gaining control of the entire IT infrastructure.

- *Identify and address organisational deficiencies*. In Daryl's case, this included the previous absence of a dedicated CISO position, misalignment between centralised security and decentralised business units, limited CEO/board involvement in cyber strategy and inadequate monitoring capabilities.

- *Draw on industry best practices and guidelines*, such as NIST CSF. This has the benefit of helping you align with industry standards, and may make it easier for you to obtain C-suite and board buy-in.

- *Protect your crown jewels*. Identifying and protecting your organisation's 'crown jewels' (critical business technologies, data, systems, and infrastructure central to operations) is vital.

- *Ensure your cyber strategy encompasses the six key organisational domains*: leadership and governance, human factors, information risk management, business continuity and crisis management, technology and operations and legal and compliance.

- *Embrace cyber resilience by design*. This approach can be valuable as it means integrating security controls from the outset rather than adding them later, with board-level championship of this approach.

- *Think assumed breach*. Effective cybersecurity extends beyond IT security to address business risks arising from digital transformation and hybrid working, requiring collaboration across departments and an 'assumed breach' mindset.

19

Cyber Strategy That Makes a Difference

A CISO would typically work on the cyber strategy every day. This does not necessarily mean a cyber strategy document, but could mean executing plans to improve and reduce risk. A cyber strategy that makes a difference is what a CISO needs to successfully defend against threat actors and the increasing attack vectors that are emerging globally.

I've been known to talk about the synergy of a giraffe and a zebra on the plains of the African Serengeti. Their strategy is to work together to avoid being eaten by lions.

Figure 19.1: Giraffe and zebras (photo from Pexels.com)

Together, they are stronger when they use their natural advantages to help each other. The giraffe has the Darwinian height advantage and unmatched peripheral vision to see the perimeter and the threat of a lion approaching. On the other hand, the zebra is closer to the ground and has sharper hearing. Ideally, both of them will alert the other to the presence of a lion before it becomes an issue.

CISOs, too, are looking to not be eaten by ravenous lions. They want to protect themselves and their organizations from risk, and a strong cyber strategy is key to them doing that.

What makes a good strategy? How do you create a strategy that encourages and enables both the giraffes and zebras in your organization to play their part in keeping the organization safe?

The CISO has many conflicting stakeholders, including the CIO, executive stakeholders, regulators, and external customers and/or partners. Each of these participants in the process will advocate for their own priorities.

A strategy will provide clarity on what will be in scope and what won't be a priority. It will need to articulate what needs to be addressed as the primary objective, but also pay some attention to how.

Every strategy will need a strategic vision that articulates cyber objectives around elements such as resourcing, including insourcing, external partnering, and outsourcing. The strategy must also be very clear on what matters – what are the priorities?

The cyber strategy will be scrutinized by the board, management, and regulators, so it needs to be both comprehensive and credible.

Cybersecurity has been described as an infinite loop. As fast as you uplift a cyber control, there will be more to do. Against this backdrop, how do you craft a strategy that provides the best combination of committed actions but also allows for iteration based on shifts in the threat landscape?

It is not possible to address every risk, and there will be new ones that keep emerging – supply chain attacks, quantum computing, **generative AI (genAI)**-enabled attacks, and so on. The CISO will not have sufficient team bandwidth to address every threat and must prioritize those that are most relevant and that pose the most risk to their organization. This is a complex and difficult task to get right.

Getting the cyber strategy right is critical, but it is equally as critical to then execute the strategy. In essence, in my view, it is all about building and executing a cyber strategy that makes a difference.

It is my pleasure to introduce **Jim Boehm**, **Chief Digital Risk Officer** at **McKinsey & Co.**, a brand-new role. I should note that when Jim started to write this chapter, he was an Expert Partner in Digital and Cyber Risk at McKinsey, and his role was 100% client-facing. Jim has therefore seen many enterprises execute a cyber strategy with his assistance. He has observed what has worked and not worked so well for different companies.

Over to you, Jim.

What makes a good cyber strategy?

Jim Boehm

Over the last 11 and a half years, I have had the incredible privilege to work with dozens of companies on their cyber strategies. These engagements have spanned a diverse array of industries, including banking, insurance, public sector, critical infrastructure, transportation and logistics, retail, consumer packaged goods, high technology, telecommunications, start-ups, and investment funds. They have also varied significantly in scale, from Dow Jones Industrial Average constituents and FTSE/DAX 100 firms to smaller private equity portfolio companies. Geographically, my work has extended across North America, Latin America, Europe, Africa, Asia, and Australia.

Throughout these engagements, I have encountered a broad spectrum of organizational structures, including differing CISO reporting lines, operating models, insourcing and outsourcing arrangements, and other organization-specific characteristics. In this chapter, I will explain what I've learned and take you through the five elements I consider key to a good cyber strategy.

What good looks like

Over time, I've developed a perspective on what makes a good cyber strategy. 'Good,' in my view, simply means the cyber strategy does what it needs to do efficiently and effectively.

To elaborate, a 'good' cyber strategy in my mind fits the need well; it has everything you need and nothing you don't, is powerful but not overwhelming, and is enviable in its simplicity. There are no broken parts or loose ends. It stands the test of time, even if it needs to be purposefully modified every now and then to stay current. Perhaps most importantly, a good strategy does not sit on the shelf but is out in the field (even if only metaphorically) where its impact is evident. In a word, a good strategy is one that makes a difference – a *real* difference – in the day in the life of a CISO and their organization.

When David asked me to distill what makes a cyber strategy a 'good' one, I ultimately winnowed the things I have learned over the years down to five essential components. Let me go through these.

Clear 'us' versus 'them'

The profession of cybersecurity exists to combat people who are trying to do harm in the digital domain. So, to be cyber secure, we have to have a clear understanding of who is 'us' and who is 'them.' For your strategy to have even a prayer of succeeding, you must have this clear first and foremost.

Your adversaries (them) are not 'the business,' 'IT,' or 'the CFO.' Rather, 'them' refers to those who want to do you harm – military units trying to hurt your company (or, in the case of collateral damage, hurt your company via callous accident), nation states trying to siphon your data, criminal groups trying to extract financial gain, black hat activists who want to create havoc, and so on.

Hopefully, your colleagues also have the same mindset – the InfoSec team is not the enemy. You are all on the same team. 'Us' is inclusive of everyone in your company (excluding malicious insiders, of course), stakeholder groups that exist to help you, your vendors and partners who are doing work on your company's behalf (though, of course, an extra level of diligence is warranted in partnering with and securing your vendor community), and peer companies who are united in your common mission of defense.

Risk-based and rational

Organizations do not exist for the purpose of cybersecurity. Rather, organizations exist for the purpose of achieving a mission (or missions) in line with their vision (or visions), whether profit-making or not. Anything that would disrupt the ability or opportunity for that organization to achieve its aims is a risk.

Since the profession of cybersecurity exists to combat those who would do harm in the digital domain, it follows that the cybersecurity strategy must inherently be risk-based. In the context of a cybersecurity strategy, 'risk-based' means allocating the most attention and resources to the specific controls that focus on elevating cybersecurity maturity in areas that are the most exposed to business and operational harm.

Of course, part of being risk-based is being rational in the asks for attention, budget, and resources. Take too little and your organization will be exposed. Take too much and your organization will suffer from opportunity cost. We still have a larger mission to achieve, after all.

Integrated

In keeping with the previous theme, as CISOs, we must adopt the mindset that security is in the service of (though not subservient to – more on that later) technology, just as technology is in the service of the business.

Your strategy cannot exist on its own in a silo, just as security as a practice cannot be an ivory tower amid a sea of risk complications and complex technologies. Your peers in the risk and technology functions need to be some of your closest collaborators (respecting, of course, the boundaries of 'credible challenge' required by most regulators), constantly working together to further the aims of the business. Risk's job is to identify and articulate business and operational risks; technology's job is to accelerate and broaden business and operational impact via the digital domain. Security must support both, and both must support security.

Security is the 'how' of risk management in the digital domain, and it is security's remit to deliver digital risk management in a way that balances effectiveness and effortlessness.

The CISO's strategy must strive to be both effective in its control and as effortless as possible for adjacent stakeholders. As such, the CISO and their team must understand and work in lockstep alongside – not in opposition to – both risk and technology to improve effectiveness while doing so in such a way that minimizes disruption and toil.

Easy to explain, easy to understand

If you are a CISO, the cyber strategy is *your* strategy. You own it and are accountable for delivering on its vision and mission. However, if you are the only person who can understand what the cyber strategy says or how it allocates resources, then it is not a good one. Your strategy exists to explain your vision and mission to everyone who is not you. Crucially, this includes those outside the security realm.

Measured, managed, and modified

This is perhaps the biggest gap I see in most cyber strategies. To make a real difference, a cyber strategy must be managed to achieve the outcome(s) it states. To know where, when, and how to tweak certain activities or efforts in the name of management, you must have both absolute and comparative metrics that have been measured over time to inform which interventions need to be made and to what extent.

Finally, to keep the strategy relevant so it can continue to make a difference as technology and the world around your organization change, you will need to modify your strategy from time to time. Again, to know what to modify and to what extent, you must have measurements marking both where you are now and where you want to go. In many ways, modification is just a more periodic but often larger form of management – even though the underlying principles are essentially the same.

These things are easy to say, but hard to do. People are hard, risks are unclear and constantly evolving, the risk and technology organizations are running at their own speed and in different directions, clarity is elusive, and measurement requires time and financial investment that will often be challenged as "better used elsewhere." But those challenges do not relieve us of our obligation to still pursue them.

So, how does a CISO move from simple catchphrases to implementation? Let's dive into each area a little more.

Clear 'us' versus 'them'

As CISOs, we must start here. Though by no means easy to achieve, this dimension is perhaps the easiest to crystallize – 'them' are those who would do you harm in the digital domain, if they are successful. 'Us' is everyone else. Not every 'us' is the same, of course, and some of those 'on the team' may need to be carefully managed and even monitored. But even those arms' length or oversight organizations that sometimes may cause us to feel pain can still contribute to our institutional accountability of managing digital risk.

I started my career in the U.S. military and had the privilege of working alongside some of the finest military personnel around the globe. Starting right from my first day at the U.S. Naval Academy, I was exposed to, and shaped by, a combined ethos of 'ship, shipmate, self' and 'mission first.' It was only after being in a theater of combat that I came to viscerally understand that which had been taught in the halls of the Academy – even our adversaries shared the same ethos among themselves.

The world is not black and white, of course, but at least the military mindset and resulting orientation to the world were easy for me to grasp as a young officer in my 20s.

Many in the security profession today share the same background as mine, but it is by no means universal. Nor does it need to be. Anyone who has ever been on any kind of team – be it sports, school, a family unit, anything really – can tap into the 'us' versus 'them' mindset. But why is it so hard to put into practice?

It is hard because people are people, and many people look for ways to assert themselves as individuals before looking for ways to collaborate. This means that in nearly every interaction, the humans involved are looking for openings to advance their own agenda, declare their own expertise, or affirm their own ego. Sometimes, the people you will be working with have suffered a string of self-perceived defeats in other arenas of their day and are simply looking to put 'points on the board' to give themselves a little boost of much-needed dopamine. These are all real and valid drivers for some of the organizational friction that can lead a CISO to consider those within their own organizations as 'them' – and vice versa. Once, I even had a CISO declare to me that he'd rather work with the attackers than with his peers! It was a silly statement on the face of it, of course, but still, his point was made.

A CISO must be the bigger leader in these hundreds of daily interactions to demonstrate why collaboration is pre-eminent, set the example for the security function and others, build collaboration capabilities – whether digital or human – and institute incentives for both good and bad behavior.

Some days, just working to clarify and shore up the relationship with those who should be easily understood as 'us' will take up the majority of the CISO's effort. But without this first and foremost job, your strategy will fail – or at least go nowhere fast.

Risk-based and rational

Despite what cyber maturity assessments would tell you, our job as CISOs is not to do ever more *without* bounds. Rather, it is to do ever more *within* bounds. This is what being risk-based means at its essence.

The 'bounds' here are the business and operational risks that need to be mitigated. There are other constraints, of course – namely, budget, talent, speed and scale of innovation, and laws and regulations – but the 'bounds' of a CISO's job are shaped and clarified by the requirements to mitigate the digital risks affecting their organization, partners, and customers. How much and how deeply to mitigate those risks is even within the risk-based bounds as well – too little, and time and resources will get consumed by addressing risk failures; too much, and the time and resource investment creates opportunity cost risk for others that might otherwise grow the business or scale an innovation in IT.

To be risk-based, then, it means that a CISO must intimately understand the business's and the technology team's strategies and concrete objectives and the full spectrum of risks associated with those strategies (hopefully organized and clarified by the risk function). By understanding and internalizing not just the words of the business and technology strategies but the spirit and intent of them, the CISO can start to shape the control environment through their strategy accordingly. The contours of that strategy then need to be circulated to and syndicated with risk and IT peers, and a great CISO will be accepting of feedback and collaboration to achieve the optimal risk effectiveness and control effortlessness outcome. One important point of feedback and collaboration is, of course, the budget, and related resource requests a CISO will make to support their strategy. These cannot be absolute numbers; they must be made in the context of the broader business environment and corporate climate. In this way, the CISO's budget is very much relevant and relative to the other strategies and organizations they will support in execution.

Similar to budget, reporting of risk also needs to be appropriate and relevant. As CISOs, we have all been asked and seen headline news reports of an absolute monetary amount that is at risk due to digital risk and/or lack of cybersecurity. While at a macro level (e.g., industry, country, etc.), these can help grab attention and start a conversation, at a company level, they are foolish. I have seen such exercises result in risk exposures in excess to a company's net worth (implying that the business would need to pack up and fold in the event of a major breach), cast incredulity on the CISO's entire strategic orientation, and, indeed, raise questions about the CISO's capacity for strategic thought, due to the exposure of the layers of 'expert' judgment that went into it, and fall by the wayside of 'interesting academic exercise but not practically useful' due to the ultimate outcome being shaped far more overwhelmingly by the business and operational risk contours and enterprise budgetary constraints.

'Raising awareness for the importance of cyber' with eye-watering numbers may have been required a few years ago, but companies today understand cyber's importance. At the board level, conversations with and among directors are only confused when trying to work through the calculations and assumptions to understand what to do about 'the number.' Even cyber insurance policy levels and capital set-asides are more calibrated to the overall economic position and exposure of a company rather than any absolute calculation focused specifically on cyber. So, my very strong opinion is that absolute cyber risk calculations at a company level are folly, and do not add value.

That said, what *does* add value is going through the risk-based exercise itself. Debating what a company's risk categories and impact levels are, and therefore what an organization's top risks are, is extremely important. Connecting those risks to the business lifecycle, through to the assets, threats, and, finally, to the controls that mitigate risk by frustrating threats, is absolutely essential for creating a risk-based strategy. So, by all means, go through the effort. Please! But just before the time comes to calculate 'the number,' take a step back instead and look at the *relative position* of the various business and operational risks that your team has evaluated to one another. *That* is valuable and is easy for those with whom you must communicate and collaborate to understand. Instead of trying to defend a number, you will instead have the opportunity to discuss why 'risk A' is worse than 'risk B,' which parts of the business 'risk A' applies to, which assets it could impact, which threats could bring it about, and which controls are needed to mitigate the risk potential. You will then be able to do the same for 'risk B,' but demonstrate why the package of controls to address 'risk A' outweighs the package of controls to address 'risk B.' The conversation will go smoothly because the board and your non-security peers will intuitively understand this comparative approach between two risks, and your strategy will be risk-based and rational.

Integrated

As much as CISOs are a very lonely bunch (believe me, I've talked with a great many!), they are very much not alone. Every CISO is one of many chief executives in an organization who has a profit or impact mission that is shared across their peers. The CISO's strategy must reflect the same; otherwise, the implementation of that strategy will be out of step with and overwhelmed by the business, risk, and technology strategies that will dominate it.

The two most important stakeholder functions for the CISO to partner with and embed their strategy in are risk and IT. Ideally, the CISO is a peer to the CRO and CIO, but more often, the CISO reports to one or the other (our internal McKinsey cybersecurity organizational benchmarking data shows that the vast majority of CISOs report to someone with a chief technology role, e.g., CIO, CTO, Chief Digital Officer).

Practically, for the CRO function, this means that digital risk (sometimes called 'cyber risk,' although this can create confusion between cyber 'threats' and 'risks') must be in the Enterprise Risk Management framework, must be integral to the risk appetite statements for each relevant enterprise risk, and must be tied directly to the **key risk indicators** (**KRIs**) for each relevant enterprise risk via risk thresholds. This means that the CRO organization should (and, in the cases of many regulated industries, must) have an independent point of view on the level of digital (cyber) risk that the company as a whole is exposed to. Importantly, the risk function – or whoever looks after risk in each entity – is entitled to its *own* view on risk levels relative to risk thresholds and appetite. Since risk retains its own view, the CISO really must understand that view and work to fit the contours of their strategic program of control to the contours of the enterprise risk environment. This is what will result in risk mitigation effectiveness.

For the technology function, practically, this means that the controls identified as rational and necessary to address the levels of risk identified must be embedded as much as possible in the design-deliver-operate-maintain-retire lifecycle of IT. This means that security personnel need to do the following:

- Attend (and contribute to!) design meetings.
- Have tools and capabilities (supported by a healthy level of training and consultative partnership) embedded in delivery pipelines (well-enabled and supported CI/CD pipelines in true product-oriented DevSecOps teams are the standard here).
- Be on-call to troubleshoot operational frictions or disruptions.
- Partner in the smooth facilitation of operations to ensure 'time to market' timelines are met and delivery is a straightforward process.
- Obsessively revisit existing control tooling and capabilities to revamp and retire whatever is no longer helping to optimize effectiveness and effortlessness.

As CISOs, our strategies need to set our security team up to deliver on both commitments to our closest peers. After all, hearkening back to the 'us' versus 'them' mandate, we're all in this together.

Easy to explain, easy to understand

It is a very rare day when I ask a CISO, "Do you have a strategy?" and I get "No" for an answer. In the last 11+ years, I can recall only 2 or 3 times in which that has been the response.

At the opposite end of the spectrum is how often I ask a CISO, "Do you have a strategy?" and they answer "Yes" – but then cannot produce a written document that goes into any amount of depth that draws clear inspiration from the strategies of their risk and IT peers, articulates their team's goals and objectives in terms of specific risk and IT goals and objectives, allocates resources according to the execution of specific 'playbooks' focused on achieving the mutual objectives, or lays out the framework and logic of measurements that will form the basis of management and modification. Many times, there is not even a document at all – just a series of sketches or pages of description that have to rely heavily on the CISO's voiceover to make any sense. Often, that voiceover is very good (which is always very encouraging!) – but that does not mean that they have a strategy.

As a CISO, you must write all this down. Sure, for your own clarity of thought – but much, much more for those around you. In so many ways, your strategy isn't even for you; it's for everyone else. You cannot deliver on all the promises, requirements, and optimizations of strategy yourself, but as a strategic leader, you need others to execute on your vision and the organization's mission on its behalf. So, it needs to be articulated clearly and specifically. This will take time, but consider that the execution and operation of your security team will be a direct reflection of the clarity and detail of your strategy. So, if your strategy is a loose collection of scribbles or an intuitive semi-rambling of thoughts and ideas, imagine what the execution of your team will look like!

Practically, you should be able to explain the security team's vision, mission, and key 'strategic imperatives' (or 'initiatives') – each with a corresponding threat and business 'why' – in a one-page memo or simple one-page PowerPoint slide graphic. I worked with one CISO in the public sector who had his one-pager laminated, and he carried it with him literally everywhere in the notebook he brought with him. I saw him take it out and share it with senior executives in his organization at least a half dozen times. The level of clarity and conviction he was able to build in those critical stakeholder management moments, and the resulting level of material support he was able to get to further his objectives, was incredibly impressive to witness and has stuck with me as a 'best practice' ever since.

The other aim of a good strategy is simplicity. The strategy should be easy to understand, MECE (i.e., mutually exclusive, collectively exhaustive) in its initiatives, structured in terms of business and technology strategy-to risk-to control-to resourcing-to measurement, written in non-technical language, and deliberately crafted to speak to both the security team and external stakeholders.

My own personal counsel to CISOs is that a full strategy should cover a three-year horizon (shorter than that and the document devolves into discussing tactics; longer than that and the digital world will have changed dramatically), but with the details refreshed every year. Importantly, work on the new strategy should begin six to nine months before the current strategy runs out – otherwise, the security team runs the risk of deviating from the path and introducing chaos.

Good strategies are hard – very hard – to get right, but partnering with those in your organizations who write great strategies (e.g., the CEO's strategy team, and the corporate communications and engagement teams) can help you understand 'what good looks like' and practice your craft. The 'C' in CISO stands for 'Chief,' after all, which means regardless of your reporting level, you are very much a strategic executive. So, your strategy and strategic communications need to reflect that.

Measured, managed, and modified

Of the five dimensions, this is probably my favorite. This is for two reasons: first, if you've done the previous items correctly, your measurement, management, and modifications over time will keep the engine of security humming nicely – and it will reinforce your own ability to understand whether you've had a job well done. Second, even if you have not followed the counsel of the previous four dimensions, if you are really good at measurement, management, and modifications over time, they can somewhat compensate for any failures in the previous dimensions and still make you a decent CISO.

At its core, measuring your security team's output enables you to make fact-based adjustments to and trade-offs between activities, areas of focus, levels of resource, work focus, and all of the other dimensions required of your role.

Practically, measurement means the calculation and reporting of metrics that allow you, your team, and your peers to understand the 'altitude and trajectory' of the security team's performance. I started my career flying, and so the concepts of 'altitude' and 'trajectory' were professionally drilled into me from the start. Within security, I like to think of 'altitude' as the risk levels I want to hit (measured via risk appetite levels, and KRIs derived from the associated risk thresholds) and 'trajectory' as the performance levels I am achieving in the service of not just risk management effectiveness but also control delivery effortlessness (measured via OKRs and KPIs derived from the associated control domains and initiative program management).

A very nice byproduct of taking this approach is that it enables you, as a CISO, to explain the health of your program in both risk and performance terms very easily to anyone in your organization who is not deep into the profession of security. I have seen this be especially helpful for CISOs who report to their boards. A board member may not be deep in security, but they can understand the consequences of a trajectory that won't get you to altitude, or one that threatens to take your altitude below your risk 'hard deck' (i.e., risk appetite and threshold levels). This enables them to then engage in a meaningful way to restore balance to the CISO and your team's efforts. "What will it take to fix our altitude/trajectory problem?" could be a good way of articulating how board members engage in this dynamic. Whether it's requesting more resources, emphasizing the importance of partnership with other stakeholders, asking for guidance on the pre-eminence of 'risk A' versus 'risk B,' or even just articulating support from other peers' programs, by taking this measurement approach, the CISO can finally engage board members in a real conversation about risk and resourcing – which, ultimately, is the board's job to help the executive team accomplish.

Once things are measured, then they can be managed. No major strategic muscle movements here – rather, periodic (e.g., monthly, weekly, every other week, etc.) checkups and regularly scheduled report reviews (e.g., quarterly) of the overall plan should be enough.

Management is getting into the trenches with your team and helping them navigate the myriad millions of 'little things' that they will need to do on a daily basis to execute on your strategy. Whether it's facilitating a meeting to integrate a new control tool into a delivery pipeline, nego-tiating with a vendor to expand the coverage of a critical tool, counseling a team member on how to expand their knowledge into an area where the security function has a current gap, or even just celebrating with the team over coffee and donuts for hitting a significant milestone, with mastery of the metrics at hand, a CISO's day-to-day should be straightforward. Each action you take can be focused on pushing a KPI here, explaining an OKR there, all in the service of creeping ever closer to achieving your KRIs. With such a mindset, even incidents can be taken in stride – with mastery of the metrics, you know where you are weak operationally and exposed in terms of risk, and so your decisions in the incident can be guided accordingly. In this way, your day-to-day may not get any easier, of course, but it does at least have a solid structure and set of facts to give you, your team, and your stakeholders a very strong sense of working your way together down a clear path.

Finally, we live in a dynamic and complex world. I am constantly stunned at the speed and changes in direction that CISOs and their teams must contend with. Remember big data? Cloud? Block-chain? Now, genAI is all the rage, and people are still talking about quantum computing. Although your strategy might be oriented toward navigating the next three years, it is highly unlikely it will remain fully intact during that time. Instead, the strategy, like business, risk, and technology, must be able to be modified over time as needed. This does not mean throwing everything out or making 180-degree pivots every 6 months, of course, but it does mean reserving some budget and revisiting priorities on a quarterly or semi-annual basis to modify and reallocate things within your strategic framework and objectives as needed. Measurement is essential to your ability to do this, too – with good measurement, modification is just another and slightly more emphatic form of management. You have your framework, you have your objectives, you have the activities that need to be done, and a line of sight into the resources and direction of travel of your key initiatives. Armed with this information, you can modify your team's approach and efforts to keep the engine of security running smoothly. Conversely, without good measurement, you and your team will feel pulled in hundreds of seemingly different and disparate directions, subject to headline exclamations, bright and shiny new technologies, or the whims of peer executives. This is definitely no place any CISO or their teams want to be.

My summary

Good, effective strategies that make a difference have these five components: clear 'us' versus 'them,' risk-based and rational, integrated, easy to explain and easy to understand, and measured, managed, and modified. Keeping these components in mind during your next cyber strategy refresh will give you a fighting chance that your strategy will make a difference and is likely to make your own day in life as a CISO just a little bit easier along the way.

David's key takeaways — Cyber strategy that makes a difference

Jim's chapter provides great insights into creating an effective cyber strategy from a leader who has many years of experience in this domain.

The essence of a cybersecurity strategy is to address the greatest risks first while, as a secondary measure, also seeking compliance. This is a juggling act, as you also must be aligned with the business strategy and ensure that your efforts are not creating too much friction for commercial processes. A good cyber strategy must set the direction for the organization's cybersecurity uplift but then also have some adaptability to adjust quickly as the threat vectors shift. However a great cyber strategy is able to address the greatest risks first, as well as enhance the customer experience and help with compliance. Sometimes achieving 2 of these objectives is possible, but every now and then you can attain a 'trifecta' and be able to pick all three winners!

Some key points from this chapter include the following:

- *Focus on external threats.* Clearly define 'us' versus 'them' in your strategy, to ensure that the focus is on the true adversaries (external threats such as nation states and criminals), rather than internal colleagues.

- *Building collaborative relationships is essential for strategy success*, particularly with business, IT, and risk teams, as internal friction can undermine the entire security mission.

- *Adopt risk-based decision making.* This requires effective cyber strategies that align with business objectives and focus on mitigating risks within reasonable bounds, avoiding both under-protection and over-investment. CISOs should aim for relative risk comparisons rather than absolute financial figures, as these are often meaningless and can damage credibility with leadership.

- *Partner closely with CROs and CIOs* to ensure that security controls are built into enterprise risk frameworks and IT lifecycles from design to retirement. Security strategies cannot exist in isolation but must be deeply embedded within the broader business, risk, and technology strategies of the organization.

- *Your strategy should be concise and clear.* A good cyber strategy must be easily explainable in a one-page summary that anyone outside of security can understand and act upon. The strategy should avoid technical jargon and clearly articulate vision, mission, and objectives with corresponding business justifications for maximum stakeholder buy-in.

- *Implement clear metrics and measurements.* These should track both 'altitude' (current risk levels) and 'trajectory' (performance toward goals) to enable fact-based decision making. Without proper metrics, security teams become reactive and subject to executive whim rather than following a strategic path.

- *An adaptive strategy is required.* Given the dynamic nature of technology and threats, strategies must be flexible enough to be modified regularly while maintaining their core framework and direction.

20

Do's and Don'ts for CISOs

The CISO is a role without a safety net and could be compared to walking on a tightrope. There is the pull of gravity, making you feel the natural pull to fall. Then there are the many stakeholders that apply pressure to each CISO, often leading to a fear of failure.

How does a CISO succeed in this environment? There is a growing number of regulators that must always be respected, and at times, your role is to ensure that progress is being communicated without overstating or understating the result. As a CISO, getting and maintaining our balance on the tightrope is a constant battle.

Let me delve into the multifaceted role of the CISO and explore the essential do's and don'ts that define success in the position. A CISO's primary responsibility is to safeguard an organization's information assets. This involves developing and implementing a comprehensive cybersecurity strategy aligned with the organisation's overall business objectives. In doing this, the modern CISO navigates a complex web of evolving cyber threats, regulatory requirements, and business needs, demanding a blend of technical expertise, leadership acumen, and communication prowess.

A crucial 'do' for a CISO is to prioritise clear and consistent communication. Cybersecurity risks and solutions must be articulated in a language that resonates with executive leadership and the board of directors, translating technical jargon into actionable insights. Transparent communication, especially during security incidents, is paramount to maintaining trust and minimising reputational damage.

Fostering a security-conscious culture is another vital 'do'. This involves more than just implementing technical controls; it requires cultivating a workforce that understands and embraces cybersecurity best practices. Regular security awareness training, coupled with clear policies and procedures, helps in this regard and empowers employees to become active participants in the organisation's defense. The culture should also be one of vigilance, where employees are encouraged to report suspicious activity without fear of reprisal.

Linked to this is another key 'do' for CISOs: building strong relationships. Collaboration with other departments, including IT, legal, and compliance, is essential to ensure alignment on security goals. Developing relationships with key stakeholders, both internal and external, also facilitates effective communication and collaboration during security incidents.

An effective cybersecurity strategy hinges on a thorough understanding of the organisation's risk profile. Regular risk assessments are essential to identify vulnerabilities and prioritize mitigation efforts. This involves not only evaluating internal systems and processes but also considering the risks posed by third-party vendors. As such, another key 'do' is to establish a robust vendor risk management program, ensuring that external partners adhere to the organisation's security standards.

Let's move on to 'don'ts'. While technology plays a crucial role in cybersecurity, a common 'don't' is to rely solely on technological solutions. Security is not just a technology problem; it's a people problem. Human error remains a significant factor in security breaches (highlighting the need for continuous training and awareness programs). A CISO must recognise this human element and invest in strategies to address it.

Another critical 'don't' is to underestimate the ever-evolving nature of the threats we face. Cybercriminals are constantly developing new tactics and techniques. This requires CISOs to stay informed and adapt their strategies accordingly, meaning that continuous learning and professional development are essential for CISOs. This includes staying abreast of industry best practices, participating in threat intelligence sharing networks, and fostering a culture of continuous improvement within the security team.

Finally, a significant 'don't' for CISOs is to become complacent. The cybersecurity environment is constantly changing, and complacency can lead to significant vulnerabilities. Regularly reviewing and updating the security strategy, coupled with ongoing monitoring and testing, is essential to maintain a strong security posture.

This is how I see what CISOs could consider do's and don'ts. I'm certain that every leader will have a different list of areas to focus on.

Allow me to introduce **Yabing Wang**, who is the CISO and CIO (**VP of Security and IT Services**) at **Justworks**, a tech-driven payroll company dedicated to supporting small businesses. As an active professional, she also serves multiple advisory boards and has published a book, *97 Things Every Application Security Professional Should Know*.

With over 25 years in technology and more than 20 years of leadership experience in cybersecurity, Yabing has excelled in enabling businesses through the development of technology capabilities and innovative services while effectively managing security and operational risks. Yabing has established global security practices and enhanced cyber resilience at multiple Fortune 100 companies, including Allstate Insurance Company, Alight Solutions, Carrier Corporation, and H-E-B.

Yabing has exceptionally deep cybersecurity expertise. I'd welcome her insights into what she sees as CISO do's and don'ts from her extensive hands-on experience.

Do's and don'ts for CISOs

Yabing Wang

When I stepped into my first CISO role years ago, a friend offered me some sobering advice: **"Don't be too hard on yourself. Every CISO fails their first time."** I remember thinking, *No way. That won't be me. I will not fail.*

Looking back now, I realize he had a very valuable point. Perhaps *failure* is too strong a word, but the underlying truth remains – regardless of your previous experience, whether you've worked under a CISO with partial responsibility or came from outside cybersecurity entirely, there are critical nuances you simply cannot grasp until you're in the seat yourself.

The role demands a lot that's impossible to fully understand from the outside. Every challenge becomes a learning opportunity, and each experience makes you a more effective CISO.

Through conversations with many CISO peers across the United States and globally, it's obvious that success in the CISO role isn't black and white. Just as cybersecurity is full of complexities, there's no single 'right' or 'wrong' way to be a great CISO.

However, we can still try to map it out from the collective wisdom out there. Let's explore do's and don'ts for CISOs. Let's embrace the learning curve. This isn't about avoiding mistakes; it's about growing from them.

Where to start

When I first became a CISO, I turned to several CISO friends for advice. Later, as I took on CISO roles at other companies, I found myself returning to the same practices, from "what should I do (or avoid) in my first 90 days" to "what should I focus on more (or less) throughout my CISO journey." Let's explore these lessons together.

First 90 days

Congratulations! You got the offer! You're now a first-time CISO!

As an experienced leader, your instinct is likely to create a 30/60/90-day plan, and that's great! But before you dive in, be aware of some common pitfalls.

You probably take pride in being a change agent and action-oriented thinker. You understand the significance of the CISO role and are eager to make an impact within your first 90 days. Subconsciously, you may also feel the need to prove yourself – to show that, despite being new to the role, you're fully capable of handling this critical position. But here's the truth: **You don't need to prove yourself**. The company chose you over other candidates because they already trust you to do the job. The more you rush into delivering results to demonstrate your capability, the more it becomes about *your* success, and the less it's about the business.

Similarly, one of the best pieces of advice I've learned from my peers is: **Don't make changes too quickly**. You don't yet understand the company culture or how people respond to change management. This is especially critical when considering blocking measures right away. A misstep here can create roadblocks that hinder the long-term success of your cybersecurity program.

Instead, **slow down** and **focus on building relationships first**. Engage with your peers, leaders, and stakeholders. Listen, ask questions, and find ways to support them. When CISOs position themselves as partners and business enablers, rather than enforcers, business leaders are more likely to trust their judgment. And when that trust and credibility are established, securing buy-in and alignment for future changes becomes much easier. Cybersecurity is as much about collaboration and influence as it is about policies and controls. By taking the time to understand the business and its people, you set the stage for long-term success.

Rather than rushing into action, take the time to assess and learn, with these 'do's':

- **Assess the current security posture:** Conduct interviews, review key documents, and, if needed, bring in external experts to assess the company's current security posture. Use these insights to build a strategic, multi-year roadmap while understanding what's critical, and what's urgent.

- **Evaluate your team:** Identify your top performers, understand their strengths and weaknesses, and consider how to build a strong, high-functioning security organization.

- **Learn about the business:** Most importantly, immerse yourself in the business. You won't grasp everything in 90 days, maybe not even in your first year, but the learning must start immediately. While cybersecurity frameworks, industry best practices, and technical knowledge are transferable, every company has its own business model, process complexities, technology debt, and company culture. A successful CISO adapts their experience to fit the new business environment, rather than assuming *"I've been there, I've done that."*

Your first 90 days aren't about proving yourself. It's about understanding, building relationships, and laying the foundation for long-term success. It's not easy to slow down, but let's try!

Now you are established as a CISO

As CISOs navigate increasing personal accountability, awareness of risks you face and proactive self-protection are just as critical as defending the organization.

Regulatory bodies such as the Securities and Exchange Commission (SEC), the Federal Trade Commission (FTC), and the Department of Justice (DOJ) are increasingly holding CISOs personally accountable for cybersecurity failures, citing negligence, misrepresentation, or compliance violations. Considering recent legal cases where CISOs have faced scrutiny in court, many security leaders are realizing that our responsibility extends beyond just protecting the organization: we must also **protect ourselves as individuals**. Here are a few suggestions to help you do that:

- **Ensure you're covered by Directors & Officers (D&O) insurance**: If your CISO role qualifies as an executive position, make sure your title is explicitly covered under the company's D&O insurance. In my first CISO role, I wasn't initially covered, and I didn't negotiate it either. I later managed to add my title to the policy. Is this a must-have during offer negotiations? It depends. However, you should assess the risk and explore ways to mitigate it if you can't secure D&O coverage.

- **Consider having your own legal counsel**: Some CISOs hire personal lawyers as an additional layer of protection, and some hire one because they don't have D&O coverage. If you have strong legal and insurance protections and trust your company's leadership, this may not be necessary. However, establishing a relationship with an external lawyer is always a good idea. You don't have to retain one immediately, but having someone to consult when needed can be invaluable.

- **Engage your company's legal team early and often**: Work closely with the legal department to ensure compliance with regulatory, legal, and contractual obligations. Never make company-wide legal decisions alone. Always consult legal counsel, even if you have a law degree yourself. While the legal team ultimately serves the company, not you, their guidance and involvement can be crucial for your protection.

- **Prioritize clear, accurate, and documented communication:** Transparency and integrity in communication are powerful tools for a CISO's personal protection. Be mindful of what's 'on the record,' but document key decisions, alignment, and misalignment, especially during incidents. Keeping accurate, detailed records of who, what, when, why, and how in major security discussions and actions can be more helpful than harmful in the long run.

To maintain our personal growth as CISOs, there's another consideration to keep in mind: when should we consider moving on? In this situation, deciding when to make a career move depends on many factors, including whether your leadership style aligns with the company culture and whether your expectations as a CISO are in sync with those of your CEO or boss. However, two key factors stand out for me:

- Have I accomplished what I set out to do? Have I made the impact I intended? If a company takes a year or more to implement change, and I find that the culture is resistant to transformation, staying longer may not be worthwhile.

- Am I still being challenged? Am I continuing to grow, take on new responsibilities, and expand my impact? If the answer is *yes*, then it's a sign this is still the right place for me.

Is 18-24 months the average tenure for a CISO? Maybe. But what truly matters is recognizing that not every company is the right fit. It's always a mutual selection process. Always aim for a role that aligns with your passion and goals, a team you enjoy working with, and a challenge that pushes you to grow.

We all want to leave the world better than we found it, and it's just as important to listen to your heart on the timing of your career moves.

Partner, advisor, and problem solver

When the CISO role was first established in the 1990s, it began in banks, and the role was heavily compliance-focused, as financial institutions prioritized regulatory adherence. This positioned the CISO as a policymaker (establishing rules to meet regulatory requirements) and an enforcer (ensuring policies were followed, often with a rigid approach, like police).

As modern business involves fast technological advancement, the CISO role has evolved and continues to evolve significantly as well. Therefore, we wear many hats:

- **Operator**: Executing cybersecurity initiatives effectively
- **Risk advisor**: Articulating risks and advising the business on mitigation
- **Risk manager**: Balancing protection with operational needs
- **Strategist**: Defining security strategy aligning with business goals
- **Business enabler**: Ensuring security facilitates, rather than obstructs
- **Communicator**: Educating everyone to protect the company

Ultimately, the best CISOs go beyond compliance and enforcement. We become trusted business leaders who drive security, innovation, and business success.

Let's look at some key 'do's' (and a few 'don'ts') related to the CISO role itself.

Be a partner for business, not the police

For decades, CISOs believed their primary mission was to protect the company and secure customer data. If something introduced additional risk, the standard response was often "No, you can't do that."

However, many modern CISOs no longer see themselves as purely compliance-driven enforcers. Instead, they balance business risk with security needs, ensuring that security measures enable innovation rather than hinder it. To drive the point home, if a company in the insurance industry designs an app with such strict security controls that underwriters can't generate quotes or new customers can't be onboarded, security has become a roadblock instead of a business enabler.

Having spent years as an architect, I never approached challenges with a simple "no" to business requirements. Instead, the architect's role was to figure out multiple options and help the business select the best solution. I carried that mindset into my CISO role. **Rather than saying "No, you can't do that," I prefer to say** *"Yes, and here's how we can do it securely."*

When security and business leaders collaborate to find the best possible solution with minimal risk, it may not be the absolute best from either perspective, but it will be the most balanced and sustainable way forward.

A great CISO is not just an enforcer but an enabler, someone who understands business objectives, integrates security into products or processes and helps drive innovation by enabling secure technology adoption. Obtaining a seat at the table of business strategies helps CISOs significantly in becoming enablers.

You can also be an innovator in security, and even in your business. Who says security can't be a revenue generator for your company?

Be the advisor on enterprise risk management

There's no doubt that a big part of the CISO role is a risk function. As CISOs manage cyber risks and contribute to enterprise risk management, a key question arises: Are CISOs the final decision-makers on risk acceptance, or are we simply advisors?

This is a complex question with no one-size-fits-all answer. The level of decision-making authority a CISO holds depends on the organization's structure and governance model. While some CISOs may have the authority to make certain risk decisions, in most cases, we serve primarily as advisors and help business leaders understand and manage risk effectively. A CISO should be cautious not to overstep in this regard by making business decisions unless explicitly authorized to do so. Overstepping can strain relationships with executives and business leaders, undermine your credibility within the organization, and expose you to unnecessary liability risks.

Instead, a successful CISO influences risk decisions through clear communication, strong governance, and strategic alignment with business objectives. What a CISO should do and *what matters most* in this area is to **define a clear governance framework and execute a consistent decision-making process** to ensure that cybersecurity remains an integral part of enterprise risk management. For example, the business executive owns the risk. The CISO's role is to identify, articulate, and advise on the risk, including recommending appropriate mitigation strategies.

A CISO can assess the risks and grant a temporary exception, or they may disagree with the risk owner's decision to move forward without mitigation. In such cases, it's the CISO's responsibility to escalate the matter to the Enterprise Risk Committee (ERC) and ensure the CEO makes the final call when necessary. If the company decides to accept the risk based on its current state, this should be properly documented, with a follow-up review in six months to reassess it.

As a risk manager and advisor, a CISO must also maintain a risk register, which is a common best practice in cybersecurity. However, since it's easy to document technical gaps and identified vulnerabilities, many risk registers tend to focus heavily on technology-related issues while overlooking weak controls in business processes.

Don't focus purely on technical gaps. Go beyond the technical aspects and identify and understand critical business processes, assess where controls are missing or not strong enough to ensure business resilience, and **abstract technical gaps into enterprise-level risks that leadership should care about**. For example, senior management does not care whether a single application grants excessive user access or if a system fails to remove a former employee. What does warrant attention is the enterprise-level risk: "We lack a consistent approach to identity and access management (IAM), resulting in overly permissive access across our environment. This increases our attack surfaces, raises the risk of data breaches, and could lead to non-compliance with multiple regulations."

To sum up, while CISOs influence and shape risk decisions, true risk ownership often lies with business leaders. The key is ensuring a structured and transparent risk governance process that balances security, business objectives, and enterprise risk tolerance.

Be a problem solver for both business and technical problems

I come from a technical background, with a master's degree in computer science and five years of experience as a software engineer before transitioning into cybersecurity in 2002. Over the years, I worked as a security engineer and security architect before stepping into leadership roles. People like me are naturally passionate about solving problems. However, for CISOs with a strong technical background, one of the common pitfalls (a CISO 'don't') is **relying too heavily on technical solutions to address challenges.**

When things break, our instinct is to focus on fixing the technical problem, sometimes at the expense of the broader business issue we were originally trying to solve. As CISOs, we need to *balance* our technical expertise with business acumen, ensuring that **cybersecurity decisions align with strategic business objectives**, rather than aiming for technical perfection.

In most organizations, only a small percentage of employees are technical. Most business leaders don't speak in technical terms or fully grasp cybersecurity issues. That's why one of the most critical skills of a CISO is to **translate technical gaps into business risks,** articulating the *criticality* and *priority* of addressing these risks at the enterprise level.

Your team identifies critical vulnerabilities through a vulnerability scanner. Your product engineering team struggles to fit remediation into their priorities. Instead of presenting items like this as part of a list of technical issues, you should frame it in business risk terms, for example, "These vulnerabilities are exposed to the internet and are actively exploitable. If left unaddressed, attackers could easily compromise our product and exfiltrate customer data." By framing security risks in terms of business impact, CISOs can drive alignment, gain executive buy-in, and ensure security is prioritized alongside other business objectives.

Effective CISOs don't just solve technical problems; they try to address business problems and align security with business value.

Be more strategic than tactical

Not all CISOs have the same role. Some are hired in response to a breach, tasked with fixing tactical problems and restoring security. While this kind of problem-solving can be exciting, the role itself may be too focused on the short term. That's why it's essential to ask: Once the immediate crisis is resolved, what is the long-term role of the CISO?

Leaders typically fall into three categories:

- Strategic-oriented leaders, focused on long-term vision and business alignment
- Program management-focused leaders, prioritizing execution and driving initiatives forward
- Operational-heavy leaders, ensuring day-to-day security operations run effectively

While every leader needs a balance of these qualities, I believe a strategic focus is the most critical for long-term CISO success. Operational excellence can be delegated – we can hire strong operational leaders to ensure cyber resilience through detection, incident response, and threat management capabilities. Program execution can also be achieved by skilled leaders driving and delivering security initiatives, while CISOs provide oversight. As the executive responsible for cybersecurity, **the CISO must be strategic** – setting direction, leading the security strategy, collaborating with leadership, and ensuring security's multi-year roadmap aligns with business values and goals. This is crucial for modern CISOs.

CISOs don't have unlimited budgets. Even if they did, bad actors would still find ways in. That's why strategic resource allocation is essential. Focusing only on fixing current issues is too tactical. CISOs must assess risks holistically, prioritizing the most critical and high-impact mitigations. Some budget should always be reserved for strategic initiatives, ensuring long-term security resilience. There's no simple formula for this distribution. It depends on risk prioritization and business impact. A skilled CISO knows where to accept short-term pain for long-term gain, ensuring cybersecurity becomes a business enabler rather than just an operational cost.

The more strategic you are, the more long-term success you'll achieve. In my observations, the most successful CISOs tend to be those who are not only technically skilled but also highly business-oriented and strategically driven.

Build and prioritize cybersecurity programs

Every organization operates at a different cybersecurity maturity level at certain points in time. As a CISO, it's crucial to assess whether you need to build foundational programs immediately or prioritize certain initiatives to address the most critical risks and the biggest gaps.

Essentials you need

Here, I'll go through some of the essential programs you will need to focus on as a CISO.

Security operations

Regardless of how advanced your cyber defense is, a strong **security operations** program is non-negotiable. For this, start by ensuring you and your team have visibility of your environment (e.g., devices, workloads, applications, users, data, activities, etc.) by getting logs or alerts in your Security Incident and Event Management (SIEM) engine. Tune and filter out false positives to focus on meaningful alerts. It's also important to ensure the incident response plan is documented and practiced often.

Risk management

In some organizations, CISOs are only responsible for managing cyber risks, while in other corporations, CISOs manage cyber risks, technology operations risks, and sometimes even enterprise risks. Either way, you should do the following as a CISO:

- Build a governance framework to guide a standardized approach to conducting risk assessment, prioritizing risks, following a risk approval process, and monitoring and tracking risk mitigations. Please avoid having too many steering or governance committees for different purposes; leverage a few to address critical risks across the enterprise instead.

- Help the organization understand the company's risk appetite and advise on defining the company's risk tolerance.

- Build a third-party risk management (TPRM) program with stakeholders such as legal and procurement to manage risks brought by vendors and suppliers. Apply your TPRM framework with a clear governance process, including risk assessment before onboarding, contract management, vendor performance management, continuous monitoring of vendor risks, and a solid vendor incident management practice.

- Depending on your industry, you may need to establish a strong compliance program to address compliance risks and meet regulations such as SOC 2, SOX, PCI, HIPAA, and others. Note, however, that compliance is a baseline, not a security strategy. Furthermore, a compliance-driven approach can limit innovation – if security is seen as just a regulatory burden, teams may resist or only do the bare minimum. Don't drive the security program only by compliance requirements; use compliance as a tool, not a crutch. Sometimes you'll need to pull the compliance lever to drive action, but don't overuse it.

Exposure management

Vulnerabilities, misconfigurations, and end-of-life (outdated) hardware or software create open doors for threat actors. A strong exposure management program should take a holistic approach built on four pillars:

- Identifying exposures across the environment
- Prioritizing risks based on business impact and compensating controls
- Remediating those issues following a defined Service-Level Agreement (SLA) based on prioritization
- Reporting and measuring remediation progress and managing residual risks accordingly

Exposure management is always challenging but essential. It requires strong risk alignment and prioritization to ensure focus on the most critical threats to the organization. It's important to recognize, as a CISO, that not all exposures need to be or can be remediated, and attempting to do so wastes time and resources.

Note that default severity ratings from discovery tools should not be taken at face value. Instead, CISOs must help their organizations define their own criteria for criticality and direct efforts toward addressing the truly high-impact risks.

A healthy security culture

Transitioning from a technical leader in security architecture and engineering to becoming a CISO required a significant mental shift for me. I could no longer rely solely on technical enforcement to protect the organization. The reality is that everyone in the organization interacts with the digital world daily, and anyone can be the weakest link. A healthy security culture is therefore another essential and should be built on responsibility, not obligation. When employees embrace security as 'the right thing to do,' they are more engaged and motivated. A strong security culture is one where employees become cyber-smart and security-aware, teams remain vigilant in their daily work, and security is embedded into product design and implementation from the start.

A resilient security posture requires both cultural awareness and technical controls to reduce attack surfaces and manage the risks, and one cannot succeed without the other. We need a mindset where everyone takes responsibility for security, alongside well-designed security measures and enforcement. Only when these two elements work together can we truly strengthen the organization's resilience against cyber threats.

Other important programs

There are other important programs to consider too. For each organization, the timing and comprehensiveness of each program will be different depending on the maturity level. You should evaluate the current state of the organization and build the strategy and roadmap to address it (at least incorporating some part of each program).

Identity and access management (IAM)

With hybrid or cloud-first environments, firewalls alone are no longer sufficient – identity has become the new perimeter. A comprehensive IAM program should include automated provisioning and de-provisioning with identity governance, multi-factor authentication (MFA) enforcement wherever possible, role-based (or rule-based) access controls for critical systems, credential protection (passwords, secrets, keys), and privileged access and non-human identity management. IAM plays a vital role in securing access and protecting data. You should make it one of the most strategic security investments.

Data protection

Modern businesses depend on data to drive decision-making, making a **data protection program** fundamental. The rapid adoption of AI has created a double exposure: AI systems consume more sensitive data than ever before, while simultaneously generating vast amounts of new data, dramatically increasing potential data exposure risks. Instead of restricting data usage, security should focus on protecting data while enabling business insights. As a CISO, ask these questions: Where is the data? Where is the data going? Do we have the right data protection in place?

You can design a data protection program with these components:

- Data Security Posture Management (DSPM) to discover, classify, and tag sensitive data
- Security controls to apply encryption, tokenization, masking, and obfuscation to protect data
- Data Loss Prevention (DLP) to prevent unauthorized data exfiltration

Of course, IAM is also a major contributor to data security, ensuring that only the right people have access to the right data at the right time.

Enterprise and cloud security

Today, everything operates on endpoints (laptops, desktops, mobile devices, IoT) or infrastructure (on-premises data centers or cloud environments). An enterprise and cloud security program ensures that all assets are protected, no matter where they reside.

Having security detection and response software running on all endpoints (EDR) and infrastructure is generally the first step for all cybersecurity. You should build on that, layering security controls across endpoints, cloud, and enterprise infrastructure.

Another important common practice is to build a secure network and apply Zero Trust and deny-by-default principles to infrastructure builds.

Product security

Security should be embedded throughout the product development lifecycle. Whether your product is an online service or part of the Internet of Things (IoT), by integrating security into the development pipeline, you can proactively reduce risk and enhance product resilience, without stifling innovation.

To maintain an effective product security program, elements such as code analysis and security testing (for example, static application security testing (SAST), dynamic application security testing (DAST), software composition analysis (SCA)), threat modelling, software supply chain security with open source dependency management, API security, and mobile application security are key.

AI governance and security

While the adoption of generative AI continues to surge, organizational approaches to AI governance and security differ significantly.

I'd suggest establishing an AI Center of Excellence (COE) with dedicated experts who are always on top of AI tools, capabilities, and training for the organization. As CISO, you should leverage this COE and proactively lead in AI governance, security, and monitoring to navigate the evolving risks it presents effectively.

Leadership and beyond

As CISOs, we rely on hard skills such as program management, risk management, finance management, problem-solving, and others. But equally important are the leadership skills we must continually practice, not just for our organizations, but for the broader security community. The stronger our leadership, the greater our ability to influence and inspire others. That's how we can elevate both our organizations and the cybersecurity community as a whole.

Relationship building

As an executive, a significant portion of your time should be dedicated to communication, collaboration, and relationship-building with management, peers, and stakeholders. For CISOs, this is even more crucial. Not only do you need to navigate the organization effectively, but you also need to invest time in building strong relationships across all levels of the company. Why? Because cybersecurity is not a one-team effort. A small security team alone cannot protect the entire organization. The earlier you mobilize the entire company as part of the security effort, the stronger and more resilient your defense against threats will be.

Here are a few key relationship 'do's' for you (and one 'don't'):

- **Identify and engage decision-makers**: Understand who holds decision-making power within the company. If possible, have regular meetings with the CEO, CFO, General Counsel (GC), CPO, CTO, and others. They are the most influential leaders for security decisions. If direct access to these roles is limited, identify other key decision-makers and establish a consistent communication cadence with them.

- **Build trust with the inner circle of decision-makers**: Decision-makers often trust certain individuals within the company. Find out who these people are and establish relationships with them, aligning with them first before introducing major security initiatives to leadership. A well-positioned advocate can help influence and accelerate buy-in for your initiatives.

- **Engage business stakeholders proactively**: Always ask stakeholders, "What can the CISO or cybersecurity team do to support your business goals?

  When business teams encounter security-related roadblocks, the solution is not to offer blanket exceptions. Instead, you should provide secure, business-friendly solutions, responding in a timely, collaborative manner.

- **Don't avoid building relationships with those you don't like:** To deliver and support shared executive and organizational goals, you don't need to be best friends with everyone, but you do need to figure out how to work together and support each other. A good leader can collaborate effectively with a diverse group of people, even those with differing opinions, priorities, or personalities. Avoiding difficult relationships only creates roadblocks to succes.

You can start by taking the first step here: schedule a meeting with someone you may not see eye to eye with, listen to their challenges, and try to understand their perspectives. Find common ground with them and identify ways cybersecurity can support their goals. Offering help is a simple gesture of collaboration and can be the foundation of a positive relationship.

Successful CISOs don't operate in silos. They align security with business objectives and build credibility through mutual support and commitment. By strategically investing in communication and collaboration, CISOs can turn the entire company into a unified cybersecurity force, making security a shared responsibility rather than a siloed function.

Contribute to the security community

While collaboration within a company is essential, it's also, perhaps even more so, crucial for CISOs and security professionals to actively engage with the broader security community.

Cyber threats evolve rapidly, and defending against bad actors in isolation can weaken our ability to adapt and respond effectively. By participating in security communities, we can gain insights, share intelligence, and collectively strengthen cybersecurity defenses across industries.

There are multiple ways to proactively engage in the community. Here are a few ideas for you:

- **Join Information Sharing and Analysis Centers (ISACs)**: By subscribing to relevant ISACs, you gain insights into industry-specific threats. (A few examples are FS-ISAC (for financial services), Health-ISAC, and Auto-ISAC (for the automotive industry).) You can contribute by sharing relevant threat intelligence from your organization, helping to strengthen collective defense across your industry.

- **Participate in CISO peer groups**: Engage with CISO groups such as Evanta, CISO Society, CISOs Connect, and the Professional Association of CISOs (PAC). Beyond discussions at events, you can also join Slack, WhatsApp, and other private forums to learn from peers in real time.

- **Speak at cybersecurity conferences**: Share your insights, experiences, and perspectives at conferences to help others grow. Speaking on panels or delivering talks not only strengthens the community but also enhances your credibility as a thought leader.

- **Advise start-ups**: Consider becoming a board advisor or board member for cybersecurity start-ups. While you can't spend time talking to every vendor as a CISO, learning from start-ups helps to keep you ahead of industry innovations. Advising young companies is one of the best ways to give back to the cybersecurity community.

The more CISOs engage with the external security community, the stronger our collective defense becomes. By sharing knowledge, learning from peers, and staying ahead of industry changes, you can better protect your organization while contributing to the greater cybersecurity mission.

Communicate effectively with transparency

A CISO's success is not just about building security programs. It's about influence, communication, and advocacy. To drive cybersecurity initiatives effectively, a CISO needs to be a top-notch communicator, which means adopting multiple personas:

- **The Salesperson**: While most CISOs don't sell the company's products or services (except for field CISOs in some organizations), every CISO must 'sell' security initiatives and strategies to key stakeholders. This includes advocating for security investments by highlighting risks and financial consequences of inaction, securing buy-in from executives by aligning security goals with business objectives, and influencing teams across the organization to prioritize security measures. A great CISO understands that even the best security strategy won't succeed without stakeholder support, and that requires selling the value of security in business terms.

- **The Translator**: CISOs must translate technical complexities into business language to show how security impacts the company's bottom line. A good CISO can explain technical risks and solutions to technology leaders and can communicate business risks and mitigation strategies to customer support, finance, or operations leaders in language that they understand. A great CISO connects the dots between security, business, technology, and risks to ensure that cybersecurity isn't seen as a siloed function but as an integral part of enterprise success.

- **The Storyteller**: Data and reports alone don't inspire action; stories do. A great CISO knows that effective communication is not just about presenting facts but about crafting a compelling narrative that resonates with different audiences. Other than reporting, a lot of times, a CISO's communication is about an ask or a necessary change. To get people's support and engagement, CISOs should be able to articulate who, why, what, where, and how, and give context and paint a big picture. Whether an analogy is used or not, the right story should emphasize the cyber risks to get attention that leads to action.

When presenting to the board, CISOs must blend all these key personas to deliver clear, impactful messaging. Here are some key 'do's' to help you with this:

- **Keep messaging simple and concise**: Board members are not technical and have limited time. Focus on what truly matters. Don't try to cover everything.

- **Avoid these common mistakes**:

    - Too many details – stick to high-level insights and key takeaways

    - Too many metrics – present only a few meaningful risk indicators

    - Technical jargon – speak in business language, not security acronyms

- **Be honest, transparent, and confident**: Acknowledge risks and provide a clear plan to address them. Deliver your message with confidence and clarity. The board values leadership, not fear. Make sure the board can walk away with an understanding of the risks, priorities, and necessary actions.

A CISO's role extends far beyond technical execution. Clear communication with transparency, including selling security, translating risks, and telling compelling stories are valuable skills that enable you to better engage with stakeholders, leading to better decision-making and a lasting security impact across the organization.

Metrics matter

I'd like to consider a CISO as the General Manager (GM) of cybersecurity. As a GM, metrics are the key to running the business and are essential for measuring progress against objectives and key results (OKRs). At the same time, metrics play a crucial role in demonstrating the maturity of security programs and communicating residual risk to the organization.

With countless potential metrics to track, the challenge lies in selecting the right ones to hold teams accountable and drive priorities, as well as choosing meaningful metrics for executive leadership and the board. It's important to distinguish what to collect and what to communicate.

Internal security teams need granular operational metrics to track security effectiveness, response time, and program maturity. Executive management and the board only need high-level risk metrics that provide visibility into critical risks and mitigations, without overwhelming them with excessive details. It's the CISO's responsibility to abstract the right data, ensuring that leadership has the visibility needed to make informed decisions.

While data-driven decision-making is essential, it's important to realize that selecting, interpreting, and presenting the right metrics is an art. A great CISO knows that metrics should not just track activities. They should tell a compelling story about security risks, priorities, and progress. Use metrics, but use them wisely.

Talent development

As an experienced leader, you already know that your success depends on having a strong and capable team. Here are a few key leadership strategies that have helped me along the way:

- Instead of providing solutions, ask questions that challenge your team to think critically and propose the best options. You're no longer an architect or engineer. Your job is to lead, not solve every problem yourself. A great coach doesn't give answers but guides others to find their own solutions because this builds confidence and problem-solving skills.

- Recognize, acknowledge, and advocate for your team. People thrive when their contributions are valued. If your team is large, you may not know everyone very well, but you can create a culture of strong leadership where every manager in your team shares the same vision and leads with the same principles. When your leaders and the team feel supported, they will, in turn, have the motivation to excel and contribute to everyone's success.

- No matter how long you plan to stay, start identifying potential successors from day one. Look for high-potential leaders and invest in their growth, exposure, and leadership development. Empowering a strong successor benefits both the organization and you. They can take on more day-to-day management, which helps you focus on strategic work to support the business, such as working more with the CEO and board, and building peer relationships, while providing value to enable business leaders. If possible, it's also worth figuring out what the opportunities could be if security can become a revenue generator, or spending time helping sales, and building trust with customers.

- Build security talent for the future. Cybersecurity professionals come from various backgrounds, not just formal degrees. I've seen many successes. One is to mentor employees internally who are interested in cybersecurity. You can also take the approach of hiring for skills and mindset rather than just credentials – junior roles are great for discovering untapped talent. If possible, establish partnerships with universities to create internship programs or real-world cybersecurity projects. This approach builds a strong talent pipeline and ensures a continuous flow of skilled professionals into your organization.

Final thoughts

I've had the privilege of learning from many great CISOs, including Charles Blauner, Jim Routh, Shamla Naidoo, Debbie Wheeler, Jason Witty, and more. Their insights, leadership, and experiences have shaped my approach to cybersecurity leadership.

My experiences across multiple companies have also provided valuable lessons, reinforcing that no two organizations are the same, and every challenge brings new opportunities to grow. I'm incredibly grateful to be contributing to David's book, a collection of wisdom from global CISOs and cybersecurity leaders. I hope that our collective experiences provide you with valuable perspectives, making your CISO journey not only more effective but also more fun and exciting!

David's key takeaways — Do's and don'ts for the CISO

There are some valuable real-life lessons to be learnt from this chapter, with some great practical tips from Yabing that the CISO should take into consideration using their own lived experience in these positions.

Taking inspiration from Yabing, I've split the key takeaways from this chapter into two groupings: tips for the new CISO and some guidance for the more advanced CISO. The first three points are more tactical guidance for the first year of a CISO role, while points 4-7 are focused on the strategic mindset shifts that experienced CISOs need to develop for long-term effectiveness.

The more advanced guidance assumes you've already established yourself and are ready to think at a higher strategic level. Otherwise, you may want to loop back and focus on the initial guidance.

For new CISOs:

- *Resist the 'Prove Yourself' trap* – this refers to the psychological challenge new CISOs face when starting the role. Resist the urge to rush into action and immediately demonstrate capability. The company already trusts your abilities.
- *Assess maturity first.* As a new CISO walking into the organisation, spend time assessing the current cybersecurity posture and combine that with learning about the business to create a strategy and roadmaps. Be sure to prioritise understanding the company's security posture, team, and business operations over quick wins.
- *Build and evaluate your team* – it is a critical early task for any new CISO to understand their inherited team. Identify their strengths and weaknesses, and formulate strategies to create a high-performing security organisation.

For more experienced/advanced CISOs:

- *Think business problems, not technical problems* – this is about evolving your leadership mindset. If you come from a technical background, always remind yourself that, as a CISO, you're not solving technical problems; you're solving business problems now. Your job is to be a business partner, rather than a police officer. Lift your head up. Zoom out. Be strategic!
- *Choose metrics suitable for executive leadership and the board.* You also need to select metrics that you need to keep teams accountable. Focus on the results (improving your security posture, cyber resilience, and enabling the business).

- *Leverage storytelling*. Your job is to drive action through narrative, so you need a compelling one that resonates with different audiences. Your story should articulate the 'who, why, what, where, and how' of cybersecurity risks and necessary changes.

- *Keep it simple* – specifically, when presenting to boards as a CISO, keep messages simple and concise, always avoiding technical jargon and excessive details. Deliver honest, transparent communication with confidence.

21
Developing Cyber Talent

The CISO always has a shortage of A+ talent – that is, those who consistently deliver. In a day in the life of the CISO, you are confronted with demands that always exceed your organisation's supply when it comes to managing resources. There are regulatory remediation projects that are delayed, incidents to manage, and investigations to conclude. The demands are endless, and it's only possible to cope when there is an adequate supply of talent.

As a CISO, where do you prioritise this effort in your busy day? There is always going to be another issue or incident to deal with, so there is never going to be a clear window in which you can spend your time just building and developing your team.

Unfortunately, talent often does not just simply walk in through the front door. Having dedicated time to focus on talent development is critical for a CISO. They need to understand where to find this talent and how to develop managers into leaders.

My own definition of talent has developed from many years in C-Suite roles and in growing staff. When staff can learn new approaches, techniques and skills, and still deliver at a high level, then they are your top talent:

Talent = Top Tier Delivery + Learning Agility

We know that there is a well-documented global shortage of talent, so it is impossible to rely on the market to fill your gaps. The only approach that you can rely on is growing this talent. I've seen different paths to this, from enterprises that hired 10-20 graduates and put them through intense training and experience, to other organisations that have aggressively invested in developing their existing staff through cyber and cloud certifications.

Building the talent pipeline, offering competitive compensation, creating a positive work environment and providing opportunities for career growth are key parts of the CISO's role. Then, ensuring that you are generous with recognition helps you to retain that talent. We have to remember that a career in cybersecurity is often stressful and a thankless job. The effort that you make day in and day out might get overlooked and may not be seen as worthy of praise, but it is extremely important nonetheless.

Introducing **Maryam Bechtel, CISO** for **AGL Energy**, a critical infrastructure provider. She has responsibility across the enterprise. Maryam has worked internationally, in Germany and Sweden, before coming to settle in Australia with Deloitte, and later with NBN as Executive Manager for Cyber Operations. She also serves on several advisory boards, including ISACA, AISA and Women in Security Network.

Maryam has a personal passion for developing cyber talent. Let's hear her perspective on how this can be tackled and what she does to drive this transformation.

Developing cyber talent

Maryam Betchel

The rapidly increasing demand for cybersecurity professionals has led to a critical global talent shortage. This shortage is particularly felt in industries such as energy, where safeguarding critical infrastructure is paramount, and cyber threats continue to rise in volume and become more sophisticated. The cybersecurity landscape is shifting, and it's not just about technical skills anymore. It's about creating a team that is both skilled and aligned with business goals, and that can adapt quickly to developing cyber threats.

As a CISO, you are dependent on the effectiveness of the team that supports you. Cyber talent can be what makes your role a success or not. It doesn't matter what technology or partners you have. Talent is the most critical, fundamental ingredient. This is why I continue to prioritise my investment in talent development.

How do I define talent?

Talent is like a Swiss Army knife; that is, it's a very valuable, agile tool and it can get great results. Your talent has a track record of getting things done.

I have also commonly encountered talent that has been placed in the wrong role. When they are reappointed and put into the right role and environment, then they can thrive and do very well. My job is to help create the right environment in which people have trust, good communication and celebrate success. Cyber staff who are talented can get great results, beyond what is written down in a job description. Essentially, you want people who are willing and aspire to push themselves beyond what their job description says.

The talent you will need

In the current climate, CISOs and other cybersecurity professionals need to evolve from mere 'cyber guards' to proactive business enablers and trusted advisors. Cybersecurity is no longer a siloed function; it is integral to the broader success of the organisation. This shift requires building teams with a mix of technical expertise and business acumen.

As a CISO, you need to align your cybersecurity strategy with the organisation's objectives, ensuring that the security measures you implement don't impede, but rather enable innovation.

When considering the staff I will need in the future, my perspective is shaped by an ongoing reflection on how my own role is evolving. Rising expectations of the CISO role will require new joiners to bring skills that the current team does not have. A good example is a cyber leader who has great analytical skills to be able to develop and manage new operational cyber metrics and the emerging developments in artificial intelligence (AI)/machine learning (ML) that will be necessary to produce advanced analytics.

In the age of AI, there is much uncertainty in terms of how jobs will evolve. I would still stress that great interpersonal and communication skills are key. These soft skills will continue to be important. I've noted a great example below, and that is the use of storytelling.

The importance of storytelling in cybersecurity

Storytelling is a crucial skill for cybersecurity professionals. Cyber is not a problem that can be solved solely by the cybersecurity or technology teams; it is a team sport and everyone's responsibility. As such, to truly protect an organization from evolving threats, it's essential to bring the whole organization along. This requires influencing and empowering all employees by telling the right story.

A compelling story about why cybersecurity matters, how everyone has a role to play and how individual actions contribute to the overall safety of the organization can help inspire collective responsibility. In this way, effective storytelling fosters a sense of shared mission, ensuring that each employee understands their role in keeping the organization, and themselves, safe in the face of cyber threats.

To be able to be a good CISO, this is a soft skill that needs to be nurtured and practiced. This skill can be used effectively both with executive stakeholders and with the board, as well as more generally.

Identifying the right cyber talent

Building a strong cybersecurity team requires more than just hiring people with certifications and technical expertise. There are three other key traits essential for building an effective team:

- **Passion for the work:** Passion drives learning, and the field of cybersecurity is always evolving. Candidates who are genuinely interested in the field are more likely to stay engaged, continually learn and adapt to new challenges.

- **Eagerness to learn:** Cybersecurity is dynamic, with new tools and techniques emerging regularly. A strong candidate will embrace continuous learning and readily adapt to new technologies and methods.

- **Proactive problem-solving:** Cybersecurity requires a proactive approach. Rather than waiting for threats to surface, effective professionals are always thinking ahead, identifying potential vulnerabilities, and mitigating risks before they become problems.

For me personally, I'd want the talent to be good at all three of these traits, but I'd consider two where the candidate has outstanding experience from an advanced company with a strong reputation in cybersecurity.

I'd note here that while having a strong proactive drive to look around corners is very important, leaning too far in this direction can lead to burnout, so good habits around taking breaks and holidays should be encouraged. Personal resilience is a key ingredient for high performance. In my view, heroes are no use to the CISO! I want staff to be fresh and excited about work and not jaded.

While certifications such as CISSP, CISM and CEH are valuable, they are not always necessary, particularly for entry-level roles. Experience, passion, and willingness to learn are often just as crucial. The right attitude can often outweigh formal credentials in this rapidly changing field.

Crafting effective job descriptions

Well-crafted job descriptions are vital in attracting the right talent; overemphasising technical jargon or rigid experience requirements can deter candidates with the right mindset, however. Striking a balance between technical skills and soft skills is key. By focusing on qualities such as adaptability, problem-solving and curiosity, you'll attract a broader, more diverse pool of candidates.

I'd add that in an interview, a potential hire who worries too much about the wording of the job description may be a red flag, signifying that they are too fixated on having a clear scope. In my view, the best job descriptions have degrees of freedom and lots of scope for self-initiative.

Sourcing and recruiting cyber talent

Sourcing and recruiting the right cyber talent requires a multifaceted approach and a blend of more traditional methods with digital channels. Networking at industry events, tapping into professional organisations, and leveraging social media platforms such as LinkedIn are essential. But don't overlook internal talent. Many of my best team members initially joined through secondments or transfers from other business units, bringing with them invaluable institutional knowledge and a fresh perspective on cybersecurity.

When I receive many CVs in my inbox, how do I sort through these to decide where to focus? I usually start by looking at experience as a key criterion. I consider how to get the balance right for 'tried and tested' versus 'emerging' talent. For some roles, I will want to get proven talent, and in other cases, I'm happy to consider up-and-coming talent. As an example, take a cyber transformation leadership role. In this scenario, I'm very happy to take on a leader with experience outside of cybersecurity. For a cybersecurity operation leadership role, however, then more demonstrable experience is going to be my preference.

Interviewing and assessment

When assessing candidates, I emphasise not only technical competence but also cultural fit. The right attitude and values are crucial to long-term success. As I mentioned earlier, passionate individuals who are eager to grow can often outperform candidates with a perfect resume. I prioritise those who demonstrate initiative and a collaborative mindset – traits that are just as important as technical prowess in today's fast-paced, interconnected world.

Another key element in my interview process is assessing problem-solving skills. Rather than just asking theoretical questions, I prefer situational challenges where candidates demonstrate their ability to think critically and address real-world problems. This approach helps to reveal their thought process, communication skills and their ability to collaborate under pressure.

Onboarding and retention

Once you've hired the right candidates, effective onboarding is essential. I recommend setting **SMART (Specific, Measurable, Achievable, Relevant and Time-bound)** goals early on to ensure alignment and clear expectations. This framework helps avoid misunderstandings and sets the stage for success.

In addition to clear goal setting, fostering an environment of continuous feedback, growth and support is key to retaining this top talent. Cybersecurity is a high-stakes field, and burnout can be a real concern. Offering career development opportunities, flexible work arrangements and mental health support can help keep your team engaged and motivated.

Diversity and inclusion

Diversity is key to building strong cybersecurity teams. Cybersecurity challenges are complex and multifaceted, and diverse teams offer different perspectives and approaches.

It's crucial to not only embrace diversity in hiring but also ensure representation in leadership positions, especially for women. Strong female role models at senior levels are vital for encouraging the next generation of cybersecurity professionals. Beyond gender, diversity also extends to other aspects such as race, ethnicity, and background. Diverse teams are proven to be more creative, innovative and effective at problem-solving, all of which are essential qualities for tackling evolving cybersecurity threats.

In addition to promoting diversity, it's important to address any microaggressions and casual racism within the workplace. Subtle forms of discrimination like these can undermine team morale, hinder collaboration, and create an unhealthy work environment. As a leader, you need to set the right example by fostering an inclusive culture where such behavior is not tolerated. By addressing these issues head-on, through training, open discussions, and clear policies, you create a safer and more respectful environment for all employees. Only by acknowledging and confronting these challenges can we ensure that everyone, regardless of their background, feels valued and empowered to succeed.

My conclusion

The demand for cybersecurity talent continues to grow, and the talent shortage presents significant challenges. However, by adapting your hiring strategy, focusing on the right traits, and embracing diversity and inclusion, you can build a team that is not only technically skilled but also aligned with your business's broader goals. It's about creating an environment where passion, growth and collaboration thrive, ensuring that your organisation remains secure in the face of ever-changing cyber threats.

Making cyber talent a priority is strategically important for the CISO. It is easy to see that, in a standard day in the life of a CISO, this is overtaken by other issues and incidents. But without a great team, the CISO is purely a figurehead and unable to act and indeed defend the enterprise.

David's perspectives on developing cyber talent

There are a couple of additional things that I would like to add to what Maryam has covered on developing cyber talent. In my view, this is such a critical topic and the CISO must be outstanding at this competency, but I know for most this is something to work on. So, in this vein, please allow me to add a few additional perspectives.

What good looks like for me

What does good look like? In my 'advisor' capacity, one of the portfolio companies that I work for is JS Careers and I assist them with finding and screening great talent across tech, cyber and data.

For these discussions, which are nearly every day, I meet with potential candidates and in a short time must decide whether they meet or even exceed requirements.

Having worked across 20+ countries in my career in a CIO and CISO capacity, I have a good sense of talent across different cultures. However, language aside, there are a few attributes that I always look for:

- Like Maryam, I look for a learning mindset – a candidate with curiosity who looks around corners (certifications and number of degrees can point to this)
- The drive to deliver, and deliver the right thing
- Exceptional stakeholder engagement

When a candidate has these three attributes then I often refer to them as a 'Painkiller', meaning that they will help an enterprise transform and grow. (For simplicity I label talent as a 'Painkiller' or 'Vitamin'. In contrast to a 'Painkiller', a 'Vitamin' makes you feel better but doesn't take away all the root causes of problems.)

When I consider which companies have outstanding talent, which is a hard question, my mind shifts to some of the largest financial institutions, but as they also spend more money on tooling, this may be an unfair comparison. When I look at just raw talent, then Israel as a country exceeds all.

Why has Israel been extremely successful in developing cyber talent? What lessons are there from them for an enterprise to consider? Let me explain.

Lessons from the Israeli cyber industry

Israel undoubtedly has a significant natural advantage in the calibre of human resources. This all starts with personal 'skin in the game'. Cybersecurity in Israel is seen as an essential survival competency. Hence, most teenagers in Israel regard cyber as a career of choice.

After high school, they want to join military units, join a cybersecurity unit, attend universities and graduate to work in cyber. Joining or getting a cyber startup going with an idea or concept that they have developed during this period is also attractive.

Now, what lessons can we apply from the Israeli experience?

As a CISO, you can create a positive culture that tries to emulate this environment. For instance, develop your own teams by giving them stronger recognition, highlighting both the challenge and reward of cybersecurity. Focus on, over time, developing this into a culture that will start to have others within your own companies and beyond seeing cyber as the place to work.

Some further ideas for replicating this interest, excitement and enthusiasm around cybersecurity are noted in the following subsections.

New starters

As new grads come onboard, don't give them the 'rubbish' chores but instead design immersive training programs that simulate real attack scenarios, encourage innovative thinking under pressure and provide hands-on experience with actual security challenges rather than theoretical knowledge.

If we treat our new grads and starters with extra care, they can develop faster. Let me take you back to my experience in supervising HSBC cyber graduates – we had 20-25 of these talented new hires that were assigned globally to strategically important locations. Each of the grads was given 3-4 rotations in the first two years, with the responsibility to perform these cyber roles and not just observe. My role was to mentor the cyber grads and provide them with coaching, then to help match them to their next rotations based upon their own career interests and personal strengths.

I also matched the grads with experienced cybersecurity leaders who then also mentored them and provided personal coaching. Then, on top of that, I organised a monthly session where senior executives provided them with career stories with an open Q&A on what worked and what did not work for them. All this had the dual benefit of both illuminating cybersecurity for the grads and further encouraging them into the profession, as well as making our cybersecurity leadership pay attention to this next generation of talent.

External partnerships

For many CISOs, external partnerships are seen as a 'nice to have', but you'll find that if you put yourself into select knowledge-sharing situations, you can help drive an overall uplift of cyber-security in your sector and country.

There are wonderful opportunities, with initiatives such as CI-ISAC and FS-ISAC to develop strong ecosystems between companies and government, as well as to influence what is taught in the tertiary education curriculum.

A culture of innovation

Try to build a culture where team members are encouraged to think creatively about security challenges, to approach problems from an adversarial (presumed breach) perspective and to develop innovative solutions, rather than relying solely on established protocols.

You want all the brains you can get on the big problems – this is how you can start to ensure that the focus is on delivery of the right things. A great example from my experience is that we had our new grads use some gamified eLearning on cybersecurity and the cloud. One of these lessons ended with a very simple question around our own playbook coverage for a use case from the training, and the realisation of 'oops, we don't currently have this covered'.

The grads' enthusiasm was infectious, their curiosity and exploratory drive, and this also encour-aged our existing staff to also want to 'sharpen their own swords'.

Focus on problem-solving ability

Israel's famous Unit 8200 has a very competitive selection procedure that looks for young recruits with outstanding technical, analytical and problem-solving talent. They focus particularly on strong problem-solving capabilities and analytical thinking, rather than traditional credentials and qualifications.

The key has been that they create an environment where cybersecurity professionals develop both technical expertise and leadership skills through challenging, real-world experiences. At the same time, they maintain a culture that encourages continuous learning.

Not a panacea

Note that Israel still suffers from a cyber resource shortage; it is not immune to this problem. The difference is that its trainees are just better and more numerous than those we have generally in other countries.

It is not that they are paid more – their cyber salaries are competitive but only rank as 9th highest. The USA, Australia and Switzerland lead the world with the highest salaries (according to a 2024 article on Analytics Insight: `https://www.analyticsinsight.net/cyber-security/10-countries-paying-highest-salaries-to-cyber-security-professionals`).

These are clear areas that we can invest in as a CISO to help encourage the next generation of talent. A second major item I want to raise in this additional perspectives section is the spectre of AI and how this impacts the focus on cyber talent.

AI talent

As this book is being written, new AI models that have intelligence matching PhD students are becoming available. There are also new agentic AI models emerging in business environments and starting to compete with humans for positions.

This is not the time for CISOs to give up on attracting and retaining talent and just focus on AI. Instead, CISOs need to do both – be a master of developing cyber talent that is both human and bot.

There is an emerging school of thought that the CISO (or CIO) can act as a HR Director for agentic AI. I wanted to raise this as this has significant implications for the role of the CISO. What I mean by this is that in this new model, the:

- CISO will need to help their business partners 'hire' the right AI agents by evaluating their capabilities, limitations, and fit for specific business needs.
- CISO will need to implement frameworks for measuring AI agent performance management, providing feedback to help continuously improve their capabilities.
- CISO will need to orchestrate how AI agents collaborate with human teams.
- CISO will establish governance frameworks to ensure AI agents operate within ethical boundaries and organisational values.

- CISO will manage the 'career path' of AI agents, determining when they should be assigned new responsibilities or upgraded with enhanced capabilities.

- CISO acts as conflict mediator when AI agents produce unexpected outcomes or conflicts arise between systems. Processes will be needed to mediate these issues.

In this future-facing working model, the CISO has potentially taken on a broader responsibility to develop cyber talent, alongside AI agents that operate in this hybrid environment.

CISOs may be one of the early adopters of AI LLM models and agentic AI, so why not try to position yourself to help safely execute this for the enterprise?

The key word here is *safely*, as if AI agents are not closely managed then they create new risks for the enterprise. This will be a new challenge for the CISO to consider.

In my view, the CISO is uniquely positioned to lead organisational AI adoption because they possess the necessary risk management mindset, technical expertise, and cross-functional influence required for safe AI deployment.

While other organisational peers may prioritise speed or efficiency in AI deployment, the CISO's primary concern with security and risk management ensures that AI agents are implemented with appropriate guardrails, monitoring and governance structures.

With these additional perspectives shared, let me wrap up this chapter with my key takeaways.

David's key takeaways — Developing cyber talent

For many CISOs, talent management may not be their strongest competency, and their promotion to this level likely wasn't due to this being a strength. But you now have accountability for the security of your enterprise, and it all boils down to who you want on your team to be able to have the best chance to succeed in your role. Maryam has shared some excellent advice on this in her chapter.

As Maryam has said, cybersecurity is a team sport, and it is for that reason that you absolutely must build the very best team around you that is possible.

A few key points to highlight from this chapter include the following:

- *Talent is your most critical asset* – this is not a HR slogan but the absolute truth; technology and partnerships mean nothing without the right people. Your personal success as a CISO depends on building a skilled team that can adapt to evolving threats and deliver beyond job descriptions.

- *Seek 'painkiller' DNA*. In hiring, look out for three key traits: passion for the work, eagerness to learn and proactive problem-solving abilities. These are what I would call 'Painkiller' attributes, and they often matter more than relevant certifications, especially when combined with strong interpersonal and storytelling skills.

- *Create a positive environment*. You must create an environment that attracts and retains top talent. Build a culture of trust, recognition, and continuous learning where cybersecurity is seen as challenging and rewarding work. Avoid team burnout by promoting work-life balance and providing career development opportunities and support.

- *Diversity gives you strategic strength* – having a diverse team is important. Diverse teams bring different perspectives, essential for tackling complex cyber challenges, and can also be a competitive advantage. Fostering inclusivity within your team is equally important.

- *Learn from Israel's cyber talent development model*. Create a 'skin in the game' mentality by giving new starters meaningful challenges rather than mundane tasks, establishing external partnerships for knowledge sharing, and focusing on developing both technical expertise and leadership skills through real-world experiences.

- *Prepare for the AI-human hybrid future* – you can do this by positioning yourself as the 'HR Director for Agentic AI', developing frameworks to evaluate, manage, and govern AI agents while ensuring they operate safely within your organization. Your risk management expertise makes you uniquely qualified to lead safe AI adoption.

22

Managing Critical Vulnerabilities

At the heart of cybersecurity management is the principle of reducing exposure through a risk-based approach, prioritising the most critical and systemic vulnerabilities. Although conceptually straightforward, this is rarely simple in practice. It often becomes a perpetual cycle, with no definitive end.

For CISOs and CIOs, the obligation to remediate is unambiguous, yet executing this duty frequently places them at odds with business stakeholders whose priorities may not align.

There is typically a clear consensus on the urgency of addressing critical vulnerabilities, particularly zero-day threats. The challenge lies with medium-severity issues: those that are individually less alarming but still capable of accumulating into significant systemic risk if neglected.

On any given day, a CISO must evaluate where to focus resources, considering questions such as:

- Are there critical weaknesses today that could be exploited?
- Have all assets been evaluated for vulnerabilities?
- Are roles and responsibilities clearly defined?
- Once detected, what is a reasonable remediation timeframe for a vulnerability?

While this activity impacts other technology teams and business stakeholders, it remains a responsibility that the CISO must master and consistently manage. It may not be high-profile work, but it is vital that it is performed with rigour rather than treated as a routine exercise.

Boards and management may not be exposed to the full complexity of this topic, and for the average staff member, managing the patching of personal devices is a very different challenge from overseeing enterprise systems.

The CISO must remain aware of both the security requirements for managing vulnerabilities and the need to maintain customer experience and avoid unnecessary impact on critical business systems. This dual awareness makes the role demanding, even without direct trade-offs. When vulnerabilities are managed well, the result is often seamless operations, with little visible sign of the effort involved.

Vulnerability management becomes an even greater concern when **end-of-life (EOL)** equipment or software is in the environment. Without vendor support, these assets cannot be patched and present an attractive target for threat actors.

It is my pleasure to introduce **Steven Brown, former CISO** at Macquarie Group and now **Executive Director** at **Altura Consulting**.

In this chapter, Steve offers us a foundation for building an effective approach to managing critical vulnerabilities, drawing on best practices from a variety of sources.

Managing critical vulnerabilities

Steven Brown

I have developed this chapter to provide you with a strong foundation for building a resilient approach to managing critical vulnerabilities in your organisation. This aims to enhance your organisation's visibility into its risk landscape and bolster overall cybersecurity resilience through effective risk mitigation.

The material I share here is informed by best practices drawn from an extensive array of authoritative sources, including cybersecurity researchers, leading corporations, industry and standards bodies, regulatory guidance, cybersecurity software vendors, threat intelligence providers and incident response teams. However, I should emphasise that none of the content here, including the practical suggestions, should be construed as direct advice. Each organisation must conduct its own due diligence to determine the strategies and measures most appropriate to its specific context and needs.

Vulnerability and exposure management

When we talk about managing critical vulnerabilities, it's often framed under two primary terms:

- **Vulnerability management**: Identifying and addressing specific weaknesses within your systems
- **Exposure management**: Builds on vulnerability management by considering the potential impact these weaknesses might have on your organisation's overall security posture

At the core, both involve identifying the vulnerabilities present in your environment and figuring out how best to handle them. I've focused this chapter on both vulnerability management and exposure management, though the terms are used interchangeably throughout.

There is another term you might sometimes hear in this regard too: patch management. While exposure management looks at the entire spectrum of vulnerabilities, including those that don't have a straightforward patch, such as misconfigurations, patch management is a more narrowly scoped concept focused specifically on deploying patches for technology systems.

Despite the approach I have taken in this chapter, I'd recommend picking a single term, whether it's 'vulnerability management' or 'exposure management,' and using it consistently across your organisation. Consistency here goes a long way in making sure everyone's aligned on scope and priorities.

What is a vulnerability?

For completeness, let me share my definition of what a vulnerability is. A vulnerability, in my view, is any flaw or weakness that increases the likelihood of a negative effect on the **confidentiality, integrity or availability** (**CIA**) of your systems. Think of it as anything that could open the door for a threat actor to gain unauthorised access or disrupt your operations. This obviously includes classic examples such as software bugs, but also misconfigurations or what we sometimes call 'configuration drift', where your systems unintentionally stray from their secure baseline settings over time.

When we use the word 'critical,' we're typically referring to vulnerabilities that demand prompt attention.

Now, it's true that low-rated vulnerabilities often sit lower on the priority list, but it's still essential to assess, track and formally manage them. This is because a low-rated issue today can easily become critical tomorrow if, say, a new exploit emerges that targets it directly.

I have found it useful to maintain a clearly defined process and reporting system to document which issues genuinely require no action. These then provide justification for that position if needed.

The scope of exposure management

Exposure management generally takes a broad perspective, examining all technology systems that could influence your organisation's confidentiality, integrity and availability:

- **IT infrastructure**, including hardware, firmware, software, networks, applications and related technologies used to build and maintain those systems (such as runtime containers, **virtual machines** (**VMs**), software development pipelines including software build components and third-party components)
- **Databases and data stores**, which house the organisation's information assets
- **End user devices**, such as laptops, desktops and mobiles, that may access or contain your organisation's systems or data

- **Operational technology (OT)**, including industrial control systems, SCADA systems and other such technologies that are critical to operational processes (or may pose a contagion risk to other critical systems if impacted)
- **Internet of Things (IoT)** connected devices and sensors that may interact with physical and digital environments
- **Third-party systems** that may critically impact your organisation if compromised (either directly or through contagion risk)

More recently, there has also been growing attention to the vulnerabilities inherent in AI models, an area still maturing but of increasing significance to comprehensive risk management.

> Define a top-level classification of systems that fall under your exposure management umbrella and use it consistently across your metrics and reports. Be crystal clear on what's included, what's out of scope and how you're handling those exclusions. Using an industry-standard grouping can also help keep your IT teams aligned and avoid debates on definitions.

It's worth noting that the scope might stretch beyond what many would consider 'technology' in the traditional sense. Take IoT devices installed throughout your buildings, for example. These often sit under other departments, such as facilities or physical security.

In my experience, what I call non-technology systems, covering areas such as business resilience, supply chain logistics, regulatory compliance and even tax and accounting, are usually owned by different parts of the organisation. That said, if there's a tech component to these systems (say, an automated building access platform or financial processing software), it absolutely should fall under your exposure management purview.

Also, keep in mind that while vulnerability management and identity governance (e.g., **identity and access management (IAM)** and **privileged access management (PAM)**) are typically separate domains, the line between them isn't always clear. Weak passwords or poorly configured identity systems can pose real risks that your exposure management function should at least be aware of and track.

> Document your scope comprehensively, both what's in and what's out, and be explicit about ownership. This avoids gaps in risk visibility and makes sure everyone knows who's accountable for what.

How to manage critical vulnerabilities

In this section, I'll share a few of my thoughts on how I go about managing critical vulnerabilities from a risk perspective.

The risk management framework

In any mature organisation, cybersecurity risks, including vulnerability management, should be woven directly into the broader enterprise risk management framework. Depending on how this framework is set up, cybersecurity and vulnerability management might be classified as top-level risks themselves, or they might sit as sub-risks under broader buckets such as operational risk or technology risk.

An effective risk management framework isn't just about maintaining a register of risks. It should prescribe where risks are recorded, who they get escalated to, what levels of risk are acceptable or not, who's responsible for fixing them, how quickly that needs to happen and what happens if they remain unaddressed. In my experience, without clear answers to these questions, you may end up with critical exposures falling through the cracks.

Here are a few areas to probe when you're embedding vulnerability management into your organisation's risk framework:

- **Terminology:** Does your framework define common terms such as 'control,' 'control owner,' 'issue,' 'risk,' 'threat' and 'priority'? Having this nailed down is critical to making sure everyone interprets and treats risks consistently.

- **Risk appetite:** Has your organisation documented its position on risk appetite? More specifically, is there clarity on what levels of cybersecurity and vulnerability risk are acceptable versus unacceptable? And is this based on qualitative judgment, quantitative thresholds or both?

- **Strategic versus preventable risk:** Does your risk framework make a distinction between 'strategic' risks, where you knowingly accept some risk exposure to pursue a business objective, and 'preventable' risks, which add no real business value and should simply be avoided? (This distinction is well articulated by Kaplan and Mikes in their *Harvard Business Review* article *Managing Risks: A New Framework* (June 2012): `https://hbr.org/2012/06/managing-risks-a-new-framework`.)

- **Explicit recognition in the framework**: Are cybersecurity and vulnerability management clearly defined in your risk taxonomies or hierarchies? Is it clear who ultimately owns these risks, whether that's the CISO, business unit heads or IT leads, and what their responsibilities are? Are there any regulatory requirements that dictate these ownership and accountability structures?

- **Governance**: Does your organisation have the right committees, forums or board-level mechanisms in place to give visibility and oversight to cybersecurity risks? Just as importantly, do these groups have documented charters that spell out their purpose, scope, responsibilities and whether they're advisory or actual decision-making bodies?

It's essential to sit down with your **chief risk officer (CRO)** or whoever holds an equivalent role, and work through these questions together. You want to make certain that your cybersecurity programme and vulnerability management efforts are tightly aligned with your organisation's overall risk strategy. Similarly, make sure that whatever conclusions you reach are properly documented and clearly communicated to all the relevant stakeholders. This is the best way to avoid unpleasant surprises down the line.

Be deliberate in defining roles and responsibilities across the entire vulnerability management process. Make it clear who is accountable for setting the scope, maintaining the asset inventory, identifying vulnerabilities, applying the necessary fixes and escalating risks up the management chain. In my experience, any ambiguity in these areas could be a route to unmanaged risk, which is a situation you will want to avoid.

The importance of identifying assets

A fundamental part of managing critical vulnerabilities is knowing exactly what assets you have. You can't protect what you can't see. It's often difficult to understand how important some assets are until they've been properly identified, logged, and evaluated.

Take something as mundane as an air-conditioning unit. This hardly sounds strategic, right? But if it's the only thing keeping your server room from overheating, a simple failure could quickly lead to a full-scale outage of your local IT environment.

I generally break assets into three main buckets:

- **Managed assets:** These are the ones that are formally catalogued, tracked and maintained by the IT team.

- **Unmanaged assets:** This is the stuff that isn't in your official inventories, such as overlooked equipment, rogue devices, untracked software or even malicious implants.

- **Temporal assets:** These are anything inherently short-lived, such as certain cloud instances, containers or ephemeral VMs. These spin up and down regularly but can still introduce real risk during their lifetime.

Taken together (including externally managed platforms), these assets constitute your organisation's total attack surface. Effectively managing this surface involves identifying and mitigating risks to reduce the likelihood of a breach.

It is also important to recognise that responsibilities or processes for managing vulnerabilities can vary significantly depending on whether the assets in question are owned by your organisation or by a third party, which can introduce additional complexity in determining who holds accountability for addressing those risks.

Here's a quick look at how responsibilities might shake out:

- **Managed assets:** Typically, the technology team owns the **configuration management database (CMDB)**, which tracks these assets across their entire lifecycle, creation, active use, retirement and destruction. Cybersecurity builds (or should build) upon this foundation by continuously scanning these assets and generating reports on their security posture. Ideally, the CMDB should also be integrated with systems capable of detecting or automatically blocking unauthorised infrastructure from the outset.

- **Unmanaged assets:** Here, CMDB owners and network teams usually lead the charge. They're responsible for spotting and either onboarding or blocking unknown devices and software on the network. If you have preventative controls that automatically block these, your cybersecurity team can rely on those as a compensating measure, but it's still essential to quantify and report the residual risk.

- **Temporal assets:** In a perfect world, these would be governed by the same policies as your long-lived infrastructure. But, for example, many organisations are still maturing their cloud practices, meaning they may have separate teams overseeing cloud management and development. This could lead to fragmented approaches that need to be tied back together.

Document your strategy and responsibilities across all asset types. If you can, use a real-time CMDB as your single source of truth, not just for traditional infrastructure but for private and public cloud assets as well. Make sure this is consistent across all layers: networks, operating systems, VMs, containers, serverless, you name it. And don't stop at static inventories. Incorporate real-time controls throughout the entire asset lifecycle, from development pipelines to production, and regularly scan for exceptions. Be explicit about who handles orphaned or unmanaged assets.

Leverage network controls and Zero Trust principles to block unknown or unmanaged devices, software and accounts from accessing your environment. Just as importantly, have clear escalation and remediation paths, and keep a record of who owns these activities. That's what ensures accountability doesn't slip through the cracks.

When you decide an asset is out of scope for regular management or reporting, make sure this exclusion still aligns with your core vulnerability management risk objectives. Even officially exempted assets can pose a significant risk. These should be documented thoroughly, treated as accepted risks with clear expiry dates and escalated up to senior management as needed. The point is to keep your risk story honest and visible, with no sweeping of anything under the rug.

Let me add some thoughts on third-party suppliers, because frankly, they've become one of the biggest sources of cyber risk for just about every enterprise. Third-party systems and services absolutely need to be in scope when you're managing critical vulnerabilities. Any time you rely on external providers, whether that's outsourcing asset management or using third-party-owned or hosted services such as SaaS platforms, you're effectively extending your risk perimeter. That means you also need to extend your vigilance.

Most regulators these days expect organisations to oversee the cybersecurity risks of their third-party suppliers just as rigorously as they manage their own internal risks. In practice, this often means running regular assessments, reviewing audit reports and making sure those suppliers meet your security standards. Of course, the specific approach can vary depending on the type of service and your regulatory obligations.

When it comes to SaaS, the underlying infrastructure is generally expected to be the responsibility of the third-party provider. But don't just assume that's safely handled; this needs to be spelt out explicitly in your contracts. Clear, enforceable terms on security responsibilities, combined with complementary technical controls on your side, such as robust network segmentation and tight user access management, are essential.

For example, you might require your SaaS provider to run their own vulnerability management program and notify you promptly about any critical risks, exposures or incidents that could impact your data. This should all be formally documented as part of your vulnerability management scope and strategy. Make sure your approach also accounts for misconfigurations and access risks, two of the most common and dangerous gaps in third-party environments, and that it lines up with any regulatory expectations you're under.

> Third parties can dramatically expand your attack surface, so build them into your exposure management process with the same level of scrutiny you'd apply to your own internal systems.

Identifying vulnerabilities

Once you have a clear framework for determining which assets fall within the scope of vulnerability management, you will need to implement methods and technologies for identifying or scanning for vulnerabilities on those assets. The appropriate approach varies by asset type, for which I have detailed some common methods as follows.

Information sources

Information sources play a foundational role in vulnerability management. It is crucial to establish reliable channels for acquiring vulnerability and patch information, including vendor websites and feeds relevant to deployed systems, open source vulnerability databases, official security bulletins, the **National Vulnerability Database (NVD)** and various threat intelligence feeds.

Threat intelligence integration

Integrating threat intelligence enhances your awareness of evolving threats. Taking this approach facilitates the identification of vulnerabilities that are currently being exploited in the wild, thereby informing you of adjustments that you may need to make to the vulnerability management process. Incorporating threat intelligence may also support the scanning of environments for **indicators of compromise (IoCs)**.

SIEM integration

Integration with **security information and event management (SIEM)** systems can further strengthen your vulnerability detection, response and mitigation capabilities by correlating vulnerability data with broader security events.

Configuration audits

Regular configuration audits are another key measure. Assessing system configurations against established best practices and security baselines can uncover misconfigurations that represent vulnerabilities. Automated tools (such as OpenSCAP with ComplianceAsCode baselines) allow such audits to be conducted with a frequency and thoroughness that manual methods cannot sustain.

Real-time vulnerability scanning

Given the rapid evolution of cyber threats, the timeliness of vulnerability information is paramount. Real-time vulnerability scanning, supported by up-to-date tools and data, ensures emerging threats are identified quickly. The sheer scale of modern technology environments and the volume of known vulnerabilities make manual processes for this impractical and insufficient.

Scanning for old and new risks

It is also important to scan for both old and new risks. Regular scanning should target newly disclosed vulnerabilities on relevant systems, as well as long-standing vulnerabilities that may persist in new system iterations. Embedding these controls within technology lifecycles, such as within the software development lifecycle, helps prevent known vulnerabilities from advancing into production environments.

External testing

External testing examines systems from the perspective of an external attacker to identify exploitable vulnerabilities. This includes automated assessments and manual penetration testing, the latter of which can uncover vulnerabilities that automated tools might overlook. Such testing may also identify newly discovered, unmanaged, external-facing infrastructure for which you need to have a process to manage.

Internal testing

Internal testing focuses on vulnerabilities within the organisation's own network, including hardware, software and IaaS environments. Common approaches for this involve agent-based scanners (installed directly on devices), agentless network-based scanners and side-scanning techniques leveraging snapshots or backups. Each method has distinct advantages and limitations; selecting the most suitable approach requires consideration of your organisation's particular operational needs.

Simulation testing

Simulation testing, such as breach and attack simulations, provides insights into how vulnerabilities might be exploited in practice, thereby allowing you to evaluate the effectiveness of existing security measures. This includes both people-driven exercises, such as red team operations, and software-based simulations, which can be especially valuable in detecting vulnerabilities arising from the misconfiguration of interconnected systems.

Tailoring vulnerability identification measures to asset type

A robust exposure management function employs a suite of identification techniques carefully tailored to the specific asset types. I've listed popular approaches by asset type in the following table:

Asset type	Vulnerability identification measures
Hardware	• Security advisories from manufacturers. • Using hardware-specific scanning tools (e.g., CHIPSEC).
Firmware	• Firmware update notifications and security advisories from manufacturers. • Vulnerability scanning tools that include firmware checks.
Software and applications	• **Static application security testing (SAST)** for identifying vulnerabilities in source code. • **Dynamic application security testing (DAST)** for runtime analysis. • Open source software vulnerability feeds (e.g., OSS Index, GitHub security alerts). • Monitoring vendor updates and security advisories. • Third-party threat intelligence and vulnerability feeds. • Application testing (e.g., OWASP ZAP), including web page scanning. • Integration of vulnerability scanning tools within the CI/CD pipeline. • Agent-based vulnerability scanners. • Configuration audits and hardening checks. • API security testing.

Asset type	Vulnerability identification measures
Networks	• Network vulnerability scanners (e.g., Nessus, Qualys, Tenable, etc.). • Penetration testing. • Configuration audits.
Databases and data stores	• Database-specific vulnerability scanners. • Monitoring vendor updates and security advisories. • Configuration audits and hardening checks. • Database-specific penetration tests.
End user devices	• Vulnerability scanning tools that include end user device checks. • Endpoint security solutions that provide vulnerability information. • Monitoring vendor updates and security advisories. • Monitoring operating system and application updates and security advisories.
Industrial control systems (ICSs) and SCADA	• Specialised OT vulnerability scanners. • Monitoring vendor updates and security advisories. • Configuration and security audits.
Internet of Things (IoT)	• IoT-specific vulnerability scanners and network-based vulnerability scanners. • Monitoring for firmware and software updates and security advisories from manufacturers. • Penetration testing of IoT devices and networks.
IaaS/PaaS	• **Cloud security posture management (CSPM)** tools. • PaaS-specific vulnerability scanners. • Penetration testing and configuration audits. • Monitoring for updates and security advisories.

Asset type	Vulnerability identification measures
Third-party systems and SaaS	• Regular security assessments and audits of third-party systems, including reviewing the configurations of your SaaS tenant, ensuring that all settings you control are correctly and securely configured. • Fourth-party monitoring services for third-party environments and systems. • Vulnerability scanning and penetration testing of third-party systems and integrations. • Reviewing results from independent audits/tests of third-party systems. • Monitoring security advisories and updates. • Implementing and reviewing **service-level agreements (SLAs)** and contractual security requirements to be notified of vulnerabilities. • API security testing.

Table 22.1: Vulnerability identification measures by asset type

Taken together, this tailored approach to vulnerability identification ensures that each asset type is managed with techniques suited to its specific characteristics, helping you to establish a comprehensive, resilient foundation for exposure management across your technology environments.

Assessing and prioritising vulnerabilities

Assessing and prioritising vulnerabilities must fundamentally be a risk-based exercise, as not all vulnerabilities present the same level of threat to an organisation. Prioritisation focused on the potential impact and exploitability of each vulnerability ensures that the most critical issues are addressed first (a practice commonly referred to as 'risk-based vulnerability management').

Vulnerability scoring

Vulnerability scoring involves evaluating vulnerabilities using established scoring frameworks such as the **Common Vulnerability Scoring System (CVSS)**, the OWASP Risk Rating Methodology or the **Common Weakness Scoring System (CWSS)**. Many of these frameworks include options to incorporate environment-specific factors to better reflect unique risks relevant to your organisation.

CVSS provides a widely adopted, standardised method for rating the severity of vulnerabilities and helps inform remediation priorities.

The OWASP Risk Rating Methodology offers a structured framework for assessing the risks associated with vulnerabilities in web applications.

CWSS facilitates the consistent and flexible prioritisation of software weaknesses.

To manage and prioritise identified vulnerabilities effectively, organisations typically aggregate all findings into a centralised system and apply formulaic methods (including drawing on the frameworks I mentioned previously) to calculate a total risk score for each vulnerability. This enables consistent, transparent and comprehensive reporting. Such scoring generally draws upon several key factors.

The first is the base vulnerability rating, such as the raw CVSS score, which usually does not reflect the specific context of an organisation's environment. Environmental metrics within CVSS can be applied to adjust that raw score to better match your context (such as confidentiality requirements of the affected data), however, and inform remediation priorities.

The second factor is asset criticality: assessing the importance of the systems where vulnerabilities are found, with particular attention to the confidentiality, integrity and availability requirements of those assets and any sensitive data they process, such as **personally identifiable information** **(PII)**.

Exploitability is another crucial consideration; the existence of known exploits of a particular vulnerability elevates the urgency of remediation. Although exploitability is typically incorporated into standard scoring systems, these assessments often lag behind the latest developments, necessitating additional threat intelligence feeds to capture newly discovered exploits. The level of external exposure also plays a significant role, as vulnerabilities in systems accessible via the internet are inherently more likely to be targeted by attackers.

Dealing with false positives

It's important to establish a robust feedback mechanism from those responsible for investigating and remediating identified vulnerabilities, which feeds back into the central repository. This will help to ensure that genuine risks are neither overlooked nor misclassified.

To preserve the integrity of the vulnerability management process, if you do get any false positives and/or exceptions, these should be accurately recorded. Clear documentation and communication of false positives to relevant stakeholders helps to prevent misallocation of resources and in detecting trends that may indicate underlying technical, procedural or human errors. Similarly, documentation on exceptions, instances where known vulnerabilities are temporarily accepted due to operational constraints, should also be carefully reviewed and approved at a senior level to ensure that residual risks are acknowledged and periodically reassessed as circumstances evolve.

The need for continuous re-evaluation

Continuous re-evaluation of vulnerability scores (and risk assessments) is critical, given that CVSS scores and other vulnerability metrics can change rapidly in response to new threat intelligence or discovered exploits. This ensures that even older vulnerabilities and previously granted exceptions are monitored and revisited if their risk profiles shift.

Note that recalculations should be driven by new scoring or exploitability information and not solely tied to the schedules of vulnerability scans.

Establishing escalation procedures for vulnerabilities

It's essential to establish clear escalation procedures to ensure that critical vulnerabilities are addressed with the requisite urgency. Any delays can be promptly reported to higher levels of management.

With the structured pathway these procedures provide you, you will be better equipped to safeguard the organisation's risk posture by ensuring timely intervention and oversight.

Tracking and reporting on vulnerabilities

Rigorous tracking and aggregation underpin the entire vulnerability management process. Ensuring that all identified vulnerabilities, including those ultimately classified as false positives or exceptions, are systematically recorded and addressed helps to guarantee full coverage and prevent critical issues from being inadvertently overlooked. This also helps provide assurance that no potentially material exposure remains unmanaged, thereby minimising the likelihood of unexpected security incidents.

Let me highlight this – tracking of vulnerability data and asset information should be *exhaustive*, capturing 100% of inputs and changes over time. This includes recording the outcomes of aggregations, transformations, exclusions, duplicate handling and exemptions, along with maintaining a complete history and timestamp for each operation. Comprehensive tracking such as this supports you with the evolving analysis of critical vulnerabilities as both asset landscapes and threat environments change, as well as facilitating future audits.

Your reporting should also be able to explain and break down changes in vulnerability counts, due to the following:

- Retired assets, new assets and existing (long-lived) assets
- Managed and unmanaged asset changes
- Changes in vulnerability ratings for existing vulnerabilities
- Duplicate vulnerabilities, which often occur when running multiple scans
- Excepted or exempted assets or vulnerabilities
- False positives
- Remediated vulnerabilities
- Newly announced vulnerabilities (on existing assets)
- Old/known vulnerabilities newly identified (introduced) on existing assets

With appropriate data storage, the level of detail I have described for vulnerability management reporting here can be reliably maintained. This should also enable the production of meaningful dashboards and communication that convey status and progress effectively.

It may be necessary to incorporate qualitative risk estimates into reporting for unknown or unmanaged assets until more useful quantitative methods become available.

Regardless of the approach, it is prudent to ensure clear traceability from the total population of assets and vulnerabilities down to the subset that requires immediate attention.

Establishing metrics and targets

Alongside the aggregated data on your organisation's current vulnerability posture, it is beneficial to establish clear risk-based targets that are referred to in communications and progress reports.

This may include remediation timelines, remediation efforts and overall risk exposure. Take the following examples:

- **Risk-based remediation targets**:
  - **Critical vulnerabilities:** Remediation within 24–48 hours
  - **High-risk vulnerabilities:** Remediation within 7–14 days
  - **Medium-risk vulnerabilities:** Remediation within 30 days

- **Low-risk vulnerabilities:** Remediation within 90 days (or periodic aggregate review and approval for non-actioned low vulnerabilities)

- **Exposure management metrics:**

  - **Percentage of assets with vulnerabilities:** Target X% for critical, Y% for high, etc.

  - **Patch compliance rate:** Percentage of vulnerabilities or assets where critical/high-risk vulnerabilities are overdue for remediation

  - **Percentage of unmanaged assets:** This might include the percentage of new unmanaged assets (indicating process improvements required)

  - **Systems coverage:** Percentage of scanned/unscanned systems (at least for critical and external-facing systems)

- **Ageing metrics:**

  - **Average time to remediation:** The average time taken to remediate critical and high-risk vulnerabilities

  - **Vulnerability recurrence rate:** The percentage of vulnerabilities or assets for which previously remediated vulnerabilities have reappeared

- **Enterprise-wide risk metrics:**

  - **Overall risk score:** Based on the current level of risk (previous aggregating metrics)

  - **Audit and compliance:** Number of open audit and compliance findings

> Periodically review and adjust these metrics and targets to align with evolving threats, regulatory requirements and organisational risk goals.

Communicating vulnerabilities

You will likely need to communicate vulnerability information to various stakeholders, including the organisation's board (or equivalent), the C-suite, business/division heads, key risk managers and technology owners.

Your communications should be tailored to each group based on their role, providing an appropriate level of detail and focusing on only the information they need to know.

Setting specific targets for vulnerability management, such as those suggested in the previous section, helps in aligning your efforts with organisational goals and, as such, in communicating your efforts to others.

Trending and ageing information will be particularly useful for most stakeholders. (As the ageing example metrics in the previous section suggest, 'ageing' may refer to how long a vulnerability has existed within your environment, how long a vulnerability has been known or how long an asset has had a critical vulnerability.)

What you share will depend on the stakeholder:

- **The board**: May only need to see high-level summary information, including historical comparisons and trending and ageing information that clearly explains whether the organisation is within the risk appetite (green), close to the risk appetite maximum (orange) or outside of the risk appetite (red).

- **Senior management and business heads**: Should receive at least as much information as the board (and ideally with a timeframe factored in that allows for their review and feedback first), as well as stakeholder-specific details of interest.

  For example, business heads will likely need to see specific information for their line of business, including any significant new risks, whether they are meeting their committed remediation timeframes, and ownership details for any delayed remediation.

- **Risk managers**: Similar reporting requirements as senior management. Organisational-wide risk managers may also need to see this level of detail across all business lines.

- **Technology owners**: These will need details relevant to their specific technology responsibilities, including clear asset-specific or owner-specific remediation requirements and any remediation delays.

Real-time communication plays a vital role in the effective remediation of critical vulnerabilities. Given the imperative to address such vulnerabilities as swiftly as possible, you need systems that offer immediate visibility into identified issues and that generate timely alerts directed to the relevant stakeholders, particularly those tasked with executing remediation activities.

Real-time communication mechanisms are especially relevant to individuals and teams responsible for taking prompt action to mitigate critical or overdue vulnerabilities, ensuring that these issues are not only identified without delay but are also prioritised and resolved quickly.

From my point of view, it's well worth considering how you might integrate vulnerability communication with your existing real-time alerting systems, corporate communication channels, software development chat platforms, and any other relevant management processes that your organisation already has in place.

In practice, you might find that only the most critical vulnerabilities demand real-time alerts. However, it's still invaluable to have a dashboard (we look at this in the next section) that shows the up-to-date status of all vulnerabilities. This gives those responsible for remediation, the technology owners, immediate feedback on their efforts and allows them to flag certain findings as false positives when justified.

Always share communications on a strict need-to-know basis, and as I mentioned earlier, ensure the level of detail you share matches what each stakeholder requires; too much or too little information can both be counterproductive.

I'd also emphasise the value of providing proactive information to these teams, not just on vulnerabilities that are already overdue but also on those approaching their due dates. This helps avoid last-minute surprises. Given the typically high volume of vulnerabilities, especially the lower-rated ones your organisation might decide not to prioritise, automated communication solutions are almost always the most practical way to handle this efficiently.

Beyond routine vulnerability status reporting, it is equally important to determine when out-of-cycle communication is warranted to keep key stakeholders adequately informed. For instance, if the organisation's overall risk posture shifts materially, such as when a newly discovered vulnerability falls outside the accepted risk appetite and has yet to be remediated, communication to senior management and potentially the board may be necessary. Similarly, if remediation activities previously committed to are delayed in a manner that undermines the organisation's risk posture, timely communication should be directed both to the responsible owners and to senior management to facilitate corrective action.

This would also apply when a significant new external vulnerability or vulnerability-related incident arises, particularly one that affects other organisations and attracts public or media attention. In these scenarios, senior management and the board may benefit from a comprehensive briefing. This should address who the issue impacts, how it arose, its actual or potential implications for the organisation, the current level of risk, the measures being undertaken to mitigate that risk, the status and anticipated completion of those measures and the expected timing of subsequent updates.

Disciplined communication practices such as those I have covered in this section ensure that leadership remains fully informed and able to make decisions aligned with the organisation's risk tolerance and strategic objectives.

Remediating vulnerabilities

Once vulnerabilities have been identified, aggregated and communicated to the appropriate responsible owners, the task shifts to remediating these within agreed timeframes.

An effective way to support this process, as I mentioned in my previous tips, is using interactive, real-time dashboards or comparable tools, which provide clear visibility into outstanding vulnerabilities and their remediation status.

> In preparing a vulnerability dashboard, it is advisable to establish under what circumstances exceptions or exemptions might be permitted, and whether the dashboard can facilitate these processes, including any necessary approval workflows. Similarly, there should be mechanisms for flagging certain findings as false positives, complete with structured review, approval and reporting steps to ensure that such determinations are logical and transparent.

Let's look at how vulnerabilities can be addressed.

Preventing vulnerabilities

Far preferable to remediation is prevention. This begins with rigorous scanning and testing of systems during development and immediately prior to deployment. To be effective, systems should be scanned with up-to-date vulnerability data, and deployment should be halted if any high or critical vulnerabilities remain unresolved. You may choose to align this requirement with existing remediation timelines or adopt even stricter standards for new deployments.

Achieving this in practice typically requires integrating vulnerability detection technologies directly into the software development lifecycle and hardware deployment processes. The use of outdated or unsupported hardware and software should also be avoided. (It is essential to define clearly what constitutes 'outdated' or 'supported' technology, particularly in the case of open source software, to ensure that there is confidence in identifying and addressing vulnerabilities.)

An effective patch management process is also vital. This ensures that software and systems are updated regularly to mitigate known security weaknesses, following structured approaches such as the widely recognised 'Patch Tuesday' model introduced by Microsoft in 2003.

Fixing vulnerabilities

When vulnerabilities are found, there are multiple common avenues for remediation. These include the following:

- Applying patches or security updates to existing systems.

- Reconfiguring technology to eliminate exposure.

- Replacing vulnerable hardware, firmware, or software with alternative solutions.

- Upgrading systems to versions that do not exhibit the vulnerability.

- Removing specific vulnerable sub-components, such as unused software libraries.

- Implementing and configuring **web application firewalls** (**WAFs**) and other virtual patching solutions. These provide protection by filtering and monitoring traffic to web applications. Virtual patching offers temporary protection against vulnerabilities until permanent fixes can be applied.

- Implementing/configuring **intrusion prevention systems** (**IPSs**) in modern firewalls, to detect and block malicious activities in real time. This provides an additional layer of defence against known exploits. This may also be a temporary solution until the underlying systems can be remediated.

It is important never to assume that remediation has been fully successful merely because recommended actions were completed. Be sure that the environment is rescanned to confirm that vulnerabilities have indeed been resolved and that configurations are correctly applied.

If direct remediation is not immediately possible

In situations where a direct fix cannot be promptly applied, it becomes necessary to adopt alternative measures such as temporary patches, isolating affected systems or deploying compensating controls to reduce risk.

Organisations should establish processes to flag such temporary measures for future review, ideally setting 'expiry dates' to ensure they do not become overlooked long-term. This principle equally applies to false positive designations, safeguarding against complacency.

Sustaining the effort

Ultimately, managing vulnerabilities is an ongoing endeavour, and a continuous process rather than a finite project. While individual successes can be achieved by addressing immediate threats, the broader campaign often resembles running on a treadmill, where consistent effort helps maintain and improve your organisation's overall security health.

Sustained effort is essential. Any lapse increases risk to both day-to-day operations and long-term security. By maintaining vigilance and systematically applying the strategies I have outlined in this chapter to manage vulnerabilities, you place your organisation in a far stronger position to manage this ongoing challenge and safeguard their security posture.

> Allow me to emphasise again – managing vulnerabilities is a continuous process rather than a problem with a fixed endpoint. There will always be new threats to address, but consistent attention keeps your organisation resilient and ready.

In this chapter, I've included some approaches that have worked well for me in practice and encourage you to keep building your vulnerability management program with a similar steady focus.

David's key takeaways — Managing critical vulnerabilities

You can tell from this chapter that Steve is a very technical CISO and has a meticulous eye for detail (which you will either have yourself or should ensure that members of your staff have).

As Steve mentions, vulnerability management can feel like being on a treadmill with the incline continuing to lift as you run to catch up. You may feel that you are not making any progress and staying in the same place, but the reality is that your fitness would be much worse if this effort were not being made. The CISO has to encourage their team to be motivated and continue to make progress themselves, regardless of any such feelings!

The key points from Steve's chapter are:

- *Vulnerability management is a continuous risk-based process that requires balancing critical fixes with business needs.* It involves identifying and addressing system weaknesses, through identifying, prioritising and remediating vulnerabilities.

- *Asset identification in vulnerability management is a crucial initial step.* Steve categorises assets into three categories: managed assets (properly catalogued), unmanaged assets (overlooked/unexpected) and temporal assets (temporary like cloud instances). This forms the organisation's total attack surface, and once you have these assets mapped, you can focus on implementing methods and technologies for identifying or scanning for vulnerabilities on those assets.

- *Third-party suppliers represent a major cyber risk and should be included in the vulnerability management scope.* Organisations are typically expected by regulators to manage third-party cybersecurity risks as rigorously as their own.

- *Multiple methods should be used for identifying vulnerabilities.* This includes monitoring information sources, threat intelligence, utilising scanning and testing. Different approaches are needed for different asset types (IT infrastructure, cloud services, IoT devices, etc.)

- *Vulnerabilities should be prioritised based on multiple factors*, such as vulnerability rating, asset criticality, exploitability and level of external exposure. This helps to ensure the most critical issues are addressed first.

- *Communication on vulnerabilities should be tailored to different stakeholders*, ensuring each has no more or less than the information they need.

23

AI: The Promise and Challenge

A few years ago, the average CISO would not have used AI in their typical day. That is not true today. The advent of generative AI (genAI) means that many cyber products have an add-on AI component and more are coming as new features – regardless of whether you want this or not.

The promise of AI in this context is to help the CISO defend the enterprise better. Threat actors can also use AI tools, however, with tools for hacking (FraudGPT, WormGPT, and others) appearing. The next era has the potential to become an arms race, as enterprises look to ensure that they aren't outmaneuvered by automation applied to penetrating their attack surface.

Future cybersecurity will be machine versus machine. The massive volume that will come with better automation of attacks is best managed by machines; however, it still requires some human oversight – otherwise referred to as a human in the loop.

In defending the enterprise, CISOs face 'alert fatigue' and the potential burnout of their team from the stress and strain of cyber operations. For defenders, AI can help to identify threats by taking in broader data inputs across a larger dataset and being more accurate in identifying false positives.

Across the estate, AI presents other opportunities – the SOC team can use it to help them develop their playbooks and automate some events, for example. Even now, with AI, we are reducing the investigation of threats to minutes rather than days or hours. AI can also provide benefits in 'shifting left', i.e., by helping to develop and test safer code that is built using tools such as GitHub Copilot.

There are, however, concerns regarding validating AI models. As more and more work is automated, the task of checking it becomes longer and more complicated. It is tempting to skip steps, checks and balances in the need for speed. It's critically important that we don't see AI as simply a cost reduction tool and reduce headcount too quickly without considering the increased need for highly trained individuals to review its work.

AI tools will make some tasks simpler and faster, but we will still need highly trained humans to check the work it produces for the foreseeable future – removing manpower from the workforce has the potential to create a very large rod for our backs when we find we need the higher skill levels that are required in humans checking the machines a few years down the track.

The danger with AI is that we use it in 'autopilot' mode rather than as a 'copilot'. There will always be a degree of human judgment needed in comparing the output of different models and ensuring that there are no obvious hallucinations. For instance, when you speak to developers, they will tell you that they have adopted these tools as copilots; however, question how they can judge the code without themselves reviewing every line generated.

It is my pleasure to introduce **Jacqui Kernot, Vice President**, **Thales Cyber Security Services ANZ** and **GM Tesserent**. She began writing this chapter when she was Security Director at Accenture.

Jacqui has extensive experience in Army Intelligence, has been a Cyber Partner at EY, and Telstra's Head of Cyber. Jacqui will explore the promise and the challenge of AI and how the CISO should embrace this, but at the same time, be wary of the new potential threats it can present.

AI: the Promise and Challenge

Jacqui Kernot

When you think about the promise of generative AI and the age of AI we are entering, it's an enormous step in human evolution. It is the beginning of the beginning, although automation in various forms has been around for 30 years – perhaps more. AI has both promise and challenge, and as cyber people, we need to look at the risks and consequences of it – what is going to make a difference, and what do we need to do now to ensure we don't let the AI revolution get out of hand?

Ironically, as we focus so much on software, this is about hardware and physical requirements, as well as the development and training of the humans we will need to keep AI safe and regulated. Revolutions don't get far if they aren't grounded, and if genAI is going to evolve, it is going to be firstly about hardware and secondly about people.

There are parallels with AI now in the way that we, as technologists, created the internet (not me personally – I'm not quite that old). We were unregulated and just experimenting, and it was just unleashed onto the world. Originally, the Internet Protocol (IP) was a DARPA project designed to be resilient if parts of the network were taken out by nuclear misadventure. When the first internet browser was created, it took off quite unexpectedly. There were no regulations and no controls. When I look back at that time, we just sort of trusted people to be sensible. (Spoiler alert – no one was sensible.)

They built it for speed, not safety, security or regulatory controls. We are in a very similar place today with genAI – hopefully, with some lessons learned, but unfortunately, as the need for the eSafety commission and other regulatory bodies demonstrates, not nearly enough. The internet is still very unsafe and unregulated, and now – with genAI – we are doing a similar thing, automating processes and taking the human checks and balances out of play. Let's look at this and the challenges that AI is bringing.

AI challenges

When we think about the internet, we are still rolling back and having to look at how we retrofit safety and security onto it and what the frameworks are to do that. For example:

- For companies, or for our applications? Both?
- At the network layer? The user layer? Both and more?
- How do we get nation-states to agree on what good looks like?

These kinds of questions still haven't been answered completely about the internet. We haven't solved the problems, and now we're going into an era of genAI where we take out, in large part, the human oversight of the entire creation process.

What is interesting about AI is that most of the problem isn't about the software itself or its creation. Most of the problem is about people who design what we call guardrails, the culture of the companies and countries they work in and the 'regulations' that those countries and companies are required to adhere to (if there are any at all). How we design the regulatory framework quickly but safely around it will have a huge impact on how much of a problem we create for ourselves.

We still don't have it right with the internet or the applications that run on it, but we're going into genAI – and that's going to pick up all the mistakes and multiply them exponentially. If we don't start using AI tools, however, we will quickly get left behind, so there's a huge existential need to get moving and take advantage of their efficiencies. This creates the perfect storm – huge pressure to adopt and a lack of regulatory frameworks and insight into how they should run, as well as very few universally agreed principles on responsible AI adoption, although many companies have developed their own. We must just hope it will be enough.

The hardware problem

Another problem that we have – somewhat ironically – is hardware. In the future, infrastructure and so many different systems are going to be automated and run on AI, so it's going to be easy to interrupt a whole lot of critical functions that we all need to live (you know, hospitals, roads, traffic systems, etc.). Adding to that is the fact that we currently have a global concentration of chip supply in Taiwan, and not enough fibre optic cable or power to data centres. Ramping up capacity or building supply chain resilience in more than one country is very expensive and lengthy as a manufacturing exercise. The instability of the current world makes this a supply crisis waiting to happen.

To support the needs of AI in the very near future, the power requirements will need to be exponentially higher, not logarithmically higher. We don't have enough power generation, and we have very little redundancy in the underwater data cable systems (trunks), and the ones on land connecting cities.

If we look at creative solutions like nuclear power plants to generate the kinds of output we will need, they are a very expensive, big multi-year infrastructure project. All in all, it's hard to see how we are going to solve all the hardware problems that arise in the short and medium term.

Meanwhile, the focus is on thinking about new AI software and tools and this sudden simplification/reduction in the cost model. This is a dangerous exercise, however, if we haven't considered the infrastructure and hardware requirements, which are costly, multiyear projects, and the risk to some of the supply of the chips and power we will need to continue the genAI transformation journey. This creates difficulty with many of the operating delivery models we see in technology today, where we have offshored many tasks to reduce costs, because what we want to do is keep control of these language models in-country – a concept known as data sovereignty (more on this later).

Unfortunately, we often fail to consider hardware, power and infrastructure until it's too late. The best time to start considering this – like tree planting – is ten years ago, and the next best time is right now.

Regulatory lag

It's also important to talk about regulatory lag. We see this consistently with new technology, but the potential for AI to develop rapidly and become out of control is much higher than with previous technological step changes.

Regulatory frameworks are urgently needed – otherwise, there is a danger that models will run wild. We'll end up in the same place we are now with the internet, where it is very difficult to roll it back, but it will happen a lot faster. Once you begin building language models without the correct data governance and guardrails, or without the correct data segregation between data sets, it's very difficult – if not impossible – to 'disinfect' the language model and take the errors out. It's not simple to just roll it back.

So, it's a really hard challenge to address. In fact, if it isn't done proactively rather than reactively, as we are trying to do with safety and security across the internet, it's virtually impossible. There are always going to be inherent risks in this, as with any new technology, but we urgently need at least broad, 'light touch' regulation. In the race to adopt AI and benefit from the efficiencies, organisations will be motivated to move quickly into the promise of AI, but there's not as much incentive to avoid causing problems – not until after they happen.

Effectively, we are creating an arms race where people are starting quickly and investing a lot of money and time to obtain cost efficiencies, and reducing headcount to fund the moves, before the guardrails are in place within their organisations or any detailed, comprehensive regulatory framework is agreed.

Financial services players and other large enterprises are moving quickly down this path in particular. As their competitors are also moving, they must start running to catch up. The lack of detailed regulation and auditing against it is problematic as we go too far to roll back.

It is a bit alarming that we haven't got the regulatory framework that makes technology safe more broadly, and now we're going into an era where we'll have even fewer control points in inspection points. As I mentioned earlier, we are creating a perfect storm.

Once again, we come back to people and the importance of cultures of safety by design in technology. How do we create scrutiny and get insight to ensure we can fix problems before they become too big, without losing automation speed and efficiency?

Most AI models deployed for companies are closed source and behind firewalls in their deployment, but the advent of China's DeepSeek AI may change that rapidly. (Note, however, that there is concern, at the time of writing, that DeepSeek data might be going offshore as well, to a government which makes no secret of its intent to collect data and use it without considering individual privacy legislation.) We have seen companies be quick to restrict access to these tools; however, as with ChatGPT, it is easy to see the escalating risk of corporate data going outside the company.

There are risks with both approaches, but with the closed model, there is no insight into how they're building their models. That's what they're doing, and they're doing that because they're trying to retain proprietary IP.

We've looked at some of the key challenges around AI. Now let's have a look at AI's promise.

The AI promise

Overall, there is enormous promise in AI technologies (particularly genAI and agentic AI), as there are many manual and menial tasks that we do every day that these can potentially automate. Having a level of automation to reduce our effort on those tasks will enable creativity because when people have more free time, they are more able to think about interesting ways to do things.

Another one of the many positives of AI is that it can help to level the playing field – for small organisations particularly. It can help make smaller organizations safer, and indeed, there is evidence from smaller companies that they are using it for automation and elevating their risk posture as a result. Essentially, it can make it easier for them to defend their data and networks and simplify their move to the cloud or better security technologies. In this way, AI better enables these companies to operate without the necessity of hiring staff, which many are unable to afford to do, especially given the shortage of cybersecurity staff. (Having said that, this means that these smaller companies have even less ability to work out whether they are doing the right thing with AI and sensibly complying with relevant regulations.)

Let me explain another example where AI can have an incredible impact on an important and developing security dynamic – the requirement for data sovereignty. More and more, legislation and companies are encouraging the repatriation of data and data repositories, as we cannot trust our data to be held in places where the government of those countries does not align with our view of data access. This is especially important in critical infrastructure environments.

To a degree, insisting on data sovereignty feels a little extreme – but there is no other way to be assured we have control over our data. Broadly speaking, the problem is that technologists have never been encouraged or regulated to create controls or checkpoints, or worry about where data is stored or even who has access to it.

In the past, offshoring has been a huge part of reducing costs onshore. More and more, though, this comes with huge risks to our critical data. We have all worked in enterprises that have offshored or nearshored to reduce cost and increase scale. In theory, we should now see that this starts to reverse, and that AI technologies become the answer to cost reduction without losing data sovereignty.

The current model is flawed for Australia as the 'A' team for offshore talent is usually reserved for the larger enterprise contracts, usually out of the US and Europe; hence, there is a large variation in capability deployed on Australian clients. AI is consistent and does not have this deviation once it is trained, especially for well-known processes.

Leveraging onshore resources combined with AI models may be the perfect blend between both reducing risk and cost that we should be considering. Let's look further into how involved humans should be with AI.

Humans in the loop

Across history, we have seen that technology truly takes off when it's open source and available freely. When we think about approaches to assurance for these AI models, one that comes to mind is that there is 'adjacency', and that means having two models checking each other. In this approach, they are both masters. In theory, we have one checking the other, and the human is on the sidelines watching and stepping in where a problem arises. This is fraught with difficulty, though, especially considering the difference in speed between human and machine.

With this approach, essentially the models are talking to each other, which is not an ideal control design because the human supervisor must sometimes rest and take holidays, etc. In the end, taking this approach, there's a risk of falling into autopilot mode, rather than AI being a copilot. This defeats the human in the loop control framework entirely – but having said that, some types of AI, including agentic AI, which learns from processes and doesn't require the same level of prompt engineering, might indeed benefit from this type of control design.

What we need to be able to manage this risk is a control point that stops exactly at that point of decision. As always, in IT deployment, it is about people, processes and technology. When we forget people and processes, the end result is usually fewer effective outcomes.

As technology starts to become self-generating, we should consider that people are going to become so much more important, especially because there is no current detailed regulation to provide a control point or define what is allowed to be released without human inspection or approval.

We really need to think about the people we engage, what standards we hold them to, and how we train them. In Australia, we are looking at professional standardisation processes and how we enable better governance of personnel in the industry, as well as who we rely on in cybersecurity. We need a similar process for AI design and governance – especially governance.

This needs to be accelerated quickly because it is coming to a critical juncture right now. This is because we are now relying on companies to make responsible decisions without any penalties or consequences, and that, historically, has not worked well.

As an example, let's move to the Security Operations Centre (SOC) and look at using AI for monitoring logs. If we train the AI model and then have a human agree with any critical decision it produces, then the value of the AI model is that it can search the asset library and look for vulnerabilities on-premise and at third-party vendors. This enables better and faster vulnerability management (or exposure management – terminology we are moving to as an industry to describe the shift from addressing symptoms to being focused on outcomes and root causes).

This seems to be an obvious place for improvements and headcount reduction, but if you start removing staff too quickly, then it may become a risk. It's likely that reducing headcount is going to be the justification for most of these investments, so this argument may be a moot point; however, it's vital to consider checks and governance before moving too quickly to reduce headcount and staff.

Ultimately, the macro control is humans in the loop. We can reiterate that humans in the loop are critical, and people are important to effective technology deployments, but the reality is these projects will take the humans out of the equation, as that is where the cost efficiencies come. Don't make this mistake – just deploying AI tools will not save you a stack of money by itself. The issue is how we train and retain senior people to provide oversight when all the entry-level/training jobs have been replaced. There are a lot more questions than answers here, but it's important to think about these issues before making headcount reductions and losing capability, which will create problems for you further down the track.

Many governance tasks require a pretty senior technologist with a lot of training to be effective. How will we develop these when there's no pathway for junior technologists?

Unfortunately, if there is no regulation forcing a check or review of AI usage, it's unlikely, then, to be on the board or leadership agenda to be reviewed. It's one of the reasons we urgently need better regulation, and it also highlights the importance of us considering these things before deciding on a deployment plan.

AI in cybersecurity

In cybersecurity, what we often see is more automation than generative AI. With generative AI in mind, we can, however, analyse our processes, including taking their expected durations into account, and experiment with generative AI (with certain controls in place, of course) to see if it can help us with them. If we do this well, it can lead to good outcomes.

> There is an uptick of automation in attacks too, that we rush to put systems in place to cope with. This has a lot of visibility on it as a risk, but perhaps not enough budget. We tend not to invest in these projects as proactively as we should, and then pay for it heavily when we are underweight in defence and a new technique is used for the first time later, which we struggle to defend against.

Whether you can you make the process better is the key question. This is where agentic AI is an exciting new development, probably even more so now than generative AI.

Agentic AI refers to autonomous systems that can make decisions and take actions without constant human oversight, simulating the behaviour of intelligent agents. These AI agents are designed to operate within defined parameters and objectives. In cybersecurity, this allows them to continuously monitor environments, detect anomalies, respond to threats, and adapt to new attack patterns in real time.

For instance, IBM has launched the Autonomous Threat Operations Machine (ATOM), which autonomously detects and responds to cyber threats, reducing the need for manual intervention. Similarly, SentinelOne's Purple AI Athena brings autonomous decision-making to SOCs, enabling faster and more accurate threat responses. These advancements are particularly valuable in addressing the growing volume and complexity of cyber threats, allowing organizations to maintain strong security postures despite resource constraints.

Agentic AI can support both red team and blue team tasks. In red teaming, it can emulate adversaries that evolve strategies autonomously, while in blue teaming, it supports continuous defence with minimal latency. This autonomous, adaptive behaviour enables faster, more scalable, and more effective cyber defence operations, but it also raises challenges around trust, control, and accountability.

As an example, let's look at the role AI can take in red teaming more closely.

Red teaming

AI tools can significantly enhance the effectiveness of red teaming by automating and amplifying key aspects of threat simulation, vulnerability assessment, and adversarial emulation. For example, they can rapidly analyse vast datasets to identify potential weaknesses in systems, generate sophisticated attack scenarios, and adapt strategies in real time based on system responses.

By reducing manual effort and improving the realism and scope of exercises, AI empowers red teams to test defences more rigorously and efficiently, ultimately strengthening organizational resilience.

While AI can greatly enhance red teaming, its use also introduces significant risks. One major concern is the potential for AI-driven simulations or tools to act unpredictably or beyond intended parameters. This could possibly cause unintended disruptions or system damage. AI-generated attacks, especially those leveraging deepfakes or automated social engineering, may also blur ethical boundaries and raise legal or reputational concerns if not properly controlled.

Over-reliance on AI is another risk here, as it is more generally (remember my earlier analogy – AI should be a copilot, rather than being run on autopilot). In this case, it could lead to blind spots in threat modelling as creative or unconventional human tactics are neglected.

There's also, of course, the potential risk of AI tools used in red teaming being compromised or misused, in which case they could be repurposed by malicious actors, effectively turning a security asset into a threat.

Who is going to sign off on the liability for this?

You need people who know where to stop, and computers do not know where to stop unless you tell them specifically, nor do they always understand concepts that are 'common sense' to us. It is probably sufficient for the AI models to identify your most critical security gaps; however, it is easy to go too far, even for human penetration testers. Having a human in the loop in the use of these tools is as essential in this case as it is in others.

Let's also remember that many enterprises do not have the right data governance in place. Both data and model governance are foundational elements that need work, and this is without adding AI to this mix. It is fair to say that these processes are not mature in many companies at the time of writing.

There are parallels when you think about the movements of workloads from on-premises to the cloud, and all the cloud configuration issues that have happened as we accelerated in this area. We all fundamentally understood that the cloud should be more secure than traditional data centre technology. However, despite all the well-architected reviews and other frameworks put in place by the major vendors, there are still many cloud configuration issues that have a critical impact on enterprises. That said, moving workloads to cloud providers is so advantageous in terms of speed and cost that it continues apace – and we have now finally realised some of the security benefits of this move through identifying many of the risks it presents and developing strategies to manage them.

We are again back to people, and another issue, which is a literacy problem. There are boards and executives who are excited by how much money could be saved by using AI (as was the case with the cloud), but there are also those who are terrified of the impact of going too far, too fast. Broadly speaking, we already have a problem with technology literacy in our executive and board population in Australia, and accelerating the uptake of technology won't help to manage risk for the most part. Managing risk and ensuring good governance is a critical part of board and executive engagement, and there's general agreement that we need to better educate this population regarding technology governance as things stand, even before accelerating our journey with AI tools, which, if not properly governed, could, of course, add more risk.

There are so many different risks AI can present – from the risk of personal information loss, cyber security threats, the risk of catastrophic failure of a critical system from infections in the language model – the list goes on. How do we manage this – from understanding it better to regulatory compliance – even before we have a good map of what that should look like?

The problem with technologists is that they tend to 'move fast and break things', rather than thinking deeply about risk, and then worry about how to fix it later. Unlike some technologies that can be rolled back to earlier versions, AI is very difficult to unplug unless it's contained properly in the first place.

Seatbelts for AI

If you remember when seatbelts were introduced (for those older people), in much of our early lives, you did not have to use them. There were big bench seats, many people loaded into the car, and sometimes even into the car boot!

Today it is unthinkable to have a car with without seatbelts, but they had cars without seatbelts for decades. And, yes, there were many accidents and people unfortunately died. Cars were so convenient though! AI is similar, but if anything, more accessible – and more seductive in that the dangers are far less obvious.

That is the kind of model that we're applying when it comes to AI. Leaders start seeing it as the next frontier in terms of cost-efficiencies and their ability to make their business work, and AI will penetrate our lives in so many areas and ways. It's important to remember that the convenience of AI should not override the risks it presents. AI needs seatbelts, just as cars do.

The way forward

So, what do we do here? I'd recommend proceeding cautiously and thinking about data governance. Strengthening data governance and control will give you an advantage in utilising all AI technologies as and when use cases arrive. We urgently need broader regulatory frameworks and standards for AI control and data governance. We also need to increase board and C-level governance and engagement.

Also, in the absence of effective privacy legislation, there is an overall gap in protecting consumer data. At present, it's difficult to understand how to protect yourself completely as a consumer, and the only way is by refusing to share data wherever possible, which isn't a state that's useful for either consumers or businesses.

In my opinion, Australia has a particularly difficult problem because, at the time of writing, we are underregulated across the board from a cybersecurity and privacy standpoint. We also have a unique problem in terms of our defence posture because of the AUKUS (Australia, UK, United States Security Treaty) partnership and other strategic defence partnerships. Accordingly, we are a target, and we are less regulated and a weaker link than the other countries.

I think the only real option is to look at a macro regulatory framework, which, among other things, applies penalties to board directors for businesses that get it wrong. We need to upskill most boards around many of these areas of technology oversight, however.

Geopolitics are changing rapidly, and combined with the acceleration of AI technologies and the race for supply chain control around chips and software, we have (again) a storm brewing. One of the best ways to control some of this risk is to ensure critical data is not stored offshore, where it may become vulnerable. We also need to ensure we have the critical infrastructure uplift and investment we need to be assured our systems can run and be safe regardless of changes in national alliances or government regulation in countries we can't control.

The other key control becomes educating and informing people and continuing to highlight AI risks as well as possibilities. Many working in technology, cyber and data risk lack the business expertise to effectively challenge organisational leaders. Elevating cyber security and risk professionals in businesses is an important requirement we must address urgently, alongside uplifting board governance and technology maturity.

To finish with a more general reminder, even with the best will in the world, we are years away from being able to enable the required physical capacity for AI in a secure fashion. It's important we start thinking hard and investing in the infrastructure layer now, so that we can take advantage of the promise of AI technologies as a nation in the future.

David's key takeaways — AI: the promise and challenge

In this chapter, Jacqui presents a compelling analysis of AI's potential and challenges, emphasizing that CISOs must provide decisive leadership to ensure AI fulfills its promise rather than creating new risks and vulnerabilities.

As AI emerges as a double-edged sword with capabilities for both harm and benefit, as a security leader, you must ensure that governance frameworks are put in place around it, and, importantly, ensure that human oversight in AI implementations is maintained.

By championing security-first approaches, driving cross-organizational education, and preparing for regulatory frameworks, CISOs can help to transform AI from a potential threat into a powerful tool that enhances both security postures and business outcomes.

Jacqui's key points are:

- *Don't wait for formal regulations to establish governance frameworks.* Develop internal standards for AI usage that provide proper guardrails, data governance, and human oversight, positioning your organisation to readily adapt when external regulations arrive.

- *Resist the temptation to fully automate security operations for cost savings.* Instead, consider how AI can be used in cybersecurity as a copilot (rather than in autopilot mode).

- *Consider implementing an 'adjacency' model* – where AI systems provide recommendations, but critical decisions maintain human approval, especially in areas like vulnerability management and threat detection.

- *Develop talent strategically.* Create deliberate pathways to develop AI governance expertise within your security team. As junior roles become automated, establish training that allows staff to develop the specialised oversight skills needed for AI governance.

- *Assess where your critical data resides and implement controls to ensure sovereignty* – particularly for sensitive information. Also consider how AI adoption might enable repatriation of offshore functions without sacrificing efficiency.

- *Proactively emphasize the need for technology governance as well as AI literacy among executives and board members.* This is important as managing risk and ensuring good governance is a key part of board and executive engagement.

- *Balance adoption speed with safety.* Leverage AI to strengthen security operations, particularly for resource-constrained teams, but be sure to maintain rigorous testing protocols and controls. Start with clearly defined use cases where AI can augment rather than replace human expertise.

Part 4

Advice from CISO 'Yoda Masters'

Welcome to the final part of this book. This has insightful contributions from CISO 'Yoda Masters': highly respected, experienced, and wise cybersecurity leaders who have reached the pinnacle of their profession and now serve as mentors and guides to others. Just like the Jedi Master Yoda from *Star Wars*, they have decades of wisdom and are truly battle-tested leaders.

The advice in this part includes career lessons on strategic vision, crisis management, and resilience. In their careers, these CISOs have shaped best practices, navigated complex organisational challenges, and served as trusted advisors to organisations. Everyone can gain invaluable wisdom from these industry 'Yoda Masters', no matter your experience level.

This part has the following chapters:

- *Chapter 24, Protecting the USA*
- *Chapter 25, Why Risk Management Matters*
- *Chapter 26, Driving Cyber Transformation*
- *Chapter 27, My Metrics Playbook*
- *Chapter 28, Career Resilience*
- *Chapter 29, Lessons in Leading Yourself, Cyber Teams and Through Crisis*

Unlock this book's exclusive benefits now

UNLOCK NOW

Scan this QR code or go to `https://packtpub.com/unlock`, then search this book by name.

Note: Have your purchase invoice ready before you start.

24

Protecting the USA

The USA has arguably one of the strongest histories as it relates to cybersecurity. It has been at the forefront of this as the founding nation of the internet and much of the digital revolution that we are seeing globally.

Being a global leader of technology innovation, the USA has been a rapid adopter of new technologies, which then quickly become embedded in its everyday operations. As a nation, it has been a global economic powerhouse, the home of advanced digitally-enabled companies operating internationally, including financial institutions and multinational corporations. These are the household names that, in the West, are commonly known as the 'Magnificent Seven' – Alphabet, Amazon, Apple, Meta, Microsoft, NVIDIA, and Tesla.

Given its substantial intellectual property holdings, high concentration of high-net-worth individuals, and considerable global influence as a leading democratic power, the USA is among the most frequently targeted nations for cyberattacks.

In response to these persistent threats, the USA has developed and deployed advanced cyber defence capabilities. Paradoxically, this strength has made it an even more attractive target for adversarial nations seeking to measure themselves against a global benchmark.

This chapter is about protecting the USA, and it is my absolute pleasure to introduce **Camilo Sandoval**, who has had the privilege to serve as **White House Senior Advisor** and **3rd Chief Information Security Officer** of the United States of America.

Camilo has extensive experience across the public and private sectors, including serving as the past Chief Information Officer for the **Department of Veterans Affairs (VA)**, which oversaw a $4.5 billion operational budget that supported a $325 billion healthcare and financial services enterprise.

At the White House, Camilo was responsible for technology, cyber, and AI for all US federal agencies, covering all the major 24 CFO Act agencies. One of his key roles was to chair the Federal Acquisition Security Council (FASC), which was created by the Federal Acquisition Supply Chain Security Act of 2018, and for this, his efforts were aimed at uplifting the cyber and AI defences.

It is my honour to ask Camilo to speak to us about his experiences in protecting the USA. I personally have so many questions about how he managed his role with all the extreme stress that comes with the position – in particular, the decision-making processes that are required to prioritise and de-prioritise according to the cyber strategy, and considering the dynamic nature of new threats.

Camilo has unique insights into a CISO role that are unlike most that we would have an opportunity to tackle. I'm certain that there are some strategic insights and learnings that we can all take away from his rare experience.

A new type of warfighter

Camilo Sandoval

There was no siren. No red blinking lights. No explosion. Just a silent alert across a classified network: anomalous behavior detected deep within a federal agency's supply chain software. It was 4:57 am when my phone buzzed – a quiet reminder that today, like every day, we were already under attack.

As the Federal Chief Information Security Officer of the United States, I wasn't defending a physical border. I was defending the invisible lines of code and trust that held the government together and, by extension, the country. Cybersecurity wasn't a support function. It was national security.

In the Trump administration, we understood this clearly: cybersecurity wasn't about firewalls and passwords. It was about power, diplomacy, and sovereignty. Every intrusion attempt was a shot across the bow. Every vulnerability, a potential opening for adversaries to weaken the republic without ever crossing a border.

In the past, warfighters carried rifles and wore camouflage. Today, they also carry encryption keys and wear hoodies. The battlefield has expanded. It includes every federal email server, every cloud instance, every outdated endpoint connected to a critical system. It includes our hospitals, our banks, our supply chains – and our votes.

But my path to the White House didn't start in Washington. It began the day I enlisted in the U.S. Air Force after high school, trading the humidity of North Miami Beach for the snow-covered rice fields of northern Japan. I was stationed at Misawa Air Base in the early 1990s; a remote post nestled between the rugged Tōhoku mountains to the west and the roar of F-16s lifting off into the Pacific Ocean skies to the east.

As a young signals intelligence analyst assigned to the 301st Intelligence Squadron, I became part of Misawa's Cryptologic Operations Centera joint mission with the **National Security Agency (NSA)**. In that world of silence and scrutiny, I discovered that true power often comes from listening, rather than speaking. That precision matters more than volume. And that information dominance – not ammunition – was quickly becoming the decisive weapon.

Years later, while serving at Fort Meade, I began to fully grasp the shift underway. What we were doing back in Japan wasn't just signals intelligence; it was the early edge of something new. The NSA was evolving, transitioning from its Cold War roots into the front line of America's cyber-security mission.

The lessons I learned in uniform shaped every chapter that followed – through college and grad-uate school, through grueling 100-hour weeks on Wall Street, and later, through one of the most consequential presidential campaigns in modern history, all the way to the Situation Room of the White House.

By the time I returned to federal service as a senior political appointee in the Trump administration, I wasn't there to climb the ladder; I was there to tackle the toughest problems facing the country. I didn't come to Washington as part of the establishment. I came with a mission, backed by the American people who elected President Donald Trump to disrupt the status quo and fix what wasn't working. I knew the bureaucracy would try to control everything, but that's not how you drive innovation, and it's certainly not how you secure a nation in the digital age.

In this chapter, I take you inside my journey from the battlefields of signals intelligence to the halls of the White House, where I confronted cyberattacks, rebuilt broken systems, and led the mission to defend America's digital front lines.

The CIO at the VA: rebuilding trust through technology

I joined the VA in 2017 following the presidential inauguration and, soon after, assumed the role of Chief Information Officer at the nation's largest integrated healthcare and financial services organization. With a workforce of over 325,000 serving more than 10 million veterans, we oper-ated at a scale rivaling the most complex enterprises in the private sector. Our annual technology budget, $4.5 billion, matched or exceeded that of global Fortune 500 firms such as Delta Air Lines, Capital One, and Mitsubishi UFJ Financial Group. Backed by 16,000 IT professionals across 171 major hospitals and nearly 1,300 clinics, our responsibility went far beyond managing systems – we were safeguarding the trust of those who had served. Yet behind these numbers lay a deeper challenge: an ecosystem burdened by decades of fragmented platforms, siloed data, and aging infrastructure, all of which threatened the speed, quality, and reliability of the care and benefits veterans depended on.

But this was more than just a systems issue, it was a trust and reliability issue. Veterans no longer believed the VA could deliver the timely, seamless care they deserved. Doctors inside the system had grown wary of relying on scheduling tools and electronic records that too often failed them. In Congress, skepticism ran deep; lawmakers questioned whether our modernization efforts would ever materialize.

Within the agency, many had grown cynical, convinced that meaningful reform was out of reach. And to make matters worse, internal political infighting – both within the VA and across the broader federal bureaucracy – often stalled progress before it could even begin.

My job was to modernize the VA's technology while rebuilding confidence that it could truly serve those who had already served.

The mandate

From day one, I understood that my time in Washington, D.C. was limited and that every moment had to count. My guiding principle was clear: deliver technology that veterans could feel in their daily lives and ensure that every taxpayer dollar stretched as far as possible in their service. To drive that urgency home, I placed a giant, oversized digital clock across my conference room table – a constant reminder to me and my team that our time was ticking. We weren't just managing projects; we were carrying out the mandate President Trump had campaigned on – to fix the VA and honor his promises to America's veterans. Every digital initiative had to produce real results: faster benefit payments, shorter wait times, and prescriptions filled without delay. We didn't have the luxury of abstract innovation. We were there to deliver impact, quickly and concretely, where it mattered most.

We began by fixing the foundation. The VA's legacy electronic health record system, **VistA (Veterans Health Information Systems and Technology Architecture)**, was once a groundbreaking platform, but decades of piecemeal upgrades had left it fragmented and increasingly unfit for a modern healthcare system. It reminded me of a classic 1970s pickup: dependable at cruising speed but not built for the demands of today's highways.

The 'VistA Evolution' initiative tried to modernize the system, but with over a hundred unique versions deployed across the country, it was like trying to standardize 130 different engines without overhauling the chassis. National consistency in care, data, and performance was nearly impossible.

Meanwhile, the **Department of Defense (DoD)** had already moved ahead. In 2015, it awarded a $4.3 billion contract to Cerner Corporation to launch MHS GENESIS – a commercial off-the-shelf **electronic health record** (EHR) platform designed to replace its aging systems. The VA, by contrast, was still struggling to ensure that a soldier leaving active duty could access their complete medical record once inside the VA system. Despite years of investment in efforts such as the **Bidirectional Health Information Exchange** (BHIE), true interoperability between the VA and DoD remained out of reach.

The result? Veterans still showed up at their first VA appointment with a binder full of paper records in hand. In an age of real-time data and cloud integration, this was more than inefficient – it was indefensible.

We launched what became one of the most ambitious EHR modernization efforts in federal history, but reaching that point took years of political and institutional effort.

By 2018, following intense debate inside the agency and growing frustration on Capitol Hill, the VA – with support from the Trump White House – signed a $10 billion, 10-year sole-source contract with Cerner to deploy the same platform as DoD. It was later revised to an estimated $16.1 billion to cover program oversight, system configuration, and infrastructure upgrades. This was a commitment to building a unified, lifelong medical record that would follow service members from active duty into veteran care.

However, implementation faced significant hurdles. Between 2020 and 2022, early rollouts at sites such as Spokane and Walla Walla, Washington, revealed major performance issues, from patient safety risks to user dissatisfaction. These concerns led the VA to pause all further deployments in April 2023. Meanwhile, in June 2022, Cerner was acquired by Oracle Corporation, introducing a new corporate structure and governance model that further delayed progress.

By early 2025, with the Trump administration back in office, the EHR modernization initiative had regained momentum. The VA was now poised to restart deployments by mid-year, guided by a renewed mandate and a definitive five-year plan to complete the transformation across the entire enterprise.

This effort is no longer just about replacing outdated software – it's about restoring faith in how the federal government delivers care to those who served. It represents one of the largest health IT transformations ever attempted, and we are once again aligned – across the VA, the White House, Congress, and industry to see it through.

Digital modernization with accountability

At the VA, modernization meant cloud adoption, artificial intelligence pilots, identity management reform, and cybersecurity upgrades – all happening simultaneously.

But it also meant holding vendors accountable and reorganizing internal teams to deliver on time and under budget.

I approached this transformation the same way I had led high-stakes mergers and acquisitions on Wall Street – with disciplined execution, cross-functional integration, and relentless focus on outcomes. This wasn't about acquiring shiny new platforms; it was about aligning people, process, and technology around a common mission.

We set up integrated delivery teams, instituted real-time performance dashboards, and enforced governance structures that gave us operational clarity and accountability.

Creating a culture of mission-driven technologists

Many of the technologists at the VA were former service members or long-time public servants – mission-oriented but worn down by bureaucracy. We reinvigorated their purpose, gave them space to lead, and brought in new digital talent from the private sector. I partnered directly with agency leaders and frontline personnel alike. I held regular town halls, both to talk and to listen. One thing I made clear to every stakeholder was that we work and live in a software-powered world. Government can't be an exception.

The most transformative thing we did wasn't a product launch. It was establishing a culture that aligned technology to mission, and mission to the individual veteran experience.

My time at the VA – and later, at the White House – was driven by this conviction: the systems intended to serve those who served must be seamless, resilient, and worthy of their sacrifice. The legacy I hoped to build was about honoring service through functional government, as well as implementing better technology.

Digital warfighting: the pivot to the White House

At the Department of Veterans Affairs, I came to understand a hard truth: in modern government, technology isn't support – it's the mission.

As CIO, I led one of the world's largest and most complex digital healthcare systems, serving over 10 million veterans. We modernized EHRs, expanded cloud infrastructure, and deployed artificial intelligence to streamline benefits and cut wait times. But we didn't stop there.

We partnered with the Department of Energy's Oak Ridge National Laboratory to explore high-performance and quantum computing – applying advanced analytics to accelerate suicide prevention. With this technology, we could scan millions of clinical records in minutes, identifying veterans most at risk and enabling faster, life-saving interventions.

We weren't just upgrading IT systems – we were using technology to save lives.

In a pivotal White House meeting, the President turned to me and asked, *"Why is AI important? Why should we be investing more in it?"*

I didn't hesitate.

"Because in healthcare," I said, *"AI can save lives."*

I explained, *"Imagine someone arrives at the ER in crisis. AI can instantly analyze their symptoms, scan their full medical history, and recommend treatment – decisions that once took hours can now be made in seconds."*

That speed can mean the difference between life and death. That's why we invest in AI. Because it can deliver outcomes when it matters most.

As I worked across agencies – from the US **Department of Health and Human Services (HHS)** and DoD to the **Department of Homeland Security (DHS)** and **Office of Management and Budget (OMB)** – I saw an even bigger problem emerging: federal cybersecurity was dangerously fragmented. Systems didn't talk to each other. Threat intelligence was siloed. Supply chain vulnerabilities were expanding. And foreign adversaries were evolving faster than the federal bureaucracy could keep up.

Then the world changed.

COVID-19 hit – and with it came a national digital crisis. Agencies shifted to remote operations almost overnight. Legacy systems strained under the load. And state-sponsored cyberattacks surged. Ransomware, phishing, and disinformation campaigns skyrocketed. Technology wasn't just under stress – it had become a fault line.

That's when the call came from the White House – a request for help. They needed someone who understood both the battlefield and the bureaucracy. Someone trusted within the West Wing, who could move quickly and float across political factions, build interagency coalitions, and stabilize the cyber front. I had earned that trust through my work on the 2016 Donald J. Trump for President campaign, and through a career at the intersection of national security, enterprise technology, and business execution. I didn't hesitate.

I was nominated to serve as the Federal Chief Information Security Officer of the United States – the third person in history to hold the title from the White House. My charge: defend the digital perimeter of the federal government. Protect the systems and data of 2.95 million civilian employees. Bring leadership and discipline to a fragmented cybersecurity environment.

The Trump administration had already laid down the strategic foundation for this. In 2018, we released the first fully articulated National Cyber Strategy in over 15 years – a bold declaration that cyberspace was no longer a peripheral policy area. It was a domain of persistent conflict, where adversaries such as China, Russia, Iran, and North Korea could challenge American power without firing a single shot.

This strategy rested on four pillars:

- Defend the Homeland
- Promote American prosperity
- Preserve peace through strength
- Advance American influence through a free and open internet

It called for whole-of-nation coordination, supply chain security, cyber deterrence, and integration of cybersecurity into national security decision-making. My job was to operationalize that vision, to modernize how federal agencies secure systems, manage incidents, and anticipate threats before they materialize.

That mission expanded when I was appointed Chair of the **Federal Acquisition Security Council (FASC)** – the first statutory interagency body charged with securing the federal supply chain. Created under the Federal Acquisition Supply Chain Security Act of 2018, FASC was empowered to identify, assess, and remove high-risk technologies and vendors from government systems. For the first time, the federal government had a formal mechanism to act on intelligence and enforce risk-based procurement decisions across agencies.

Our work gained momentum as the Trump administration moved decisively against Huawei and ZTE, recognizing the national security risk posed by foreign-controlled communications infrastructure:

- In August 2018, Congress passed Section 889 of the NDAA, prohibiting federal agencies and contractors from using Huawei and ZTE equipment.
- In May 2019, Executive Order 13873 declared a national emergency over foreign threats to communications infrastructure.
- On May 16, 2019, the Department of Commerce placed Huawei Technologies Co., Ltd and dozens of its affiliates on the Entity List (a trade restriction list that limits certain companies' access to U.S. goods and technologies), cutting off access to key U.S. technologies.
- The **Federal Communications Commission (FCC)** designated both Huawei and ZTE as national security threats, blocking federal subsidies from reaching them.

As FASC Chair, I led the effort to translate this into operational action – coordinating across the DHS, DoD, **Department of Justice (DOJ)**, **Office of the Director of National Intelligence (ODNI)**, **National Security Council (NSC)**, and others to identify vulnerabilities, issue removal orders, and strengthen supply chain resilience across the federal government. We were responding to real threats – just one compromised chip or backdoor-laden software module could expose sensitive systems or cripple critical infrastructure.

My approach was forged across domains, from the battlefield to the boardroom. Prioritize the mission. Move with discipline. Build trust across institutions. And never confuse process with progress.

This wasn't just policy work. It was cyber warfighting – conducted in **Sensitive Compartmented Information Facilities (SCIFs)**, through classified briefings, and in the high-stakes digital battlespace of modern geopolitics.

We weren't just defending networks. We were defending the republic.

A day in the life of the Federal CISO

There's no such thing as a 'normal' day when you're tasked with defending the digital backbone of the federal government. Every hour brings the potential for a new breach, a new vulnerability, or a foreign adversary probing our defenses.

Mornings began early – often before sunrise – with secure threat briefings, frequently held inside a SCIF, where I reviewed classified intelligence alongside counterparts from the NSA, **Federal Bureau of Investigation (FBI)**, DHS, and NSC. Indicators of compromise, zero-day exploits, ransomware payloads, insider threats – this was the operational language of the job.

In parallel, I prepared my own daily briefings – real-time cyber threat assessments and risk outlooks – for senior White House staff and key federal stakeholders. As the Federal CISO, it was my responsibility to turn raw threat intelligence into decisive action. That meant ensuring that cybersecurity priorities were understood and coordinated not only at the executive level, but across the entire federal civilian enterprise.

A major part of this work involved close coordination with the CIOs and CISOs from the 24 CFO Act agencies – the largest and most mission-critical departments in the federal government. These agencies, named under the Chief Financial Officers Act of 1990, include Cabinet-level departments such as the Departments of Defense, Homeland Security, Treasury, Justice, and Health and Human Services, as well as key independent agencies such as NASA, the Environmental Protection Agency, and the Social Security Administration. Together, they control the vast majority of the federal budget and operate the nation's most critical civilian systems, from financial services and public health to transportation, energy, and law enforcement.

These agencies are high-value targets. Their digital infrastructure holds sensitive citizen data, supports national security missions, and enables vital government services. One vulnerability in any of these systems could cascade across the federal ecosystem. That's why the 24 CFO Act agencies form the core of federal cybersecurity posture – and why coordinated action among their CIOs and CISOs was essential.

Our engagements ranged from daily syncs to classified briefings, tabletop exercises, and real-time incident response. Whether it was mitigating a live threat, sharing detection signatures, or driving implementation of Zero Trust architectures, I worked to ensure these agencies weren't just compliant – they were resilient too.

Some days focused on proactive defense and strategy. Others required immediate crisis leadership – responding to cyberattacks in flight, disinformation operations ramping up during election cycles, or widespread vulnerability disclosures requiring synchronized patching and containment.

Behind the scenes, I participated in secure deliberations where attribution, public disclosure, and international implications were debated. These were national security decisions, carried out across secure channels, under immense time pressure, with potential global impact.

There were no shortcuts. No room for confusion. No time to wait. Cyber defense at the federal level demanded more than technical knowledge – it required trust, stamina, and strategic clarity under pressure.

Again, this was cyber warfighting, executed through encrypted briefings, classified intelligence, and a coalition of leaders across the entire civilian government.

SolarWinds

Every day, the mission reset at zero. But nothing tested our readiness more than what we uncovered during the SolarWinds attack. Some days focused on long-term defense strategy. Others demanded immediate, high-risk decision-making, such as on Saturday, December 12, 2020, when I was called into an emergency National Security Council meeting at the White House.

The news was grave. Multiple federal agencies, including Treasury and Commerce, had been breached. This wasn't just a cybersecurity event. It was becoming a full-blown national security event.

Investigators believed the intrusions were carried out by Russia's foreign intelligence service (SVR), using a months-long supply chain compromise through a trusted IT vendor: SolarWinds. Malicious code had been slipped into routine software updates for the company's widely used Orion network monitoring platform, granting persistent access to agency systems. Hackers had infiltrated Microsoft email environments, monitored internal communications, and likely gone undetected since as early as June 2020.

This wasn't just a breach. It was a systemic infiltration of the federal government's software supply chain. The implications were massive. The same attacker had recently breached FireEye, stealing offensive cybersecurity tools. The concern level inside the government was 'very high'– not just about the agencies already compromised, but about what else might be vulnerable. "Everybody uses Microsoft products," one White House official noted at the time, and that meant nearly every agency could be at risk.

Within hours of the NSC meeting, I convened additional interagency sessions with **Cybersecurity and Infrastructure Security Agency (CISA)**, OMB, DoD, and other federal cyber leaders to coordinate containment.

Every decision came with trade-offs. Shutting down systems could impair mission delivery. Waiting could expose classified data or active operations. We had to move fast, with surgical precision – isolating affected systems, activating emergency protocols, and preserving evidence for attribution.

This was the kind of moment my role was designed for, where technical insight, interagency coordination, and decisive leadership had to converge in real time.

The tools of leadership

As Federal CISO, my responsibilities went beyond responding to incidents. I led systemic reforms designed to modernize and secure the federal enterprise, including:

- Zero Trust strategy implementation, through which we moved away from perimeter-based thinking to identity, access, and continuous verification frameworks.
- Supply chain risk management. As I mentioned earlier, as Chair of FASC, I helped craft interagency recommendations to identify and exclude high-risk vendors from federal procurement.
- Cyber executive orders. I collaborated on the formulation and enforcement of White House cyber policies that had a direct impact on the operational posture of over 100 agencies.

This meant leading with policy. In some cases, that required pushing through bureaucratic resistance, confronting outdated practices, and communicating difficult truths – clearly and without drama.

Decisions in the fog

One of the most intense moments for me came when I had to recommend isolating a critical cloud environment after indicators showed possible compromise.

We knew the decision would have cascading operational effects, but the threat of lateral movement was too great to ignore. We shut it down, traced the intrusion, and contained it. Days later, further forensics confirmed it was the right call.

Leadership at this level means navigating ambiguity, balancing speed, risk, and impact while keeping mission objectives intact. It also means managing people: agency CIOs and CISOs who need clear direction, and senior political and career officials who need confidence that their teams are protected.

Mission above optics

I didn't take the role to be liked. I took it to serve. Cybersecurity at this level isn't a popularity contest; it's a national obligation. Every hour lost to indecision could be a foothold gained by an adversary.

And so, I made decisions quickly, communicated transparently, and insisted on accountability – not only from others, but from myself. I never asked a team to take an action I wasn't willing to defend at the highest levels of government.

It was exhausting. It was relentless. And it was one of the greatest honors of my career.

Data, supply chains, and the future of digital national security

The SolarWinds attack wasn't just a breach – it was a revelation. It forced the federal government to confront a hard truth: in a software-powered world, the greatest vulnerabilities often hide in plain sight – embedded in code, concealed within trusted vendors, or introduced by the very updates we rely on to stay secure.

This was the wake-up call. And it changed how we thought about cybersecurity at a national level.

The new battlefield: software supply chains

As Chair of the FASC, I was tasked with something unprecedented: building a government-wide framework to identify and eliminate high-risk technologies from federal supply chains. For the first time, national security, procurement, and cybersecurity were being treated as a unified front.

It was clear that cyber risk could no longer be managed in silos. Agencies couldn't simply vet vendors at the contract stage and hope for the best. We needed continuous, lifecycle-wide scrutiny – and shared intelligence across the public and private sectors.

We developed interagency exclusion recommendations to prevent suspect vendors and compromised platforms from operating inside the federal enterprise. That required collaboration with legal counsel, procurement officers, and frontline technologists alike. But more than anything, it required political will – the courage to act before the breach, not just after.

Memory safety and secure-by-design software

One of the most forward-leaning efforts we advanced was the push for memory-safe programming languages. Decades of federal systems had been built on C and C++ – powerful, but inherently risky. Over 70% of vulnerabilities in modern systems can be traced to memory safety issues (as CISA highlights here: https://www.cisa.gov/news-events/news/urgent-need-memory-safety-software-products). And the flaws these introduced weren't just bugs; they were open doors for exploitation.

The challenge was cultural, as well as technical. Engineers were trained one way. Vendors were incentivized another. But our role as stewards of national security required us to ask more of the ecosystem – what should be *trusted,* in addition to what could be built.

Zero Trust and the end of implicit confidence

Alongside supply chain reforms, we began implementing the federal government's first Zero Trust architecture strategy. The principle was simple: trust nothing, verify everything, and continuously monitor all access.

Zero Trust was a shift in posture for us. Instead of hoping we could keep threats out, we operated as if adversaries were already inside. That changed how we architected systems, how we governed identities, and how we visualized risk. The path ahead was long, but necessary.

This approach reshaped how agencies thought about cybersecurity – not as a one-time compliance exercise, but as an ongoing, adaptive process of vigilance and verification.

Toward a new cyber doctrine

Our adversaries weren't slowing down. And neither could we.

The future of cybersecurity is proactive, not reactive. It's about resilience, not just defense. And it's about understanding that software isn't just a tool of government – it *is* government. From benefits delivery to battlefield coordination, digital infrastructure is now national infrastructure.

That's why I advocated for a long-term shift in cyber doctrine, one that combines procurement reform, technical modernization, and workforce development into a coherent national strategy. A strategy that prioritizes trusted technology, reduces dependence on vulnerable architectures, and makes cybersecurity a core part of how government leads.

Navigating politics, bureaucracy, and mission

Being the Federal CISO goes beyond a purely technical role; it's political, strategic, and relentlessly human too. Cybersecurity touches everything: national defense, economic policy, and public trust. That means the work lives at the intersection of competing priorities, institutional inertia, and political scrutiny.

You're not just defending systems. You're navigating power!

Cybersecurity in the Trump era

I served during an administration that sparked strong opinions – both inside and outside of government. But regardless of where individuals stood politically, my responsibility remained constant. In my dual-hatted role as a senior political appointee and as the Federal CIO and CISO, my mission was clear: protect the systems, safeguard the mission, and ensure that cybersecurity was never compromised by partisanship. National security doesn't belong to one party – and neither did my oath.

Some viewed the Trump-era federal government as chaotic. But behind the headlines, there were thousands of dedicated professionals—civil servants, military officers, and policy experts—working tirelessly to keep the country safe. My role was to bring them together around a unified federal technology and cybersecurity agenda, even as the broader political climate remained deeply divided. After all, we couldn't afford to operate under the illusion that IT was a back-office function. In government, a technology failure is a mission failure.

The President had made clear that national security and critical infrastructure protection were top priorities. That gave me the backing I needed to drive bold reforms: Zero Trust architecture mandates, software supply chain initiatives, and real-time threat intelligence sharing. Still, success required constant negotiation – not with the Oval Office, but with layers of bureaucracy hardened over decades.

Building coalitions inside the government

Cybersecurity within the US government is distributed across dozens of entities: DHS, OMB, DoD, **General Services Administration (GSA)**, NSA, **National Institute of Standards and Technology (NIST)**, and every civilian department. To make change stick, I had to earn the trust of agency CIOs and CISOs, many of whom were dealing with their own internal crises. Some welcomed federal direction, others resisted what they saw as 'White House overreach.'

So, I didn't dictate – I convened. I brought leaders into the process early, gave them real input, and demonstrated that the reforms weren't just mandates – they were mission enablers. My guiding principle was this: *lead with clarity, not control.*

I forged strong working relationships with key counterparts across the federal enterprise, from technologists and policy advisors to legal counsel and budget officers. I worked closely with the National Security Council, CISA, and the intelligence community to ensure that executive directives were signed, implemented, operationalized, and enforced where it mattered most.

The value of being an outsider-insider

Having worked across the military, Wall Street, and federal civilian agencies, I brought a different perspective to the job. I wasn't raised inside the Beltway. I understood how large, complex systems operate – but I also knew how to cut through red tape, challenge groupthink, and build momentum around a shared objective.

That outsider-insider dynamic gave me credibility where it mattered. I spoke the language of mission. And when I walked into a room full of stakeholders – whether they were political appointees or career executives – I made it clear I was there to get the mission done, not to posture.

Legacy and the road ahead

Leadership at the federal level is not about recognition – it's about responsibility. It's about making hard decisions when no one is watching and standing by them when everyone is. As I look back on my time as Federal CISO or CIO, I don't think about titles, headlines, or even milestones. I think about moments of clarity, moments of risk – and the people who stood with me when the stakes were highest. And I ask myself, "Did we make a difference?"

I didn't enter public service to preserve systems. I came to challenge them. To ask better questions. To push for urgency in places where complacency had settled in.

My legacy isn't measured in white papers or policy memos. It lives in the agency teams that now think like operators, not just compliance officers. In the procurement officials who ask, "Can we trust this?", not just, "Can we afford it?" Most of all, I'm proud that we elevated the conversation – that we helped move cybersecurity from the back office to the front lines of national strategy.

If you're reading this as a future CIO, CISO, or public servant, know this: the systems you inherit will be imperfect. The risks you face will be more complex than ever. And the mission will rarely wait for perfect timing or unanimous agreement. But that's what makes this work matter. Lead decisively. Communicate clearly. Build alliances, not empires. And never forget who you serve – not just the agency, organization, or business, but the country behind it.

We live in a time when code is policy. Where digital infrastructure is the front line. And where the smallest piece of compromised software can threaten the largest institutions. That's not cause for fear – it's a call to lead.

What keeps me up at night, beyond the adversary's next move, is our own inertia, our tendency to do what's familiar instead of what's necessary.

But what gives me hope is the new generation of cyber leaders – those who are willing to challenge assumptions, speak uncomfortable truths, and design systems that are secure by default.

There is a phrase I often return to: "*Stand the watch.*" It's a military tradition – a reminder that someone must always remain vigilant while others rest. That's what cybersecurity leadership is. A quiet watch. An invisible shield. A responsibility to see what others don't and act before they can.

I've spent my life in service – to the military, to veterans, and to the nation. The tools have changed, but the mission has stayed the same: protect what matters most. And now, the mission is yours.

David's key takeaways — Protecting the USA

The role of CISO for the USA is indeed a special one that requires some unique skills to take on the challenges that it entails. It has been fascinating and an absolute personal honour to get some glimpses and insights from Camilo's journey into and through this executive position that is unlike any other in the world.

Some highlights from his chapter include:

- *Cybersecurity is a matter of national security, not just an IT issue.* This was particularly relevant for Camilo, but it is true more widely, too. Modern CISOs must think beyond traditional IT support boxing. Every system you protect, every vulnerability you address, and every decision you make has strategic implications. Approach your role as a war fighter defending critical infrastructure, not as a technician managing systems.

- *Building trust through mission-focused leadership is vital.* Success as a CISO requires earning credibility across diverse stakeholders, from technical teams to executive leadership to external partners. Lead with clarity and consistency, communicate the 'why' behind difficult decisions, and always prioritise mission outcomes over personal recognition or political considerations.

- *Supply chain security is your new perimeter.* The SolarWinds attack demonstrated that trusted vendors could become attack vectors. To help mitigate the risks the supply chain can present, develop comprehensive supply chain risk management programs, implement continuous vendor assessment processes, and remember that security decisions must be made throughout the entire technology lifecycle (not just at the procurement stage).

- *Embrace Zero Trust as both an architecture and a mindset.* Move beyond perimeter-based security thinking. Implement identity-centric, continuously verified access controls, but more importantly, cultivate a culture that assumes compromise and designs resilience accordingly. Trust nothing, verify everything, and monitor continuously.

- *Speed and decisiveness beat complete information.* In crisis situations, waiting for complete information can be more dangerous than acting on incomplete data. Develop frameworks for rapid risk assessment and decision-making. Be prepared to make tough calls – such as shutting down critical systems – when, for example, the threat of lateral movement outweighs operational disruption.

- *Technology leadership requires political and coalition-building skills*; technical expertise alone isn't sufficient. You must navigate bureaucracy, build cross-functional alliances, and translate cyber risks into business language that resonates with leadership. Learn to work within political realities while maintaining focus on mission-critical objectives.

- *Modernisation must be systematic and accountable.* Whether implementing cloud adoption, AI initiatives, or legacy system upgrades, approach transformation with disciplined project management principles. Establish clear governance structures, real-time performance dashboards, and hold both internal teams and external vendors accountable for deliverables.

- *Prepare for the next generation of threats.* Stay ahead of evolving attack vectors by advocating for secure-by-design principles, memory-safe programming languages, and proactive defence strategies. Remember that your adversaries are constantly evolving– your defensive posture must be equally adaptive and forward-thinking.

25

Why Risk Management Matters

A good CISO surrounds themselves with friends and foes. They want to hear the good and bad news fast. There is little point in deceiving yourself and not having the full picture in terms of facts to make a judgment.

That being said, as CISO, you often don't have all the facts and data available, or you can't wait for this to be collected and analytics to be completed. There is a compass that every good CISO will use, and that is risk management.

Capital 'R' risk management is where you need to funnel your attention and focus. These are the largest risks that can penetrate your defenses and then leave you looking unprepared, and, worse still, can get you fired. These capital 'R' items should be obvious, but unfortunately, in a day in the life of a CISO, they can get lost in all the noise.

Your friends and foes will, intentionally or unintentionally, be sending you these snippets of information; some will be rumours, requests, and requirements. Being able to work out and calibrate these and then determine where to spend your precious time is what separates the masters from the apprentices.

Risk management can be a 'dirty' word, and you might immediately think about those colleagues who have a title such as risk executive or risk manager who have annoyed you and asked silly, stupid, or downright illogical questions. They may think that they are doing their job to protect the enterprise, but in my opinion, they are simply doing small 'r' risk management. This simply means that their focus is on 'rats and mice' items that take up your time and may be totally un-related to the capital 'R' risks.

This is why risk management matters. Risk management is all about focusing on the highest risks to the business, against the highest critical assets.

I've seen many cases and examples where CIOs and other colleagues ask the CISO to spend their time and effort on areas and domains that are not as important. There may be push from the board or management; in some cases, this is a mandate from regulators. In the end, it does not matter where this emanates – what is critically important is how you manage this so that such requests do not distract you from your primary objective of protecting your enterprise.

To do this, you need clarity of thought on your own priorities, and this should align as much as possible with your boss'. Your own strength of conviction is also important, to say "no" if needed, and stay the course. This is easy to say but often hard to maintain with all the pressures that one as a CISO can face.

It is my pleasure to introduce **Tim Callahan, SVP** and **Global CISO** at **Aflac**. Tim had a long history of serving his country in the Air Force before he started his CISO career in banking and then later in insurance in 1998. Tim has been a CISO for some 19 years, which is itself an incredible feat of resilience and tenacity. He is also chairman of the National Technology Coalition and serves in several other advisory roles.

In this chapter, Tim will share why risk management matters. This is an opinion that I've come to agree with in my career, but I admit that it was not my starting position. I've learned through my experiences, however, that risk management not just matters but is vital.

Why risk management matters

Tim Callahan

Why is the concept of **cyber risk management** so important? This discipline has been brought into more focus in recent years due to the growing realization of how cyber incidents can affect the financial health of a company. Regulatory bodies have also been driving the focus on applying sound risk management practices to the cyber threat world. The best practice has become to ensure that cyber threats are incorporated into the enterprise risk management program.

There has been another realization that it is not possible or practical for every cyber threat, existing or emerging, to be eliminated. It would be incredibly costly to go down that path. Even if cost were not a consideration, in this scenario, we would be in a constant race, as threats have grown tremendously, morphed into many areas and are still evolving.

Now that you understand some key context behind why risk management matters, allow me to explore this in more detail.

Some historical context

The information security profession for years has held the responsibility for cybersecurity even before we called it that. Cybersecurity was (and sometimes still is) generally seen as protection from adversaries. Information security encompasses that, as well as the internal processes that protect the **confidentiality, integrity, and availability** (**CIA**) of information and information systems. Technology risk management is another subcomponent of information security and generally deals with the integrity and availability of technology, systems, and information.

Risk management does not operate in silos. It is an approach that connects different practices across the organization, for instance, technology change control (an information security practice to ensure the integrity of information and systems, that is, protecting them from internal mistakes that can affect the accuracy of processing information) and business continuity – or, better labeled, business resiliency (another information security practice, which ensures the availability of information and enterprise systems).

Cyber threats can and should influence the resiliency program, especially as it relates to ransomware and other destructive attacks; however, sound information security and resiliency practices must address more than just cyber threats. Risk management is the golden thread connecting risks and assessing their overall impact on the business.

Cybersecurity is now also often seen as all about protecting the CIA of information, as well as the associated systems, hardware, and networks that process, store, and transmit that information. As such, *cybersecurity* and *information security* are terms that are often used interchangeably.

There was a time when information security professionals were not as attuned to the concept of risk management in practice. Risk management, which focuses on understanding organizational risks and applying appropriate controls to them that align with specific organizational missions and goals, emerged as the reality of cost versus reward started to become part of the conversation. It is a legitimate question of how much a company is willing to risk from a financial standpoint as it tries to balance the ever-increasing cost of cyber defense. At what point are we spending too much to mitigate the cyber threat?

Cybersecurity and risk management – interconnected disciplines

Both cybersecurity and risk management require governance oversight and active management processes. They both rely on looking at internal and external threats, and then the process to manage these incidents, should they occur.

Cybersecurity serves as a specialized application of risk management principles to information and digital assets.

Having said that, at face value, we may observe an apparent tension between these two paradigms. One may seem to advocate for comprehensive protection with minimal consideration for resource constraints or operational requirements, based on the argument that information assets warrant protection regardless of expense, while the other emphasizes informed decision-making and proportionate controls aligned with organizational objectives and budget realities.

I would argue that no fundamental contradiction exists.

I've seen that security practitioners now recognize these disciplines as fundamentally interdependent, where vulnerability in one domain directly impacts the other. Consequently, the natural tendency becomes implementing comprehensive protections across all fronts. However, recent years have demonstrated the pragmatic constraints of cost-benefit analyses as previously discussed, alongside exponential growth of security technologies influencing operational methodologies. Deploying every available tool or treating all threats with equivalent priority is impractical. This operational reality has led to the integration of risk management principles into security practice.

Most security practitioners have welcomed this integration, and many would maintain that risk-based methodologies were perpetually embedded within the profession. This is illustrated by the fact that vulnerabilities are risk-ranked – critical, high, medium, and low (acknowledging that it is likely acceptable to allow low-risk vulnerabilities to exist to focus on the more dangerous critical and high ones).

The merging of the cybersecurity and risk management disciplines has led to a greater need for rigor in documenting risk practices.

Risk management programs

Effective risk management programs provide a clearly defined process for understanding and documenting risk, as well as assessing organizational risk tolerance and determining suitable strategies for risk mitigation.

A 'risk register' is the accepted method to record risk, as an inventory of possible risks.

The register is usually refined to the top risks (maybe the top 10), but the inventory should never be lost. In fact, there should be an annual process to review the inventory of risks and determine whether anything has changed that may serve to elevate the risks.

Understanding risk begins with an 'organizational' risk assessment. In doing the assessment, risk should be considered in terms of threat (criminal or otherwise), regulatory considerations, and reputational concerns. The balance of these tends to be industry-specific.

Excelling in one of these areas doesn't guarantee success in the others. You might have bulletproof defenses against hackers but still face significant regulatory penalties for compliance gaps. Or you could check every regulatory box and block attacks yet still lose customers who simply don't trust that their data is safe with you. I've seen that customer perception matters as much as actual security – if people believe that you are vulnerable, you have a business problem regardless of your technical capabilities.

When your team does risk assessments, these need to be more than a catalog of what could go wrong. They should map out what you are already doing right, documenting existing controls that are working to reduce your exposure as well as identifying the gaps where you're flying blind, and outline what additional protections you need to build.

The assessment must also clarify your strategy for each identified threat. Some risks will demand elimination, for instance, by deploying technology that hunts down and destroys malware before it can take hold. Then, some others may warrant acceptance – this can be the case where protecting against risks would cost more than just dealing with the consequences. The key is making these choices deliberately and strategically rather than by default.

Why should I go to all this trouble?

You may be wondering at this point why you need to go to all this trouble. Personally, I used to think the same way early in my career – "Why can't I just fix the security problems and move on?" My own bias was to jump straight into deploying firewalls and patching systems without all the paperwork and meetings. But I learned the hard way that good intentions and technical skills are just not enough.

What I discovered is that without a formal risk management program, you are, in effect, flying blind. You might be working incredibly hard on what you think are the most important problems, only to find out later that the executive team was worried about completely different issues. Unfortunately, I've been in situations where I spent months perfecting our incident response capabilities while the board was losing sleep over regulatory compliance gaps I did not even know existed.

The formal risk program became my lifeline because it created a shared understanding of what the priority risks were and what 'done' looked like. I've seen many teams work hard at a control without a formal definition of 'done.' This discipline can help you to stop constantly having to justify why you are working on certain projects. You can then point to the agreed-upon risk priorities, which means budget reviews are easier discussions.

The most liberating part was finally having corporate backing for saying "no" to requests that didn't align with our risk priorities. Before that framework, every urgent request felt like it had to be accommodated. Afterward, I could confidently redirect conversations back to our established goals.

The essential elements of cybersecurity

With the current (and appropriate) focus on the expanding cyber threat, it is easy to get distracted by the technological aspect of security. There are new solutions hitting the market that can truly benefit the fight against cybercriminals.

Established security companies have been refocusing their efforts, or at least remarketing their products to enhance threat awareness or threat intelligence. Added to cyber threats are the expanding use of **artificial intelligence** (**AI**) in the enterprise and by criminals against companies (as one might expect, security companies are now marketing their solutions as AI-driven).

There is an unprecedented sense of urgency across industries to get in front of new AI threats. Boardrooms are abuzz with talk of cybersecurity in industries where just a while back, the topic would never have made the agenda of a board committee. Companies are creating and recruiting executive-level heads of security – CISOs – to bring focus to their cybersecurity efforts. This is leading them to build programs from the ground up, or in some cases, rebuild programs more attuned to current threats.

In speaking with many security professionals, I have heard of cases of rapid implementation of security technology that have not proven their value and have therefore become almost wasted effort. The pressure to do something can often lead to not ensuring that there is a solid process in place for the security technology to support. Now is not the time to abandon the essential elements of a security program; those tried-and-true enduring principles of a solid program that have proven their worth over time.

What are those essentials?

The tried-and-true approach to an effective security program is to start by conducting an enterprise information/technology risk assessment to determine and prioritize what to protect. Then, based on the risk assessment, tailor the program and protections to meet the risk tolerance defined by the company's leadership and corporate governance structure.

Defining information risk tolerance

This exercise can happen before, during, or after the risk assessment. However, it is essential to define the security strategy, roadmap, processes, and solutions. The investment in security for the company must be commensurate with the desired risk tolerance.

The CISO must lead the discussion, but the level of information risk tolerance is not a security decision. Risk tolerance is a board-level decision that will drive the cybersecurity maturity target of the company.

Assessing risk

As the CISO puts a governance framework into place, the risk assessment should be among the first steps. It is on that risk assessment that the security strategy, policy, and standards should hang.

Therefore, it is essential to get it right.

> It must be noted that the risk assessment should be refreshed annually. The initial one will likely identify areas where there are not currently controls and enable prioritization or the development of a roadmap to implement controls. The year-over-year iterative approach following that will drive decisions, adjustments, and prioritization in the roadmap to achieve the desired maturity target.

The risk assessment should, crucially, incorporate a risk register that can be extracted and used to inform enterprise risk. Here are the other elements generally needed in an enterprise information/technology risk assessment:

Element	Description
Overview	This should provide a view of the content, the overall inherent risk, and the overall residual risk that is supported in the remainder of the document.
Business profile	This outlines the industry, the business operating environment, and the business strategy. This should also address the business culture and how that culture influences the view of risk management and tolerance around cybersecurity. For instance, if the company has a strong culture of protecting its customers, that is good to know as it will influence the tolerance for cybersecurity risk.
Information/technology profile	This defines the information that is being protected, where the information resides, and the relevant technology landscape. This would also define third-party risk, as to what information and relationships exist with third-party providers.
Inherent risk within the industry	This describes the risk that applies to the industry in general and how that does or does not affect the company.
Contemporary factors affecting risk	This covers those current risks the industry is seeing, shifting risks, and emerging trends. This could include factors such as geopolitical climate, microeconomic, or any current factor that could impact risk to the company.
General controls environment	This defines and assesses current controls and documents control gaps and any remediation efforts and timelines. This should define whether the controls can be relied upon as a mitigating factor.
Internal threat/risk	This is a summary of the internal risks to information and assets, the potential damage resulting from these, and controls and mitigating factors to reduce inherent risk and residual risk.
External threat/risk	This is a summary of the external risk to information and assets, the potential damage resulting from this, and controls and mitigating factors to reduce risk – inherent risk and residual risk.
Ongoing risk assessments, testing, and measures	This section is intended to summarize all related risk assessment processes that exist, how controls are tested, and how effectiveness is measured. Another consideration is to include the process around application risk assessments, third-party risk assessments, and so on.

Table 25.1: Risk assessment outline

Adopting a controls framework

Whether before or after the risk assessment, you must determine a framework and get broad company buy-in to that framework. When you take the effort to get company buy-in to your risk framework, this will proactively prevent constantly reassessing both specific issues and how to think about the issues. There are multiple frameworks to choose from, but ensure you select one that is most applicable to your company and industry.

If you compete as an international company, you may consider the ISO 2700 model. In the US, the NIST Cybersecurity Framework has become the generally accepted framework for a cyber program. If you are a public company, the COBIT model is most accepted to address Sarbanes-Oxley general IT controls. COBIT and NIST differ in their focus and scope. COBIT focuses on IT governance and management, aiming to align IT with business goals and ensure value delivery. NIST, on the other hand, is more focused on cybersecurity risk management, providing guidance for organizations to protect their systems and data. You will most likely need to marry both frameworks, as a public company.

Once a framework is selected, you will need to go through the elements of it to determine what does and does not apply to your company. You want to include any industry-specific criteria. For instance, if you are a financial institution, you would want to ensure the Federal Financial Institution Examination Council criteria are infused into your controls.

Foundational governance documents

The other critical element of establishing a program is governance documents such as a cybersecurity policy, standards, procedures, and defined and recorded processes.

If these documents don't exist, as in a new program, you may want to use a cybersecurity principles document to get things started. These set out the enduring principles of a program. It is generally easier to get stakeholders to agree on a set of principles that should not be violated as a starting point than to get everyone to agree on a specific path forward from a blank slate.

Some examples are as follows:

- No entity should be granted access rights to a system or information that is greater than what is needed to perform the job function (entity encompasses people, machines, applications, etc.).
- No information should be retained longer than is required for regulatory, legal, or business needs.

- Access to information and systems must be properly validated, authenticated, and secure prior to access, including multifactor authentication commensurate with risk.

- No business owner can accept risk that affects other business owners. The risk acceptance responsibility must be elevated to the proper leadership level that can accept risk for all affected business entities.

There are probably no more than 20 fundamental principles on which you should get widespread approval. As you craft the other documents, policies, standards, and so on, you need to ensure there is no violation of these principles. That will ensure alignment across policy, standards, and procedures. The principles will also serve to help settle disagreements on policy elements. For instance, when you get pushback on a policy, you refer to the agreed-upon principle on which the policy is based. The discussion then becomes one about how the wording does or does not support the principle. It is a lot more effective to ask the question, "Do you still agree on the principle you agreed to?"

The cybersecurity policy should be approved by the highest governance body in the organization. In a public company, this is normally the board of directors. The policy constitutes the board's instruction to management on the minimum elements of a security program.

> The policy should be written in a series of policy elements that are numbered to form a framework that can cascade through standards, procedures, processes, and capabilities. In other words, a properly written policy should promulgate controls that are traceable back to the foundational policy.

As you are crafting your governance documents, ensure that you think through what an exception program will look like. In the early stages of a program, you will likely be getting requests for exceptions as the various constituents endeavor to comply with policy and standards. Things to consider in the exception process include the following:

- The level of leadership that exceptions require – is it the division head that must approve the request? In essence, that person must be the appropriate person to accept the risk of noncompliance.

- What the maximum duration is that an exception should be granted (hint: the most accepted practice is no greater than one year).

- The risk if the exception is granted and the risk if the exception is not granted. Both should be outlined.

- The proper owner of the exception – the person with the authority and ability to correct the exception. This is generally different from the approver of the request. All exceptions should identify this person.

- The remediation path for the exception. This should always be identified.

Another essential is a **security education and awareness** program. This program must let people know what the requirements are, as well as educate them on risks, threats, and tactics criminals will use to penetrate your company. People are the best defense against the criminal element, and security awareness helps equip them to be best prepared.

There are certainly more elements of a governance process. These will become evident once you decide on a framework and document the controls.

My conclusion

One of the most meaningful and liberating conversations I have had around cyber risk management came when Richard A. Clarke (Dick) briefed the board of directors. Good Harbor Security Risk Management, for which Dick is the Chairman, had conducted a companywide assessment of our cyber readiness and maturity posture. The assessment was comprehensive and left us with a strong set of recommendations that ultimately became our roadmap to maturity.

When Dick briefed the board on the results, he made the point that the CISO does not own the risk. The board owns the risk. The CISO can only manage the risk within the risk tolerance set by the board. Success depends on the board ensuring that there are resources allocated to the CISO to lead a program that can achieve that risk tolerance.

The statement is certainly true. That does not mean the CISO has a blank check or no culpability, but it does mean there is shared accountability for managing cyber risk.

The level of risk tolerance will drive the investment needed to manage the program within that tolerance. The CISO must use this to craft a program that demonstrably ties the investment to achieving the tolerance. The CISO must also develop metrics that effectively measure and show progress toward achieving the maturity of the program to that tolerance.

David's key takeaways – Why risk management matters

Tim has shared some great learnings from his extensive career and experience as a CISO here. Risk management is what allows the business to operate. Taking on too much risk may have a negative impact. Similarly, managing too many risks can distract an enterprise from revenue-generating processes. This is where the CISO has to live – in the intersection of technology and business risk.

As Tim suggests, rookie CISOs may see risk management as a hindrance that slows down their own progress. It is guru-level CISOs like Tim that truly understand how much risk management matters, and how important it is to get it right. In essence, risk management is a superpower for the CISO. Without risk management as your foundation, you are just an expensive technical advisor. But with this superpower, you become a strategic business leader who happens to specialize in security.

A few key points I'd like to highlight from this chapter include:

- *Getting fundamentals right matters.* While new security technologies are interesting and important, don't abandon fundamental security program elements. Ensure solid processes are in place before implementing new tools to avoid rapid technology implementations that don't prove their value.

- *Risk reduction is the goal.* Understand that the complete elimination of cyber threats is neither practical nor cost-effective. Focus on risk management principles that balance security investments with business objectives, rather than pursuing absolute security regardless of cost.

- *Start with a comprehensive enterprise risk assessment.* A thorough organizational risk assessment should consider threat, regulatory, and reputational risks specific to your industry. This assessment should, importantly, include a risk register, define existing controls, identify gaps, and document risk management strategies (elimination, acceptance, mitigation, or transference).

- *Establish a clear risk tolerance level with board leadership.* Note that risk tolerance is a board-level decision, not a security decision; however, the CISO must lead discussions on this, which will drive investment levels and program maturity targets. Remember: the board owns the risk; the CISO manages it.

- *It is important to develop foundational documents, including security principles, policies, standards, and procedures.* If these don't already exist in your organization, start with fundamental principles (no more than 20) that stakeholders can agree upon, then build all other governance documents to align with these principles. Also, include a well-defined exception process from the beginning.

- *Select and commit to an appropriate controls framework.* Choose a framework that fits your company and industry and secure broad organizational buy-in. Tailor the framework to include industry-specific requirements relevant to you and ensure it supports your risk assessment findings.

- *Develop metrics that demonstrate progress.* Create measurable indicators that show how security investments tie to achieving risk tolerance levels and program maturity. This provides accountability and demonstrates value to leadership while supporting continuous improvement efforts.

26

Driving Cyber Transformation

Driving cyber transformation is something that is easy to say and very hard to do. A cyber transformation is not just about delivering new technology; it is about delivering change across people and processes too, including embedding processes with more secure practices and staff within a new, enhanced culture.

While the average CISO typically does not come from a classic programme delivery background, nor are they trained in organisational change management, as a CISO there is a significant programme of delivery that you will need to manage across business and technology stakeholders. This is your number 1 priority, but it is likely that this may not be held to the same high level of importance by other stakeholders.

For many enterprises and institutions, the spend on cyber is usually the largest within the technology budget; thus, the CISO will need to manage large budgets and deliver risk reduction through their programme of delivery. To achieve this goal, there is a basic need to have skilled staff to help you drive this change. In some instances, a strong **Cyber Risk Quantification (CRQ)** foundation can provide the required business case to assist you in prioritising your change portfolio.

How much is too much change? That is hard to gauge. When I was at HSBC, there was a five-year programme to uplift their cyber controls. This initiative was not triggered by a breach, but a proactive programme championed by the global CIO – Darryl West.

The spend was around US$1B over that period, and the programme was generally unpopular with other technology leaders as it meant that funding capacity for other business projects was limited. Overall, it can be said that this was a successful cyber transformation, and the uplift was measured by CRQ and shared back to the board and also to regulators.

There was also a question around embedment and how well the new controls were being made to be fully operational. (The danger is that we add new layers of defence, but don't understand which ones are effective and when they aren't working.) This was nothing a good red team attack would not be able to determine via a robust test of cyber capabilities.

It is my pleasure to introduce **David Ng**, who is **Head of Group Technology Information Security** at **OCBC Bank** in Singapore. David has a successful history of driving cyber transformation as a long-serving CISO at OCBC and previously in his distinguished regulator career at the **Monetary Authority of Singapore (MAS)**.

David will share his insights around cyber transformation, and as you read this, it is interesting to think about the nuanced relationship of a CISO with a regulator. At face value, one can consider how the regulator can be a personal career threat to the CISO and can indeed directly influence the board and management by publicly questioning their competence.

I'd note that in normal situations, the regulator has an inherent power imbalance in this relationship. Most CISOs approach regulators with respect and a healthy degree of wariness. In David Ng's case, with his trusted regulator relationships, he views regulators as partners in risk management, and it is therefore interesting to reflect on his approach to driving cyber transformation given this Yoda 'superpower' that he possesses.

Cyber transformation

David Ng

"It is not what you have done that counts. It is what you have not done that matters!"

I serve as the head of group **Technology Information Security Office (TISO)** of OCBC in Singapore.

The bank started in the 1930s with the goals of providing customers with financial solutions for their personal and business needs, and to support the community it served. Today, OCBC is the longest-established Singapore bank and has grown to become a regional financial services group.

How the cybersecurity defence strategy took shape

The phrase 'a joint responsibility has no accountability' marked the beginning of OCBC's cyber transformation journey with the establishment of TISO (my role). I was hired to lead the department in August 2014 as the bank was shoring up its defences to address technology risks and the evolving cyber threats. At the same time, regulators in the countries where OCBC operates also increased their expectations as well as regulatory sophistication. Hence, the bank needed to invest prudently to preserve its banking licences so that it could continue providing financial solutions to its customers and the community it serves.

Right at the beginning of the cyber transformation journey, the department was granted a group-wide mandate to serve as an independent IT security unit overseeing the bank's overall cyber and IT defence strategy, security architecture, and cybersecurity functions. To ensure cybersecurity meets the regulators' expectations and operates at the highest global standards, I made it mandatory that the department and the cybersecurity functions that it operates reference leading industry cybersecurity frameworks and standards, such as the **National Institute of Standards and Technology (NIST)** Cybersecurity Framework.

Not only did I adopt the NIST Cybersecurity Framework but I also overlaid it with additional elements to ensure effective governance and management of cyber risks were also in place, in unison.

The various risk committees that I represented govern various cyber risks, including information security, digital risk, and risk management. The layers of governance are required to ensure that the overall cyber strategy is a living and adaptable plan.

> 💡 Lack of governance can derail due diligence. When it comes to cybersecurity, there are no second chances.

The bank formulated its first cyber transformation, CDR 1.0, which ran between 2013 and 2017, to tackle evolving cyber threats such as hacking and distributed-denial-of-service attacks.

What is CDR?

CDR stands for **Cyber Defence Roadmap**, a multi-year programme to address specific cyber threats and risks and meet regulatory expectations:

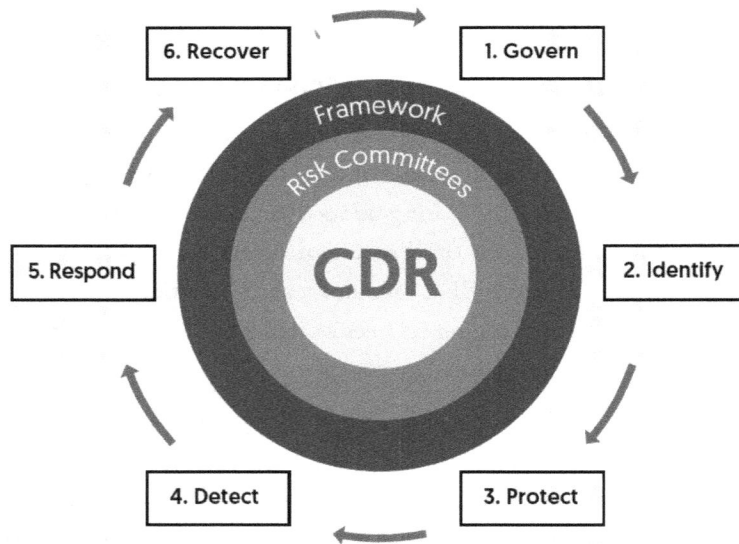

Figure 26.1: OCBC group's cybersecurity strategy

The five-year plan was underpinned by robust security measures, as well as the values of transparency and reliability for all digital interactions, with the goal of ensuring uninterrupted service and rapid recovery from IT or cyber disruptions.

84 capabilities were curated across people, processes, and technology. These were 84 additional capabilities over and above the IT and IT security capabilities that the bank had already invest-

ed in. At the outset, people and processes were the two biggest gaps, given cybersecurity was emerging back in 2012/2013.

When the TISO role was inaugurated, the first cyber transformation plan was already in execution mode. At that time, I was caught in a dichotomy to validate the plan by an external independent consultant – if the validation highlighted gaps in the plan, how would I continue with the plan and steer the transformation journey? If the validation went completely against the plan, what would it say about my colleagues who were responsible for formulating it?

The validation turned out well and the bank went on to complete the first roadmap in 2017. After completing CDR 1.0, I used two industry-renowned cybersecurity standards – (1) the control points outlined in the NIST 800-53 standard, and (2) the maturity level outlined in the US Department of Defence Capability Maturity Model Integration – to benchmark the bank's overall cyber readiness. Following the benchmarking exercise, the bank achieved an 'Integrated Picture' maturity level (utilising cyber threat intelligence to form an integrated view of its security posture and threat landscape).

Subsequently, the bank completed two iterations of the roadmap, i.e., CDR 2.0 and 3.0, with 149 capabilities implemented across people, process, and technology. Throughout the three roadmaps, the bank continued to focus on building digital trust and employing cutting-edge technologies and best practices to transform cyber protection to safeguard financial assets and customer data. What was also key in the transformation journey was that cybersecurity continued to serve as a strategic enabler to align cybersecurity objectives with business priorities.

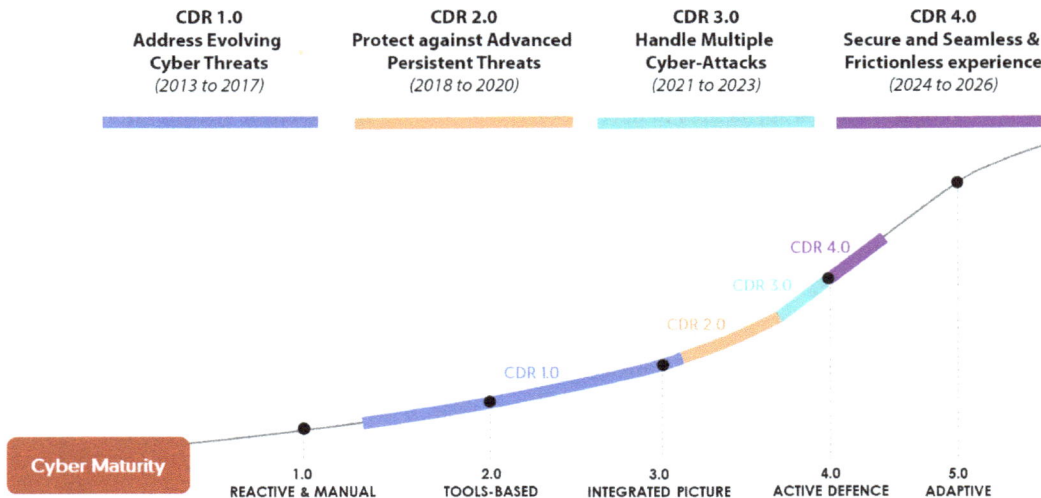

Figure 26.2: OCBC's CDR and cyber maturity levels

In the latest roadmap, CDR 4.0, 24 capabilities have been curated. CDR 4.0 is planned to be completed by the end of 2026, as you can see in *Figure 26.2*, and aims to move the bank's cybersecurity maturity beyond 'Active Defence' maturity level – by providing predictive and agile capabilities to protect, detect, and respond to imminent cyber threats.

Prioritising the implementation of capabilities

Given the risk appetite and investment priorities, I adopted a four-pronged approach to implement the various capabilities needed:

- **Addressing the evolution of the cyber threat landscape** – our team curated diverse cyber threats to be addressed in each roadmap. These threats ranged from advanced persistent threats to the emergence of blended threats and the growing risks associated with artificial intelligence attacks.

- **Cyber capability readiness and resource availability** – we recognised the importance of a well-equipped and qualified workforce to defend against existing and emerging threats as it progresses through its transformation roadmap. A key enhancement we made in this area included developing a cyber development pathway that extends beyond an employee's current job domain.

- **Enhancing existing cyber protection** – we identified current processes and technologies that needed enhancement due to the increasing sophistication of cyber threats. Enhancements included augmenting existing capabilities with new features and integrating artificial intelligence.

- **Regulatory expectations** – we proactively adapted to the evolving regulatory environment in the countries where we operate by considering the governance standards and recommended approaches in each iteration of our roadmap. These include maintaining compliance with the Cyber Security Agency of Singapore's Cyber Codes of Practice 2.0 and streamlining cyber intelligence sharing with Bank Negara Malaysia.

As a head of state in cybersecurity, implementing more capabilities doesn't mean doing them all. Dated processes can either be removed or enhanced using automation, for example. Newer capabilities, especially skillsets, need time to be nurtured. As a leader, I need to encourage my colleagues to take up the challenges and always subscribe to the 'change the ways we work' mentality.

Another notion I subscribe to is that cybersecurity is a team sport – we are stronger together! Hence, the bank collaborates regularly with regulators, academia, and industry partners to enhance its digital banking security and futureproof its investments, staying ahead of emerging threats and regulatory requirements. For example, with the emergence of quantum computing, there is growing concern about the potential danger of 'store-now-decrypt-later' attacks. In this regard, the bank signed a **Memorandum of Understanding (MoU)** with Nanyang Technological University of Singapore in November 2022 to conduct proof-of-concept projects to bolster the security of the bank's IT systems:

Figure 26.3: Signing of the research collaboration agreement between NTU Singapore and OCBC, witnessed by Deputy Prime Minister, Coordination Minister for Economic Policies, and Chairman of the National Research Foundation, Mr Hang Swee Keat

In August 2024, the bank signed another MoU with the **Monetary Authority of Singapore (MAS)**, solidifying their collaboration to explore quantum security solutions to combat cyber threats:

Figure 26.4: The MAS joined forces with OCBC, among other identified financial institutions and telecommunication operators, to explore quantum security solutions for the financial sector

As the previous examples demonstrate, I have taken a proactive approach to address this emerging risk and am working with others to address this in a careful manner. Regulators, just like auditors, are my best allies. Each of us sees light through a different lens. To be successful together, we must see the light at the same wavelength and angle.

Engaging with regulators is not rocket science. All it takes is an honest, direct, and collaborative mindset.

Cybersecurity as a business enabler

The TISO role focuses on finance, risk, service, and people to transform cybersecurity from a technology-centric approach to one that serves as a business enabler. For example, in addition to evaluating the protection offered by various solutions, the office assesses the total cost of ownership, examining the extensibility of scaling and updating capabilities to meet current and emerging cyber threats and developing regulatory expectations.

Let's look at two examples.

First, in early 2015, Singapore's financial institutions' customers were inundated with financial malware. The bank swung into action to support its community by partnering with business departments and IT to roll out IBM Trusteer Rapport to its corporate customers to help thwart the malware affecting their desktop computers and laptops.

Today, cybersecurity protects the bank's corporate assets within the boundaries of its firewall and safeguards its customers. This enablement aligns with the bank's purpose and values – to strengthen its market position by building customer trust and supporting sustainable growth across the locales where the bank operates.

Next, in 2024, the bank displaced several cyber capabilities previously hosted on-premises to a unified capability on a public cloud platform. This strategy to migrate to a public cloud platform wasn't a straightforward one as it involved many risk partners and stakeholders in the bank. It was a deliberate effort to reduce operational expenses and unify the bank's cyber defence under one security policy that served its franchise.

At the same time, the regulator expected the same or higher accountability to be established; notwithstanding the unified platform not only extends the cyber protection boundary further away from the bank's core infrastructure and critical services but also aids in consolidating and simplifying incident response and daily operations.

As I have demonstrated here, cybersecurity leaders must think strategically from the outset. I encourage leaders to view cybersecurity as an enabler, as this perspective fosters informed investment decisions that avoid costly, redundant capabilities misaligned with broader objectives. Instead of investing in boutique or single-purpose technologies, a strategic focus empowers organisations to adopt integrated solutions that bolster cyber resilience across the entire organisation. This approach also ensures that investments align with the organisation's long-term goals, preventing overspending on technologies that may not fully support their needs.

What keeps me awake at night

"How do you know?!"

"How do you know the cybersecurity capabilities implemented yesterday operate effectively today?"

"How do you know you have applied the necessary patches to all your IT systems?"

When cyber breaches occur, cybersecurity leaders spend a lot of time answering to senior management, including the board of directors and regulators, while cyber adversaries do not have anyone to account for.

Questions like the preceding ones begin with me and end with me elevating cyber protection. I have the following advice I'd like to leave with you to consider, to help you do the same:

- **Always verify** – subscribe to the 'Plan, Do, Act, Check' method. Do not make assumptions. Trust but verify. When it comes to cybersecurity, there is no second chance, as I mentioned earlier.

- **Know your business** – know your finances, know your people, know your risks, and know your operations. The start-up mindset is always necessary. I will never forget one piece of advice: 'When one is rich, their mind is poor. When one is poor, their mind is rich.' If it were your own money, for example, would you spend it like that?

- **Teamwork is essential** – the right hire brings the team to the next level. Hiring fast and hiring right is a challenging balance. Hiring right is a thousand times more important.

- **What doesn't kill you makes you stronger** – there will be many cyber events to respond to, many regulatory expectations to fulfil, and many audits to go through. While these are challenging situations or moments, they sharpen your cybersecurity standing or posture.

- **Change and learning are constant** – learn, unlearn, relearn. As technologies become obsolete, so does our skillset. Cyber adversaries can fail many times, but they only need to get it right once. However, cyber defenders must be right all the time.

- **Continue to get your hands dirty** – be 3-feet from the keyboard getting your hands dirty, while also elevating yourself to 30,000 feet to see things from a broader perspective (helping you to avoid focusing too much on a single thing).

David's key takeaways — Driving cyber transformation

David is a legend in Singapore and is highly respected. There are some extremely valuable insights from his chapter here from his deep experience at MAS in Singapore, combined with his CISO role at OCBC Bank. His insider knowledge of how regulations are crafted and enforced, which allows him to anticipate changes and build 'regulation-proof' cybersecurity policies from the start, is particularly interesting. He also possesses valuable working regulatory relationships, along with industry-wide risk assessment expertise.

David's chapter also provides us with an inspiring example of strategic foresight through his alignment of cybersecurity initiatives with regulatory expectations, before they become requirements.

Here are the key points from this chapter:

- *It's important to be proactive and anticipate threats.* As David says: "It is not what you have done that counts. It is what you have not done that matters." This is a practical and sobering approach that also implies that you are never done and speaks volumes to how David looks at cyber transformation as being an ongoing roadmap. I'd suggest this is a phrase worth repeating to your own board and management.

- *Reflect on your approach to engaging the respective regulators in your role.* How can you develop the same level of trust with them that David has been able to achieve? What can you do better to improve your rapport? Have you shared your own cyber transformation roadmap with your regulator?

- *Ensure that cybersecurity serves as a business enabler and aligns objectives strategically with business priorities.* The cloud migration example David mentions in the chapter is a great one to illustrate this, whereby resilience and security were increased, and customer experience was improved – a trifecta of benefits.

- *Invest in innovation and futureproofing.* David has adopted an approach to continuously innovate by investing in futureproof technologies to stay ahead of emerging threats and regulatory requirements. What David didn't explain was all the work that he did behind the scenes with his stakeholders to get this funding approved. (These are never easy approvals and take real long-term focus and stakeholder management.)

- *Work to build digital trust as well as resilience,* as David has done. I'd add that this is both externally with the regulator and internally with his stakeholders. This is not a short-term fix (sprint) but more akin to a marathon.

- *Approach cyber transformation in waves.* David drove strategic capability implementation in alignment with a multi-year roadmap, rather than extensive change, all at once. His strategy, focusing on automation to replace outdated processes while nurturing new skillsets and maintaining compliance, was carefully thought through and implemented.

27

My Metrics Playbook

What does life experience teach you? We all learn about ourselves and others in the process of our career. One very important aspect of our learning is the value of things. Because we have struggled or had difficulty with something, accomplishing a task is that much more rewarding. In this way, experience teaches us what is important, as well as less important.

As a CISO, there are often no guidelines that you can rely on. You have the authority (to make decisions, control resources, and take action) and responsibility (to achieve specific outcomes – in this case, to protect the enterprise), and that can be daunting and challenging. There will be lessons you learn around your own self-awareness and how you can become more personally resilient (but you are essentially on your own).

The concept of a playbook is that it provides you with a blueprint to tackle something – your metrics as a CISO, in this case, helping you to get the right balance between strategic and business-as-usual activities.

A metrics playbook can do many things. For example, it can guide you on how to engage with stakeholders to get the best outcome. This is particularly important when conflicting objectives are at play, and as the CISO, you must be able to speak the language of the business, as well as that of cyber risk. Engagement with the business to develop a cyber strategy and roadmap will require you to again make trade-offs, and there will be a focus required on some assets, while others will be left for another time.

When bad stuff happens, the CISO needs to explain and justify how they manage incidents with management, external partners and the board. Metrics help you with this. How these parties then engage effectively will have a significant bearing on the collective and individual outcomes being positive at the end.

Metrics also guide you on how and where to act. The day in the life of a CISO is full of meetings and constant interruptions. Most CISOs face consistent noise, which includes false positives and incomplete information. There is nothing more frustrating for the CISO than not having all the facts to make decisions and act. You have complete authority and responsibility, but not the facts you need to be able to respond effectively.

Introducing **Peter Troy**, recently retired from **Morgan Stanley** as **Deputy Global CISO**. Peter has also served in senior cyber roles at Lloyds Bank, Barclays and J.P. Morgan.

Peter has significant experience, some of which he will share with us in this chapter, with a focus on metrics. It is my privilege to ask Peter to share some of his secret formula for this with us.

The importance of measurement

Peter Troy

I have been very fortunate to work in some fantastic organisations with super talented people and the one thing that stood out for me in the best of them is that they were generous with their time and learnings. So, in that spirit, I will try and pass on a few gems of my lessons learned to you.

The problem that I have spent the most time in my working career fixing or improving is the ability to count things. 'Things' being a very diverse spread of people, process and technology; oh, and of course, money – never forget the money! Each of these measures breaks down again and again into categories such as location, physical/ephemeral, required, budgeted and actual. They all count the same things, but viewed through a different lens – we'll come to optics later.

So, if I could offer my young self only one piece of sound advice when starting out, it would be "start counting." Measure what you can, and that will tell you what you need to measure, which incidentally becomes a measure itself. You'll never be done, but going by the 80/20 rule, you will be in far more control of 80% of the measures you need.

If you are not measuring it, you are not managing it!

This is such a simple statement, but the most challenging thing to do at speed and with quality.

In the earlier part of my career, counting was easy because I could count in a few hours to get the numbers by the categories that were required. I didn't know the pain my boss was taking in buying me that time to count.

As the banks I worked at consolidated during the 90s, counting at scale became an art when it should have been a science. Getting to a number normally involved a bit of real counting, and some extrapolation and judgement.

This would lead to some very long discussions at meetings when a lot of caveats were thrown in with the numbers. I remember using the fruit analogy (meant to highlight groupings of similar things), and a COO paraphrasing as "so, what you're telling me is we have a lot of fruit, mostly apples, some oranges and a few pears."

COO's, auditors and regulators paraphrase a lot, so pay attention to the nuance because my fruit analogy was not as paraphrased, although I could see how they interpreted it that way. The key lesson here is all about being really clear with your message, and this is where numbers can really help!

Qualify and quantify

When you are a CISO, you spend a lot of time taking complex technical issues and translating them to various audiences, all with different levels of understanding and business backgrounds.

Boards are intentionally set up that way to ensure breadth and depth of challenge to the leaders. The narrative you craft will become a record, and so it's vital the right message is interpreted at a later cold read. (*Note the use of the word narrative over story. Story is too closely linked to fiction for my liking.*)

The two levers you must work with when crafting such a narrative are **qualification** and **quantification**. While the former is normally quite subjective and where experience and judgment come into play, the latter is empirical evidence of measurement, which is very hard to argue against.

CVSS (Common Vulnerability Scoring System) and **CVE (Common Vulnerabilities and Exposures)** can play a role in qualification, but ratings can be moderated to a degree, and you tend to be in the mature 80% of measures counted at that stage of discussion. (Note: 80% here is meant to signify that if you are at that level of debate, you probably have mature metrics, hence you are 80/20 done on building it out.)

I did a training course many moons ago (intentional use of a qualification here to obscure age) on Neurolinguistic Programming (NLP). I think I took it because it sounded cool, and I'd read too much Philip K Dick and William Gibson, along the lines that humans have underlying programming.

The learning I got from it was that the interpreter in humans is not the same. Some of us are visual, some audial and all of this is influenced as we grow up. I'm not even going near the kinetic folks, and I put that in the 20%. To get to a point, some will get the columns of numbers, some the charts and some narrative bullets. So, your best way to communicate your message is a blend of presentation styles and a good narrative, leveraging both qualification and quantification.

Be brief. Great advice I had from a long-time-ago boss was that if you can squeeze the message into a Blackberry screen, then it will get read and understood quickly. (I think I may have blown the age obfuscation with the Blackberry reference!)

The importance of thinking ahead

When you start out measuring, it pays to think ahead and collect contextual reference data at the same time as you take your measurements – it can be difficult to go back in time and get that later. Storage is cheap now, so you can be far more generous with what you measure. But know the devil is in the detail, and it's far easier to pick out an indicator from data in hindsight than it is with foresight.

Obviously, think about what the measurement you're taking represents, as there's no point spending money, time and effort to secure data only to drop it in another data store less those controls. (One real bugbear of mine was that to get a measurement from a data mining tool required 'Privileged Access', because of the sensitivity of other data shared in that store.)

For measurement reporting, you don't need to know who (used the reporting system), just how many. There's no reason why you can't exploit firm-wide deployed tooling, but by keeping measurement data separate from raw data (also known as source data), you can be much more flexible with how you distribute it. After a few years in a role and when the measurements are mature, there is nothing more satisfying than sending someone a link to simple counts rather than the need to extract data to a spreadsheet and send it over. It demonstrates to others that you know what you are doing and have confidence in the team.

Thinking ahead helps avoid these pitfalls and will ensure you can answer the subsequent questions that follow any presentation of a measurement. The best way to prepare for those questions is to make them your questions to the team. **Rigour** and **discipline** mean everything in measurement. If you don't keep questioning the counts and interrogating the numbers, then not only will you miss a building event, but the quality of your measurements will deteriorate. Nobody gets to evade the laws of thermodynamics, and you must put a lot of energy into keeping order.

Here are a couple of common questions to anticipate:

- Is that worse or better than the last report?
- Is it out of tolerance?
- What time period was this?

Trajectory and velocity

Ballistics is the science that studies the motion and effects of projectiles – such as bullets or any object launched through the air. We can think about data in this analogy. In ballistics, insufficient launch angle or initial velocity will cause a projectile to fall short of its intended target due to gravity's pull overcoming the projectile's forward momentum before it can reach the desired range. This is a good way to look at some measurements.

The trajectory refers to whether the measurement data is going up or down, depending on whether the measure is either good or bad.

Velocity refers to whether we are going too fast or too slow and undershoot or overshoot the target.

Then come the esoteric questions:

- Can we get it back in control quickly enough?
- Is there a tail?

Presenting your measurements

I was surprised by how big an impact style had. Relatively few numbers presented well are far more impactful than a table of detail.

Most companies have templates to adopt for reporting to keep the style and formatting consistent – there is nothing more tiring to your audience than having to understand your style, not just what the measurement is telling them.

Personally, I got very interested in Tufte's approach and infographics for a while and then realised the investment bank had absolutely nailed the most succinct way to present complex data using the likes of candle charts and tickers. So, we created a dashboard of sparks (spark charting, or more commonly, sparklines, can be in a line or bar chart and are used to visualise data trends in a compact form), which, at a glance, would show a rolling twelve-month volume, red and green representing high or low.

My metrics catalogue

Choose what to produce when, and keep a catalogue of the measures you have, what they tell you and how they interact with other measurements. They will ebb and flow in usefulness. It's surprising how often you must refight battles of the past, so having this catalogue to hand really saves you time and effort.

I remember being in a board meeting when the chair opened the meeting with the question, "Has everyone read and understood the deck being presented?"

It was 350+ pages. He told us he had digested every page and how long it had taken. He asked going forward that we prioritise only measurements we wanted to bring attention to or wanted a decision on and relegate all others to the appendix.

After a few cycles, we dropped the appendix as the full master documents were easily available.

I learned a lot about measurement during my spell in retail banking and working hand-in-hand with the fraud departments.

Leading indicators help you to be forward-thinking. Credential validation attacks serve as a good example because they typically occur early in the attack chain. This then allows security teams to detect and respond to threats before more damaging activities like data exfiltration or system compromise take place.

Lagging indicators tend to be easier to count, but unfortunately, they also tend to be outcomes you can't do much about – for example, the number of cyber incidents and mean time to detect them.

Periodicity is not as easy as it sounds. I would publish all board measurements a month in arrears, as accuracy is essential. You will often have to jump in your time machine and travel back to a snapshot in the past to point out that, for example, it's only possible to see May with complete clarity in June.

Extrapolation is useful to a point. You may have the trajectory and velocity looking good but bear in mind that holiday seasons and change freezes don't play well with those projections.

Optics

When you build your catalogue, categorise the measurements as **Performance**, **Profile** and **Pipeline**. Simply: it's happened, where it is now and finally where it looks like it will be, or a future known. Also differentiate performance and risk indicators; normally, the latter is influenced by multiples of the former.

Performance charting visualises speed and efficiency, while a profile chart provides detailed information on individual components and their characteristics. A pipeline chart maps out the stages and progression of a process.

To take an example, UK Finance has excellent metrics (https://www.ukfinance.org.uk/policy-and-guidance/reports-and-publications/annual-fraud-report-2025). The investment they put into their collation of measurements really pays back. Using these, we were able to benchmark to industry. They told me what the loss was as an industry, and I knew what *our* loss was and our market share, so it was a very powerful message to the board to be able to quantify where we stood – important if you need to get investment or protect the program you have.

Crafting a narrative

"There are three kinds of lies: lies, damned lies, and statistics." – Mark Twain

As this quote suggests, in crafting a narrative around your measurements, be careful not to put too much spin on it. The deadliest mistake people can make is to spin too much and then believe that spin themselves. It always pays to have a peer review group to ground you.

Analogies can also support your narrative.

Analogies

Have lots of analogies in your back pocket to use around your metrics. Analogies are a very powerful communication tool that helps you translate technical speak to someone who is less tech savvy.

Take this analogy: Think of metrics as a car dashboard. Some key things, like speed, will always be displayed, but others appear only when they have exceeded or neared a threshold. This keeps the dashboard simple to read and focussed on the topics most deserving of attention.

My first car was from 1972 (it was old when I got it) and had a volt and amperage meter for the battery. This was because batteries, alternators and electrics were very poor in those days, and you would often end up with a flat battery. So, the battery was something worth monitoring.

Finding a hook

Another way to think about this is to make the numbers come to life for the reader, and that is what I call 'finding a hook'. This can be, for example, around critical assets and how we respond to security incidents, or where poor cyber user awareness led to a near miss.

Allow me to illustrate a process to find these hooks:

1. Identify your key cyber metrics, critical security indicators like detection time, response time, incident volume, patch management and security awareness.

2. Pinpoint a pain point from these metrics – for example, that may highlight your gaps, risks through poor performance, declining trends or benchmark misses. A pain point could be a high number, a slow rate, a low score, or an unexpected trend.

3. Determine the measurable impact of that pain point, and translate this into business costs, such as financial losses, downtime, reputation damage and compliance risks.

4. Frame the problem and its impact into a concise and attention-grabbing statement or question that highlights the need for action.

Stickiness

Some measurements resonate, some don't, and finding a hook really helps land your message. '**Performance**, **profile**, **pipeline** or **hindsight**, **insight** and **foresight**' are phrases I've used to good effect.

In everything you do, have one eye on the future, as it's a journey.

My journey has been a blast, enjoy yours!

David's key takeaways — My metrics playbook

As a CISO, Peter ensures that he tackles what is most important first. In this regard, Peter has used measurements and metrics as his North Star.

A good CISO should primarily rely on facts and data. Indeed, as a CISO, you gain credibility with your stakeholders if you lead with facts – they expect data-driven security decisions backed by metrics, threat intelligence, and risk assessments. Adding your own experienced intuition to these facts is also beneficial.

Here are some of the key highlights from Peter's chapter:

- *Bean counting is a winning competency.* The ability to count and measure accurately is fundamental to success as a CISO, covering people, processes, technology, and finances. If you're not measuring it, you're not managing it effectively.

- *Measurement and reporting require constant rigor and discipline* – data quality deteriorates without regular questioning and validation. Consider trajectory (direction) and velocity (speed of change) when analysing metrics.

- *It's important to tailor your messages to your audience.* When communicating complex technical issues to different audiences, use a blend of qualification (subjective, experience-based judgment) and quantification (empirical measurements) to craft clear narratives.

- *Present data efficiently* – a few well-presented numbers are more impactful than detailed tables. Use consistent templates and consider visual tools like dashboards with spark lines for easy, at-a-glance understanding.

- *Maintain a metrics catalogue, documenting what each measure tells you and how metrics interact.* Consider both leading indicators (like phishing campaigns) and lagging indicators (outcomes) in your measurements.

- *Be mindful of data context and storage.* Collect reference data as you collect your measurements, keep measurement data separate from raw data, and ensure security controls are appropriate for the sensitivity of the information.

- *Maintain a peer review group to ensure your narrative remains grounded and accurate.* Also, use analogies effectively to translate technical concepts for non-technical audiences.

- *Segment your data analytics* – categorise measurements into Performance (what happened), Profile (current state), and Pipeline (forward outlook) to provide a comprehensive view of your security posture.

28

Career Resilience

The role of CISO is one of immense responsibility, requiring the ability to navigate a relentless stream of cybersecurity threats while balancing regulatory expectations, business objectives, and stakeholder concerns. The challenge is not just technical; it is a test of leadership, adaptability, and resilience.

CISOs operate under constant pressure, often feeling as if they are 'drinking from a firehose' as they manage the daily complexities of securing an organization's critical assets. Beyond the technical domain, they also influence an enterprise's compliance posture, overall risk management strategy, and reputation. Amid these demands, it is easy to forget that the individuals in these roles are human, managing both professional and personal stress while striving to build long-lasting careers in a fast-moving field.

There is a common understanding that the average CISO tenure is three to four years, an indication of the intensity and burnout often associated with the role. Yet, there are leaders who defy these statistics, demonstrating extraordinary resilience and dedication. One such leader is **Meg Anderson**, a seasoned cybersecurity executive with over 17 years of experience as a CISO in the financial services sector, plus a further 20 years of experience in IT beyond that. As such, Meg is a testament to the power of perseverance and strategic thinking in this demanding profession.

Meg most recently served as the **vice president** and **CISO** at **Principal Financial Group**®, where she led the company's Information Security & Risk team. Meg is also an active contributor to the broader cybersecurity community. She has served on the board of the **Financial Services Information Sharing and Analysis Center (FS-ISAC)**, chairing key committees focused on risk, strategy, governance, and nominations. Additionally, she has lent her expertise to the UnityPoint Health Information Security Committee of the board and participates in various CISO councils and advisory roles for cybersecurity venture capital firms. She is committed to the next generation of security professionals and has participated in mentorship initiatives with Cyversity and the NYU Tandon School of Engineering and within Principal.

As someone who has also been involved in FS-ISAC and understands the challenges and responsibilities of cybersecurity leadership, I greatly admire Meg's ability to navigate this space with resilience and excellence. Her career serves as an invaluable blueprint for security professionals aspiring to build longevity and impact in this field.

I look forward to the insights Meg will share in this chapter on career resilience.

Resilience is the secret ingredient

Meg Anderson

'Resilience' is often repeated as something that is required to have a strong cybersecurity program, sometimes secondary to understanding all technology assets, making sure they are protected in alignment with internal and external policies, laws, and regulations, and ensuring all security controls are working as designed. But resilience wasn't something on my mind when I accepted the job of CISO of Principal Financial Group® in 2008. When interviewing for the job, it was a lateral move for me from another area of the company where I served as a director in IT. During the interview process, I had the opportunity to ask a few questions of the **Chief Information Officer** (**CIO**), my future boss, and remember two questions distinctly.

"Will I have a peer group?" was the first question. His response was a quick "yes." He explained that he had a small and collaborative management team in place, including the heads of the infrastructure, data, financial management, mainframe, and project office teams. I would join this management team if I got the job. I don't recall him asking why I'd asked, but I was moving from an area of the company that had recently gone through some organizational change, and it left me leading a team that was a bit of an island.

By then, I had a 20-year career in that area of technology, including as a programmer, leading just about every application development team from billing, correspondence, and proposals to medical management and claims payment, then finishing up by leading a variety of support functions for our mainframe and distributed development and data warehouse teams. Despite this, I didn't have as much of a connection to my peers any longer because of changes taking place. I felt the void, often. Trusted peer relationships are critical and especially critical for the CISO, or other senior security roles, although I didn't really think about it like that at the time.

I found a basic need (think the bottom tiers of Maslow's Hierarchy of Needs: https://www.simplypsychology.org/maslow.html) in my CISO career was having a trusted group of peers both inside and outside of the company. Those are people you can depend on to bounce ideas, thoughts, and questions off, including insecurities. You can count on them to not only lift you up when needed but also tell you when you are being too hard on yourself, or conversely, point out blind spots.

Some people are very intentional about writing down potential peers and targeting them to be part of their group, while others, like me, mostly let this occur naturally. Whichever route you might choose, it's important to nurture your peer group, including ensuring there is two-way benefit. And don't be afraid to pivot away from certain peers as you outgrow the relationship or find you are not as compatible as you once were.

The second question I asked during the interview for the CISO job was whether I was expected to retire from the role. The CIO laughed out loud at that one before realizing I was serious. He told me that he was hoping I'd stay for 3–5 years because "it's a complex space." My concern at the time was that as CISO, I would don a 'security' hat and be asked to go do 'security things' while the 'cool, emerging technology things' were advanced by my technology colleagues. I didn't want to go off and stand in the corner with my security hat on and miss out, and at that time, I envisioned difficulty jumping back into a technology leadership role after pivoting to information security.

While 'missing out' did not happen, I did, in fact, end up retiring from the CISO role after 17 years in the job. At year 4, I asked my boss if he wanted me to begin to think about a successor, almost as if I would be expected to leave at year 5. I was having a lot of fun in the job, experiencing career success, and satisfying my intellectual curiosity, so I was glad when he said I was welcome to hang out in the job for as long as I wanted. I proceeded to do so and often measured my satisfaction in the role based on the amount of 'fun' I was still having. I am not sure I would say that 'having fun' in the CISO role was ever an explicit goal. There were days that were clearly no fun at all, but being able to put those bad days into perspective and learn from them is something all leaders do. For CISOs, those days might come in the form of crisis response or pressure from regulators, executives, the board, or customers; staying calm and making sound decisions even when there is high stress is something that can be learned and improved over time.

Many people ask me how I have managed to have a 17-year tenure as a CISO, let alone while at the same company, when the average tenure is widely reported to be low, commonly two to three years. I've had the chance to reflect on that question over the years, but I didn't think about resilience as being one of the main reasons until more recently.

When I think of resilience, I consider it primarily as the ability to handle the negative consequences of a situation without letting it be all-consuming and take on an outsized impact or life of its own. Security leadership requires quick thinking; taking too much time to stew or swirl when in-the-moment decisions need to be made does not typically improve the negative consequences, especially when the goal is to contain a threat. As Colin Powell, a U.S. general, chairman of the Joint Chiefs of Staff (1989–93) and secretary of state (2001–05), said: "Bad news isn't wine. It doesn't improve with age." Resilience allows CISOs to adapt to all types of situations that might arise as part of the remit of their job, and luckily, these experiences help to further strengthen their resilience.

With this backdrop, I would like to take you back to the beginning of my journey to give you a better understanding of the salient points in time that, on reflection, increased my resilience. While some definitions of resilience bring to mind an elastic band that bounces back to its original shape when pulled and released, I think instead that each time we are called upon to handle a new challenge, or are pulled like the elastic band, once that challenge has been handled, we then add that experience like an arrow in our quiver, to pull back out and take aim differently in the future.

My life before being a CISO

I began my career as a COBOL programmer in the health insurance technology team of Principal®. Beyond building skills such as logical thinking and problem solving and learning from events like late nights due to technology glitches (some caused by me) and all the things that go along with being a developer, I had opportunities to learn about the business, all that technology supported.

This was mostly before we talked about how technology enabled the business, but there were most definitely signs of what was coming as companies were ramping up their use of technology and telling their stories using examples of how technology was differentiating their products and services. Being a part of building process improvements to create efficiencies, extending systems to partners so they could self-serve, automating to speed up the business cycle, and modernizing technology to ensure it was always available were some early learnings.

As the world changed and the technology bubble of the 1990s was expanding (and then later burst), adding technology to business processes also significantly changed regulatory oversight. During my time working in technology as part of the health insurance business, I was part of a team that helped to ensure the new **Health Insurance Portability and Accountability Act (HIPAA)** requirements were met. This knowledge would serve me well as CISO and come in handy throughout my career.

One thing I learned from being involved with implementing new controls and processes to comply with HIPAA was that compliance can be an influential driver of action. While it may be more appealing or dramatic to find other motivators to enact security-related controls, compliance remains a powerful motivator. There have been more than a few times in my 17 years as a CISO when the phrase "Never let a good crisis go to waste" was muttered. While compliance is not typically a crisis, it can drive urgency, and being involved in HIPAA compliance was a good learning moment for me.

Learning how to CISO

I often tell myself, and others, that I had 'some' experience in the information security field when I became CISO at Principal. I was so grateful to be given the opportunity with what little I knew, especially as I look back, because I can't imagine this happening in today's environment. Companies must be sure they have highly qualified individuals in the CISO seat now; I don't think it would be rational, or at least not advisable, to hire someone to learn on the job for any large, global, or highly regulated company, and most definitely not for a company where all three of those adjectives apply.

Making a move to the CISO role required that I jump in with both feet and embrace the role. Even in 2008, it was clear that the scope of information security was expanding. My marching orders, so to speak, included a focus on technical upskilling for the team and bolstering team leadership. This was a challenging mandate given it was the largest team I had led to date, and I didn't feel my technical skills were a match for what a CISO needed to know, or even close to what the top talent on the team had.

I wish I could say I created a development strategy with specific plans to learn the subject matter of information security smoothly and quickly. I wish I could say I immediately sought out a mentor to help me. I wish I could say I pursued a certification to learn and test my knowledge and bring me some instant credibility as a security leader. I did none of those, or at least not in the structured manner I would suggest others now consider.

So, how did I learn to CISO? To paraphrase Chumbawamba, "I got knocked down, but I got up again." That's another definition of resilience that resonates with me!

One of the members of my new team welcomed me by carrying about five large three-inch binders of documentation to our first meeting in my office. I'm not sure what he expected me to do with this information, but I suspect it may have been a bit of a friendly scare tactic to reinforce my lack of knowledge in the field. I must admit, after that meeting I definitely wondered what I had gotten myself into. But I assured him that I appreciated the welcome 'gift basket' and would review the material over time. I also assured him that I was counting on learning from talented team members like him, and to please be patient with all the questions I was sure that I'd be asking as I settled in.

As CISO, there were not many memorable moments where I was sure I had 100% of the knowledge I needed, that all the knowledge I did have was accurate, or where I felt 100% confident in where I was heading. This is something every leader probably gets used to, but this feeling was amplified because I knew that I didn't know enough. The phrase 'fake it 'til you make it' sometimes kept me going in the early days of being a CISO. And sometimes I failed at that. For example, while I have forgotten the names, I was seated at a lunch with a group of other security professionals during the RSA Conference, a huge annual security conference. The lunch was sponsored by a security vendor, and I didn't know anyone seated at my table. Not one to shy away from participating in the conversation, I engaged in a discussion that two people at the table were having about the NIST 800-53 security framework. I had absolutely no idea what they were talking about and remembered asking why it was called 800-53 (in my head, it was 853). I got the strangest look from the gentleman next to me, so I asked a clarifying question: "Does it have 853 pages?" Wow, it is somewhat stunning how naïve I really was. Most people say no question is a stupid question, but I think most security professionals would agree that mine was stupid. Perhaps the learning there was to listen a bit longer before chiming in with questions, simply learning by listening. I didn't realize how inept this question was until about two to three years later, when my team was talking about adopting NIST 800-53. (I wish I could remember who was sitting at my table; hopefully they don't remember this as vividly as I do!) Remember, you get knocked down, but you get up again, even if you don't initially realize you were knocked down in the first place!

Aside from spending some time meeting new people at conferences and security meetups, I also learned from a few of our strategic security vendors, as well as from YouTube videos and my own mistakes. My questions were getting better, and I was able to do a better job piecing together all the aspects of information security that make up a strong program. Don't misunderstand me, most of the pieces were already in place; it was simply that I didn't fully appreciate or understand how they fit together to mitigate risk, combat threats, satisfy regulators, assure customers, and enable our business strategies. Not to mention this was a time of rapid change in the cybersecurity industry, including new tactics being used by criminals that required new ways for us to think about the strength of our program.

Digging in and making mistakes was a weekly occurrence. Debating with engineering teams, leaders, and my own peers required that I understand how our policies, technical controls, and processes fit into the bigger picture and into the task at hand, for whoever needed a decision.

Having been a developer myself, I felt I had a decent appreciation of what the developers were familiar with, and what they were unfamiliar with, when it came to information security. The things that were unfamiliar were growing as the cyber landscape exploded – threats, regulations, expectations, and so on. There were frequent debates that required escalation to higher-level decision-makers. I learned to pick my battles and to focus on the probability of the 'bad thing' happening and the impact if it did. The same person who had brought me the stack of binders turned out to be a trusted adviser for me, helping to frame out security risks without using the word "compromise," as there is no compromising on the strength of controls needed if the probability is high and/or the impact is high should that control fail. Learning to focus on the negative consequences of a security event, without creating **fear, uncertainty, and doubt** (FUD), is more of an art than a science.

Resilience came into play more than a few times when others wanted to negotiate their way out of a risky situation. I sometimes felt that those who wanted to negotiate with me suspected I was unqualified for my job and that they could sweet-talk me into getting their way. I recall a time when a risk assessment was escalated to me because an area of the company did not want to use two-factor authentication to access confidential information stored outside of the company in a virtual data room. The person who had been working with the business area had warned me that they were going to come talk to me to escalate their plea. They arrived in my office, and I heard their reasons as to why they should not have to comply with our policy, which at the time said that anything stored off-property that was classified as confidential required two-factor authentication to access it. (This was well before **Multifactor Authentication** (MFA) was required by our regulators.) This technology leader was lobbying for their business area, who did not want to store their confidential information in internal document repositories because they were concerned others in the company would access the information – an insider trading risk. Yet they were perfectly willing to accept the risk that any cybercriminal who was able to get a hold of the username and password for the site (or brute-force it) could access their confidential information. I eventually got them to a place of mutual understanding and respect. We talked about how to illustrate that this truly was a risk that had a decently high probability of occurring, which would result in a very bad day for their business area. A couple of years later, this situation came up in conversation when there was a news story about cybercrime in a virtual data room of another company. The person whom I had to say no to admitted that using two-factor authentication was the right thing to do. It's experiences like this, when as a CISO or a security leader, that help you to build skills for the next challenge. And it also gives you confidence that making a decision based on what you know about cybercrime and threats is okay, even if others think it only happens in other companies or to other people.

Sometimes we look for the math around frequency and probability, and that is not a bad thing, but CISOs learn quickly that when it happens to you, the probability becomes 100%, perhaps only due to one small oversight or control failure.

There is a lot of talk about imposter syndrome in the world of security. While I was initially less familiar with the term, once I learned more about what it meant, I realized it was something I experienced. I felt that I needed to know everything given I was the 'chief' and that I would definitely be expected to be the one with 'all the knowledge'; this was entirely self-inflicted. Sometimes I would find myself in a debate, usually with technology-focused experts, who would want to go very deep as to why the security team was asking them to look for alternative solutions, or to get out of what the security team asserted was needed. It was at times like these when I really felt stretched and needed to remember how important it is to make sure all parties in a debate or conversation feel heard. I was not really very good at this and still struggle with it today. Sometimes, I found that once the decision was made, I was not satisfied with it unless all parties understood that it was the right decision for the firm. Over time, this became less important to me as situations and experiences bore out the reason for the decision in terms of strengthening security.

I realized I was not going to be right every single time, but if I listened to all perspectives and worked with the teams and various experts to land at an optimal place for all, we were in a good place for the time being. Most decisions can be re-evaluated with new information, or even new decision-makers, in the future. This does not mean you were wrong at the time the initial decision was made, although it did sometimes feel that way.

The beginning of CISO 2.0

What I learned during this stage of my career can be summed up as building my confidence in myself. I (mostly) ditched imposter syndrome and owned my career.

I felt I finally grew into the role fully. However, the key thing about a CISO role to bear in mind is that it changes constantly. There is a myriad of polls from peer groups, surveys from vendors, and blogs written by experts that illustrate the many responsibilities that fall to CISOs in companies from large to small. Sometimes it appears that the role picks up responsibilities for things that no one else in the organization wants, either because they don't feel they're qualified for it or they feel it's too important to be a side of the desk job for them. At different times in my career, I saw these additional responsibilities as being either opportunities or things that were being dumped on me. Sometimes it's important to take one for the team; other times it's more important not to let new responsibilities distract you from the focus on cybersecurity.

One opportunity I had was to lead our data services team after the previous lead retired. I was asked whether I thought this made sense. My response was something like: "I think it's a weird responsibility for a CISO to have, but I am willing to do it." Because I was feeling confident that my cybersecurity team was operating well and independently, taking on this new role wasn't all that frightening. The team was responsible for data infrastructure and business intelligence reporting. The very real connection to cybersecurity was the data handling. I learned a fair amount from the data professionals of this team while I operated as their leader. I know they also learned more about cybersecurity. In fact, one of the leaders on this team later became my head of **Governance, Risk, and Compliance (GRC)** and is now a leading voice in the AI conversations currently in flight as head of data governance.

Looking back to this experience, which was about 10 years ago, this was an interesting responsibility to align with a CISO role, given today's data, analytics, and AI growth. What I learned from this experience was that I could take on additional responsibilities without sacrificing my focus area and ensure the team had a leader available to them when needed. This responsibility only lasted about two years because a new position was created for a chief data officer, and eventually the team moved to that area. I adapted by taking on the new responsibilities and adapted again when those responsibilities were removed.

> Many CISOs grow their role by taking on physical security, privacy, and other aligned functions. Sometimes I hear CISOs remark negatively about being given new responsibilities, or feeling put upon.
>
> While I would not suggest anyone respond by calling a new opportunity "weird" like I did, I would highly encourage you to take the plunge, accept a new responsibility, and make the best of it. Remember that change is constant, and you would not be asked to take on more responsibility unless there was confidence in you and your ability to be successful.

CISO 2.0 – take two

About four years into the CISO role, I was asked to create a charter for a new CISO group being formed by a local technology association's CIO committee. I was specifically asked not to chair the group (because my boss was chair of the CIO council, and he felt our company should not chair both groups). This was a bit of a challenge for me, in essence, to take the lead but not be the leader.

I created the draft charter and adjusted it, along with the handful of people who showed up for the first meeting. We eventually recruited another member to be the chairperson and began regular meetings. Most of the meetings included open discussion where we brought our own issues, questions, or problems, and I remember bonding with the members. Each of us participating had our hearts in it, and the group provided an outlet for us to assist others in the local area. Members were able to get affirmation or confirmation that a direction on an issue was correct, or if not correct, they would get some great ideas to course-correct. We talked about budget issues, policy, control strength, threats, vulnerabilities, and leadership issues. The importance of an external peer group like this cannot be stated strongly enough. I believe external information sharing accelerates ideas, gives CISOs a safe place to try out ideas, and share thoughts or frustrations. If you are a CISO and don't have a group like this, find one, or form one, quickly!

Beyond the local CISO group, I also benefited from our company's membership in FS-ISAC. Without going into details, we were not convinced that this organization was one that we would benefit from, but we got an offer to 'try before you buy' for six months. After six months, if we didn't feel it was worth it, we could walk away. In those first six months, we were the target of a cyber-related incident that affected many large U.S. banks that were also members of FS-ISAC. The assistance we received from the experts at FS-ISAC to better understand and remedy this incident was invaluable. We joined after our first free six months and have remained active members since.

I haven't mentioned it yet, but being a female CISO put me in the position of being a minority in just about every group or meeting I was in. This was true on day 1 and day 6,205! After being a member of FS-ISAC for a year or two, I was asked if I would run for the board. While flattered, I didn't think I was quite ready for this responsibility, nor did I want to add to my travel schedule because of the ages of my children at that time. I was asked to let the CEO know when I was ready so that he could nominate me. About three years later, I was ready to run and let the CEO know that he could nominate me.

He did so, and I was voted onto the FS-ISAC board. This was a phenomenal opportunity, and I gained another peer group. My experiences on the board helped me to grow as a cybersecurity professional, a leader in the cybersecurity community, and professionally. Everything I had learned up to this point helped me to be a better board member. This included my curiosity and ability to ask questions. My pragmatism, a trait I believe is common at Principal, was also often praised during my board service.

I was on the board for six and a half years and gained useful knowledge on how boards work, especially as the chair of the nominating and governance committee. I also realized that being female in a predominantly male profession gave other females a sense of what they could become. In fact, just a few years ago, a young woman told me that because she had seen me on stage at an FS-ISAC conference, she told herself, "I can do it." It was heartwarming to know that the confidence I learned to have in myself and the opportunities that I took inspired others.

Winding down as CISO

The great thing about a long career is that you can look back and remember significant milestones. The bad thing about a long career is that you forget so many significant milestones!

When I was promoted to vice president, something I thought was unattainable when I started my CISO career, I was given advice that was akin to "now that you've made it, your role is to help others." As I entered the later years of my career, there were more opportunities to coach and guide my team and mentor others both inside and outside the company based on my experience and view of the future of the field.

The continuous learning that I began out of necessity on the first day of my CISO career endured as a theme across the technology industry and cybersecurity field. Being in a field with rapid change for so long was not possible without the ability to adapt, learn, and grow. This growth went well beyond technical skills. Translating complex security issues into clear guidance, actionable engineering outcomes, and insights for executive leadership and boards was a constant challenge given the dynamic nature of cybersecurity and threats. Keeping myself current through a massive amount of reading and industry engagement was a necessity. The technical and leadership upskilling I was tasked with on day one was not always easy, but seeing the strong and talented team built over time was professionally rewarding and gave me a great deal of pride.

Resilience is not just about one person. Encouraging professional development, empowering team members, and rewarding and celebrating successes are huge investments in the resilience of your team. And a lot of fun when you see the outcomes!

Lessons in resilience

These and countless other experiences during my 17-year career as a CISO have taught me several key behaviors and lessons that may be useful to those considering a career across the many domains of cybersecurity:

- **Find trusted peer groups:** You won't prevent all incidents, so use your peer groups proactively and in times of trouble. The trust and camaraderie you build will serve you well. Also, use them as a sounding board or shoulders to cry on as needed. They'll understand, and it might not be easy to find others who do.

    Think about your peer group as a two-way street. There is a lot to learn from what others experience too. Drive this point home to all levels of employees on your team. Burnout in cybersecurity is widely reported; trusted colleagues can help!

- **Crisis management skills:** Remain calm under pressure, especially during crises such as data breaches or cyber-attacks. Be the leader others look to to make smart, practical, and sound decisions in times of high stress.

Until you feel you have achieved a high level of crisis management skill, look at every incident that happens around you (to competitors or supply chain partners, or what you see on the news, for example) and ask yourself what you would do if that incident happened at your company. You may have an 'oh, sh*t moment' that drives improvement in your program, or it could build your confidence that you are doing enough to make whatever happened to them a low probability for you. Use these walk-throughs to tell stories to your executives and boards, make tweaks to your controls and playbooks, and give your team a pat on the back when it's clear you are in a position of strength.

> Learn to recognize the crises that will help to accelerate initiatives that may have gone stale or need more attention. Leverage these moments to strike while the iron is hot.

- **Risk-based decision-making:** Making informed decisions by listening to the impact on your business and weighing the opportunity, experience, or reward against security risks should become a habit. Quantifying the risk and reward can be impactful. Don't rely on fear-driven tactics.

> Don't forget that FUD does come in handy at times; there are people who want the dramatic view of what could go wrong to illustrate a point or spur action. Use this selectively.

- **Take the time to appreciate how far you've come:** The CISO job requires preparing for uncertainty, so there is no such thing as knowing all you need to know. Think about all you have absorbed, learned, and experienced. There will be more to come. Stay open to new ideas. The CISO role is varied and is likely to open new doors for you, and maybe additional responsibilities. Take them. Give them back if you need to. Your career may be comprised more of twists and turns than being simply linear, and that's okay.

- **Culture matters:** Listening and learning the perspectives of others are two key competencies required of a CISO. Understanding requires seeing the world from multiple points of view. Adapting your view is equally important to helping others to see that the world is not always safe and secure.

When you have the time to be proactive and plan communications or actions, use this time wisely. This will build your confidence and help you remain consistently 'on message,' which will earn you trust. Being approachable with your team and others across your company will pay dividends by setting an example and building the reputation you'll need to keep your company ahead of issues, whether they be cybercriminals, regulators, or stakeholder demands. A positive culture also creates the environment where you and others will want to do your best work, so investing in it as a foundation to your success is a winning strategy!

It will be interesting to see where the role of the CISO goes in the next decade, but one thing I strongly believe is that the need to be resilient will persist. I hope you can use my experiences to reflect on your own path, make adjustments, or confidently drive forward. I'd love to hear from you on LinkedIn if reading my chapter has made a difference for you.

I have confidence that the next generation of cybersecurity professionals will learn from those who came before them. My ask is to please continue to pass on your experience and wisdom as you gain knowledge and resilience. The universe needs cybersecurity.

David's key takeaways – Career resilience

Meg has an admirable career that extends far beyond the normal boundaries of her peers. Resilience is indeed her secret ingredient; the question is how you too can build this attribute so that this becomes your strength.

This chapter was written by Meg as she was in the process of retiring from her long-standing CISO career. Her generous sharing of her professional experiences in this chapter is hard to boil down into a few pages; however, she has accomplished this splendidly.

There are very valuable learnings we can take away from this chapter, from Meg taking the opportunity to move into cybersecurity for a few years to becoming a significant, longstanding CISO.

Some key points from her reflections include:

- *Build your support network* - cultivate connections both inside and outside your organization to bounce ideas off of, receive encouragement, and gain different perspectives. These relationships provide crucial support during challenges and help combat burnout in cybersecurity.

- *Embrace continuous learning.* The cybersecurity field evolves fast, requiring ongoing education. Be willing to admit knowledge gaps, ask questions (even 'stupid' ones), and learn from mistakes to build expertise over time.

- *Develop crisis management skills.* Remain calm under pressure during security incidents. This will help you to make sound decisions quickly, without allowing negative situations to become all-consuming. Use incidents at other organizations as learning opportunities.

- *Focus on the probability and impact of security events rather than relying solely on fear-based tactics.* Quantify risks when possible and help business leaders understand security trade-offs.

- *Build team resilience.* Resilience is not just an individual thing; encourage professional development, empower team members, and celebrate successes to strengthen your entire security organisation.

- *Choose business enablement.* While compliance is a powerful motivator for implementing security controls, understand how security measures enable business strategies, rather than just satisfying regulations.

- *Recognise your own personal growth.* The CISO role evolves constantly, so take time to appreciate how far you've come. Stay open to new responsibilities and opportunities that enhance your perspective, even if they seem unusual for a security leader.

29

Lessons in Leading Yourself, Cyber Teams and Through Crisis

Cybersecurity is a tough career. I've personally been a CIO for more than 20 years across Financial Services and Pharmaceutical, as well as being a CISO and Global Head of Tech & Cyber Risk. The CISO role was the toughest that I ever had, and it was at HSBC, which is a target for nation-states.

The role can be challenging, complex and at times stressful. You feel a huge responsibility to protect the enterprise and the jobs of the people who work there.

Unfortunately, when attacks occur, they are often at inconvenient times – at 4 pm on a Friday, or as you are sitting down for Saturday lunch with the family, for example. These are the real facts of the role. You never get thanked for this either; prompt response is a responsibility of your position, even a reason for being.

To be able to sustain a CISO role requires incredible personal resilience to maintain performance despite pressure from regulators, stakeholders, management and the board. Successful attacks, whether these are on your organisation or on others, will only accelerate the concern that is felt by these parties.

I'd actually argue that resilience is not enough. It takes a team to defend well against cyberattacks and you need to be a strong leader to bring the organisation along the journey with you, on good and bad days.

Cyber incidents are also often not along the same attack vectors, and therefore, a CISO requires a curious mind to be able to continuously stay on top of new attack approaches and technology to manage risks and issues effectively.

CIOs and CISOs typically have a career horizon of 2-4 years. There are many reasons for this churn, but these transitions have become nearly normal and commonplace.

Now, just imagine doing the same CISO role for 16 years in the same company.

Let me introduce **Richard Johnson**, a true legend. As I write this, he has been a **Group CISO** at **Westpac** for more than 5840 days. When we talked about a day in the life of a CISO in all the preceding chapters, there is no doubt that Richard has seen it all.

Richard has not only survived these ~5840 days, but he has thrived. Richard has a deep technical background and served as Head of Architecture, Research and Cybercrime at Westpac. Prior to this, he was Chief Security Engineer at Bankers Trust.

I invited Richard to share some of his rich history and stories of his career here so that we can all take away lessons on CISO career longevity from him. He is indeed a rarity in this day and age, and each of us will learn something from his incredibly sage advice.

Lessons in leading yourself, cyber teams and through crisis

Richard Johnson

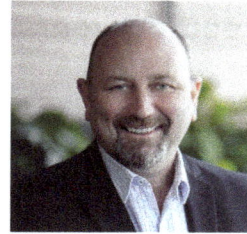

As I'm writing this, I'm in my sixteenth year as Group Chief Information Security Officer for Westpac, an Australian bank and financial services firm. I joined the organisation about 22 years ago, when the company I was working for was acquired by Westpac – in the process, our humble team of four became the core of a newly hired team of 33, which was pretty exciting at the time. Four days later, cybercriminals set up the first-ever phishing site impersonating one of our brands. And that turned out to be the start of twenty-plus years of intense cyber competition – pitting the criminal ingenuity of the attackers against the resourcefulness and dedication of the defenders. That competition continues to this day.

As you might imagine, over that period of fairly intense change and growth, I've had plenty of opportunity to learn a lot about myself, leading people, leading security functions and leading through crisis. This chapter sets out some key lessons that I have drawn from those experiences. My hope is that sharing these experiences may help you in your own journey and help you navigate more swiftly toward your goal, whatever that might be for you.

Personally, I find quotes a powerful tool for conveying meaning and communicating experience. A wise colleague, Professor John Yearwood, once told me, "Narrative is a compression function for experience" – that is, stories take complex experiences and distil them down into easily communicated, memorable form. So, you'll see in this chapter that I've structured some of the key lessons that life has taught me around those key phrases that help make them memorable for me – including a couple of my own.

Leading yourself

"Do something generally useful, and which you enjoy" ~ Mrs Johnson

Growing up, I wasn't sure what I wanted to do. I really liked messing around with computers, but there were not a lot of full-time computer jobs back then. I liked being outside in nature, but didn't want that every day as a job. Having just graduated high school, but with no idea what to do next, my mum made a helpful observation: "Well, just do something you enjoy, and which is generally useful". In part, that was helpful because it took a lot of the pressure off; you don't have to have a complete 10-year plan in place before you do something – you can start with just the next step in a direction that broadly feels right to you.

At the time, I looked around and saw that lots of roles involved working with money (of which I had none), and that seemed like a good candidate for something generally useful to lots of people. So, I pursued an Economics degree at Sydney University and joined the Australian Army Reserve, via the University Regiment, to pick up some other skills, earn money for rent and get to spend some time outside.

That wise advice from Mum has proven helpful throughout my career. Often, faced with a large, unbounded problem, many of us feel the need to come up with a complete, detailed plan before starting to act. That can easily turn into analysis paralysis – and the problem can get worse in the meantime. Instead, if you can get comfortable with the uncertainty, you don't need a complete plan: identify roughly which direction you want to travel in and just do something generally useful, and that you find agreeable, to move along that path.

"Navigate toward things which create energy for you" ~ Richard Johnson

Freshly armed with an Economics degree, I still didn't know what I wanted to do. So I followed the path of least resistance. That led me into accounting: I joined one of the big firms, completed my Professional Year to complete my Chartered Accounting accreditation, and became part of a financial audit team.

Only one year into the job, I found myself in a dusty, hot Compactus filing room, digging through boxes of assorted receipts looking for a missing cheque stub. I had a moment of clarity: "What am I *doing*?" That prompted some reflection on the start of my career – on my choices and where they were taking me.

I managed to negotiate my way out of financial audit into an exciting new role – in the emerging field of computer audit. When I say "emerging", I mean "tiny". In the entire firm at the time, there were four people in this team. However, the culture of the team was very exciting, I found the leader inspirational and we were breaking new ground, so I was quickly drawn in.

Learning this lesson about creating energy from what you do was important. There are elements in any role that can create energy for you, which in turn amplifies what you get from that role and what you bring to it, in a kind of positive reinforcement loop. That energizing element can be the skills you use, the challenge in the tasks, the level of change and variety (high or low) in the work, your boss, your colleagues, your customers, the nobleness of the cause (or not) and whether the mission of the team resonates for you. Those same things, though, can also be mismatched, and that becomes quickly draining – they draw energy away from you, and what you bring to your role and what you take from it both deteriorate.

That impact on your energy doesn't just affect your work; it seeps out into the rest of your life too. So, being aware of this and navigating your career toward things that create energy for you is crucial to your happiness.

For me, that is cyber. (And you might already be seeing the kinds of attributes that pulled me toward the CISO role.)

"We are what we do." ~ Will Durant, drawing on Aristotle

It wasn't just energy that prompted me to rethink where I worked. Being in audit had conditioned me to consistently look for faults, errors and to always assume mistakes had been made. It was rewiring my brain, and I realised that this mindset was seeping out into the rest of my life. Every time I went to dinner with friends, I studied the bill diligently to check it for errors, to make sure there wasn't an extra item and to make sure that any surcharges were correct. What I'd noticed is what is now called neuroplasticity: that the brain constantly changes itself throughout the course of our lives, influenced by our experiences and thoughts. That can be a long-term process – in *Outliers* (2008), Malcolm Gladwell argues that 10,000 hours is required to achieve mastery of a skill – but it is one of the most powerful forces in our lives. And the modern science of neuroplasticity begins from that much older wisdom: 'we are what we repeatedly do'.

That realisation prompted me to reconsider who I wanted to be (and who I didn't want to be!), and therefore what I wanted to repeatedly do, as a pathway toward that. Those reflections also influenced my choice to move into cyber.

"No one makes you feel anything – how you react and respond is up to you."
~ Dr. Baxter

My shift into a dedicated cyber role was quite fortuitous. A colleague from a previous role had recently moved from IT Audit into cyber. He was looking to add a security engineer to his team, and he asked if I knew anyone who would be willing to take it on (and we both knew he really meant me) – I readily agreed.

Of course, we didn't call it 'cyber' then. In the early 2000s, the field was still transitioning from being known as 'computer security' or 'IT security', to the shiny, new 'information security' – reflecting that what we were protecting was much broader than just the systems themselves. It would be another decade or so before Hollywood got hold of it, and rebranded our field as 'cyber', making it all 'sexy'.

So, I found myself for the first time in an engineering role, building production computer systems. I knew a lot, but this was new ground and I had to learn quickly. I spent my daily commute and much of my weekends reading everything I could get my hands on regarding networking, application development, operating systems, Information Technology and computer architecture, trying to absorb everything before I needed it on the job.

Out of (what felt like) nowhere, I started experiencing some intense physical symptoms, including tachycardia, blurred vision and chest pain. After initially ignoring them (as so many do), the symptoms became more frequent and I realised something was wrong; I thought I might be dying. So, I sought out my excellent regular doctor and asked him for help.

After running some tests, he confirmed I wasn't about to die. He turned our conversation toward what else was going on in my life, whether there had been any recent changes and particularly asking whether there was any stress at work. I shared the story of my recent shift into security engineering, and the overwhelming intensity of trying to learn things quickly and swiftly implementing changes into production. On reflection, I thought that I was stressed, but Dr Baxter quickly spotted that my symptoms were, in fact, anxiety.

The conversation from there was very helpful. He helped me understand that we don't control our inputs, which deliver the potential for stress, but we do have control over our reactions and response. He continued: "Stressors are unlimited. You cannot stop them, however, how you deal with them is the one thing that you (and you alone) can control". You can choose how you react; if something bad happens, feel the emotion, reflect and then pivot that emotion and energy to action. It's important to always look for opportunities. You control what you do and how you feel. No one can *make you* feel anything.

We talked briefly about how I felt unqualified for the role I was hired into and the imposter syndrome I was feeling. Listening carefully, he then challenged me gently: "Do you trust the judgement of the people who hired you?" Yes, of course I did. And in that light, it seemed reasonable that I might trust their assessment of my capability too – and particularly my future potential (particularly my willingness and ability to learn and grow into the role).

Leading people

> *"The Leader always knows what to do (especially when he doesn't)"* ~ *Warrant Officer Class 2 Jones*

As a young man of 19 years, the Australian Army Reserve surprisingly decided to invest in me and selected me for officer training, which was a great honour. That involved learning to lead a platoon of 30 soldiers through a wide range of increasingly challenging training exercises. These were routinely multi-day patrol, ambush and combat exercises, usually in hot, rugged terrain – except when it was freezing and pouring with rain – all of which was both physically and mentally gruelling. I loved it.

On one of those occasions, we were two days into an exercise out in the bush on a scorching summer's day in the Singleton area. My platoon and I finally arrived at a water resupply point, exhausted and parched. When we reached the point indicated on the map, the water was nowhere to be found. We checked: we were in the right position; someone must have messed up and failed to get our water here. Typical.

Morale collapsed immediately. My platoon slumped down to the ground, disgruntled and despairing. I was also swept up in their frustration. I recall kicking a tree and loudly blaming whoever was responsible for our water not being delivered.

At this point, the Warrant Officer responsible for training me on this exercise approached me: "Mr Johnson, may I have a word?". The two of us stepped away from the group for a bit to talk out of earshot.

He asked about the state of my platoon – clearly, they were down. And he asked how I was feeling – and I was upset too. And then the real question: "Do you think you being visibly upset right now is helping your soldiers?" That caught me by surprise. No. Clearly, it wasn't – by expressing my frustration in front of them, I was basically signalling to the rest of the team that I didn't know how to solve this problem for them.

"Mr Johnson, the Leader is the Captain of his submarine. And the Captain of the submarine always knows what to do (especially when he doesn't)". In a time of crisis and challenge, the team looks to their leader for signals on how to feel and how to approach the problems. Great leaders express confidence that a way through will be found, that the team isn't stuck, and thereby motivate the team to continue. That doesn't mean that you already have an end-to-end plan, but that you organise the team in the direction of something that will help. "Now, Mr Johnson, get on the radio, figure out where the hell the water got sent, ask them to hold position and plot a route to get us there".

This was a valuable life lesson about practical leadership, which resonated and has stuck with me and served me well ever since. And the next resupply point had *plenty* of water.

"The leader's role is to be at the centre of the battle" ~ *Sun Tzu*

Some people assume that leaders are inherently distant – perhaps inspired by an image of generals in the wars of the early 20th century, planning distant battles on giant map tables half a world away from the front lines, or of omniscient, distant executives, an unseen source of emphatic instructions.

I don't ascribe to that way of thinking at all. In my view, great leaders are present with their people, making key decisions and visible in the action. Their people draw energy from seeing them side by side with them. Good leaders articulate a vision and a path to get there. They navigate past obstacles. They look after their troops and lead them back home again.

When people see their leaders do this, they are drawn to them and will more readily follow them again, adding their own discretionary effort to advance a collective mission.

"Culture eats strategy for breakfast." ~ *Peter Drucker*

Culture can be a bit abstract; to make it more concrete, I like to think of it as all of the shared habits and beliefs of a group: What is the purpose of our work? Why do we choose to be here? What do we believe is important? What does success look like? How will we behave toward each other on our journey to get there?

My people leadership philosophy has always been to try and create the kind of culture that I would want to join if I were just starting out. My choices, what I say, how I behave and what my team sees me prioritise all help shape that culture. What I reinforce and recognise in others also does, as does where I visibly intervene to adjust things. There are many things each of us can do to influence the culture of the teams we are part of, hopefully in a positive direction, if done authentically and consistently, over time.

Clearly, strategy is also important. But culture determines organisational capability – an effective, cohesive, motivating culture can execute on its strategy dramatically faster. A cohesive team with high *Esprit de Corps* has a force multiplier effect – both increasing individual contributions and helping individuals collaborate more effectively toward shared outcomes.

I also take a holistic and long-term view of the working relationship I have with my team. We all have a job role to perform, but we are also whole people with hopes and dreams and fears and outside interests. If you have young children, then getting to swimming lessons at 3 pm on Wednesday can be mission-critical for you. We should embrace the whole person, not just the role: support your people and they will reward you by sticking with you over the long term. In my experience, if you support the whole person, not just the 'employee', then they routinely do amazing things in return – sometimes bringing incredible energy and determination to their work.

Leading security functions

"Relentless competence. Repeat." ~ *Richard Johnson*

How often have you observed leaders who think the only path to greatness is through dramatic change? They construct grand, detailed plans, and then burn through huge amounts of energy getting them endorsed and funded. Inevitably, execution becomes difficult and the world changes during delivery, meaning that the final result can be quite different to what was originally planned. There's certainly a time and place for these kinds of programs, and they can be incredibly important – but I want to highlight that this isn't the only path available to a leader.

If you know your goal and you are prepared to play the long game, then repeatedly making incremental improvements over time can be incredibly powerful. Continuously compounded improvement is, in my experience, a deeply under-valued strategy.

In my teams, we focus on being reliable, consistent, and resilient, continuously delivering small increments of change. When we design projects and portfolios, we always aim to deliver a series of visible improvements every quarter, and strenuously avoid a pattern of 'design and build for two years, and then the value appears all at once'.

That will help you demonstrate success, accrue capability, and if you deliver strongly with that, a virtuous cycle builds. The delivery of early outcomes helps generate confidence among those allocating resources, both that the benefits will be realised and that the team executing is trustworthy.

This long-term, incremental approach can be very powerful. When the team I lead was formed in 2003, it had 33 people; twenty years later, it was more than 500. And the relevance and value of that team has soared as the universe changed around us with the emergence of cybercrime, bad actors and self-propagating worms, as well as the acceleration of advanced persistent threats in the last decade.

From the 'a bunch of geeks in an ivory tower' stereotype, security functions like ours are now a strategically important capability supporting an organisation's core value proposition. Trust is at the foundation of any organisation's business and protecting that is critical.

"Fortune favours the prepared mind." ~ Louis Pasteur

Part of our 'relentless competence' approach is also anticipating what might go wrong and being prepared for it as best we can.

Very often, specialist teams can spot oncoming problems from quite a distance out. While those potential future problems are clear to an expert, they might be well below the activation threshold for a large-scale organisational response to be reasonable, particularly if there is significant uncertainty about the likelihood of the problem eventuating.

In these circumstances, it's valuable to be proactive and transparent about the challenges we anticipate and provide our recommended actions to mitigate or avoid them. Where the problem has the potential to be material, it can be helpful to proactively monitor developments in the external environment – to maximise the early warning before a risk eventuates. And when the problem is later sufficiently clear that a more intense response is needed, you can be ready with a well-developed proposal: "Here's one we prepared earlier".

This technique can be helpful beyond risk management. If you can figure out the answers to the questions that the organisation hasn't even asked yet, you can be well positioned to quickly deliver a lot of value, including beyond your core role.

"Get the fundamentals right" ~ attributed variously

Over the last 25 years, the pace of change in technology has been incredible. Coming from a world in which desk phones and computers were only accessible while in the physical office, the always-on connectivity to a globally available set of applications through high-definition super-computers *in our pockets* might seem like something of a miracle to our younger selves.

While the technology continues to evolve at pace, the fundamentals of cybersecurity have remained remarkably stable: a layered defence is the best strategy. It is still very valuable to focus on these elements first:

1. Be clear on what technology and data you have, and what (or who) you're defending against.

2. Ensure you've got the basics under control – patching, configuration management, multi-factor authentication, network segmentation.

3. Then build up defence in depth – layered controls – until you find the right point on the risk/return curve for your organisation.

A strong level of internal and external collaboration is essential to achieve our goal of a layered defence and all-around protection. It doesn't make sense to build barbed wire defences 12 feet tall around 85% of your perimeter – all you will achieve is channeling the attacks toward your weakest point.

It's important to get the fundamentals in place, not focus on the newest shiny security tools. For example, the single biggest threat that employees are likely to encounter on any given day is an email-borne threat like phishing. We want to enable our people to identify and act as our distributed early warning system – if we can get 100 employees to report a phishing email, and we didn't send it out as part of a simulation, that alerts us to something we need to investigate.

"I'll take one independent test over a thousand expert opinions" – Werner von Braun

In cyber (and in technology generally, for that matter), there is no shortage of expert opinions. It doesn't take much to get someone to provide an opinion about how a system *should* work, or how a design *should* be done, or what the result of something *should* be. But it's worth keeping in mind that these opinions are inevitably general statements derived from principles – and incomplete information means that they can be substantially incorrect.

Designers and implementers make assumptions. Technology changes very quickly. Systems are constantly in flux. People troubleshoot and adjust and fix forward. So, the design intent and the actual system inevitably drift apart, and that drift starts very soon after implementation.

Cyber is still a maturing field of study, and so, while expert opinions can be interesting and useful, in my experience, they are no substitute for *actually* going and testing systems and their behaviour.

So: test things. All the time. At every opportunity. And do so from the attacker's perspective – you need to consider how your tank will fare against incoming fire in battle, and not just based on what it looks like from the inside.

In particular, don't just assume your systems are set up as designed: test them, fix the gaps, and then test again. Repeat.

More generally, don't take anyone's word for how things should work – assumptions can be dangerous! Go and get it tested, or at least collect data from the running system, and find out. Trust but verify.

> *"In the land of the blind, the one-eyed man is king." ~ Desiderius Erasmus*

You may have noticed my strong preference for obtaining meaningful data and using that as the primary basis for decision-making. It will, therefore, likely be unsurprising that one of my key strategies is obtaining access to ground-truth data from systems, as much as possible. Where necessary, I'll fight hard to get my systems (or worst case, my people) access to the telemetry from everything critical in the environment – to bring that data together and inform action.

With accurate and complete data, we have better situational awareness. We can see where the strength in the environment is, and where there may be areas of weakness; we can see what things are operating normally and where things are deviating from the baseline. This is clearly useful for operations, but it can also be used to inform tactics and strategy. My team's cybersecurity strategy is fundamentally threat-driven – we use all of the data available to us about attackers, assets, vulnerabilities and security controls to develop a threat assessment, and then we focus our efforts on controls that reduce the most important threats. This approach is fundamentally underpinned by great data – hence our ongoing focus on acquiring enduring access to it.

> *"Against a common enemy, only a coordinated defence makes sense."*
> ~ Richard Johnson

As a field, cyber naturally encourages us to focus on the problems and the work yet to be done. It's therefore particularly important for us to occasionally look in the rearview mirror and reflect on the progress that we have made – as that sense of progress is an important source of energy.

So, I find it helpful to think back to previous incidents and reflect on how much stronger our capabilities and defences are now. A key example for me was the first phishing website mimicking one of our brands on the 4th of July 2003. It was quite poorly constructed, and not at all sophisticated, but it was novel – and we had to develop new techniques to get rid of it. Similar phishing attacks soon targeted our peer organisations.

With other CISOs of Australian banks, we quickly realized that this was a common problem, and that it would be helpful to share what we knew and what tactics were seeing some success. The first meeting of that group happened shortly after and we realized that it was going to be valuable to work together, through a coordinated response to what was quickly becoming an ongoing threat.

It's a truism in cyber that the attackers evolve and improve – and so we must do the same. It's been important to me that strengthening collaboration among peers is a priority, and I'm thankful that my peers have (generally) agreed. As a result, while the attacks we face today have become more advanced, the level of collaboration among us has kept pace. A core of Australian banking cyber teams still meet multiple times a year. Beyond that, we are now part of more than a dozen other information-sharing communities – some real-time and online, some primarily meeting-based and many that are hybrid. My organisation invests strongly in working relationships with regulators, law enforcement, various other government agencies and departments and industry bodies. That collaboration has been critically useful in major global cyber incidents – like WannaCry and NotPetya (2017) and the log4j vulnerability (2021) – as an early warning mechanism, for situational awareness and sharing tactics and content. (During a global incident, even someone sharing their internal explanation to management can save you critical minutes.) And these groups collectively benefit from the broader collaboration globally among security researchers, security product vendors, governments and others. You can never have enough friends.

Based on the rest of this chapter, though, you won't be surprised to hear that I think we must not stop here. We cannot assume our current approach will continue to be adequate, despite those past successes.

The set of threats we all face is continuing to grow – in both volume and sophistication, and as new attackers join the fray. 'Relentless competence' requires continuous improvement; in information sharing, sharing threat insight rapidly at the earliest stages of an incident is a key opportunity for improvement. In trying to protect others, minutes matter, and any detail could make the difference.

I've talked a lot about collaboration between peer organisations, but the same logic applies at several other levels. Within your own organisation, investing in relationships between functions can be vital to enabling effective collaboration, reducing the time to detect some kinds of incidents. Similarly, collaboration across industries and between countries often grants access to unique insights and useful capabilities. The more diversity of knowledge, skill and information we can bring to our problems, the stronger our collective defence.

Our adversaries collaborate freely and in the open. So often, though, companies, governments and other defenders can exhibit a nervousness about sharing cyber information, particularly during incidents. This asymmetry creates an advantage for the attackers. We therefore must continue to explain why sharing matters, and find ways to connect: against a common enemy, only a coordinated defence makes sense. We are at our strongest when we work together, as my experiences have repeatedly demonstrated.

Leading through crisis

"Hey, they're lighting their arrows! ... Can they even do that?" ~ Gary Larson

There's an old *Far Side* cartoon that depicts two Wild West types under attack from archers with flaming arrows, sheltering behind barrels and wagons. The quote above is the caption of the comic, the exclamation of one of the participants.

This comic epitomises to me what it is like to work in cybersecurity.

In our chosen field, our adversary can do whatever they want – they are criminals after all, so they are typically unconcerned with legal constraints and risks (unlike us!).

And they are *our* adversary. The same threat actors who attack me will likely attack you. The ones that attack our customers and employees will attack yours. In many cases, our customers may even be the same people. So, if one of us can improve their security awareness, then everyone wins.

It's therefore vital that we adopt a similarly adaptive approach – and share what we learn. We must continue to be curious about what is happening and inventive in finding new ways to respond to new and changing threats. Many of the cyber tactics and technologies that my team uses to protect us every day had not been invented ten years ago; I am sure that some of the tactics we will rely on in a decade are only just emerging now. A proactive flexibility, underpinned by collaboration, will be critical to our collective success.

> *"War is the realm of uncertainty; three quarters of the factors on which action in war is based are wrapped in a fog of uncertainty." ~ Carl von Clausewitz.*

During an incident, communication is everything – at a time when information is often hard to come by. This is known as the 'fog of war' effect, as an organisation is working hard to understand the cause and scope of an incident or attack, set against a constant and very real need for information and certainty – from customers, the community, shareholders, regulators and the media. Being clear about what you know and what you don't yet know is paramount, as is telling people when you will communicate next. Even if there is no new news, providing that transparency and dependability helps.

A critical form of communication we should focus on is communication among the community of defenders. When an organisation is affected, it's critical that they're able to privately share what they know about the underlying issue, so that other organisations can review their systems too and bolster where needed. (When we talk to our colleagues in the US, we hear that litigation and regulation have stifled that as an unintended consequence.) We need to focus on sharing more and more fully.

> *"Never waste a good crisis" ~ attributed variously*

This is a common refrain, so I won't dwell excessively.

A crisis is clearly unpleasant. Certainly, the vast majority of our work in cyber is directed toward preventing, mitigating and containing crises – and that is yeoman's work.

However, not all crises can be prevented; some things are simply beyond anyone's control. Being prepared to learn from adversity – particularly in the immediate aftermath – can at least ensure that some improvements for the organisation (and you) can come from it.

Some of the best, most rapid capability improvements I've seen cyber teams able to achieve have been born out of crises. It's possible to do amazing things that are simply implausible during normal time (for a range of reasons) and deliver significant leaps ahead in capability. It can make possible the implementation of some of those 'here's one we prepared earlier' plans.

Closing thoughts

I hope that some of my own lessons have been helpful to you. As you can see, I have been very fortunate to benefit from the wisdom of many others through my life and career – and in turn, I hope that some of that may now help you too.

In learning to better lead yourself, your people, a cyber function and through crisis, you can influence and significantly improve the lives of the people around you.

Good luck, and I hope you have a calm, incident-free day.

David's key takeaways — Lessons in leading yourself, cyber teams and through crisis

Richard is a Yoda-like master CISO who has weathered countless security breaches, regulatory changes and enterprise transformations and this scar tissue brings invaluable wisdom. In this chapter, he has shared real-world lessons from adversity that textbooks cannot teach, real gems that each of us can take away and reflect on.

These lessons provide peer CISOs and aspiring security leaders with invaluable practical guidance, the kind that can only come from someone who has 'been there and done that' through the most challenging of scenarios.

Some highlights from his chapter include:

- *It is possible to have a long career as a CISO* – Richard has achieved the remarkable feat of serving as Group CISO at Westpac for 16+ years, demonstrating exceptional resilience and leadership in a role where the typical career horizon is 2-4 years.

- *Personal resilience is essential for a CISO* – you can't easily eliminate stressors, but you can manage your reactions to them. From a CISO who has thrived and not just survived, the strength of your own personal resilience is paramount.

- *Great leaders are present with their teams at the centre of the battle* – providing direction and confidence even in uncertainty. A CISO can't operate as a General that sits outside of the conflict zone and watches from afar. How you support your cyber team in these battles makes a real difference to their morale and your own ability to be on top of the points of conflict.

- *Culture is vitally important* – particularly a culture that embraces people fully, rather than just as employees. This can lead to greater discretionary effort and loyalty.

- *Despite rapid technological evolution, cybersecurity fundamentals remain stable* – know what you're defending, master the basics (patching, authentication, etc.) and build defence in depth.

- *Focus on continuous delivery of small, visible improvements that build trust and compound over time*, rather than relying solely on dramatic transformations.

- *Collaborate externally for collective defence* – in cybersecurity, organisations face common enemies, making cross-industry collaboration and coordinated defense essential.

30

Sunset

Sunset signifies the end of the day; for the CISO, it usually means a global handoff of cyber operations to the team operating to manage cyber incidents and investigate issues.

Figure 30.1: Sunset at Darwin Sailing Club (Photo Credit – David Gee)

Having said this, evening, however, also represents a heightened danger period. Historically, more cyber activity and attacks occur after-hours when cybersecurity teams are often at a lower staff ratio and response times can be slower (according to Arctic Wolf's 2025 Security Operations Report, 51% of alerts are generated outside of traditional business hours: `https://arcticwolf.com/resource/aw/security-operations-report-2025`). As such, sunset for CISOs is also a reminder that cybersecurity is a continuous process, and in some ways, we never stop performing our role. In that spirit, the CISO will be working with their team on setting priorities for the next day, reviewing upcoming security initiatives, and ensuring that any critical security tasks are properly scheduled or delegated.

The reality is that you are not a machine and do need to take a rest. When there is an emergency, your day may seem to extend without end, but on a normal day, getting some rest is going to make you a better manager and leader.

At the end of every workday, you should have a sense of accomplishment, and your thoughts will turn to readying yourself for the home front, perhaps with happy hour beckoning. As the world slows down, it is also an ideal time to exercise mindfulness in terms of reflection and learning. These two concepts are related but subtly different. From my experience, *reflection* is a deeper and more thoughtful analysis, while learning is what you want to take from this going forward as actionable takeaways.

Now that we have set the scene for the CISO, let me return to the narrative of this book. Indeed, it has been an exceptionally long day in the life of a CISO. Across this day, you have followed many CISOs and heard about their personal stories and their career lessons learnt. Let's take the time to sit back and reflect on these.

My reflection on key themes

From my own experience in writing this book and working with the leaders who have contributed to it, please allow me to summarise what my own reflections are.

The leaders in this book are diverse in terms of geography, company and industry. A handful know each other, but it is true to say that they are not a group of my personal friends who have all worked together. As such, the mentorship advice contained in this book is quite naturally diverse and not 'groupthink'.

My reflections fall into five key themes. As you read my reflections in this section, this may prompt you to revisit specific chapters that relate to your own relevant situation and plans. The key themes I have identified are as follows:

- Leadership evolution
- Focus on the basics
- Managing a crisis
- The balancing act
- Your personal resilience

Let me explain these.

Leadership evolution

Leadership evolution is a common lesson that you will have seen across many chapters. There is an overarching key theme of each of the CISOs and cybersecurity leaders moving from (usually) technical roles to becoming strategic business partners. One exception was **Catherine Rowe**, who talked in her chapter (Chapter 8, *Diverse Paths to Cybersecurity Leadership*) about her shift from her non-technical legal, privacy and compliance career to the role of CISO. This highlighted to me that transferable skills such as governance, stakeholder management and logical thinking are all superpowers for the CISO.

Leadership all starts with the right talent. The key role that the CISO plays in creating an environment that helps their talent to develop and grow can serve as the very foundation of their leadership evolution. **Maryam Betchel** shares in her chapter (Chapter 21, *Developing Cyber Talent*) some good guidelines to accelerate this growth. Your own leadership cannot develop if your team itself is weak; you must surround yourself with the most talented resources that you can find and then insist on strong teamwork.

The evolution journey from humble beginnings was a theme that I heard repeatedly, but particularly so in **Krzysztof Kostienko**'s chapter (Chapter 6, *The Journey to CISO: From Humble Beginnings to Leadership*). In the chapter, Krzysztof shared insights into his own journey to becoming a CISO, including highlighting the importance of building trust and developing your soft skills.

The very notion of stepping up into a new global role and making the switch from individual contributor to leader was a key aspect of **Sam Coco's** story (Chapter 7, *Stepping Up into a Global Role*). In his chapter, he talked about being ready for opportunities when they arrive, as well as an approach to building your new team as a leader and earning trust.

Getting a good start as a CISO is so important, I devoted a whole chapter to it in my first book, *The Aspiring CIO and CISO*, offering a first-90-day plan for the CISO. It was therefore fascinating for me to read **Keith Howard's** story (Chapter 3, *Priorities for the New CISO*) about his first six months as a CISO and how he tackled his priorities, as well as the five key priority items he'd recommend focusing on as a new CISO.

"Every CISO fails their first time!" is the career advice **Yabing Wang** recounts in her chapter (Chapter 20, *Do's and Don'ts for CISOs*). Yabing also shared her recommendations for the first 90 days in a new CISO role and went beyond that to cover the stages of growing your presence and stature as a CISO through to being a trusted advanced CISO.

A follow-on from this thread is that your leadership evolution can be iterative. Success can emerge from failure if you take the time to reflect on it and adapt, as **Dr Matthew Ryan** explained in his chapter (Chapter 17, *So, You Got Fired*). His perspective aligns with that Yabing shared in her chapter in this way, on failure almost being a rite of passage for the CISO.

It is to be expected that the new CISO will have skills, knowledge, experience and behaviour gaps when they attain their new role. **Teresa Walsh's** letter to the new CISO (Chapter 4, *Cyber Threat Intelligence That Is Actionable*) is a great example of how to embrace this positively and address this through intelligence gathering and analysis.

Osamu Terai's insight into being a CISO in Japan (Chapter 12, *A CISO in Japan)* is a great example of another kind of leadership evolution, where the step up to CISO is based on seniority and not just merit. There are long-standing practices that have made this criterion the norm in the country.

If you have picked up this book, then becoming a CISO is likely the natural expected path for you (if you are not already a CISO), but being a CISO may not be the end of your career journey. You can also evolve from this position, with many paths to consider, as **Abbas Kudrati** explained in his chapter (Chapter 16, *Alternative Career Paths to Consider*), providing alternative CISO career options such as consulting, vCISO roles, and several other options. Abbas highlights that each of these paths provides additional challenge and learning opportunities to help you continue your leadership evolution.

Focus on the basics

A focus on the basics is critical for a CISO because the majority of successful cyberattacks exploit fundamental security gaps. This may include unpatched systems, weak access controls, and poor employee training. Very often, it is the case that basic security hygiene can have the highest-impact investment for reducing your organisational risk.

While **Sandro Bucchianeri's** chapter (Chapter 11, *Being Brilliant at the Basics*) explicitly focusses on being brilliant at the basics, I noted this was a key theme across many chapters. Sandro argued strongly that getting the basics right, rather than focusing on shiny new things, makes a real difference.

Similarly, "Get the fundamentals right" is a direct quote from **Richard Johnson's** chapter (Chapter 29, *Lessons in Leading Yourself, Cyber Teams and Through Crisis*). He goes on to emphasise "Relentless competence. Repeat", with an approach to playing the long game, then repeatedly making incremental improvements. This can be very powerful. Richard also specifically highlights in his chapter: "Ensure you've got the basics under control – patching, configuration management, multi-factor authentication, network segmentation."

Strategy, in my view, is an excellent example of a focus on the basics. A strategy is choosing where to focus and not focus. A CISO who tries to operate tactically without a strategic foundation often finds themselves constantly reactive. They will then struggle to demonstrate value and have difficulty securing organisational investment support for necessary initiatives. In his chapter, **Jim Boehm** (Chapter 19, *Cyber Strategy That Makes A Difference*) shares that a good strategy is one that "does what it needs to do efficiently and effectively". He goes on to add that *"it has everything that you need and nothing that you don't"*. A good strategy must be easily explainable, risk-based and serve the collaborative efforts of business and technology stakeholders.

A strategy doesn't need to be overly complex, but it should clearly articulate how cybersecurity enables and protects business operations. Making hard choices is the basis of a good strategy, and **Adam Cartwright's** chapter (Chapter 10, *How To Defend With Less*) is all about defending with less funding. When we understand our most critical assets and are able to assign investment appropriately, then this can be impactful. Of course, not over-investing in defences when these are sufficiently mature is part of this decision-making process.

Peter Troy (Chapter 27, *My Metrics Playbook*), in his chapter, chose to particularly highlight the importance of appropriate metrics and data, another basic. A great point of his is "if you are not measuring it, you are not managing it". Fact-based decision-making is key to managing cybersecurity. This is a basic requirement that the CISO must have to succeed, and I have seen that this capability is not always strong within our industry.

Risk management is another basic fundamental that we must get right as CISOs, from the board down to our staff. It really does matter. **Tim Callahan** focused on this (Chapter 25, *Why Risk Management Matters*) and highlighted that "without a formal risk management program, you are, in effect, flying blind". Tim also discusses risk exceptions, and personally, I have seen this risk management practice be poorly managed when this 'basic' is not given the appropriate attention. I've seen examples where 700+ risk exceptions have been documented in the risk register, but have no risk mitigation plans or any committed date to address. (After the challenge, more than 95% of these were removed and mitigated.)

Managing a crisis

Managing crises is integral to the role of a CISO. You must lead your teams to effectively handle incidents, communicate with management, and maintain team morale under pressure. One of the most humbling realisations for the CISO is that their technical expertise alone is not enough.

Being great at managing a crisis in the heat of a battle is a true 'moment of truth'. When you do this well, everyone notices and, unfortunately, they also notice times that you do not do this well. **Richard Johnson** shared his view that the leader should be found in the centre of the battle (Chapter 29, *Lessons in Leading Yourself, Cyber Teams and Through Crisis*). He noted that "great leaders are present with their people, making key decisions and visible in the action". Richard also advised "never waste a crisis". He stressed that when a crisis does occur, ensure that some improvements come from it.

What is bigger than a cyber crisis? That is a global crisis, and the COVID-19 story that **Camilo Sandoval** shared in his chapter is particularly insightful (Chapter 24, *Protecting the USA*). As CISO for the USA, dealing with the national digital crisis that ensued at a time of intensifying nation-state attacks was a challenge that Camilo rose to. (Let me remind everyone how severe the cyber activities were during this period. There was intensive cyber activity against governments, corporations and individuals.) Camilo also explained his crisis leadership in dealing with incidents such as SolarWinds.

For every CISO, the nightmare situation is to be attacked by a nation-state actor. They are motivated, well-funded and are highly skilled at their craft. This is the crisis that **James McLeary** shared in his chapter (Chapter 2, *Hand-To-Hand Combat with Lazarus*), on being hacked by Lazarus, the North Korean threat actors. He managed this crisis and survived to tell us his story. His example really brought to life the crisis internally and externally with the regulator and other third-party partners. Reading this story might have made you acutely aware of your own level of (or lack of) preparedness.

Following a major crisis comes the rebuild. **Daryl Pereira**, in his chapter (Chapter 18, *Rebuilding After A Breach*), shares his story of architecting after a significant crisis. This highlights that long after the dust of a crisis has settled, there is a medium- to long-term period of rebuilding cybersecurity defences. This is not a short-term fix, despite this often being what is expected by the board and management.

The balancing act

There are many different types of balancing acts CISOs must navigate.

Many cybersecurity professionals struggle with the transition from tactical to strategic thinking. This is an important balancing act, however, as your security decisions as CISO can ripple through business operations and affect regulatory compliance. For CISOs, the 'perfect' security solution isn't always the right business decision.

The CISO must be confident in their team, but also, at the same time, always verify too, and when they present to the board and management, they cannot easily talk in absolute terms given the ambiguity they face. It is indeed a real balancing act.

Having a foot forward and backwards at the same time and feeling 'stretched' is akin to the yoga pose 'Warrior II' which in Hindi is Virabhadrasana II (वीरभद्रासन द्वितीय). It looks easy but in fact the pose is extremely challenging to hold for a few minutes. The pose grounds the yoga practitioner in the present moment and encourages them to face challenges with grace and composure – very much like what the CISO must do.

CISOs face an internal balancing act between the confidence needed to make critical decisions and the humility to question their assumptions. In **Stéphane Nappo's** chapter (Chapter 9, *Overcoming Doubt*), he recommends that we embrace doubt "as a tool for clarity, control and strategic foresight" and notes that overconfidence is "of great help for attackers". Indeed, Stéphane reframes doubt as a strategic asset, and he recommends that we create psychological safety for teams to admit their knowledge gaps.

Dr David Ng, in his chapter (Chapter 26, *Driving Cyber Transformation*), shared his story about driving a cyber transformation over a sustained period. He talks about the continuous nature of this journey, but what I really like is that he highlights the reality with his sobering quote: "It is not what you have done that counts. It is what you have **not done** that matters!". The transformation and successful execution of the strategic plan is countered by your mind remembering that there is so much more to fix and address.

Allow me to introduce another yoga term – *'drishti'*. This is the act of maintaining a focus on a single point while you are balancing and stretching yourself. In that way, you have an internal awareness alongside an external focus. This analogy shows us how effective cyber transformation requires both 'outward' vigilance toward threats and 'inward' perspective (awareness of organisational culture, processes, and capabilities). In David Ng's example, a cyber-resilient organisation cultivates the capacity to maintain a security focus while remaining sensitive to business needs, user experience and operational efficiency.

A tool to achieve this objective is stakeholder management. This topic is covered by many of the leaders, and **Shamane Tan**, in particular, shares her framework that is most effective for the CISO to strive to be outstanding at stakeholder management. In her chapter (Chapter 13, *Navigating the C-Suite, Boards and DOPE Dynamics*), she explains how you can engage your board and management through storytelling to simplify matters and meet the audience where they are. This can also encourage them to take ownership. Her approach is a clever way to build alignment by tailoring your communication to their personas. She uses analogies and has a strong focus on critical business outcomes.

In terms of a balancing act, it is hard to go past managing vulnerabilities. In his chapter, **Steven Brown** outlined the struggles to reduce risk exposure while being aligned with business stakeholders and shared an approach to help you do this (Chapter 22, *Managing Critical Vulnerabilities*). He, like Shamane, highlights that the reporting for managing vulnerabilities needs to be carefully tailored for the different audiences that receive communications on it – too much or too little is very much in the eyes of the beholder.

When you are the CISO, it is often the case that you are pulled down into the depths of detail. It is critical, however, that you can reset your horizon and look at problems from a top-down viewpoint, as well as exploring more in-depth detail where necessary. **Phoram Mehta** shared in his chapter (Chapter 14, *Systems Thinking for CISOs*) his approach to using systems thinking – a holistic approach that can provide you with a larger, more joined-up perspective.

To be the juggler of technology and business priorities requires the CISO to take on the role of change agent. **Fal Ghancha** shares his experiences in taking the high road in terms of the CISO working to have cyber branded as a critical business enabler and strategic investment in his chapter (Chapter 15, *The CISO as a Change Agent*). To make this shift from being seen as purely an IT expense requires a CISO to always view matters through both a business lens and a security lens.

In her chapter, **Silvia Lam Ihensekhien** also explained how security should align with business objectives rather than being seen as a 'blocker' (Chapter 5, *How I Got To Be CISO*). She outlined how to be a great CISO too, and this includes her thoughts about business acumen: "Understanding the business is crucial as different businesses have different priorities. Cybersecurity should be seen as a business enabler, integrated and aligned with business operations".

The AI era we now find ourselves in is a new challenge for the CISO in terms of getting the balance right, balancing adoption speed with safety. **Jacqui Kernot's** chapter (Chapter 23, *AI: The Promise and Challenge*) illuminates both the challenges and promises of AI, with her thoughts on the way forward for AI, in relation to cybersecurity.

Your personal resilience

The role of the CISO is one of the most stressful in IT. For this reason, your own personal resilience is a key factor for CISO success. This is a job where, every day in the life of a CISO, there is constant high-stakes pressure from cyber threats, regulatory demands and executive expectations. You are expected to make critical decisions under stress (often without full information) during security incidents that can threaten business operations.

The CISO also faces the unique challenge of being accountable for a risk that they cannot eliminate. To do this job over the long term requires strong stress management as well as emotional resilience. In this book, there are some good lessons on how to manage the stress of the CISO role and avoid burnout.

Meg Anderson, in her chapter (Chapter 28, *Career Resilience*), shared her own career stories about resilience being the secret ingredient to her longstanding CISO role. A quote of hers I love, that sums up the need for resilience so well, is: "When I think of resilience, I consider it primarily as the ability to handle the negative consequences of a situation without letting it be all-consuming and take on an outsized impact or life of its own". Meg keeps everything in perspective and explains that each time you find yourself stretched and under pressure in a situation, you can see that challenge as just another arrow to place in your quiver and use in the future. She also stresses the need as a CISO to build your team's resilience – by taking up this challenge, you also help build your own personal resilience as you surround yourself with a team that can adapt well to scenarios in front of them.

Richard Johnson's chapter on leading yourself and cyber teams through crisis (Chapter 29, *Lessons in Leading Yourself, Cyber Teams and Through Crisis*) also touches on stress and the need for resiliency as a CISO. Richard, like Meg, has the extraordinary experience of being CISO at his bank for over 16 years. He explained that: "We don't control our inputs, which deliver the potential for stress, but we do have control over our reactions and response". He also noted that "Stressors are unlimited. You cannot stop them; however, how you deal with them is the one thing that you (and you alone) can control. You can choose how you react".

His message is that when bad things happen, you will still feel the emotion, but you can choose to reflect on this and then turn that emotion and energy into positive action. That is such great practical and pragmatic advice for us all!

Now, reflecting on all of these key themes, allow me to share what my own key learnings from the contributors to this book are.

My key learnings

I acknowledge that everyone will probably have different insights from the experience of reading this book, and these learnings will be contextual to where you are in your own career and the aspirations that you have. My key learnings are framed in terms of a retired executive who wished I could have learnt these lessons earlier in my own career (for many items, I did end up learning these through experience, but it would have been much easier if a mentor had just plain told me!).

Strategic thinking over technology depth

Since most cyber leaders commence their careers in technical roles, they then often struggle with the 'soft skills'. Strategic thinking is one such critical soft skill for the CISO. Being able to work with, and navigate, the business with critical thinking is going to be more important to your career than a deep understanding of technical details.

Communication is your superpower

Successful CISOs learn that their ability to translate complex security concepts into business language that executives understand is vital to their role. There are many CISOs that are great at their role but then struggle in the boardroom and this can lead to their demise.

When you have made the effort to build strong relationships across your enterprise, then this pays back when you have an incident or require their support.

Politics, unfortunately, matters

A great CISO operates within the framework of their enterprise; they are not an 'island' and cannot operate independently. If you take the time to understand the business and how revenue is generated, this does help you start to be more aligned with business thinking. How you operate within these dynamics, then, can assist you in ensuring your strategic priorities gain funding support.

Incident response is everything

When you are a CISO, you are in the spotlight – and your own leadership is under the microscope of the board, management, peers, staff and regulators. How you react to incidents and learn from these episodes of managing crises is key.

The CISO must be curious and always a lifelong learner. Without these attributes, your job will be at risk.

Risk management is an art

When you are the CISO, you must educate everyone, including your own team and management, that it is impossible to eliminate all risk. As a business partner, we must understand all risks and be able to help articulate what acceptable risks are. For instance, we might agree to accept a higher risk during a time of extreme business transformation. While this is not ideal, it is unrealistic to seek perfection and purely become the department of "no".

These are my five key personal learnings. You may have some different key learnings, and that is good. It's most important that you make these learnings relevant and act on them appropriately.

Your day's reflection

As you reflect on your personal learnings and takeaways from the chapters that you have read, you may be prompted to consider your own career goals and ambitions. I have no doubt that these reflections are highly personal and that you will be both generous and hard on yourself.

Whenever there is an opportunity to learn from an experienced mentor, like all those in this book, then there will be a multitude of ideas to consider. But allow me to add a couple of practical words of caution to bear in mind when you are working with a mentor:

- **Don't expect them to make your decisions** – you want your mentors to help guide your thinking, but not do the actual thinking for you. I'd suggest that you keep asking yourself what you would do in any scenario. Then, apply your personal judgment to the decision.

- **Don't assume their path is your path** – every career is different, and while there are many diverse stories in this book, what their career trajectory has been and the decision-making style that worked for them in their context may not work for you in yours. To blindly copy their approach without adapting it to your situation and within your own company can backfire.

My final thoughts

Finally, to close, I've asked myself a question: what haven't the CISOs and other cybersecurity leaders talked about across all the chapters of this book? There are a few topics that I noticed did not get much attention – these include DevSecOps, data security and crytopgraphy. However, this is not a complete surprise; these are topics that usually don't get the airtime when CISOs must prioritise their time wisely. What this does highlight is that a day in the life of a CISO is full of challenges and activity. It can be hard to have bandwidth in your thinking time to focus when there is so much being handled.

In my first book, *The Aspiring CIO and CISO*, I shared the following graphic, which illustrates the many 'hot topics' that can take the attention of the CISO. This highlights the critical nature of ruthless prioritization. So, allow me to reflect on time management and priority management.

A day in the life of a CISO

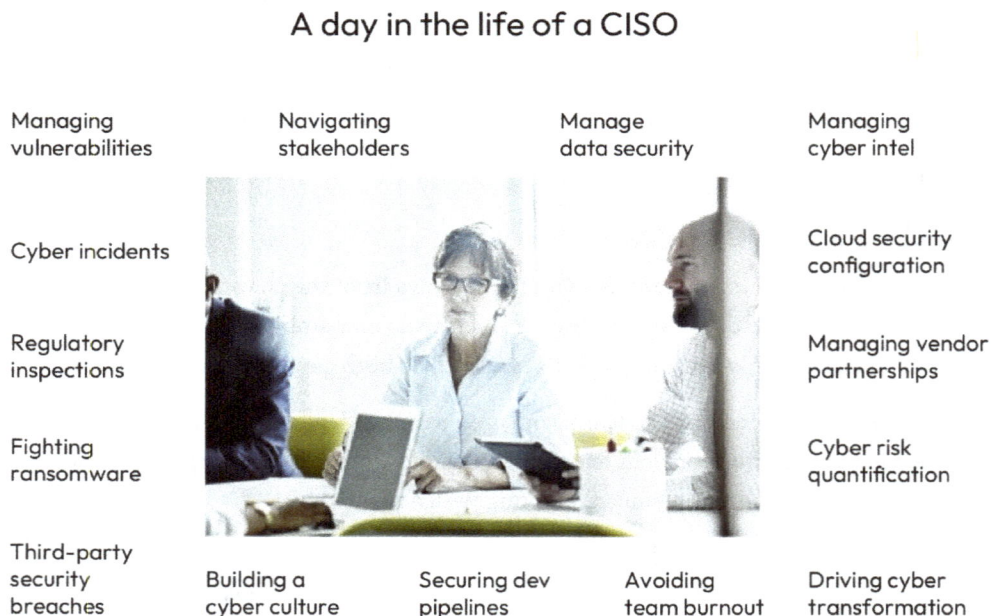

Figure 30.2: CISO responsibilities

As a leader we must never use the excuse of 'I do not have time to take to improve myself'. Hence I would now like to leave you with some thoughts on how you can start to action your own learnings, before you say that you do not have the time to carve out to tackle this. In my view, as I've said, this is all about ruthless prioritisation. A day in the life of a CISO must be a constant battle of *priority management* and *time management*. These are not the same thing! These are subtly distinct, but which is more important?

For a CISO, I would say that *priority management* is significantly more important than *time management,* because cybersecurity is inherently reactive – threats don't follow schedules, and a zero-day vulnerability will always trump your planned vendor meeting.

In my own experience, *priority management* is strategic; it helps you identify what will have the greatest impact on your organisational security posture and business objectives. *Time management,* on the other hand, is more akin to your own tactical execution. CISOs must learn to operate with limited budgets and team capacity, making the ability to quickly assess what matters most essential. On any day, this will be different: critical patching, incident response or a regulatory compliance initiative.

While, for the CISO, *time management* remains valuable for efficiency and cyber strategic thinking space, strong priority frameworks are what truly separate effective CISOs from those who execute efficiently on the wrong things.

Thanks for supporting this book and, in doing so, making an investment in yourself as a better leader!

Best wishes on your career journey,

David J. Gee

31

Unlock Your Book's Exclusive Benefits

Your copy of this book comes with the following exclusive benefits:

- ☁ Next-gen Packt Reader
- ✦ AI assistant (beta)
- ▦ DRM-free PDF/ePub downloads

Use the following guide to unlock them if you haven't already. The process takes just a few minutes and needs to be done only once.

How to unlock these benefits in three easy steps

Step 1

Have your purchase invoice for this book ready, as you'll need it in *Step 3*. If you received a physical invoice, scan it on your phone and have it ready as either a PDF, JPG, or PNG.

For more help on finding your invoice, visit https://www.packtpub.com/unlock-benefits/help.

> **Note:** Did you buy this book directly from Packt? You don't need an invoice. After completing Step 2, you can jump straight to your exclusive content.

Step 2

Scan this QR code or go to `https://packtpub.com/unlock`.

On the page that opens (which will look similar to Figure 31.1 if you're on desktop), search for this book by name. Make sure you select the correct edition.

Figure 31.1: Packt unlock landing page on desktop

Step 3

Once you've selected your book, sign in to your Packt account or create a new one for free. Once you're logged in, upload your invoice. It can be in PDF, PNG, or JPG format and must be no larger than 10 MB. Follow the rest of the instructions on the screen to complete the process.

Need help?

If you get stuck and need help, visit `https://www.packtpub.com/unlock-benefits/help` for a detailed FAQ on how to find your invoices and more. The following QR code will take you to the help page directly:

Note: If you are still facing issues, reach out to `customercare@packt.com`.

‹packt›

Other Books You May Enjoy

If you enjoyed this book, you may be interested in these other books by Packt:

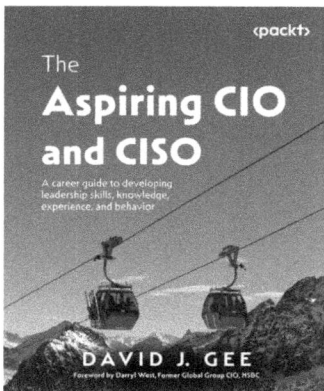

The Aspiring CIO and CISO

David J. Gee

ISBN: 978-1-83546-919-4

- Develop a compelling personal brand for CIO and CISO roles
- Gain mentorship through expert tips, techniques, and proven strategies to navigate executive leadership
- Be well prepared for interviews, with insights into interview questions as well as questions you can ask
- Gain insights into managing high-stakes situations and leading your organization through crises
- Practice leadership through real-life CISO and CIO scenarios
- Find out how to establish and leverage professional networks crucial for your advancement to CIO or CISO roles

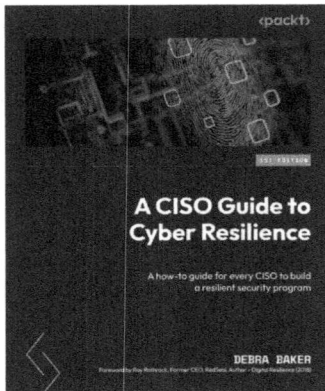

A CISO Guide to Cyber Resilience

Debra Baker

ISBN: 978-1-83546-692-6

- Defend against cybersecurity attacks and expedite the recovery process
- Protect your network from ransomware and phishing
- Understand products required to lower cyber risk
- Establish and maintain vital offline backups for ransomware recovery
- Understand the importance of regular patching and vulnerability prioritization
- Set up security awareness training
- Create and integrate security policies into organizational processes

Packt is searching for authors like you

If you're interested in becoming an author for Packt, please visit authors.packtpub.com and apply today. We have worked with thousands of developers and tech professionals, just like you, to help them share their insight with the global tech community. You can make a general application, apply for a specific hot topic that we are recruiting an author for, or submit your own idea.

Share your thoughts

Now you've finished *A Day in the Life of a CISO*, we'd love to hear your thoughts! Scan the QR code below to go straight to the Amazon review page for this book and share your feedback or leave a review on the site that you purchased it from.

https://packt.link/r/1806110695

Your review is important to us and the tech community and will help us make sure we're delivering excellent quality content.

‹packt› _secpro

Stay Relevant in a Rapidly Changing Cybersecurity World – Join Thousands of SecPro Subscribers

_secpro is the trusted weekly newsletter for cybersecurity professionals who want to stay informed about real-world threats, cutting-edge research, and actionable defensive strategies.

Each issue delivers high-signal, expert insights on topics like:

- Threat intelligence and emerging attack vectors
- Red and blue team tactics
- Zero Trust, MITRE ATT&CK, and adversary simulations
- Security automation, incident response, and more!

Whether you're a penetration tester, SOC analyst, security engineer, or CISO, _secpro keeps you ahead of the latest developments — no fluff, just real answers that matter.

Scan the QR code to subscribe for free and get expert cybersecurity insights straight to your inbox:

https://secpro.substack.com

Index

www.ingramcontent.com/pod-product-compliance
Lightning Source LLC
Chambersburg PA
CBHW081217220326

41598CB00037B/6805